FREDERICK II

FREDERICK II

Bust of Frederick II recently discovered in Barletta by A. Praendi

FREDERICK II

OF

HOHENSTAUFEN

A LIFE

By

GEORGINA MASSON

London : SECKER & WARBURG : 1957

Printed in England by
Western Printing Services Ltd, Bristol
and
first published 1957
by
Martin Secker & Warburg Ltd
7 John Street, London
W.C.1

CONTENTS

5

CONTENTS

LIST OF ILLUSTRATIONS

To J.D., T.A., and P.,
without whom this would never have been written

GUELFS · PLANTAGENETS · HOHENSTAUFENS · HAUTVILLES

GUELFS

Henry the Lion of Saxony & Bavaria 1129–1195 = Matilda of England

- Henry of Saxony Count-Palatine of the Rhine
- Emp. Otto IV of Brunswick =1) Beatrice of Hohenstaufen =2) Mary of Brabant

PLANTAGENETS

Henry II 1135–1189 = Eleanor of Aquitaine

- Matilda = Henry the Lion
- Richard Cœur de Lion
- Joan = William II of Sicily
- John = Margaret of Angoulême
- Richard of Cornwall
- Isabella = Emp. Frederick II
  - Henry III 1207–1272
- Eleanor = Simon de Montfort

HOHENSTAUFENS

Emp. Frederick I = Beatrice of Burgundy 1123–1190 Barbarossa

Emp. Henry VI = Constance Hauteville

- Emp. Philip IV = Irene d. of Isaac II Angelus (Emp of East)
- Beatrice = Emp. Otto IV
- Emp. Frederick II 1194–1250 =
  1) Constance of Aragon
  2) Yolande de Brienne of Jerusalem
  3) Isabella of England
  4) ? Bianca Lancia

Children / descendants of Frederick II:
- 1) Henry VII = Margaret of Austria; 2) Conrad IV = Elizabeth of Bavaria; 3) Margaret = Margrave of Meissen; 3) Henry
  - Frederick ?son
  - Conradin 1252–1268
- Manfred = 1) Beatrice of Savoy =2) Helen of Epirus
  - 1) Constance = Peter III of Aragon & Sicily (island) d. 1285
  - 2) Errico; 2) Frederick; 3) Beatrice = Marquis of Saluzzo; 3) Azzolino
- Constance = (Emp. of East) John Vatatzes

Illegitimate Children by Unknown Mothers

- Richard of Theate
- Enzio = Adalasia of Torres & Gallura =3) d. of Ezzelino d. 1272
- Frederick of Antioch = Margaret of Polo & Saracinesco 1292–1256
- Catherine = Marquis of Caretto
- Violante = Richard Aquino Count of Caserta
- Margaret = Thomas of Aquino Count of Acerra
- Blanche four d. 1278

HAUTVILLES

Roger II 1095–1154 = 1) Albiria of Castile 2) Sybil of Burgundy 3) Beatrice of Rethel

- William I = Margaret of Navarre
  - William II = Joan of England; William III
- Roger, lover of Emma of Lecce
- Tancred = Sybil of Acerra
  - Roger betrothed to Irene d. of Isaac II Angelus (Emp of East)
  - Albiria = 1) Walter de Brienne III 2) Count of Tricarico =3) Count of Tiguano
  - William III
    - Walter IV de Brienne 1205–1244
    - 1) daughter? 1) daughter? 2) Count of Tricarico

Illegitimate lines marked thus: – – – – – –

NB ~ These are not complete genealogical tables. In order to simplify, only members of families who are mentioned in the book appear in this table.

FOREWORD

IN attempting to cover so vast a canvas as that represented by the life of Frederick II of Hohenstaufen, selection is inevitable; his many-sided genius was described by Dr. M. Schipa in the *Cambridge Mediaeval History* as: "It is easy too to sum up his achievements: that by his all but successful resistance and his constant appeal to public opinion in his manifestoes and letters he undermined the political prestige of the Papacy, that in the verse-making of his courtiers and himself Italian literature took its rise, and in his building and his magnificence lay for the fine arts the fertile seeds of a new era, and that with his Byzantine and Norman inheritance he created 'the state as a work of art'. But all these lists seem pettifogging beside the creative spirit that brought order where it passed, and inspired and compelled obedience. The power, which in the rout of able and illustrious men shines through the crannies, in him pours out as through a rift in nature. Among the rulers in the centuries between Charlemagne and Napoleon he has no equal." I have, therefore, concentrated my efforts upon trying to produce as clear a picture as possible of the man himself, of the influences which shaped his character, the atmosphere in which he lived, and of the impact of his extraordinary personality upon his contemporaries and posterity.

I would like to thank Miss J. Pybus for her kindness in reading the manuscript and her helpful suggestions. Also the Hon. Stephen Runciman for his advice about the relationships of the Brienne family, Dr. D. Storm Rice for his interpretation of a cufic inscription, Professore G. Pepe for advice on the reformation letter. Mr. A. Lyall, Mr. B. Kennedy Cook and Mr. H. Brewster are among many friends who have given me encouragement and assistance. To Prince Doria Pamphilj I am greatly indebted for his kindness and hospitality in allowing me to visit Melfi and Lagopesole.

For many of the illustrations I am indebted to the authorities of the Vatican Library, the Gabinetto Fotografico Nazionale of the Italian Ministry of Public Instruction, the Soprintendenza alle Gallerie of Naples, the Director of the Museum of Capua for allowing me to photograph the sculptures of the Capuan gate, and to the Soprintendenza delle Monumenti of Apulia for assistance in photographing Castel del Monte, also Professor C. A. Willemsen for the loan of his photographs. And finally I must thank Conte S. Fago Golfarelli of the Ente Nazionale Italiano di Turismo for his help and advice during my many travels in Italy.

Rome, May 1957

PROLOGUE

THE splendour of the gold and the jewels, the magnificent vestments, and the gem-encrusted robes of silk, which shimmered in the light of the tapers burning on the high altar, seemed to fill Sant' Ambrogio with sunlight and to dispel from the shadowy old church the gloom and mist of the cold day without. All Milan was in the streets on this day in January 1186 to see the arrival of the splendid personages who filled their oldest church to overflowing; they had come to witness a double event of world importance—the marriage of Henry the son of the Emperor Frederick Barbarossa to King Roger's daughter Constance, the presumptive heiress to the fabulously wealthy Kingdom of Sicily; and their joint coronation with the iron crown of Lombardy.

The marriage was to provide a happy ending to the wars which the emperors had conducted against the Norman kings of Sicily in their attempts to make this upstart but wealthy kingdom part of their imperial domains, while the coronation, which was taking place in Milan by special petition of its citizens, signified the end of the struggle between the Emperor and the rebellious cities of the Lombard league.

A new city had arisen from the ruins to which the Emperor had reduced Milan when he had sacked it twenty years ago; and as he rode through the streets on his way to welcome his son's bride, Frederick Barbarossa might have drawn comfort for his defeat at the hands of the Milanese at the battle of Legnano nine years before with the thought that a people of such courage and energy had been an enemy worthy even of an emperor.

A forest of scaffolding rose in the centre of the city where the cathedral was being rebuilt, though not yet far enough advanced to serve as the setting for the day's ceremonies. Perhaps it was as well, as the absence of the Archbishop, Uberto Crivelli, now Pope Urban III, whose right it was to perform the coronation of the kings of Lombardy, would be less conspicuous; though many of his fellow townsmen must

15

have been wondering what he would be thinking of the day's events.

For this marriage might one day mean the union of the Kingdom of Sicily with the Empire, effecting the encirclement of the papal states by a single great world power that could then reduce the Apostolic See to the position of a mere cipher. When Urban's predecessors had blessed Norman Count Roger's conquest of Sicily from the Saracens—even endowing him with considerable spiritual independence in his own realm, by making over to him and his successors many of the functions of a papal legate—they had always been careful to maintain that Sicily was a fief of the Church, hoping thus to keep the military prowess of the Normans and the riches of their kingdom as a counterweight to the threat of the imperial power.

No wonder that the marriage was taking place without the blessing of the Pope, and that the Guelf partisans even whispered that Constance had been made to forswear her vows as a nun in order to marry the Emperor's son. The reigning King of Sicily, her nephew William II, though young, was still childless after eight years of marriage, and Constance was the sole remaining legitimate heir who could succeed to the kingdom after his death. She had in fact lived for years in the convent of the Basilean nuns of St. Saviour near the Royal Palace in Palermo; but in the twelfth century it was quite common for ladies of high rank to live in convents without taking vows. She was over thirty at the time of her marriage, and would probably have lived tranquilly with the nuns until her death if her nephew's childlessness had not made her marriage a matter of dynastic importance for the survival of the heritage of the house of d'Hauteville.

No record has come down to us to indicate what Constance's feelings were about this sudden upheaval in her life, and her marriage to a man whom she had never seen, but who already at the age of twenty was known even in far away Sicily to be very different from his father—"not affable or benevolent with the peoples". In the violent clash of opinions between the rival faction for, or against, her marriage to the Emperor's son, apparently Constance's voice had never been heard. When in the end the English Grand Chancellor, Walter of the Mill, won the struggle against his rival the Vice-Chancellor Matteo

d'Aiello by describing to King William the horrors of the civil
war that would rend Sicily upon the King's death if the succession was not assured, Constance dutifully set out to marry the
strong man whose power could curb the Sicilian barons and preserve her throne. She was handed over to the papal envoys at
Rieti in 1185 with five hundred pack-horses and sumpter mules
laden with treasure, jewels, ermine and other precious furs—
"a dower worthy of the heiress of a great kingdom, and the
bride of an Emperor".

As she made her way up to the high altar of Sant' Ambrogio,
Constance personified to the watching congregation all the
exotic glamour with which the conquest of Sicily had surrounded her family—which in later times earned for her father
and his successors the title of "baptised Sultans". Tall and fair
with the very white skin of her Norse ancestry, Constance was
distinguished by the gracious manners of a princess educated
at a court which was the most luxurious and sophisticated in
western Europe. Her robes of brocaded and embroidered
silks, and her superb jewels, recalled the Byzantine magnificence
which reigned there; while the modesty of her bearing, which
was favourably commented upon by the chroniclers, carried with
it a hint of the seclusion of women that was the custom at the
court of Palermo.

After the marriage ceremony the Patriarch of Aquileia
placed the historic iron crown of Lombardy upon Henry and
Constance's heads. His part in the day's ceremonies brought
down upon him a papal interdict—but he was a worldly and
ambitious prelate and he must have calculated that the favour
of twenty-year-old Henry, the future Emperor, was worth
more than that of an ageing Pope. Constance also received the
crown of Germany at the hands of a German bishop. Then to
the pealing of bells the newly married couple, accompanied by the
Emperor, made their way to the state banquet which took place
in a large wooden pavilion which had been specially erected
near the church. The half-reconstructed city was in no state to
entertain the tremendous throng that had come to see the
wedding; there was no hall large enough to hold them all. Even
Sant' Ambrogio had been used as a granary until the wedding,
and had to be hastily cleaned out and refurbished to do honour
to the occasion.

The marriage had in effect thrown down the gauntlet to the Pope, and the Hohenstaufens did not wait for the papal wrath to descend upon them. Refusing to give back to the Church the Tuscan lands of the patrimony of Countess Matilda, Henry, who was henceforth to occupy himself with the Italian provinces of the Empire, marched towards Rome, while his father returned to Germany.

The Pope, who at this time was in Verona, placed the Patriarch of Aquileia under an interdict for performing the marriage ceremony without his permission and for usurping his functions as Archbishop of Milan for the Lombard coronation. The bull of excommunication of the Emperor was in preparation when it was delayed by his loyal subjects of Verona sending a delegation to the Pope with a petition which said—"Holy Father, we are friends and servants of our lord Emperor and we have promised to defend him and not to allow any wrong to be done to him in our presence. We therefore warmly pray your Holiness not to excommunicate him within our walls." The blow of excommunication never fell upon Barbarossa, because one of far greater magnitude now overwhelmed the whole Christian world. Jerusalem surrendered to Saladin after his victory of Hattin, and once more the Holy Places were occupied by the infidel.

In the wave of horror that swept Europe, the Pope died, the quarrels of the Christian princes took second place, and the gallant old Emperor set out at the head of the armies of the Third Crusade to meet his death by drowning as he tried to urge his troops to greater speed while crossing a river on their march through Asia Minor in 1190.

King William of Sicily had died in the previous year. In spite of their oath of allegiance to Constance and her husband taken during his lifetime at Troia, the Sicilian nobles under the leadership of Tancred (an illegitimate grandson of King Roger) had seized power and placed Tancred on the throne. They were supported in their action by the party of Matteo d'Aiello, who had been against the German marriage from the start, and even, somewhat covertly, by the Pope who saw in this insurrection his chance to break the dreaded association of the Kingdom of Sicily with the Empire. There was some legal justification for Tancred's usurpation, as the d'Hauteville accession to

power among the Norman adventurers who had conquered
southern Italy had originally been made on the elective
principle.

In the spring of 1191 Henry and Constance came to Rome
for their coronation as Emperor and Empress. In May the
Emperor laid siege to Naples as a preliminary step in his
campaign to regain his wife's kingdom. The citizens of
Salerno asked for the honour of playing host to the Empress,
and she took up her residence in this town which was the key
to the way south—perhaps her continued failure to produce an
heir influenced the decision, as Salerno was the home of the
most famous school of medicine in Europe.

The siege of Naples made little progress and the imperial
army was decimated by a sickness which finally nearly killed
the Emperor himself; and the rumour that he was dead created
panic among his supporters.

Henry's attempts to recall his wife to his side were frustrated
by the Salernitans, who, perceiving which way the wind was
blowing, suddenly changed sides. A hostile crowd surrounded
the tower to which Constance had withdrawn as a precaution.
She was saying her prayers, but when the shouts from without
could no longer be ignored, she showed herself to be a worthy
descendant of her Norman forebears, whose wives had cam-
paigned beside their husbands. She came out to try and calm
the people with kind words, turning to threats when they would
not listen to her; and only retiring when she was greeted by a
shower of arrows. The magistrates of Salerno then put her
on board a ship for Messina, handing this valuable hostage
over to Tancred, who to his credit received her with all honour.
After some months, and prolonged representations from the
Pope, Tancred eventually sent her back to her husband in
Germany loaded with gifts.

The Norman kingdom had proved a tougher nut to crack
than Henry had anticipated and he did not return to the attack
until three years later, when the treasure acquired from the
ransom of Richard Cœur de Lion had enabled him to equip a
powerful army, and Tancred's death left the Sicilians with the
widowed Queen Sybil and her son William, a child of seven, as
leaders. In these circumstances Henry's progress was rapid,
and by promises of a general amnesty and the reversion of the

County of Lecce to William—which was his father's by right of maternal inheritance—the Emperor was soon installed in the Royal Palace at Palermo and invested with the Sicilian regalia by Walter of the Mill, to whose efforts he really owed it.

The coronation celebrations were barely ended and the Sicilian nobles and clergy who had attended it were all still assembled in the capital, when Henry, on the pretext of a conspiracy against him, seized them. The child William was blinded and castrated, and all the nobles who had been present at the coronation of Tancred were burnt alive. This mass execution of hundreds of the Sicilian aristocracy was carried out in a field only a few hundred yards from Henry's own residence in the Royal Palace. Not content simply with wreaking his vengeance on the living, Henry had the body of Tancred and his eldest son Roger dragged from their graves and beheaded in full view of the populace.

This reign of terror began on the feast of St. Stephen, the day after Christmas 1194, but some time must have passed before Henry knew that it was also the birthday of his own son, whose fame as the Emperor Frederick II of Hohenstaufen was to do much to blot out of Sicilian minds the bitter memories of his father.

PART I

The Rise to Power

Chapter I

CHILDHOOD AND ADOLESCENCE
1194–1212

FREDERICK was born into a world of change. The period of
the Crusades which had exemplified the spirit of a unified
Europe, fired by a single ideal, was drawing to an end. His
own father had helped to destroy that ideal by his imprisonment of the returning crusader king—Richard Cœur de Lion—
only a short time before Frederick's birth. The next Crusade—
the fourth—was to be directed against the Christian Empire
of the East, to forward the mercenary schemes of Venice.

The modern powers of Europe were taking shape. During
the first fourteen years of his reign, Philip Augustus had already
consolidated the central power in a united France. England
still held the Angevin domains in France, but within ten years
she was destined to lose them through the incapacity of her
King—John—who signed the Magna Carta when Frederick
was twenty-one years old.

The realms of learning were gradually being invaded by
laymen; law schools already existed at Bologna and canon
law was studied at Paris. Around these beginnings the first
universities arose. The Church was also beginning to lose
ground in its domination over the minds of men—the riches
and worldly power of the Roman prelates had for some time been
provoking bitter comment and criticism among laymen, and the
goliardic poets wrote scurrilous verses, parodying the most
sacred subjects, in their attacks upon churchmen. Poverty and
simplicity had been forgotten as Christian virtues; and Francis,
the son of a merchant of Assisi, was still enjoying the gay life
of his native town when Frederick was born. Eleven years
later he took "the lady poverty to wife" to become one of the
greatest saints the world has ever seen.

In the East, the great Saladin had died the year before

Frederick's birth, and the Byzantine Empire of the Comneni was falling into decay. On the steppes of Mongolia, Genghis Khan was fighting for the mastery of the Tartar tribes which was to give him the leadership of Asia.

Frederick's birth took place in the March of Ancona at Jesi, a little windswept town not far from the Adriatic coast of Italy. His father had wanted him to be born in Sicily; when, after years of childless marriage, it became certain that Constance was pregnant, Henry recalled her to her native kingdom. The long journey from Germany to southern Italy must have been hard on a woman of over forty who was pregnant for the first time, and Constance was suddenly overtaken by the pangs of childbirth in this remote place. She knew that the factions which had been hostile to her marriage would welcome any opportunity to discredit the birth, and the fact that this was her first pregnancy, in an age when women were often mothers at fifteen, would offer every advantage to slanderous tongues. It was vital that there should be plenty of witnesses who could testify to the fact that Frederick really was Constance's child, and by birth the legitimate heir to the Norman kings.

Taking all this into consideration, the traditional chroniclers' accounts of the strange circumstances which surrounded Frederick's birth are generally considered to be based on fact, though there is no actual documentary confirmation. They relate that a tent or pavilion was hastily erected in the market-place of Jesi, to which any matron of the town was allowed entrance to witness the birth, and that afterwards Constance showed herself to the people in the open market-place with her breasts bare, suckling the child. In a period when the emperor was still accorded the ancient Roman title of "divine" the drama of the scene must have been tremendous, and Frederick probably owed to it the lack of success of his enemies' attempts in later years to declare that he was in reality the son of the butcher of Jesi.

Acting on Henry's orders, Constance left the child in the care of Conrad of Urslingen, Duke of Spoleto by Henry's creation, and went on to Bari to meet her husband, where they underwent yet another joint coronation on Easter Sunday. The Emperor had brought with him a hundred and sixty horses laden with treasure seized in Sicily, including the regalia and personal treasure of the Norman kings; for the imperial coronation mantle of future emperors was none other than King Roger's, which was probably looted by Henry at this time. Its Arabic inscriptions and sumptuous embroidery give some idea of the Oriental magnificence of life at the court of Palermo, which made even an emperor covetous. Besides the treasure Henry brought with him Sicilian prisoners and hostages, destined for a life of imprisonment in the Hohenstaufen strongholds of Swabia; among them were Queen Sybil and her daughters, the maimed child William, and the Greek Princess Irene, who was the widow of Roger, Tancred's eldest son.

In spite of these precautions and what he described in a letter to the German bishops as the "pacification of Sicily, which by our care is now restored to a state of prosperity; to the glory of him who laid his arms upon the cross and died for us", Henry was evidently uneasy about his hold upon the southern Italian kingdom. He continued his policy of germanisation, awarding key fiefs to old companions in arms. He had already made his brother Philip Duke of Tuscany, and even tried to propitiate the Pope by sending an embassy and swearing to undertake a Crusade; though this also gave him a good excuse for bringing yet another German army into southern Italy.

Finally Henry set out for Germany, leaving Constance as head of a regency council which included Conrad of Urslingen and the Chancellor, Walter of Palear. On his way he stopped at several places in central Italy, and it is possible that at one of them he saw his son for the first and last time. The Emperor's main object in returning home was to obtain the child's election as King of the Romans, the title borne by the Emperor-elect. (Barbarossa had succeeded in having Henry himself elected at the age of five.) Henry counted on using the looted Sicilian treasure in bribes as an added inducement in securing this first step towards the child's ultimate succession to the Empire which for all their ambitions no emperor had yet succeeded in making hereditary. He was successful, and Frederick was elected while he was still a babe in arms, even before his christening at Assisi, where he was given the name of his two grandfathers— Frederick Roger—in the presence of fifteen prelates, cardinals and bishops.

On leaving Bari, Constance returned to Sicily, as its effective sovereign, for the first time since her marriage. The little that is known about her indicates that she was a strong-willed woman, proud of her heritage and capable of taking clear-sighted action to defend it. What her feelings must have been when she arrived in Palermo to find the aftermath of the whole-sale slaughter of St. Stephen's Day is not easy to imagine. Henry's ferocious cruelty, however, had not stamped out Sicilian resistance to his rule. Whether then, or at any other time, Constance took part in the Sicilian independence move-ment has never really been established—though there may have been some secret understanding between her and the Admiral Margitone and a certain Count Giordano, who now led the island revolt; while Queen Sybil's brother, Count Richard of Acerra, followed suit on the mainland.

Next year Henry returned, and with his crusading army put down the rebellion, treating its leaders with such a refinement of cruelty as to shock the public opinion even of those days. After his defeat and capture, Richard of Acerra was dragged by horses through the streets of Capua and, still living, hung by the feet for two days, until a court fool put an end to his agonies by tying a weight to his neck and strangling him. In Germany the luckless Sicilian hostages were blinded; while in Sicily the leaders were tortured to death in Henry and Constance's pre-sence. Count Giordano was put on a red-hot iron throne, and a red-hot crown was hammered with nails into his head, an allusion, apparently, to Henry's suspicions that he had planned to succeed him in the sovereignty of the island.

Henry now seemed to be convinced that all resistance had finally been crushed and he allowed the crusading army to sail, only to find that the nobles rose once more against him. It was an awkward moment, but by adopting a conciliatory atti-tude and promising a general amnesty he succeeded, sur-prisingly, in regaining control of the situation. This time he seems to have suspected Constance's participation in the rising, for he ordered the Chancellor, Walter of Palear, to have her confined in the Palace of Palermo. It is impossible to con-jecture what further cruelties he might not have perpetrated if the Emperor had not died suddenly after a short illness.

He knew that he was dying and that instead of creating an empire as great as that of the Caesars, to be handed on to a son fully grown, he was now leaving to a woman and a child not yet three, a heritage of unfulfilled schemes and deadly hatred. During the last days of his life he tried to propitiate his enemies—he even sent an embassy to Richard Cœur de Lion to release him from the oath of vassalage extracted from him at the time of his captivity. Henry also foresaw the powerful position which the Church could now assume in the affairs of Sicily, and he tried to disarm its opposition to his son's succession by making a will in which he gave way to all the Pope's demands that he had previously refused, even going so far as to declare the Holy See heir to the Realm of Sicily if Frederick should die without children.

This will was subsequently suppressed by his German friends who hoped to rule the country, ostensibly in the name of the Empire, but they had counted without Constance. This clear-sighted woman immediately seized the reins of power. She knew that she and the child would need a powerful protector if they were to survive at all, let alone rule, and her first action was to send an embassy to the Pope to obtain his recognition of her son's right to the succession by sanctioning his coronation. Celestine III profited from her desperate need to drive a hard bargain; he even resuscitated the story of Frederick's being the son of the butcher of Jesi, and Constance had to swear upon oath that he was her legitimate child before the Pope would come to terms at all. She was forced to acknowledge that her kingdom was a papal fief and to pay for it an annual tribute of a thousand scifati, and she had also to abandon many of the special concessions which had given the Norman kings a measure of spiritual independence in their own realm, and nearly all the ecclesiastical rights of the crown in the nomination of the Sicilian bishops.

Celestine died before the agreement could be ratified, and Constance had a serious illness from which she rallied sufficiently, however, to push through a settlement with the new Pope, Innocent III, and to hold a joint coronation of herself and her little son in Palermo early in the summer of 1198. But it soon became evident that Constance's illness was mortal. With great courage she tried to plan ahead to prevent the chaos into which the rival factions would throw Sicily as soon as her authority had gone. She died in Palermo on the 27th of November 1198, and by the terms of her will Frederick, who was not yet four, became the ward of the Pope.

The situation after her death was even more disastrous than that foreseen by Walter of the Mill. The ultimate result of Constance's marriage had been to let loose upon the kingdom a band of German adventurers and soldiers of fortune, whom her husband had introduced into the country in his efforts to subdue it; many of them were sheer freebooters who had well earned the hatred of Constance and her people. As soon as she was reasonably sure of papal support, Constance banished them all— from their leader Markward of Anweiler, whom Henry had made Seneschal of the Empire, to their Sicilian adherents such as Walter of Palear, who had imprisoned her at her husband's command.

A similar wave of anti-German feeling had swept the whole of Italy at Henry's death. The people had risen against the German lords whom he had installed—his own brother Philip, Duke of Tuscany, had to flee for his life from Montefiascone, where he had stopped on his way to take Frederick to Germany for his coronation as King of the Romans. If the news of his father's death had broken only a few days later Frederick would already have been confided to his uncle's care and have been on his way to Germany to be brought up as a German prince; instead, he was later handed over to his mother's emissaries and taken to Palermo to be brought up as the Norman king of a realm which was the cross-roads between the West and the Saracen and Byzantine East. By such a narrow margin can the course of history be changed. If Frederick had later succeeded to the Empire after receiving the orthodox education of a German princeling, his political aims and his whole philosophy of life would have been entirely different and he would have been a less remarkable but probably a much happier man.

Innocent III had made one additional stipulation in his agreement with Constance, the recall of Walter of Palear to court. Constance complied, and it says much for her common sense that, although she must have hated him personally for his part in her imprisonment and for his pro-German sympathies, she realised that he was an able and forceful man, whose favour must be ensured if any sort of stable government was to continue after her death. Palear again took up his duties as

Chancellor and was made a member of the household council, which was vested with the powers of regency to govern the kingdom during Frederick's minority. Palear was Bishop of Troia and, according to the custom of the times, all his fellow members were also ecclesiastics. They were the Archbishops of Monreale, Reggio, Palermo, and Capua; but Palear was the dominating character in a council of elderly men, some of whom died not long after taking office, leaving the way clear for him to indulge his own ambitions and those of his family.

In the chaos which now descended upon Sicily it is sometimes a little difficult to establish who was fighting whom. Apart from the counts and barons who took immediate advantage of this opportunity to rob the central power for their own benefit, the various conflicting parties finally sorted themselves into two groups, until this balance was upset by the Pope unwisely introducing a third. The Germans under Markward of An-weiler tried to seize the country upon the pretext that they represented the imperial power to which it rightly belonged as a result of Constance's marriage to Henry. They were aided and abetted by one of the great maritime powers, Pisa, who hoped to profit from the situation by grabbing ports for her own use. The Moslems soon threw in their lot with this group as they naturally feared that the Pope might take advantage of his guardianship to strike at them. The Norman ele-ment welcomed the Pope's intervention, as it was certain that he would do everything in his power to expel the Germans in order to break the link between the kingdom and the Empire.

The situation had resolved itself into a straight fight between these two groups, with a papal army supporting Palear as the leader of the Regency Council representing Frederick and backed by the Normans. Then the Pope made the mistake of insisting upon the restitution of the County of Lecce to the heir of Tancred, one of his daughters who had escaped at the time of Henry VI's death and married a renowned soldier, Walter de Brienne, who was also a relative of the King of France. With the Pope's support Walter now invaded southern Italy at the head of a French army with the intention of regaining his wife's inheritance. He at once won a victory over the German opposi-tion near Capua, and marched south to continue the struggle.

Innocent had apparently thought that by backing Walter

he had found an economical method of ridding himself and
southern Italy of the Germans and that he had safeguarded the
rights of his ward Frederick sufficiently by making Walter
swear that he would limit his claims on his wife's behalf to the
County of Lecce and make no attempt to set up either her or her
heirs as pretenders to the Sicilian throne because of their
d'Hauteville descent. Palear did not share the Pope's opinion
on this point, and his fear that Walter's ultimate pretensions
might deprive him of his virtual position of regent drove him
into opposing the Pope and making a bargain with Markward
of Anweiler.

The exact conditions of this agreement will probably never
be known, and Palear may subsequently have tried to go back on
it; but later events speak for themselves. When in 1201 Palear
left Sicily, Markward seized Palermo and laid siege to the
fortress of Castellamare, to which Frederick had been taken for
safety, in the care of Palear's brother Gentile of Manupello.
At the crucial moment Gentile unaccountably absented himself
—he maintained later that he had gone to Messina in order to
obtain provisions with which to stand a siege. In his absence
the Castellan, without any attempt at resistance, gave up the
castle, and Frederick, to Markward of Anweiler.

It is significant that it is in these circumstances of treachery
that Frederick first emerges as a personality. Of his actual life
up to now little is known, beyond chroniclers' accounts of
poverty, verging upon destitution, to which the chaos of the
civil war had reduced him. They said that he owed his very food
to the kindness of the citizens of Palermo, who took it in turns
to keep him in their houses, one for a week, another for a
month, according to what each could afford.

Frederick was now seven years old, and since his mother's
death had been the centre around which a collection of schemers
had laid their plans for their own advancement. Officially he
was the Pope's ward, and a legate, Cardinal Gregory of Galgano, had been appointed to supervise his upbringing. But the
Pope and his legate were mainly occupied in protecting the
Church's interests among the shifting sands of Sicilian politics,
while Frederick's personal household, his "familiars" as they
were called, were mostly relations or hangers-on of Walter of
Palear.

Even at this early age Frederick probably had already realised that the men who surrounded him were only out for themselves. Even if he had not, the treachery that permitted his seizure by Markward of Anweiler, without any effort at the defence of a coast fortress from which he could in the last resort have escaped by sea to Messina, must have brought it home to him. It is certain that he knew, and feared, the danger of falling into Markward's hands; an eyewitness account of the actual scene leaves this in no possible doubt.

A letter from one of Frederick's "familiars" addressed to the Pope describes the scene: "When by the treachery of those who had care of him, they had penetrated into the inmost part of the palace and came forward to lay their hands upon him, and it was clear to him that he was now in the hands of his enemies, he, who had hardly emerged from the age when he had been rocked to sleep with lullabies, defended himself with tears and force. Nor did he forget his royal estate when, like a mouse who fears the pursuit of a ferocious animal, he threw himself upon those who were about to seize him, trying with all his force to ward off the arm of him who dared to lay his hand upon the sacred body of the Lord's anointed; then rending his clothes from off him, filled with impotent rage, he tore at his soft flesh with his sharp nails."

A child of seven's consciousness of himself as "the Lord's anointed" seems incredible today, but the man who had witnessed the scene knew Frederick intimately, and he wrote immediately afterwards when Frederick was a helpless child, prisoner of his enemies, and not in the light of after-years when he had become a powerful sovereign. The writer was apparently convinced of Frederick's sense of his own royalty and of the outrage committed against him. The boy who could think and act thus was later to sacrifice his personal tranquillity and even his own kingdom to his interpretation of his duties as an emperor.

Within a few months of seizing Frederick, Markward of Anweiler died as the result of an unsuccessful operation for the stone. He had a bitter hatred of Constance and had tried to discredit Frederick's legitimacy with the Pope in the hope of getting the kingdom for himself, and his early death may well have saved Frederick from mutilation or death. William Cap-

parone, who followed Markward, was a man of less force of
character, with no personal animosity towards Frederick or his
family, and in any event he drew what authority he had from
his control of the young king's person; apart from making sure
of that, it is probable that he left the child much to his own
devices.

How Frederick spent the next five years of his life is a
mystery, but he emerged from them a man already formed;
skilled, as his father had been, in the exercise of arms, a magnificent horseman, an omnivorous reader, and passionately
interested in nature and the study of the universe. In his
avidity for knowledge he would talk to, and argue with, anyone he pleased; though he was impatient of any kind of restraint
and had coarse manners and habits.

Some elements of the normal education of a nobleman of his
period Frederick had. His Latin tutor, William Franciscus,
who was already with him in 1201, held the post again in 1206.
Frederick had a natural love of learning; years afterwards he
said: "Before I assumed the responsibilities of government
[which he did at fourteen] I sought after knowledge and
breathed her balsamic perfumes." This rather flowery phrase-
ology has an Oriental flavour about it, and it is certain that
Frederick must have known many Moslems, for they made up
a large part of the population of Palermo. When he was a man
he spoke Arabic with ease, and it was evident that his tastes and
his beliefs had been influenced, and his devotion to science
greatly fostered, by his Moslem friends, though he owed his
introduction to the latter, at a very early age, to the papal
legate, Gregory of Galgano.

The Palermo in which Frederick ran wild from the age of
seven to twelve was like a city of the *Arabian Nights*. It had
been under Moslem dominion for nearly two centuries when
Count Roger I conquered it in 1091. Under this ruler the
Moslem population, except in Palermo itself, was reduced to a
status little better than serfdom, but with his characteristically
Norman capacity for organisation and utilising the best of what
came to his hands, Roger soon discovered that the Moslems
made the most efficient civil servants. His son King Roger II,
the Great, was not only himself an administrator of a high order,
but a great patron of the arts and science; and under him the

A reconstruction of the palace and gardens of the Cuba at Palermo, from a painting by A. Lentini

Fountain in the palace of the Ziza at Palermo

Bust believed to be of Frederick II as a young man, found recently in Apulia

Sicilian court became a world centre of learning and culture for Christians and Moslems alike, second only to that of the Arab kingdoms in Spain. Many of the translations of Greek and Arabic scientific works made during the twelfth century came from the Sicilian court. First under King Roger II, later under his successors, Eugene the Emir and Henricus Aristippus translated the writings of Ptolemy, Plato, and Aristotle from Greek into Latin; while the Moslem Idrissi compiled his famous "Geography", after fifteen years of research, at King Roger's command.

Contemporary writers, both Arab and Christian, describe the predominance of the Moslem influence at Roger II's court. Nor was this limited to administration and learning; the whole tenor of life was Oriental rather than Western. For luxurious living the Arabs were far in advance of the Europe of those days, and Roger rapidly acquired a taste for the pleasures and refinements of Moslem life. He lived like a sultan, with a harem guarded by eunuchs; in palaces which from contemporary descriptions must have been very like those of Granada with colonnaded courts, enclosed gardens and fountains; there was even a court with a lion fountain like that of the Alhambra. Roger II's son and grandson, William I and William II, who succeeded him, added to these palaces and gardens until they surrounded Palermo, in the words of an Arab poet, "like a necklace of jewels around the throat of a beautiful maiden".

This was the setting of Frederick's childhood. In winter he probably lived in the castle of Palermo, perhaps even in the suite of rooms which King Roger II had decorated for himself with glittering mosaics of men and animals and birds. During the summer the household probably took refuge from the great heat in the palace of the Favara or Maredolce, so called because it was surrounded on three sides by an immense artificial lake, or in the Cuba, with its Oriental dome, which was built in the midst of sweet swift-flowing waters brought underground from cool springs in the mountains.

Here on summer evenings when the perfumed muscat wine was flowing freely, Frederick may have looked on while Capparone and his friends were entertained by a troupe of the Arab musicians and dancing girls for which Sicily was famous. The pavilions of the Favara and the Cuba, which stood on

B

small artificial islands among palm trees, had been created
for evenings such as this, with the brilliant moonlight and the
golden beams of the torches reflected in the waters, while the
musicians sang Arab love songs to the sound of the lute, and
the dancing girls stamped their feet and danced to the rhythm of
the clicking of their fingers. . . . "Long draughts of cooling
water cannot compare with my content when I kiss the lips of
my beloved . . . her breath is scented with amber and by its
fragrance I know that she is here."[1] No wonder that in later
life Frederick was to call down upon himself the horror of the
pious when he said that God would not have chosen Palestine
for his own if he could have seen "My own Kingdom of Sicily".

The Cuba, the Favara, and two other palaces—the Ziza and
the Menâni—were all built in the enormous royal park which
extended for miles into the foothills surrounding Monte
Matazzaro. It was planted with aromatic trees and shrubs, bay
trees, and myrtles, and in the spring was perfumed with heavy
scents from the groves of oranges, lemons, and limes; while the
pink foam of the almond blossom was reflected in the living
waters of the fountains and artificial rivers and lakes. No
vestige of it now remains, and the palaces which survive are
either ruined or desecrated; but the memory of its beauty lives
on in the pleasure gardens of the later Moslem kings—the
gardens of the great Moguls in Kashmir and in the Aguedal
of the Moorish sultans at Marrakech.

This fantastic garden was the kingdom of Frederick's childhood; in it he could escape from the human beings whom he
could not trust, and the birds and animals replaced the companionship of family and friends that he had never known.
The loneliness of his life must have been overwhelming, and
from it probably grew his love, which was so strange for those
times, for birds and animals, and for the natural beauty of the
countryside. When, later, he wrote a book on falconry, he
displayed an extraordinary knowledge of the life of birds and
their habits; the foundation of which had probably been laid
in the royal park of Palermo. When he was Emperor he built
for himself hunting lodges in wild and lonely places of great
natural beauty, which he called his "places of solace"; he rested
there whenever he could get away from the cares of state. This
habit of escaping from the trials of mankind into the tran-

quillity of the natural world was an inheritance from his childhood.

Frederick's life at this time was quite unlike that of a future king—he did not live in the aristocratic isolation of a court. He ran wild. According to a courtier's description of him when he was about thirteen years old, he had coarse manners and habits formed by the rough company he kept. Circumstances, and his own lively curiosity, brought him into contact with people of every sort and kind and he had the opportunity of knowing how the people lived and what they thought and felt in a way that few other kings have ever done. The last legitimate Norman king had died only eleven years before Frederick fell into the hands of Markward of Anweiler, and the people probably left Frederick in no doubt as to what they thought about the Germans and Capparone and his followers. When they compared present conditions with the peace and prosperity of the good old times which they had known under his Norman forebears, their tales must have fed his hatred of the men who controlled his kingdom, and fired him with impatience to be rid of them. His passionate nature must have turned inward upon itself, for he dared not show his feelings, but there is something appealing about the fact that, like a boy of thirteen of any period, he used to sit up at night reading adventure stories—the history of his forebears' exploits and of the Sicilian fleet, probably from the old chroniclers' dramatic accounts.

This strange childhood both made and marred Frederick for life; it was a forcing house which formed his character so that when he came of age at fourteen, he was in many ways already a man; and it enabled him to undertake, successfully, the subjugation and government of an empire only four years later. But he paid for it by a life of isolation, spent in a world of his own, far in advance of the time in which he lived. In spite of great personal charm, Frederick seemed unable to break through the barrier which separated him from the rest of mankind; he had few friends and, apart from his own children, with one possible exception, it is doubtful if he ever loved anyone.

All his contemporaries were evidently astonished by Frederick's extraordinary precocity. It is mentioned several times in letters, but the most striking evidence comes in a letter from the Pope, dated the 26th February 1208. In it Innocent III described Frederick: "As was said of the Caesars, his peers, power comes before its time, and from the door of puberty with swift steps he enters the years of discretion and with his powers anticipates the years." Innocent had never seen Frederick and owed his knowledge to Cardinal Cencio Savelli, who was then legate in Sicily. About two years before the date of this letter Frederick had been returned to the guardianship of the Pope, as the result of a rapprochement between Innocent III and Walter of Palear, who resumed the work of the Chancellorship.

The Frederick of 1208 is described in a contemporary letter, a letter written when Frederick was an unknown boy with poor prospects, a dependant of the Pope, no more than the titular head of a state, where the writ even of his powerful Chancellor ran not much further than the gates of Palermo.

The identity of the writer is not known for certainty, but he was evidently an intimate of the court, for he wrote: "As you have been long in doubt, by reason of the varying descriptions of the habits of the king; of his stature, aspect, and life; and as you wish to have more precise information from me; although this calls for something in a higher and more polished style, I have persuaded myself to undertake it to show you how ready I am to please you. The stature, then, of the king is neither small nor taller than one would expect at his age. But the Universal Author of nature has given him robust limbs and a strong body, with which his vigorous spirit can achieve whatever he undertakes. He is never idle, but passes the whole day in some occupation or other, and so that his vigour may increase with practice, he fortifies his agile body with every kind of exercise and practice of arms. He either employs his arms or carries them, drawing his shortsword, in whose use he is expert; he makes play of defending himself from an attack. He is a good shot with the bow and often practises archery. He loves fast thoroughbred horses: and I believe that no one knows better than he how to curb them with the bridle and then set them at full gallop. This is how he spends his days from morn to eve, and then begins afresh the following day.

"To this is added a regal majesty and majestic features and mien, to which are united a kindly and gracious air, a serene brow, brilliant eyes, and expressive face, a burning spirit, and a ready wit. Nevertheless his actions are sometimes odd and vulgar, though this is not due to nature but to contact with rough company. The royal will can by its fundamental character easily alter all this for the better, and all that is vulgar will little by little be changed to good. He is intolerant of admonitions, and judges himself capable of acting according to his own free will, and considers it shameful for himself to be subject to a guardian and to be considered a boy. Which leads to his not obeying his tutor's commands, and transgressing with the freedom customary to kings, he talks with all and argues in a manner which diminishes the veneration of his majesty. However he has virtue in advance of his age, and though not adult, he is well versed in knowledge and has the gift of wisdom, which usually comes only with the passage of years. In him, then, the number of the years do not count, nor is there need to await maturity, because as a man he is full of knowledge, and as a ruler of majesty."

On his fourteenth birthday, the 26th of December 1208, Frederick came of age, and nine months later he was married to a wife of the Pope's choosing, Constance of Aragon. She was the widow of the King of Hungary, ten years older than Frederick, and he does not seem to have been enthusiastic about the match; but it was agreed that she should bring five hundred knights in her train, under the leadership of her brother Alfonso Count of Provence, and that they should be at the disposal of her husband. Knights provided the striking power of an army, and judged by the standards of the day it was a sizeable force with which Frederick might set about the restoration of order in his kingdom in real earnest.

With the piled-up determination acquired during the years of his minority, when he had been forced to watch, inactive while his kingdom became a prey to anyone sufficiently powerful to help himself to the pickings, Frederick lost no time about setting matters to rights when he came of age. Already when he went to meet Constance on the 19th of August, he had led an expedition to restore order in the island—he had signed the marriage contract early in 1209 in Syracuse—and by the time that the marriage took place he had succeeded in getting quite a large part of the lands of his personal demesne in the island returned to him.

The marriage was celebrated in Palermo with great splendour, nobles from all over the realm coming to witness it. There was evidently a considerable amount of curiosity about Frederick himself—this young king who had grown up in complete obscurity but who for all that was the grandson of the two greatest men of the last century, Barbarossa and Roger the Great.

The wedding also offered an opportunity for pageantry and display, calculated to appeal to the barons, and this alliance with the powerful house of Aragon signified the return of the Kingdom of Sicily to the stage of world politics. Since the death of King William the brilliant court of Palermo had suffered a complete eclipse, and the townsmen and merchants must have looked forward to the prosperity which a stable government and the gaieties of a cultivated court would bring, even though the nobles might be less enthusiastic at the prospect of the reinforcement of the royal power by a train of foreign knights.

What the two principal figures, the bride and bridegroom, made of each other, no indiscretions of chroniclers or courtiers have survived to tell—Constance, a woman of twenty-four who had already reigned as queen, whose brother's title—Count of Provence—stood for all that was chivalrous and cultivated, and was associated with the poetry and romance of the Courts of Love; and Frederick, a boy of fourteen who spent his days in the practice of arms and hunting, and his nights in reading history, who had vulgar habits and rough manners, and who probably for the first time in his life now met a sophisticated woman of the world.

The years which separated them would at any other age have made little difference; but between a boy of fourteen and a young woman in her early twenties, who had already been married and had a son, it represented a tremendous gap. In all his life until then Frederick had been accustomed only to the company of rough soldiers, scheming priests and politicians, and the people of Palermo itself. We do not know what friends and acquaintances he had picked up in the course of the years; but even in his adult life, when he was the most polished and courtly monarch of his day, he could relapse into phrases such as "I have never fattened a pig but I have relieved him of his bacon!" —which was surely a relic of the years when he had run wild in the streets and market-places of Palermo. Memories of this period must have been in his mind when he wrote letters of advice to his young son Conrad, whom he had left alone in Germany. In them he warned his son against becoming too familiar with huntsmen and falconers—the "rough company" which he had frequented in his own youth—perhaps he remembered the embarrassment which some youthful *faux pas* of his own had caused among the polished company of the court which his first wife had brought with her to Sicily.

The arrival of Constance with her train of knights, court ladies, and troubadours, opened up a new world to Frederick, very different from that of the ecclesiastics and the soldiery to which he had been accustomed. It is significant that from the time of his marriage to Constance all descriptions of Frederick's person and manners emphasise his charm and personal fascination. His fastidious habits and passion for personal cleanliness later became a legend, as did his sybaritic tastes. Within three years his marriage transformed Frederick from a rough uncouth boy into the "Puer Apuliae" whose glamour captivated Germany.

There was nothing romantic about the marriage—it was purely political—but it gave Frederick what he lacked—the polish of a courtier. It introduced him to what was most civilised in European life and to the conventions of courtly love. In a few years Constance gave birth to a son, Henry. It was not long after that Frederick's first illegitimate child, Enzo, was born, the first evidence of the existence of the sensual side of Frederick's nature which later exceeded the limits even of the licence recognised as the prerogative of kings and emperors in his day.

Although the marriage was purely political, it inevitably had a profound effect upon Frederick's personal life; for the first time since his mother's death there existed someone else whose interests were entirely bound up with his own. The tie became stronger with the birth of a son, and it would to some extent have relieved Frederick of the awful burden of loneliness which had marred his childhood.

Constance herself had to depend a great deal more upon her young husband than she had anticipated, for within two months of the wedding her brother and nearly all of the five hundred

knights who had accompanied them from Aragon were dead—
victims of one of those violent epidemics which so often attacked
foreigners in the kingdom of Sicily and changed the course of
history. After this tragic event Frederick and Constance left
Palermo to escape the infection and went to live in Catania.

Although Frederick knew what a blow the knights' deaths
represented to his hopes of a rapid reordering of his kingdom—
their coming had been the deciding factor in his acceptance of a
marriage which had not aroused his enthusiasm—his reactions
were the same as they would have been at any period later in
his life. He spent his days hunting either in the woods of Murgo
or around the lakes and marshes of Lentini, one of the wildest
and most beautiful places in the neighbourhood of Catania.
But while behaving apparently as if he was still a boy interested
only in hunting and studying the wild life of the country round,
Frederick, as was to be the case throughout his life, was in fact
pursuing the aims of his policy unchanged, with the reduced
means at his disposal. So now he was preparing the way for an
alliance with Genoa by making a Genoese count, Alaman da
Costa, whom he had first met in Syracuse the year before, a
member of the royal council.

Frederick knew that he was going to need the help of every
ally he could make because, either just before or just after the
death of Alfonso of Provence, he had issued an edict com-
manding all landowners to submit their title-deeds to the royal
curia for examination. It was a blow which he had no doubt
planned during the years while he watched his royal demesne
and prerogatives slowly being whittled away by the grasping
nobles, or given by Palear to his adherents. It was characteristic of Frederick to choose this legal and unostentatious
way of setting about the return to normal conditions in the
kingdom, while being well aware of the storm which it would
inevitably provoke.

When he could no longer call upon a force of Aragonese
knights for support, the Calabrian barons made no attempt to
hide their feelings about this boy-king's ideas of taking lands,
including his own, back from them. The most powerful among
them were the Counts of Gerace and Tropea. Anfuso de Roto
of Tropea apparently insulted Frederick to his face, and his
astonishment must have been unbounded when he suddenly

found himself, and many others of the most powerful nobles of the realm, seized and imprisoned. The news spread fast and created a sensation. The Abbot of Cassino delayed the departure of his chamberlain, who was due to leave for the court bearing presents and compliments for the king on the occasion of his marriage.

Frederick was well within his legal rights, but he was not content to leave it at that. He addressed a circular letter, outlining the reasons for his action, to the prelates and nobles of his realm, beginning with the Abbot of Cassino. In the letter he wrote: "It is said that the Barons and the people do not approve of our action—but we remember already to have written to you before to tell you of the malignity which existed —but now it has become manifest. They plotted against us— the Count Paolo and Count Ruggiero of Gerace. The Count of Tropea, Anfuso de Roto, said 'I will make my seat in Calabria and be equal to the King'; he wanted to be Admiral and to have the castles of Mente and Monticino. As we refused, hoping to keep the small part of our demesne left to us, he shouted threats at us. Think then on your fidelity if we are not justified? Is there anyone in Calabria who does not know that Count Anfuso has taken nearly all our demesne and has destroyed churches and sacred church lands? Taking persons and fortresses and turning the houses of God into the dens of thieves."

This circular letter was signed at Messina on the 14th of January 1210. The last document to bear the signature of Walter of Palear was dated a few days previously, and from now on, although he retained the title of Chancellor, Palear was made to reside in his see of Catania. It was the parting of the ways.

Once before a circular letter had been sent out on Frederick's behalf; it was addressed to the princes of Christendom, and dispatched in the summer of 1201 during the confused and threatening period when Palear had left Sicily and Markward of Anweiler was at the gates of Palermo. It asked the princes' help for the child king of Sicily—an orphan and a "lamb among the wolves", and it was written in Frederick's name by one of the familiars of his household, perhaps a clerk who had been trained in the papal chancellory, whence such letters were

increasingly being issued. Did Frederick know of the existence
of that first circular letter? And was its author still a member
of his household to whom he turned when he took this first
completely independent action of his own? In any event, with
the dispatch of his circular letter Frederick instituted a practice
that was subsequently to become one of his most powerful
weapons of policy.

Warning of a far greater danger which was now approaching
Frederick's kingdom from without had already reached Palear
from the Pope in December. Malcontents who disliked
Frederick's energetic policy, and some of the Germans, who
still clung to their fiefs in the northern marches of the realm,
had been seen in the camp of the Guelf Emperor Otto IV, and
were known to have invited him to the Sicilian kingdom. Otto
was on his way to Rome for his imperial coronation at the head
of a powerful army and, although he was chief of the party
which was traditionally faithful to the papacy, Innocent III had
rightly mistrusted his intentions from the first.

Since Henry VI's death, Germany had been devastated by
civil war between the Guelf and Ghibelline claimants to the
imperial throne. To begin with, Philip of Hohenstaufen had
loyally tried to support his nephew Frederick's legal claim; but
the leaders of the Ghibelline faction had elected Philip Emperor
in place of Frederick, because they felt that their cause was
doomed to failure if they fought on the behalf of a child in far-
away Sicily. After eleven weary years Philip had established
his supremacy, only to be murdered by a disappointed suitor of
his daughter. Sheer weariness imposed a compromise solution
upon the warring factions; the Guelf claimant, Otto of Brunswick, was betrothed to Philip's daughter, thus uniting Guelf
and Hohenstaufen. Beatrice was regarded as the heiress of the
Hohenstaufens and apparently Frederick was completely forgotten. Otto was finally elected Emperor, with the Pope's
concurrence, on condition that he laid no claim to the Kingdom
of Sicily.

Success after so many years of struggle appears to have gone
to Otto's head, for he planned to extend his dominions not only
to the full extent of Barbarossa's empire, but to go back on his
word to the Pope, and to seize the Kingdom of Sicily as well.
The German princes wanted no more war, and the Ghibellines,

who could still remember Barbarossa, were outraged at the Guelf Emperor's intention of wresting even his mother's Kingdom of Sicily from Barbarossa's grandson. The deciding factor, however, was the Pope's attitude; if even a Guelf Emperor was to renew the menace of the union of the Empire and Sicily, it would be far better to replace him by Frederick, who was only a boy and had been brought up as Innocent's own ward, far away from Ghibelline influences.

The Pope had already prepared the way by warning the bishops of Germany that if the Emperor was excommunicated they were released from their oath of obedience. Otto's invasion of the papal province of Tuscany, and Apulia in the Kingdom of Sicily, was the signal for his excommunication.

By the autumn of 1211, Otto had occupied the whole of the mainland part of Frederick's kingdom. He had been sent an invitation by the Moslems to invade the island of Sicily and was preparing to cross the straits of Messina, when he received the news that at a General Council held in September at Nuremberg, the princes had declared him deposed and elected Frederick emperor in his stead. The Pope, Philip Augustus of France, who opposed the Guelf succession owing to their kinship with his English enemies, and the war-weariness of the German princes were the influences which had been at work to bring about this surprising revolution within two years of Otto's final succession to the Empire and his coronation. He realised the full seriousness of the situation, and by the 1st of November he was already on his way back to Germany.

In the midst of the consternation which reigned in Sicily, with galleys riding at anchor in Palermo harbour ready to carry Constance and their newly born son Henry, and probably Frederick himself, to Africa if Otto's invasion should prove successful, the King preserved an astonishing calm. He chose this particular moment, the nadir of his fortunes, to have the sun and moon, emblems of world dominion, emblazoned on his coat of arms.

Few dramatic gestures of this kind can ever have received so rapid and complete a fulfilment. Early in 1212 the German ambassadors, Conrad of Ursberg and Anselm of Justingen, arrived in Italy with the offer of the imperial crown. Frederick was just eighteen when Anselm arrived in Palermo, and his hold upon the island of Sicily, let alone the rest of his kingdom, was shaky indeed. No wonder that his councillors and his wife advised him to decline the offer.

Frederick himself had no ties with his father's country; he had grown up among people who had good reason to hate the Germans and who had probably succeeded in inculcating something of their feelings in him, as his terror and outrage at the time of his seizure by Markward bore witness. Moreover Frederick had just begun to set his realm in order when it was again thrown into chaos by the invasion of Otto and his German army, which threatened Frederick's very existence. But it was this last threat, probably, that decided Frederick, in spite of all advice to the contrary, to accept the offer of the Empire. His sense of outrage at Otto's unprovoked attack and his own ardent spirit may have had something to do with it, but with judgement astonishing in one so lacking in political experience, he took the long view. He saw that disappointment at his refusal would consolidate Otto's position in Germany, so that he could return with reinforcements to attack Sicily again.

Innocent III was well aware of the perils involved in giving his support to Frederick, and if he or his advisers had had any real idea of the character and feelings of the young man who had recently been his ward, they would have tried any other means to achieve the basic aim of their Italian policy—to prevent the unification of the Sicilian Kingdom with the Empire and the consequent territorial encirclement of the Papal States. Instead, promises of subservience were extracted from Frederick. Ratification of agreements made by previous Norman kings and of his mother's concordat with the Pope and agreement to pay tribute were evidently not considered a sufficient guarantee; he was required to make an act of submission as well. This he did in Messina in February 1212: "We swear in the presence of the Papal Legate fidelity to you and your successors, and promise that if you or your successors come to some part of the realm, and we, called by you, can come without peril to your presence we will personally do liege homage to you." The agreement went on to lay down the conditions governing the election of the Sicilian bishops. This had long been a bone of contention between the popes and the kings of Sicily, and already trouble had sprung up between Frederick and Innocent over the election of the Archbishop of Palermo. Even the present agreement did not settle matters, as it laid down that after their selection by the chapter, all bishops had to be confirmed in their office both by the Pope and the King, thus leaving the way open for continual friction in future.

Frederick's son Henry, who was only a few months old, was solemnly crowned King of Sicily, Constance was made regent, and Walter of Palear recalled to court. From now on Frederick bore the title of Emperor-elect, and at the end of February he set out on the hazardous journey to Germany, to win the Empire in real earnest.

Frederick sailed from Messina with very few companions, but their number included one man whose devotion to him never failed and who seems to have been one of the very few human beings with whom Frederick was on terms of real affection and friendship. Surprisingly enough he was a priest, Berard of Castacca, who later became Archbishop of Palermo. He had known Frederick for some years and as Bishop of Bari he had for a time been a member of the regency council. Now he was created papal legate to accompany him, a fact which says much for his powers of diplomacy and for the affection which he inspired in Frederick.

The hostility of Pisa, whose galleys were on the look-out for him, forced Frederick to land at Gaeta and to continue his journey by road to Rome. The old Appian Way was flanked with the ruins of Rome's imperial grandeur, and the young heir to the title of the Caesars was received in the city with all the honours due to an Emperor-elect. But in the midst of these remains of ancient greatness and the promise of his own imperial future, Frederick was effectively reminded of the mediaeval present and of the true seat of power—on Easter Sunday he was called upon to perform the act of feudal homage to Innocent as his suzerain for the fief of Sicily.

On his knees before the Pope, he placed his hands within those of Innocent, and bowed his head before the penetrating gaze of this small intrepid man whose indomitable will had raised the papacy to heights of power which it was never again to equal. The pale oval of the Pope's face, with its long dominating nose, oblique eyes, tiny ascetic mouth, and forceful

chin, looked down upon the smooth beardless one of a youth
with brilliant blue eyes and red-gold hair. Apparently Innocent only saw there the immaturity, the sensual mouth and the
humility of the pose—the pride which outmatched his own, and
the ruthless determination, escaped him. One of the Church's
greatest statesmen, for all his experience, failed to take the
measure of this youth of eighteen.

If the Pope had sensed the piled-up resentment which years
of bitterness had wrought upon a proud and passionate spirit,
only held in check by the determination of intellect and will,
even at this late hour he would have searched for some other
means to carry out his policy, or, failing this, he might have
risked all in a generous gesture and left Frederick unconditionally free to go and claim the Empire. Instead Innocent
added fuel to the fires of Frederick's pent-up suspicion and
resentment by making him swear to relinquish the one remnant
of his heritage which even in the darkest times had been his in
name—his beloved Kingdom of Sicily.

The schooling of his desolate childhood served Frederick
well on this occasion. Innocent never seems to have guessed
that this well-disciplined young king who agreed to make over
to his infant son his Kingdom of Sicily, as soon as he himself
was crowned Emperor, even promising that during the child's
minority the kingdom should be administered by a regent of the
Pope's choosing, was inwardly determined to do no such
thing.

In Frederick's eyes the chaos in which he had found his
realm was the result of the Pope's negligence and pursuit of the
Church's interest to the exclusion of his duties as guardian.
The fact that the Pope was in a position to exact a promise from
him to surrender his kingdom and his own son to the tutelage
from which he himself had just emerged was as bitter a blow
to a young man of Frederick's temperament as could be imagined. He who at thirteen had been "intolerant of admonitions
and judged himself capable of acting of his own free will, and
considered it shameful to be subject to a guardian" found that
as Emperor-elect the bonds were still there, and he had not
even yet achieved the shadow of power, but was still a puppet
in the hands of the Pope.

Frederick must have been thankful to leave Rome and continue his journey. His friendship with the Genoese Count Aleman da Costa now stood him in good stead; he sailed from Civitavecchia in a Genoese galley, whose crew succeeded in smuggling the future Emperor across the Ligurian Sea to their home port, past the watchful eyes of their Pisan rivals. Frederick was given a great welcome in Genoa, and stayed there for three months in the house of Niccolo Doria. The Dorias were the leaders of the Ghibelline faction in the city, and they remained faithful to Frederick even when Genoa became a papal stronghold. Probably it was on this occasion that Frederick first met Percival Doria, who later became one of that intimate circle of poets, wits, and men of learning which made Frederick's court the most brilliant of his day.

With characteristic business acumen the Genoese came to an agreement with Frederick, whereby he stated that upon his accession as Emperor he would confirm all the privileges granted to Genoa by previous emperors, and the city made him a gift of a large sum of money.

In July Frederick left Genoa for the last part of his journey, which was to prove the most dangerous stage of all, for the Milanese were on the watch to try and prevent another member of the hated house of Hohenstaufen from reaching Germany and becoming Emperor, and they patrolled the Lombard plain. The normal route across the Alps by the Brenner was also closed to Frederick by the presence of Otto and his army at Trent.

On Saturday, the 28th of July, Frederick and his train were welcomed into the city of Pavia to the pealing of church bells. Already in Lombardy the glamour of the south surrounded him, and to the solid townsfolk of Pavia he was the "Puero Sicilie", the Boy of Sicily. He stayed in Pavia overnight and the following evening, as soon as it was dark, he set out with an armed band of townsmen for a ford on the Lambro river where a rendezvous had been arranged with a force from Cremona, a city which had always been strongly Ghibelline. After a long night's ride, Frederick and his small force were resting on the banks of the river, waiting to make contact with the Cremonese at dawn, when they were surprised by a band of Milanese. In the mêlée which followed, Frederick, who could by now see the Cremonese approaching the opposite bank of the Lambro, leapt on a horse and, riding bareback, swam the river to safety and a triumphant welcome in Cremona.

For a while after this, Frederick disappears completely from our view; and to this day the exact route by which he crossed the Alps is not known, but it was at Chur, in the heart of his hereditary Duchy of Swabia, that we next see him, as he starts upon his conquest of the Empire.

Chapter II

THE EMPIRE

1212–1220

NO foreign king taking possession of a newly conquered realm could have been more of a stranger to the country which he was called upon to rule than Frederick of Hohenstaufen when he arrived in Germany. He knew nothing of the internal politics or even the character and language of the people of his father's country, which could not have presented a greater contrast to the semi-Oriental Sicily in which he had been brought up.

In his grandfather, Barbarossa's, day the Emperor himself and many German nobles could not speak with ease Latin, which was the language of diplomacy and officialdom. By Frederick's time there had been an increase in learning in Germany, but many contemporary chroniclers paint a picture of a country sunk in barbarous anarchy, in which constantly warring nobles would forswear the most sacred oaths and sink to any depths in order to gain money or power. The government of Sicily had been a difficult proposition, but it paled in comparison with what confronted Frederick in Germany.

Some of the epithets which the Guelfs applied to him— "the Priest's King", "the Boy from Apulia"—give the key to what many of these tough barons must have thought of a beard-less youth of eighteen, a Pope's protégé, who had come without an army to try and govern them. A young man too who, had they known it, spoke several foreign languages and was addicted to learning.

In spite of Otto's excommunication and Frederick's election, the ex-Emperor still enjoyed a good deal of support in Germany; eighty princes had attended the diet which he had held in Frankfurt upon his return from Italy, and he disposed of a considerable army—which had lately overrun all Italy to the

Straits of Messina. Moreover, he had the advantage of experience as a military leader, whereas Frederick had none.

The immediate odds seemed heavily in Otto's favour, and
it looked as if Frederick would be faced with a struggle of years
if he was eventually to obtain the Empire, and the ultimate
issue was far from sure. But that strange providence which
had brought Frederick unscathed through his adventurous
journey across Italy had already been working in his favour
before he reached Germany.

In August Otto's marriage to Beatrice of Hohenstaufen,
his trump card in the struggle for the Empire, had taken place
with all possible pomp and circumstance. Within a few days
of the marriage Beatrice, who was still in her teens, died
mysteriously. With her went Otto's hopes of dividing the
Hohenstaufen inheritance and allegiance, and her sudden
death, so shortly after her marriage to a man who was under the
ban of excommunication, was regarded in a superstitious age
as a sign of divine displeasure.

Luck again favoured Frederick in his first active venture in
Germany. Upon his arrival in Swabia he had been received by
the Bishop of Chur and welcomed into the great Abbey of St.
Gall, but so far no city had acclaimed him. Daring greatly, he
rode with only 300 men straight for Constance; it was touch and
go, and failure for Frederick at this stage would have been
disastrous. Otto had come to Uberlingen near Lake Constance
in preparation for a state entry into the City of Constance itself. Frederick, with only a small band of followers, presented
himself at the city gates a few hours before Otto was due to
arrive. At first Frederick was refused entrance, but when the
Papal Nuncio, Bishop Berard of Bari, who accompanied him,
had read aloud the Pope's sentence of excommunication against
Otto the gates were opened, and the Bishop of Constance
received Frederick and his band.

Three hours later Otto arrived with a magnificent entourage
for the ceremonial entry, only to find the city gates barred
against him. A touch of the ridiculous was added to his dis-
comfiture by the fact that he and his train had to go hungry
away, while Frederick and his friends sat down to the banquet
which had been prepared for them. It was the type of story
which loses nothing in the telling, and the news of it soon spread.

The story of Constance probably preceded Frederick on the road to Basle, where he was to hold his first official court, for the Bishop of Strasburg came out of the city to meet him with a train of five hundred knights. Here for the first time the lay lords began to follow the example of the ecclesiastical princes who had been the first to support the young Emperor-elect.

Some idea of the practical problems which beset Frederick at this juncture may be judged by a single instance of the financial difficulties which he had to face. His uncle Philip had bought his ascendancy over Otto in the Empire by mortgaging many of the Hohenstaufen hereditary lands and giving away the royal privileges of taxation and toll rights in order to reward his supporters. Otto had been helped by English gold. Frederick arrived to find his family and the state finances in chaos, but to win over the greedy German nobles money was essential. The Duke of Lorraine was one of the first great lay princes to declare his allegiance, and as a reward Frederick made him a gift of three thousand silver marks. He raised the money on security given by the Archbishop of Mainz, the Bishop of Worms, the Count of Hapsburg, Anselm of Justingen and some other Swabian supporters, and by mortgaging the town of Rosheim in Alsace.

After holding court at Basle, Frederick went to live in Barbarossa's castle of Hagenau in Alsace, which seems later to have become his favourite place of residence in his northern realms. It had two great advantages from Frederick's point of view—there were magnificent forests for hunting and one of the finest libraries in the Empire. It was a great walled castle, grand and imposing, with a suite of state rooms floored with red marble. Barbarossa had built a special chapel to house the imperial regalia, whose emptiness—the crown jewels were still in Otto's possession—served as a reminder to the young Emperor-elect of all that lay ahead of him before it could be filled with its treasures again, while the grim castle in the grey October mists of a northern autumn, so different from the garden palaces of Palermo which at the same season would have been bathed in sunlight, pointed the contrast of all that Frederick had left behind him in embarking upon this imperial adventure.

Further signs of success, however, were not long in coming.

Frederick was joined by no less a person than Otto's own chancellor, Conrad of Scharfenburg, an ambitious and able man who was also Bishop of Metz and Speyer. Before he became Otto's chancellor Conrad had served under Philip of Hohenstaufen, and his political experience was of great value to Frederick at this time, while the mere fact that a man so personally ambitious had deserted Otto to join his rival must have decided many waverers as to which way the wind of success was blowing. Frederick took him immediately into his service, confirming him in the chancellorship, which he held for the eight years that Frederick remained in Germany, later accompanying him to Rome for his coronation.

In November Frederick made his debut in the realms of international politics. At Vaucouleurs he met the son of King Philip Augustus of France, the future King Louis VIII, who came as his father's representative to negotiate a treaty with the Emperor-elect. The meeting was, politically, a very friendly one, for Philip Augustus and Otto were enemies, and the King of France had done everything in his power to assist in Frederick's election. It is difficult however to believe that, personally, the two men could have appealed to each other—Louis, small and puny, set in a mould of cold and pious austerity (he was the father of St. Louis), and Frederick, young, athletic and devoted to the pleasant things of life. A treaty of alliance was drawn up, by which Frederick undertook not to make peace with Otto or his nephew, King John of England, without previous agreement with the King of France.

Either then, or shortly afterwards, this agreement brought to Frederick one thing which he badly needed—a large sum of ready money. He had by then moved to Frankfurt, where on the 5th of December he was acclaimed as Emperor; and there, after his acclamation, he distributed the enormous sum of twenty thousand silver marks in largesse among his followers. It was a gift from the King of France, whose envoys had been present while the princes and nobles of the Empire took an oath of fidelity to Frederick and swore never to accept Otto again as Emperor, Lord, King or Regent.

There was something flamboyant about this gesture, but it was wise policy; the whole country got to hear of it, and the impression it created was all the greater because Otto was notoriously mean. The chroniclers shrewdly noted that the gift brought Frederick great popularity.

Frederick was becoming something of a legendary figure; luck seemed to follow him wherever he went. Young, handsome, liberal, the heir to a great name, gifted with a personal fascination which he seemed to be able to call up at will, he was as different from the parsimonious Otto as day from night, and a war-weary country began to see in him the hope of a change from the continual strife of civil war. The minstrels sang songs about him, and suddenly the derogatory nickname of the "Boy from Apulia" was charged with the glamour of the sunlit south, the ancient land of the Caesars.

Without military force and beset by considerable financial difficulties, Frederick displayed great political acumen in setting about the conquest of Germany by peaceful means. He wooed his German subjects in a manner which he never troubled to assume with his Sicilians. With conscious use of his charm, he made graceful gestures—such as inviting a defeated foe, who was his prisoner, to dine every evening at his own table. This he did with Thibault, the new Duke of Lorraine, who unlike his father had become hostile to Frederick and rebelled against him. They used to sup together in complete intimacy over a period of several months, attended by the Duke's squire who carried his cloak.

But the body upon which Frederick concentrated his main efforts and political activities was the Church. It was the greatest single power in the country and had owned since the eleventh century more than half the land in Germany. The Rhineland archbishops ranked as princes of the Empire immediately after the King himself; and owing to their higher standard of education most of the administrative offices were in the hands of priests.

It is significant that the first political act of great importance to which Frederick put his signature, on the 12th of July 1213, was the Bull of Eger, which was in effect a reaffirmation of the Charter of Speyer signed by Otto as the primary condition of his recognition as Emperor by the Pope. The propitiation of Innocent and the ecclesiastical princes in Germany was the aim that Frederick set out to achieve by this act which, in effect, relinquished all the ground gained for the imperial power by

Frederick Barbarossa and Henry VI from the Church. The principle of the Emperor's right to interfere in the nomination of bishops was maintained, but in other respects the Bull of Eger went far towards creating an ecclesiastical state, or states, within the realm of Germany. The right of appeal to Rome on Church matters was freely allowed, and the spiritual domain Frederick abandoned almost entirely to the Pope. In Italy the territorial extent of the papal states was recognised.

Frederick's wooing of the German Church continued throughout the eight years in which he lived in the country. Originally it was dictated by his need for a solid body of support upon which to build up his personal position in the country; then as he came to realise the peculiar character of the German monarchy and the implications of the elective principle, he saw how necessary was the goodwill of the ecclesiastical princes to ensure what was later to become his main aim—the election of his son Henry as King of the Romans and as his own successor. This was probably present in Frederick's mind from the outset; although he had sworn to the Pope not to unite the Empire and the Kingdom of Sicily under one person, and Henry had been crowned King of Sicily when his father left the country in 1212.

From very early on Frederick seems to have made a clear distinction in his own mind between the functions of an emperor and those of a ruler of Germany. Unfortunately for the peace of Europe the Empire in its wider sense appealed to him as much as his own Kingdom of Sicily, whereas ruling Germany did not. The reasons for his preference were partly political and partly personal. The mediaeval idea of the Empire with its lofty aims and high-sounding titles had always held a fatal appeal for the Hohenstaufens and Frederick's Italian background and upbringing made it all the more understandable that the imperial office, as the successor of the Caesars, should hold a special attraction for him. Moreover the political conception of centralisation and unification of power came naturally to him. He had all the instincts of a despot, perhaps because he could prove himself to be a very efficient and even upon occasion a benevolent one. He had no liking for the form of government which made him the first among his peers, as he would have been among the German princes; this characteristic also later rendered his attempt to govern the independent barons of Outremer as King of Jerusalem singularly unsuccessful.

On the personal side there is no doubt that whereas Frederick loved his own Kingdom of Sicily, he never really cared for Germany. The fact that during the thirty-eight years in which he ruled as Emperor he lived in the country for only nine of them and that he finally tried to shift the whole centre of power to Italy is evidence of this. In his letters he was explicit on the subject. Years later, at the time of the Tartar invasion, he complained that he had to give up the joys of his own realm, which offered every pleasure, for the "stern seas and mountains of Germany". The luxury of life in Sicily, which was then the most civilised country in Europe, must have made Germany seem all the more barbarous to a man of Frederick's aesthetic and sybaritic tastes. As was natural in one who had lived in the sunshine of the Mediterranean until he was eighteen, Frederick found the dark cold winters of Germany insupportably long and depressing.

The years of civil war between Otto and Philip of Hohenstaufen had resulted in a great weakening of the central power, which even in peaceful times was always hard put to it to keep control in Germany, and a corresponding increase in the independence of the princes, who enjoyed what almost amounted to sovereign rights within the boundaries of their own estates. This process of the decentralisation of power was not new in German history; it occurred whenever a minor or a weakling held the title of emperor. It was due to the fact that whereas the kingship was elective, the possessions of the lay vassals had gradually come to descend by hereditary right, so that the heads of the great families enjoyed power and popularity almost equal to that of the Emperor. It was a state of affairs which the princes and the Pope were naturally anxious to preserve for their own ends, but which each dynasty that produced a succession of emperors tried to circumvent by obtaining the election of their heirs at a very early age and thus ensuring the succession in the family.

But the mere fact than an election had to take place before the titles of King of the Romans and Emperor could be passed on from father to son weakened the monarchy at the root, for even the strongest emperor was indebted, and usually had to make concessions, to some of the electors to achieve his aim. At other times the princes deliberately elected a weakling in order to maintain their own position; and when the elected heir was a minor—as occurred after the deaths of Henry III and Frederick's father Henry VI—the conditions of chaos which reigned strengthened the princes' position even more. Thus at a time when the central power was gradually evolving in England and in France, the growth of the monarchy in Germany was stultified.

These factors certainly strengthened Frederick's preference for the Kingdom of Sicily, where they did not obtain; but before he could evolve any sort of policy his own claim to the kingship and Empire had to be consolidated. Here again fate played into his hands. At Bouvines, on the 27th of July 1214, Philip Augustus defeated the armies of Otto and a small contingent of the English forces. When Otto fled from the field of battle all hopes of his being able effectually to oppose Frederick were gone, and Philip Augustus gave symbolical expression to this fact when, on the evening after the battle, he dispatched to Frederick the tattered remnants of the imperial banner.

Frederick did not take part, militarily, in this great victory, but shortly afterwards he launched out on his first large campaign. He left Worms with an army which the chroniclers described in glowing terms as "the greatest ever seen". On the 23rd of August he was before Aix-la-Chapelle, where in May Otto had married Mary, daughter of the Duke of Brabant. Frederick planned an invasion of the Duke's territories, but the threat was enough; the Duke of Brabant capitulated and gave Frederick his own son as hostage. In September Frederick crossed the Meuse, defeated the Duke of Limburg and the Counts of Juliers and Cleves, and retook the castle of Trifels, which had been one of his father's strongholds, where he had held Richard Cœur de Lion prisoner. By October Frederick was back in Speyer, having completed a swift and successful expedition against Otto's supporters in the north-western provinces.

In November Frederick held another court at Basle. A little more than two years had passed since that first court after the adventure of Constance. He had come a long way in the interval, his position in Germany was assured, and Otto was reduced to a mere shadow. He had made powerful allies, and had just returned with honour from his military campaign. Feudatories from the far corners of his vast realms were coming in to make their personal act of obedience; the prelates and representatives of the Kingdom of Arles thronged the court at Basle, and Frederick confirmed to them the privileges granted by his predecessors.

Frederick was crowned King of the Romans at Aix-la-Chapelle in July 1215. The papal legate, the Archbishop of Mainz, anointed him upon the throne of Charlemagne and placed the silver crown of Germany upon his head. It was a moment charged with emotion—the orphan boy who in his childhood had been so destitute as to stand in need of the charity of the burghers of Palermo, who had been man-handled by the rough soldiers of Markward of Anweiler, who had nearly had to flee his country before the advance of Otto and his invading army— now without the struggle of civil war, with hardly a blow struck on German soil, almost as if events had moved by their own volition, was the anointed King of Germany, surrounded by the mystic pageantry of the coronation service and holding in his hands the sword and sceptre of kingship. It was the cul- mination of the first phase in his career, the necessary preliminary to the great ambition, the crowning at the hands of the Pope in Rome which alone would give him the right to the full style and title of *Romanorum Imperator et Semper Augustus*. Suddenly, at the vital moment, with a dramatic gesture, Frederick took the Cross and declared that he would lead a Crusade to free the Holy Places from the infidel.

Of all the acts in Frederick's life this sudden vow to lead a Crusade is perhaps the most inexplicable. His upbringing in a half-Moslem country, and the consistent interest in, and sym- pathy for, the Moslem world which he showed throughout his life, indicate that he could never have shared the sentiments of other Christian princes for the hated infidel. At the time the Church had put no pressure on him to go on a Crusade, and the Pope at this particular moment was content to see him set about the reordering of Germany.

Though always at his least guarded in moments of success, it was on the whole unlike Frederick, in later life at any rate, to rush headlong into unpremeditated action. But at the time of his coronation he was still only twenty-one. The extraordinary run of luck which, after so long a period of adversity, he had in the previous three years experienced may, particularly in view of his superstitious character, well have encouraged him in the conviction of the divine right of his mission as Emperor. Though a far from orthodox son of the Church, even in the midst of his struggles with the popes Frederick always observed with decorum all the outward attributes of a Catholic prince. It would probably never have occurred to him to do otherwise; Catholicism was one of the attributes of an emperor, and to his conception of the Empire he was to sacrifice himself, his realm, and the peace of the world.

At the time of his coronation Frederick's absorption in the past history of the Empire was evident. Charlemagne had been canonised by an anti-Pope during the reign of Frederick Barbarossa, and after his coronation Frederick had the body of his great predecessor placed in a magnificent new reliquary, adorned with gold and silver and the effigies of succeeding emperors, including his own. He created some astonishment by doffing his royal robes and climbing up with one of the workmen on to the scaffolding, and himself working with hammer and nails to secure the lid of the reliquary. With all his new dignities there was still something in Frederick of the inquiring mind of the boy of thirteen who would insist upon talking and asking questions of all and sundry in Palermo, and in his sudden decision to take the Cross his youth should probably be given equal weight with other factors.

There was also, of course, the more mundane consideration that the crusader's vow should win for him the approval of the Pope and the ecclesiastical princes. Possibly even at this very early stage he had already evolved the idea that it would provide him with an excuse for having his son Henry brought to Germany, on the pretext that his succession to the ancestral Duchy of Swabia, if nothing more, would be ensured if Frederick died while campaigning in the Holy Land.

While Frederick was being crowned in Aix-la-Chapelle, Otto, the former Emperor, was living on the charity of the citizens of Cologne, and his new wife was adding to his unpaid debts by spending her days playing dice. When Frederick arrived at the gates of Cologne, the citizens decided that they had had enough of their embarrassing guests. They offered to pay Otto's debts and to give him six hundred marks if he would leave. As Frederick entered the town in triumph, Otto and his wife slipped out of another gate disguised as pilgrims.

For a few days in November of 1215, the eyes of the world turned once again to Rome where, as the crowning event of his remarkable Papacy, Innocent III had called the fourth Lateran Council. Two thousand, two hundred and eighty-three delegates were present, and the crush was so great that the Archbishop of Amalfi was killed. Frederick's representative was Berard, now Archbishop, of Palermo, who had accompanied him on the fateful journey to Germany. There were also representatives of the Latin Emperor of the East, and of the Kings of France, England, Hungary, Aragon, Cyprus and Jerusalem. Here the theory of transubstantiation was formally stated, which put so much power into the hands of the mediaeval priesthood, and which Frederick was later to assail in a far less reverent spirit than John Wycliffe.[2]

One of the questions debated at this Council was Frederick's accession to the Empire; a Milanese lawyer rose to support Otto's claims; he was quickly followed by Frederick's representative, and the situation degenerated so rapidly as to have all the makings of a brawl. The Pope with great dignity rose and left the council chamber, followed by the clergy. After a recess, Frederick's title to the Empire was confirmed.

Among the few laymen present at the Lateran Council was a man who for the next twenty years was to be the great intermediary between Frederick and the papacy, the Grand Master of the Teutonic Knights—Hermann von Salza. Although he and the Emperor had never so far met, Frederick must have had highly favourable reports of him, for he was now charged with the delicate mission, fraught with possible political repercussions, of going to see the Empress Constance and the Regency Council in Sicily, to arrange for her and the little King Henry to join Frederick in Germany. It was natural enough, now that he was firmly established in the country, that Frederick should want his wife and child to join him; but any mention of Henry's going to Germany immediately resuscitated the bogy of the union of Sicily and the Empire in the mind of the Pope, and on the 1st of July 1216, Frederick promised that as soon as he had been crowned Emperor in Rome he would definitely make over the Kingdom of Sicily to his son Henry.

A fortnight later Innocent died in Perugia after a short illness, just about the same time as Constance and the six-year-old Henry set out from Messina on their long journey. The anarchy into which the mainland provinces of the Kingdom of Sicily, through which they had to pass, had fallen bore eloquent witness to the unhappy lot of a country whose king was absent, and whose place was nominally filled by a child. Whole provinces were overrun by rebellious counts who had joined Otto on his march south, and were still in active rebellion against Frederick's legate, the Bishop of Worms.

It is not certain that Hermann von Salza accompanied Constance and Henry on the journey, but he arrived at Frederick's court in Nuremberg in December. When the two men met face to face, immediately a friendship sprung up between them. Von Salza was about twenty-five years older than Frederick, he had been Grand Master of the Teutonic Knights since before 1211, and he had just returned from seven very active years in the Near East. Frederick's vow to lead a Crusade was naturally a matter of prime importance to the Order, not only for its aim of reconquering the Holy Places from the Moslems, but because it might vitally affect the complicated rivalries which divided the three Military Orders of St. John, the Templars, and the Teutonic Knights themselves. The Teutonic Order had been the latest to arrive upon the scene and a bitter enmity existed between them and the Templars. Von Salza's personal success with Frederick is attested by the fact that at the court of Nuremberg he gave special privileges to the Teutonic Order.

Shortly after his son Henry's arrival in Germany in 1217, Frederick created him Duke of Swabia. Probably at the court held in January in Nuremberg, he was presented to the nobles of the Empire. It was the first outward sign of Frederick's secret determination to obtain Henry's election as King of the Romans. It is doubtful whether Frederick would have dared so soon to make an overt move of this kind if Innocent III had still been alive, but the new Pope Honorius III was a man of a totally different type, a sound financial administrator and a pious churchman, but lacking the genius of his predecessor. Moreover Frederick knew him well; as Cardinal Cencius Savelli, he had been one of the papal legates in Sicily delegated by the Pope to care for Frederick during his minority.

Gradually Henry's name disappeared from the state documents of Sicily, and Frederick began to push him forward as much as possible in Germany, associating his name with his own in acts and donations. For the next four years the basis of Frederick's policy was to get Henry elected, and to the pursuance of this aim he sacrificed everything else. He may already have decided that the tendency towards decentralisation in Germany was too strong for him to try and stem the tide, and that the best course to follow was to make sure of the basic essential of Henry's succession, thus leaving himself free to pursue the wider aims of the Empire and to consolidate and reorganise the Kingdom of Sicily.[3]

Frederick's actions during these years certainly support this theory; they were one long series of concessions to the princes, particularly the ecclesiastical princes, who could be counted upon to give him firmer support because they were not taken up with dynastic and family interests. In many cases he may not fully have appreciated the ultimate effects of his actions. For instance, in 1215 he had allowed two imperial fiefs to be transferred to the see of Ratisbon. The abbess of an abbey which held some of the lands brought a plea against the transfer before Frederick in the following year, and he reversed the judgement with a rider that in future the lands of the Empire were inalienable. This might appear to have reinforced the imperial power, but in actual fact the transfer of lands within the Empire had up to then been a purely administrative matter; from now on the Emperor could not dispose of imperial lands as he wished, whereas the princes could allot their fiefs at will. At the beginning of the century the Emperor's permission was necessary before the holder of a fief could cede land to anyone; by 1224 Henry's administration allowed the Count of Zell to acquire lands from any free man.

The ecclesiastical princes, who succeeded in winning more freedom and privileges from Frederick than anyone else, were very able diplomats and knowing that the Emperor needed their support, no doubt represented the concessions that they won from him as means to enable them better to serve him and the Empire. In the past the German Church had preserved its

independence in the face of Roman thunders, and backed
Frederick Barbarossa against the Pope, and it must be admitted
that they did the same for his grandson, in spite of his continuous absence from Germany for fifteen years and the shortness of his subsequent visits, until the fateful day of his deposition at the Council of Lyons after his second excommunication.

If some of the concessions that Frederick made were against
his wish and better judgement, he on his side was clever enough
to conceal the fact, realising that to give with grace and an air
of magnanimity contributed to the popularity which he wished
to achieve. If, however, he later realised that he had gone too
far and was seriously endangering his own rights, he would
reverse his judgements on the plea of his own youth and inex-
perience.

On the 19th of May 1218 Otto died; for the last two years
he had been living on his estates in Brunswick, he had practically no supporters left, and he had divided his time between
fighting with the Danes and the Archbishop of Magdeburg.
His end could not have been more miserable. As he lay dying
he was surrounded by priests who scourged him, and between
sobbing the words of the *Miserere* he called to them to lay on
the stripes more heavily. It was only seven years since he had
been crowned in Rome, overrun all Italy, and threatened
Frederick from the Straits of Messina.

In December, at the court of Fulda the last partisans of Otto
recognised the new Emperor. There was now only one man
who abstained, Otto's brother Henry, Duke of Saxony, who
was also Count Palatine of the Rhine. He still held out and
kept in his possession the imperial regalia. Frederick had to
get the Pope to command him to return the crown and other
insignia and finally an accord was reached, whereby Henry of
Saxony was constituted Vicar-General of the Empire, and at
the court held at Goslar in June of the next year the crown of
Charlemagne and all the imperial regalia were finally placed
in Frederick's hands.

The office of Vicar-General really only became operative in
the absence of the Emperor, and as at this time Frederick talked
incessantly of his plans for the Crusade, the appointment was
aimed not only at obtaining the final pacification of Germany
by an agreement with the Duke of Saxony, but at reassuring

the Pope of Frederick's definite intention of leading the Crusade.
It is not possible to ascertain just how far the secret negotiations
with the princes for Henry's election had proceeded at this
stage, but they were probably well under way, as already by the
beginning of 1219 the Pope had his suspicions—Henry had
now been made regent of the Kingdom of Burgundy—to which
he gave voice in a letter to Frederick.

Frederick's reply, which was written in May, was at the same
time bold and cautious. He frankly admitted having made
approaches to the princes on behalf of his son but went on to
say: "This is not with the aim of uniting the realm to the
Empire, but that while we are absent in the service of Jesus
Christ, that the Empire may be better governed, and if we die,
that our son may have better means of keeping his patrimony
in Germany." The Pope was not taken in, and Frederick
was required to renew the promise which he had repeatedly
made to Innocent III to give the Kingdom of Sicily to his son
and to provide a vicar to govern it until Henry's majority.

By February 1220 Frederick was evidently sufficiently sure
of his ground in Germany to begin putting out feelers for the
Pope's reactions to what, surely, had been his secret intention
all along—to keep the Kingdom of Sicily for himself during
his own lifetime. His first letter, written on the 10th of February, was very cautious; he said: "As it could happen that our
son might die without leaving a child or brother, we reserve to
ourselves the power in this case to succeed to him in the realm,
not by virtue of the right of Empire, but by the title of legitimate succession, whereby a father takes the inheritance of his
son, always recognising that we hold the realm from the Church
and will take the oath of fidelity for it."

This clause was represented simply as a proviso in the case
of the remote possibility of Henry's dying before his father,
otherwise Frederick agreed to fall in with the Pope's wishes.
It was sufficient, however, to awaken the Pope to action—
he had not known Frederick as a boy for nothing—and immediately he took Henry officially under his protection as King of
Sicily. The ink on this document was barely dry before another
letter arrived at the papal court at Viterbo from Frederick,
written on the 19th of February, within a few days of the first.
In it he ceased to beat about the bush and came right out with

what was in his mind—"Nevertheless we want even more from your goodwill and the devotion of which we have given proof towards the Church and yourself, and when we are in your presence we hope to obtain from your beatitude the favourable issue to our demand that we may keep to ourselves the Realm of Sicily for our life."

This letter was timed to arrive in Viterbo about the end of April, when the court was to meet at Frankfurt, and the stage be set for Henry's "surprise" election on the 23rd. Frederick was not present when the election actually took place; but this was simply a diplomatic ruse to give verisimilitude to the account which he later gave to the Pope of the election's having occurred without his knowledge and volition, almost by a process of spontaneous combustion of affection and gratitude among the princes.

The princes, especially the ecclesiastical ones, had every reason to feel grateful towards Frederick, as three days after the election—the date actually coincided with the first official use of Henry's new style and title of King of the Romans—he signed the "Privilegium in favorem principum ecclesiasticorum" and sealed it with the great seal of the golden bull, which was reserved for the most solemn documents, and on which Frederick was portrayed upon a plaque of pure gold, seated on his throne, holding the orb and sceptre.

By this privilege Frederick completed the processes begun by the Bull of Eger of creating in the Church lands an ecclesiastical state within the state of Germany, from which in effect all imperial authority was excluded. Ostensibly the privilege was designed to right abuses which had in the past crept into the laws and customs regulating the position of the Church and its relations with the Emperor. In actual fact it went far beyond this scope and accorded many further privileges to the Church. The ecclesiastical princes could coin their own money, extract tolls and dues, and make wills freely, leaving their belongings where they wished. If they excommunicated a man and he was not absolved within six weeks, automatically he was subject to the ban of the Empire.

The privilege comprised a large body of laws and regulations treating with every aspect of Church rights in relation to the ownership of land, taxation, and its relations with the sovereign.

The throne room in the castle of Gioia del Colle

The Throne at Gioia del Colle

Bust of Pietro della Vigna from the Capuan Gate

Head called the "Fidelity of Capua" from the Capuan Gate

The work of preparation must have required weeks if not months and its ultimate effects were so far-reaching that the fragmentation of Germany into principalities can be said originally to date from the 26th of April 1220. It was the price which Frederick paid for Henry's election, and its very elaboration is proof, if any further were needed, of the slowly nurtured schemes by which Frederick ultimately arrived at this goal which would set him free to pursue his imperial plans and return to Sicily.

Judged by modern standards, Frederick's behaviour in this matter is indefensible. It is true that he himself had actually been elected in 1211 by the princes without any intervention on his part, or without making any promises to Innocent III, but once he had accepted the offer of the Empire he had promised formally on several occasions to the Pope to relinquish Sicily to his son. Moreover it is very doubtful if Frederick would have been able to establish himself in Germany without the Pope's support. But it should be remembered that Innocent, and every other statesman of the thirteenth century, with the possible exception of St. Louis, followed the rule of expediency. Innocent had traded on Constance's precarious position after Henry VI's death to extract from her a repeal of the privileges in the matter of the Sicilian church, which had been freely granted to the Norman kings by his predecessors. In spite of his public protestations to the contrary, Frederick can have felt no gratitude to Innocent, who had made use of his powerful position to extract promises from him just as he had done from his mother, and simply used him as a pawn in the game of Church politics. Inexcusable as Frederick's conduct may seem today, it would have appeared not only justifiable to himself, but nothing out-of-the-ordinary to the practice of the time.

All this did not, however, prevent both Frederick and the German princes from awaiting the Pope's reactions with a certain amount of trepidation. Three months passed before Frederick wrote with specious excuses to inform Honorius officially of Henry's election, and to explain his delay in writing. He pretended that the messenger he had sent the day after the election had been held up by illness—as if he had no others at his disposal. The story of the election's taking place in his absence was combined with abject protestations that nothing was

c

further from his thoughts than the union of Sicily with the Empire. "Our Mother the Church should have no fear or mistrust on the subject of a possible union of the realm and Empire, because we ourselves desire the separation . . . we will oppose all our efforts lest their union should occur at any time, as you will see by our acts, which will be such that Mother Church may justly rejoice at having procreated a son such as us. Because even supposing that the Church had no rights over the Realm, and that we should die without leaving legitimate heirs, we would make a donation of the realm to the Roman Church rather than to the Empire."

The letter was written on the 13th of July. On the 31st of July the messenger, who was the Chancellor of the Empire, Conrad of Scharfenburg, himself wrote to the Pope explaining that his departure was delayed by a tertiary fever (to which he had only fallen victim in July). The Chancellor was evidently very uneasy as to the Pope's reactions, as in the letter he said that he hoped that Honorius would forgive him for having served Frederick better than the Pope, but he added that the ecclesiastical princes thought that the election of the son of a prince protected by the Pope could not be displeasing to him.

Frederick had gambled, but only when he was sure of his ground. Otto's death had simplified the situation by removing the last effective rallying-point of any possible opposition to himself in Germany, thus strengthening his position to the extent that he felt that he could go ahead with his plans for Henry's election. But outside Germany there still remained the Pope, to whose predecessor he had solemnly sworn to relinquish the Kingdom of Sicily to his son. As long as Innocent III had occupied the Holy See, it is doubtful if Frederick would have dared, at least so soon, to bring about Henry's election; but, in spite of his protesting gestures, Honorius was of a very different metal and the Emperor knew it. He also knew that a Crusade, which would win Jerusalem back for Christianity, was the dominating desire of the new Pope's life; and no one else in Europe but himself could bring the prestige, and the resources, which alone could guarantee its success.

Already Frederick had succeeded twice in delaying the Crusade to which he had been formally committed since the

Lateran Council; and he had succeeded in allaying the Pope's suspicions as to his real intentions until Henry's election was a *fait accompli*, and the preparations for his own coronation in Rome so far advanced that it would be difficult for Honorius to evade it. Now he calculated that the Pope's desire to see the Crusade safely launched at last would override all other considerations in his mind; and that if a face-saving formula was invented, he would be prepared to accept it, and to proceed with the coronation, in the hope that once it was accomplished, the newly consecrated Emperor would depart for the Holy Land.

Frederick was right. The date of the imperial coronation was fixed for the autumn, and the preparations for departure for Rome and the long journey to Sicily began. In August the court was at Augsburg, the traditional place of departure from Germany for the Kings of the Romans on their way to Rome. Henry, who was now eight years old, was left in the charge of bishops and the great officers of state, or *ministeriales*, who were trusted henchmen of the house of Hohenstaufen. Looking back on his own childhood, Frederick would have been inhuman if he did not feel a qualm at leaving his son to a life which would in many ways be so similar to his own at the same age in the Palace of Palermo. For Constance the parting must have been bitter indeed; her son by her first husband, the King of Hungary, had died in tragic circumstances when as a widow she had fled with him to Austria from the persecutions of her brother-in-law; and now she was leaving Henry to fulfil the ambitious plans of his father. She never saw her son again.

In the first days of September Frederick crossed the Brenner, on the third he was in Bozen (the modern Bolzano), and as the royal cortège progressed through Italy it was met by nobles, princes, bishops, embassies from Venice and Genoa, and the representatives of the Italian cities. It was almost exactly eight years to the day since Frederick had left Italy, escaping like a thief in the night with a handful of followers, through remote Alpine passes. Now in the gorgeous golden days of an Italian autumn he proceeded in stately fashion through the countryside where the grapes, ripe for the vintage, hung like triumphal garlands from tree to tree.

The Emperor-elect, coming to receive the imperial crown,

was in a mood of august benevolence, and as he progressed through northern Italy he dispensed royal grants and diplomas with a liberal hand. The aura of Caesarean prodigality which had preceded his coronation at Aix-la-Chapelle and won him the enthusiasm of Germany, was again in evidence. It had served him well in the past, and no doubt it was consciously cultivated; but the thought of returning to Sicily, triumphant, after the years of strain and scheming in Germany, gave to it reality in the mind of Frederick as well.

Encamped on the shores of Lake Garda, Frederick wrote to the Pope to thank him for all his kindnesses, and, to disarm criticism before their meeting, he announced that he had undergone out of reverence to the Pope the necessary penances for having delayed the Crusade; though he safeguarded himself by saying that he was not to blame. The emissaries of the Doge of Venice came to greet him and a treaty was signed, which provided for mutual redress in the case of hostile acts by the subjects of either state, extradition of fugitives, and freedom from custom dues for the Venetians within the Empire. In return the Doge promised an annual tribute of money, pepper, and a robe.

Representatives of the Lombard cities waited upon Frederick at the imperial camp at Modena; they had all recognised him, but Milan refused him the coronation with the iron crown of Lombardy. With the exception of this rebuff, the welcome which Frederick received was tremendous, the pomp and ceremony of the imperial cortège was well calculated to appeal to the crowd, but the envoys of the cities were bent on more serious matters than mere junketings, and the jockeying for favours was at fever heat.

The Genoese, conscious of the important part which they had played in Frederick's adventurous journey to Germany, confidently asked for the confirmation of their privileges. Those within the Empire were granted anew, and the control of the whole Ligurian coast from Monaco to Porto Venere, but to their dismay no mention was made of trading rights in Sicily. Grants were also made to their deadly rivals the Pisans, in spite of their previous hostility, and Frederick's generosity on this occasion attached Pisa to his cause for life. Even Frederick's diplomacy appears to have given way under the strain of so many and such contrasting requests. He first granted the right of garrisoning their castle and fosse to the citizens of Faenza, and then revoked it upon the representations of Forli. The imperial Chancellor Conrad had his hands full smoothing down ruffled susceptibilities.

In October Frederick dispatched an embassy to the Pope; it was to be the first of many, headed by Hermann von Salza. The next prolonged stop on his journey south was significant; it was at Bologna, whose university was famed throughout Europe for its study of Roman law, and the most celebrated of its jurists, Roffredo of Benevento, later joined his court. In November, when he was almost at the gates of Rome, Frederick received an embassy from the Pope; further assurances about the Crusade and upon his promise not to join Sicily to the Empire were required of him, and the date of the coronation was fixed for the 22nd of November.

At last the goal was reached and the imperial retinue encamped upon Monte Malo, the modern Monte Mario. It was the second, and last, time in his life that Frederick came to Rome, though his determination to follow in the footsteps of the Caesars was to be the guiding principle of his life. From the heights of Monte Mario the city was laid out like a map at his feet; the Colosseum, the Pantheon, and the other classical buildings and ruins were clearly distinguishable among the mediaeval buildings which clung to their sides like so many barnacles. Much that fell victim to the quarrying activities of the Renaissance was still standing in his day, and like any modern tourist with his Baedeker Frederick could have picked out the various monuments with the aid of the *Mirabilia Urbis Romae*, the mediaeval guide book which had been written about fifty years earlier. No chronicler has recorded whether he ever made a closer inspection of the marvels of the city whose classical and architectural aspects were beginning to be appreciated as well as the religious ones of the relics and the scenes of martyrdom of saints. If he did, it would have been this ancient aspect of Rome which would have interested Frederick most, as the classical tendencies of the Capuan gate, the Apulian castles, and his image on the Augustals later bore witness.

Little time for day-dreaming or archaeological excursions was left to Frederick during the few days he had in Rome. The day before the coronation he had a long series of discussions with the Pope on outstanding matters of business. Here the solution for the Sicilian problem was thrashed out, which Frederick must have already evolved in his own mind when he wrote to Honorius the previous February: "and when we are in your presence we hope to obtain from your Holiness the favourable issue". Frederick had admitted that Sicily was a papal fief, which his father had never done. He now went further and proposed that Sicily should have its own government and administration by Sicilian nationals, its own great seal, and that Henry's name should still be associated with it in a purely honorific fashion. Frederick had ceded to the Pope the shadow of power and kept the reality for himself by maintaining that his own person was to be the only link rather as the Crown in our own time is the only link between the members of the British Commonwealth.

Honorius accepted, and Frederick on his side maintained the administrative separation between Sicily and the Empire until the very last years of his reign, when his titanic struggle with the Popes was reaching its climax. Eighteen years after Frederick's coronation Henry's name was still formally associated with his father's in Sicilian documents and this practice continued right up until Henry's death, even during the last years when after his rebellion in Germany he was his father's prisoner. During all these negotiations Von Salza had been constantly at Frederick's elbow, and the measure of the latter's gratitude may be judged by the fact that in the midst of such great affairs he remembered to approach the Pope with a request for the restitution of the right of the Teutonic Knights to wear the same white mantle as the Templars, a matter of continual jealousy between the two orders.

The coronation, the last which Rome was to see for nearly a century, was of unparalleled splendour—and tranquillity. For once the day was not marred by tumults between the Roman populace and the Emperor's German entourage. This was due to Frederick's recognition of the importance of "bread and circuses" to the Roman mob; largesse was their privilege at an imperial coronation, and largesse and a magnificent spectacle they got, in full measure. Its lack had caused Barbarossa to be crowned in secret and had provoked bloody affrays at Otto's coronation, but Frederick was sufficiently Italian to appreciate its importance.

The coronation brought an even more cosmopolitan gather-ing to Rome than usual, though the Italian aspect dominated and the prelates and nobles of the Kingdom of Sicily had flocked to the city for the occasion. Riding in procession Frederick and Constance descended the ancient Via Triumphalis; before entering the city the Emperor-elect had to promise to uphold the rights of the Roman citizens. At the Porta Collina he was met by the clergy, who escorted him to St. Peter's; largesse was scattered to the crowds thronging the way, and on the steps of the basilica the Senator and counsellors of Rome[4] came to hold the Emperor's horse as he made his way up them to kiss the feet of the waiting Pope and to present to him the tradi-tional tribute of gold. The Pope embraced Frederick and together they proceeded towards the church, then Frederick went into a side chapel to take the oath to defend the Church and to be received as a canon of St. Peter's—perhaps one of the most surprising, as well as most talented, men ever to have held such an office.

Clad in the imperial robes and swathed in the magnificent mantle of his grandfather King Roger, enriched with Oriental embroideries of tigers and camels, Frederick now entered the silver doors of the basilica, and was anointed. After a special prayer for the King, the Pope crowned him first with a mitre and then with the crown of Charlemagne, and finally placed in his hand the sword which he brandished to show that he was the defender of the Holy See. The bestowal of the sceptre and orb followed. After this the Empress Constance was crowned in her turn.

In the celebration of the high mass which followed, in recog-nition of the spiritual aspect of the imperial office, Frederick removed the insignia of his rank, and clad in priestly vestments surmounted by the dazzling folds of a blue and gold dalmatic upon which were embroidered the Transfiguration and Adora-tion and the symbols of universal power—the sun and moon—he assisted the Pope as a subdeacon in the service. The Emperor and Empress received communion from the Pope, and the kiss of peace, then, with tapers quenched, the excommunication of all heretics and their abetters was proclaimed, and finally

Frederick took the Cross from the hands of Cardinal Hugo of Ostia, and swore to lead the Crusade in the following August.

Once they were outside the basilica there took place the ceremony which had raised such disputes between former popes and emperors, and which had so much significance for the mediaeval mind. Frederick advanced and held the stirrup for Honorius to mount, then he led the Pope's horse forward a few paces before mounting himself. Characteristically Frederick did not boggle at this performance, he was now the anointed Emperor and he had kept his Kingdom of Sicily as well. The fruits of eight years' scheming and diplomacy were within his grasp, and he did not grudge a little play-acting for the benefit of the ageing Pope. The substance of power was what interested Frederick, not the mediaeval symbols by which his contemporaries laid such store.

The magnificent cavalcade set off, with Honorius leading, and the Emperor and Empress following him through the narrow streets which led towards the Tiber. At the church of Santa Maria in Transpontina they parted, the Pope and Emperor exchanged a final embrace; then Frederick rode back on his white charger to his camp on Monte Mario, and the Pope returned to his palace.

Did the old Pope reflect upon the strange turn of the wheel of fortune which had brought him and Frederick together again in such momentous circumstances? Looking back to fourteen years ago, did he remember the gauche and poverty-stricken boy whom he had known in Palermo, who was only King of Sicily in name but whom he had that day consecrated Emperor of domains which rivalled those of the ancient Caesars, washed by the waters of the English Channel, the Mediterranean and the Baltic?

Perhaps Honorious was more concerned with what he regarded as the triumph that he had achieved for the Church. This was the Emperor's promulgation, on the day of his coronation, of ten laws which were based upon those of the Lateran Council. At Honorius's request Frederick had given lay sanction to the laws in defence of ecclesiastical liberties, such as immunity from lay courts and taxation. He had reinforced the laws against heresy, also the humanitarian laws which protected strangers, seafarers against wreckers, and the peasants, who could no longer have their ploughs and cattle seized.

Frederick had been prepared to make concessions, now that his son was safely elected King of the Romans and he himself was on his way to the realm as its king, and he had the added incentive that in so doing he was able to present the world with the spectacle of Church and State acting in unison for the suppression of heresy and rebellion, which were then regarded as being closely linked. Rebellion he might well be called upon to face in the reorganisation of the realm which lay immediately before him, while the provisions against heresy could be conveniently applied in his future dealings with the Lombard communes, where heresy had in fact deep roots, but who were also guilty of what in his eyes was a far greater offence—rebellion against the imperial authority.

The coronation over, Frederick could hardly contain his impatience to return to his kingdom which he had come so near to losing for ever. Three days later he struck camp and, proceeding by the ancient Via Labicana, he first set foot once more on Sicilian soil when he crossed the Liri at Ceprano.

PART II

Prelude to the Struggle

Chapter III

THE REALM
1220–1225

FREDERICK had been preparing for years for this brisk,
December day, and as the small imperial cavalcade wound
its way down the rugged valley of the Garigliano he had his
plans all cut and dried for the resettlement—for he was well
aware that that was what lay ahead—of his realm. As the
monastery of Cassino, on its towering height, came into view,
he could reflect with satisfaction that already its outpost fortresses of Rocca d'Evandro and Atina had been returned to him,
not without demur, by the Abbot; and that the frontiers of his
realm were further secured by his having demanded and obtained
from Count Roger of Aquila the restitution of the castles of
Suessa, Teano and Mondragone. But he knew too that this
was only the beginning.

The return of these fortresses without strife or bloodshed
was an eloquent witness to the uneasiness with which the
nobles, and even faithful churchmen such as the Abbot of
Cassino, viewed Frederick's return to his realm. Many of
them had travelled to Rome to demonstrate their fealty to
him at the time of his coronation; others had welcomed him
upon his arrival, the majority of them in the hope that their past
treachery and avarice during his minority and absence in
Germany might be forgotten. Most of them were very well
aware that now they no longer had a boy to deal with, but a
man of twenty-six who had proved himself an able diplomatist
and statesman and who, by his political acumen, had not only
earned for himself the most magnificent title which the western
world could bestow—but had managed to retain the Realm of
Sicily and the papal benediction as well.

Some measure of the reputation which Frederick had by now

achieved was demonstrated by the fact that he was returning
to a country—nearly all of whose nobility had at some time
betrayed him—not as his father had done at the head of a
German army but accompanied by his wife and a small court
of intimates such as Hermann von Salza, Berard the Archbishop
of Palermo, and the newly joined Roffredo of Benevento, and
their attendants. They had travelled fast, urged on by Frederick's impatience, and by the 15th of December they had reached
Capua.

Capua in the thirteenth century was neither the city of the
fleshpots which Hannibal knew nor the battered and somewhat
sordid town of today, but the flourishing centre of the richly
agricultural Terra di Lavoro, strategically important for its
impregnable position, almost encircled as it is by a coil of the
winding Volturno river. It was the first important town in the
realm of Sicily, which lay upon the Via Labicana, the route
that Frederick and his suite had taken from the papal states—
and here they halted.

The stop was not, as might have been expected, simply a
pause for the weary travellers, who had been *en route* since
they left Augsburg four months earlier, to draw breath before
sailing to the capital of Palermo and the comfort of one of the
royal residences. The plans for the reconstruction of the Realm
of Sicily matured during the years in Germany would brook
no delay and here in this provincial town Frederick began at
once to put them into effect. At the first court to be held in the
kingdom for eight years, he promulgated the laws, an ordinance
of twenty chapters, which laid down the foundations upon which
the entire reorganisation of Sicily for the next thirty years
was to be built. They were to be the framework of the first
modern European state.

H. A. L. Fisher has described Frederick as "the greatest
single force in the Middle Ages". He had already, before the
return to Sicily, shown great political ability. Later he was to
display the all-round intellectual brilliance which distinguished
the complete man of the Renaissance and the benevolent despots
of the eighteenth century.

But for the immediate task in hand he possessed two qualities
which were to be even more useful to him as a ruler, common
sense and an ability to organise. These qualities he had inherited

from those Norman ancestors who had created an ordered and prosperous realm from the patchwork of states that, by their military daring, they had conquered.

Common-sense and an instinctive understanding of organisation had dictated the basic principles of the laws which Frederick now promulgated at Capua. The fact that they were already prepared right down to the last detail, and that he seized the earliest opportunity of making them public in the first town of the realm in which he could stop, show clearly the impatience with which he had been waiting for this moment, and his determination immediately to bring home to his subjects the unpalatable truth that the time of lawlessness and freebooting was at an end, and that in future they would have to deal with a king who intended to rule in fact as well as name.

The results of the thirty years of anarchy which confronted Frederick upon his return to Sicily might well have convinced most men that the only way of restoring order was to use force. Instead, with one shrewd stroke he produced order out of chaos, not by the brute force of a foreign army, but by decreeing a return to the legal and political *status quo* of the time of William II, the last legitimate Norman king. Frederick's ordinance of twenty chapters practically resuscitated the laws in force during that reign. Its main provisions laid down that: Justice should mainly be administered by court judges, dependants of the Crown. Cities could no longer elect their own mayors, royal bailiffs were appointed in their stead. Taxes reverted to what they had been at the death of Frederick's mother Constance. In general the rights of the various categories of subjects were to revert to those which they had enjoyed at the death of William; for instance, that of bearing arms was limited to those who had done so in his day. Other laws struck hard at the usurped power of the nobles; royal castles which they had seized, or others which they had built since William's death, had to be handed over to the Crown, and the royal consent was necessary if they were to leave even the strongholds to which they were legally entitled with a greater force than that of four unarmed men; but worse was to follow for them in the most important law of all. This was the *de resignandis privilegis*, which required that all privileges accorded to anyone whatsoever since the end of William's reign (with the sole exception of the Abbey of San Giovanni di Fiore) should be submitted for confirmation to the Royal Chancery before Easter 1221 for the mainland provinces, and before Whitsun of the same year for the island of Sicily. This sweeping decree covered the whole gamut of royal privileges from the greatest fiefs down to small individual grants for the collection of tolls and other perquisites, but naturally the blow fell hardest upon those who had been in a position of power and had gained most—the nobles and the Church.

Much of the power of the Norman kings had been based upon their possession of a vast and rich demesne. This had been frittered away in privileges accorded by a succession of usurpers and officials who had governed during Frederick's minority and absence in Germany or had been seized outright by force, or spurious legal means and faked documents by the barons and ecclesiastics. Frederick's new laws not only struck at the root of this trouble, but afforded an ideal means whereby the Royal Chancery could obtain a precise record of the titles of what legal fiefs and privileges really did exist.

Donations made at the expense of the demesne were automatically revoked. Illegible donations were rewritten, and such privileges as were renewed in Frederick's name had a new clause inserted to the effect that they could be revoked at the Emperor's pleasure.

The laws promulgated at Capua not only regulated the present tenure of fiefs but provided for their future control by the Emperor. Their holders could neither marry, nor could their children inherit direct, without the sovereign's consent. This last provision afforded Frederick the possibility of a constant reversion of fiefs, and the means of keeping rigid control over not only the actual holder, but his heir as well.

In pursuance of his determination to regain for the royal demesne all that had been lost by it during the years of chaos and his own minority, after the Court of Capua Frederick also instituted searching inquiries to discover the whereabouts of the villeins and burgesses belonging to it who had emigrated to other areas since William II's death. This mediaeval practice of considering men as chattels tied to the land is repulsive to modern eyes, but it constituted an important aspect of the economy of the times, and the recuperation of the actual demesne lands would have lost much of its value if the manpower was lacking to cultivate them.

The old Norman laws had laid down a series of ordinances whereby a fleet could be created, manned and kept in good sea-going condition. Certain fief holders, cities and towns of the realm were bound to furnish timbers or money for shipbuilding and also money for the maintenance of the fleet, these dues being known as "lignamia" and "marinaria"; they were also each responsible for producing a certain quota of sailors to man the fleet. Frederick caused the provisions of these laws to be brought into full force again, with such effect that by the end of 1221 he already had two squadrons at sea. One is tempted to wonder if his plans for the restoration of the old Norman sea power had been maturing in Frederick's mind since the days when as a boy of thirteen he sat up late at night reading Sicilian history.

The edict promulgated at Capua, which required the return of castles built since William II's death, also laid the basis of a state army. No sooner had Frederick obtained possession of them than they were knocked down or converted into royal fortresses. It was not his custom, as had been done in the past, to turn them over to a faithful vassal; they now belonged directly to the Crown, and were maintained, victualled and garrisoned by it. The repair of these castles was provided for, certainly later in Frederick's reign, by a comprehensive series of ordinances which laid down that the men of neighbouring villages and towns should be responsible for the actual work. In times of peace—and this was a remarkable innovation—they were either uninhabited, or maintained by a Castellan and skeleton staff. Thus, immediately upon his return to Sicily, Frederick laid the basis of what was, in effect, a navy and a department for national defence.

The general effect of the new laws was to bring about a return to the Norman system of administration that had made the Kingdom of Sicily one of the richest and most pros-perous in Europe. The Normans themselves had not attempted to impose a ready-made foreign style of government upon the provinces which they had conquered, but with practical good sense they had taken the best of what they had found in the mixture of Byzantine, Lombard, and Saracen systems, under which the southern Italian provinces had been governed, and had welded them together into a homogeneous and easily workable system of administration.

So now Frederick, with his inherited Norman instinct for the basic essentials of good government, did not attempt to create a new system, but seized upon the best of what had already existed. The fact that he arrived in the realm with a sound basis upon which the entire future framework of an organised state could be built, demonstrates the extraordinary energy of the man, who, even while he was engaged upon the administration of a vast empire—which he had also taken over in a chaotic state—found still the time to devote himself to a profound study of the Sicilian administration and to draw from it the essential elements for its regeneration.

The Capua laws were not accepted without protest. But it was the order to hand over the castles built since William II's death that provoked armed rebellion. Count Rainer of Manente, a Tuscan whom Frederick's mother had befriended and introduced into the Kingdom of Sicily and who had subsequently sided with Markward of Anweiler and Capparone, belonged to this last category. He had made use of his position during Frederick's minority to feather his own nest at the expense of the demesne, later he raised a rebellion after the departure of Frederick's wife Constance to Germany, and finally he had the effrontery to present himself at the court in Germany without even troubling to ask Frederick for a safe conduct. His behaviour at court was so insolent that Frederick, with a forbearance which had its origin in the fear of what further trouble the arrogant count could stir up in Sicily, kept him at court as a hostage for the return of the demesne lands that he had usurped.

Nevertheless Count Rainer maintained contact with his Tuscan relatives who continued to incite trouble in Sicily, sending arms and reinforcements to the island dissidents. Frederick finally settled the matter by instructing the Pisans to give no further passage to Tuscan troops to Sicily, and his own port and harbour authorities to arrest any who landed there. Count Rainer's family even enlisted the Pope's support in their attempts to have him set free, but Frederick resolutely refused to do so until the usurped lands of the demesne had been returned to his control.

A very much tougher proposition than the usurping Rainer was Thomas of Celano, count of the rugged and mountainous province of Molise, which marches with the Abruzzi. Thomas possessed extensive lands in both provinces and could put an army of nearly fifteen hundred knights and squires into the field. For years this redoubtable man had preserved his independence in his own lands, and the only master he had acknowledged had been the Emperor Otto, during his brief Italian expedition. Aware that the oath of fealty to Otto had branded him for ever in Frederick's eyes and confident in the natural strength of the impregnable castles with which his mountain fastnesses were studded, Thomas of Molise did not present himself in Rome to take the oath of fealty at Frederick's coronation, though he sounded out the ground by dispatching his son on his behalf.

Frederick would accept no substitute oath of fealty, in spite of the attempted mediation of the Pope. Warned in advance, the Count of Molise entrenched his forces in two of his strongest castles—Bojano and Roccamandolfi. Here he remained while Frederick, by persuasion or by using the forces of the barons who had already done homage to him, gained possession of the key fortresses of the Terra di Lavoro, and established an effective control of the administration of the province by placing it in the hands of the newly created Justiciar, Count Landulf of Aquino, and his brother Thomas, who was made chief justice and created Count of Acerra.

In entrusting the control of this important frontier province (which roughly corresponded to the modern Campania) to the Counts of Aquino, Frederick had rewarded a family that had always remained faithful to his own and whose devotion to the Hohenstaufen cause was to remain unbroken until his death.[5]

The campaign against the Count of Molise began in the spring of 1221, with the newly-created Count of Acerra in command of the royal forces. Bojano was taken by assault, but the campaign dragged on for two years, even necessitating Frederick's personal intervention. As one strong point was seized or surrendered, the Count fled to another. The difficulties which the royal forces encountered before he was finally sub-

dued demonstrated better than anything else the gravity of the
situation which could have faced a weaker man than Frederick in
his attempts to restore order in the realm, and the wisdom of
the new laws which created state strongholds throughout the
country and curtailed the powers of the feudal barons.

The beginning of the end came when the Count of Molise's
wife opened the gates of Roccamandolfi and threw herself and
her son upon Frederick's mercy. The Count himself still held
out in Ovindoli, but finally a diplomatic settlement was reached
by the Count's possessions being vested in his wife, and his
sons handed over to Hermann von Salza, to be given up to
Frederick as hostages if the Count, who had fled, did not
finally comply with the requirements of the settlement. Later
he was cited to appear before the royal court to sustain his
claims and answer for his behaviour; he failed to come and
Frederick confiscated Molise and his other lands. Finally in
1227 they were granted to Conrad of Hohenlohe.

In the spring of 1221 Frederick went to the island of Sicily
and in May he held a court at Messina. At Capua the broad
lines for the reorganisation and government of the state had
been traced. At Messina Frederick concerned himself with
municipal administration, probably with an eye upon the Pope,
for the regulations promulgated were of the type concerned
with public morals and restrictions against Jews which would
be pleasing to the Church, and indeed paralleled those of the
fourth Lateran Council though some of them also fitted into
Frederick's own concept of an orderly and well-administered
state.

Strolling players and minstrels were to be outlawed if they
disturbed the peace with ribald songs, blasphemers were to be
strictly punished, prostitutes were not to be allowed to reside
in towns or to use the public baths on the same days as respect-
able women. Jews—and certainly here Frederick had his eye
upon papal approval—had to wear sky-blue tunics and a yellow
patch on their clothes and let their beards grow so that they
might be easily distinguishable; this regulation was also an
extension of the Lateran Council decrees against Moslems.

Frederick then set off on a tour of inspection of the principal
towns of the island, stopping at Catania, Caltagirone, Palermo,
Girgenti, and returning again to Palermo where he confirmed

the privileges granted in his name in 1200 and 1210. Although he later created Naples the capital of his kingdom, because it was more easily accessible to the rest of Europe, Frederick always seems to have remembered with gratitude the city of Palermo which sheltered him during the hardest years of his life and whose citizens had fed him when he was in want.

From Palermo Frederick returned to Catania, probably to oversee an operation which was as vital to the interests of the realm as the subjugation of the Count of Molise—the expulsion of the Genoese from Syracuse, which they had held since 1204. The Sicilian barons had not been the only people to profit by the undefended state of Sicily during Frederick's minority; the great maritime powers of Genoa and Pisa had also had their share. Hatred of the Pisans, who supported the Emperor Otto, had led the Genoese to assist Frederick in his journey to Germany. Their consequent friendship with him, added to their possession of Syracuse, had given the Genoese a predominant position in the island, where they had greater interests at stake than Pisa. They had already taken considerable umbrage at Frederick's refusal to renew their privileges and trading rights for the Realm of Sicily when he was encamped at Modena on his way to Rome, though he had confirmed those which they enjoyed in the Empire, and had tried to soften the blow by awarding them control of the whole Ligurian coast.

Frederick valued the friendship of the Genoese, but the prosperity of the realm was paramount. The chaos of the last thirty years had been reflected in the degeneration of Sicilian trade to such an extent that the country which had once been so prosperous was now on the verge of bankruptcy. Much of what Sicily had lost had been diverted into the pockets of the maritime powers—particularly the Geneose—and for the regeneration of the country it was essential that her commercial life should be restored to prosperity—an impossibility so long as the practical monopoly of her trade, and the lion's share of the profits, passed into the hands of foreigners.

The Genoese were ejected from Syracuse. In accordance with the provisions of the *de resignandis privilegis* promulgated at Capua, Genoa's concessions in Palermo, Messina, Trapani and other ports were withdrawn, and her warehouses confiscated by the state. Pisa suffered the same treatment in the matter of privileges, but as her possessions were insignificant by comparison she suffered less.

The indignation of the Genoese who, with some justification, had expected preferential treatment, knew no bounds. William Porco, the Admiral of Sicily who had accompanied Constance and the young King Henry to Germany, was also a Genoese, and he fled the country. He evidently bore a heavy grudge against Frederick as he seized the first available opportunity to return to Sicilian waters as a pirate and to aid and abet the Emperor's enemies.

In the midst of his multifarious activities for the reorganisation of the realm, Frederick had yet another preoccupation which had already started to absorb some of the resources which he had begun so laboriously to build up. In May when he was at Messina he had already sent some ships carrying reinforcements, under the leadership of the Duke of Bavaria and the Bishop of Passau, to assist the armies of the fifth Crusade fighting near Damietta. Further ships with food and soldiers followed, commanded by Anselm of Justingen, who had been created marshal as a reward for his services as the German ambassador who had announced to Frederick his election as Emperor.

All were carefully instructed not to take part in any serious military engagement until the arrival of the Sicilian fleet under the command of the new admiral, Henry of Malta, and the Chancellor, Walter of Palear, in July. Unfortunately the leaders of the Crusade took no heed of Frederick's warning and by their impetuosity provoked the disastrous loss of Damietta before the arrival of the Sicilian fleet. Too late by a margin of only a few days, the Sicilians did all they could to succour the defeated army of Crusaders, and on the return journey Walter of Palear fled to Venice, where he died in poverty, rather than face his young master with the news of the disaster. The office of Chancellor of Sicily expired with him. For the rest of his reign Frederick never renewed it, probably because, once granted, it was not transferable during the lifetime of the holder. Frederick had on several occasions dispensed with the services of Walter of Palear, and sent him to reside in his see of Catania, but as long as he lived he was still the legal Chancellor of Sicily, and Frederick had no intention of allowing another man to aspire to the power which Palear had once enjoyed without the possibility of being able to dismiss him if he so desired.

August, the month in which Frederick had sworn at his coronation to lead the Crusade, had come and passed with his taking no more active part in it than the dispatch of admittedly impressive reinforcements and supplies to its predecessor. From past experience, Frederick had become expert in finding good reasons for delaying this perilous undertaking—perilous not only for the inevitable risks of battle and sickness involved in a campaign in the Near East, but for the even more insidious ones attendant upon a sovereign's absence from his own kingdom, which were all the more dangerous for Frederick because of his recent prolonged sojourn in Germany and the unsettled state of the realm.

Frederick's departure on a Crusade at this stage would inevitably have thrown Sicily back into a state of chaos, with the newly-subjected barons reverting to their lawless and predatory habits as soon as the controlling presence of the Emperor had been removed. Nor would the finances of the state have been capable of supporting the tremendous drain that the arming, supplying and maintaining of an army in Palestine would have involved. Even though the actual manpower of the Crusading army was to be furnished by the Empire, Sicilian wheat and gold were necessary to supply them with the sinews of war.

After Henry of Malta had returned from the Damietta expedition, Frederick set him another task which, characteristically enough, fulfilled two objects. He was made commander of the forces that were dispatched to subdue the Moslem population of the western part of the island of Sicily. This action was as essential to the order and well-being of the realm as the subjection of the Count of Molise and the control of the Genoese and Pisan trading stations, and it was a far more difficult proposition. It had, however, another outstanding virtue from Frederick's point of view—he was fighting the Infidel, as he had sworn to do, not in far-away Palestine, but here in the midst of a Christian realm, and a few hundred miles from Rome, where their very existence was surely more of an affront to Christianity than in the Orient.

Perhaps at the outset Frederick had not quite realised the full difficulties of the campaign which confronted him before the wild mountainous block of the western provinces, where the Moslems had installed themselves, could be effectively brought under his control. In 1220, even before his coronation in Rome, Frederick had been besieged with complaints from the Archbishop of Monreale, whose lands, at the very gates of Palermo, were subject to constant raids by the Saracens from their mountain fastnesses. Giato, one of the principal strongholds, was not much more than ten miles distant from Monreale, and many of the farms, castles, and villages that rightfully belonged to the archbishopric had been seized and held by the Moslem freebooters. The same conditions reigned throughout much of western Sicily where, profiting from the internal disorders, the Moslems had seized and held lands for more than twenty years.

Henry of Malta was successful in the first stage of the campaign against the Moslems; he captured Giato, and Frederick returned to the mainland for the winter, evidently under the impression that the subjection of the Moslems would present no further difficulties.

It was during this winter sojourn upon the Italian mainland that Frederick met—so the story runs—St. Francis of Assisi. There is no documentary evidence of this meeting, but a widespread tradition and a plaque recently discovered in Bari Castle agree upon the main points of what is said to have occurred.

The Saint had recently made a pilgrimage to the Holy Land and even secured an interview with the Sultan of Egypt, al-Kamil. On his return journey he came to Bari, where Frederick was holding court in the castle by the sea. Either by Frederick's invitation or upon his own initiative, St. Francis came to see the Emperor and apparently was allotted a tower room in the castle as lodging. Frederick with characteristic scepticism arranged for a beautiful woman to be introduced into the Saint's bedroom, and watched proceedings through a spyhole. According to some legends St. Francis put the temptress to flight with a fiery shield; others say that he called for a brazier and, spreading the red-hot coals on the floor, lay upon them and invited the lady to join him.

When the castle was being restored in 1950, a stone was discovered, under many coats of plaster and whitewash, above the door of the tower room. It was dated 1635, and upon it was written in Latin: "Here Francis, dressed in an ash-grey robe, subdued with fire a lascivious girl temptress, like unto a ferocious Hydra. He, who prudently extinguished with flames, Venus born of the waters, who near the waters assailed him; with his strength, in this castle, made the retreat of chastity impregnable."

Although the plaque with this inscription was put up four centuries after the event, it may have replaced some earlier inscription, as the castle had been subjected to many repairs and alterations. In any event it is a fact that the tradition was still so strong four hundred years later that it was recorded in this fashion and that it persisted long after the stone was covered and its very existence forgotten. The legend goes on to provide a happy ending to the story. Apparently Frederick was so much impressed to see that St. Francis really lived according to the precepts which he preached that he spent the rest of the night talking to the Saint. It is a pity that no courtier was present at this extraordinary conversation between the sceptical young Emperor, who was already known for his sensual and sybaritic tastes, and the man who had forsaken the world and taken Lady Poverty to wife, who was to bear upon his own body the stigmata of the Crucifixion.

In every outward aspect no two men could have been more different. But, for all his love of luxury and the pleasures of life, Frederick had the intellect and tastes of a scholar, and a scholar's approach to truth. Shams and bogus piety were abhorrent to him, and he was capable of self-sacrifice in pursuance of what he considered to be his sacred duty as Emperor. Later, during his great struggle with the Church, one of the most potent weapons of Frederick's propaganda were his attacks upon the riches and corrupt lives of the religious hierarchy, and there is no reason to doubt his sincerity in making them. Saint and Emperor in fact—whether or not they met—had attitudes in common. Both he and St. Francis aimed at combating the riches and corruption of the Church, though their motives were widely divergent. It is even possible that the Emperor drew some of the inspiration for his subsequent, and most telling, broadsides against the Church from that night spent in discussion with the Saint.

The currents of reform were surging strongly beneath the surface of the mediaeval order in thirteenth-century Europe. By submitting to the discipline of the Church, St. Francis saved himself and his followers from the stigma of heresy which fell upon the Patarenes, Waldensians, and the Albigenses—men with whom St. Francis had much in common—who were persecuted by Church and Emperor alike. Frederick too had much in common with these sects, and it is one of the tragic ironies of history that he persecuted them because he regarded them as rebels against the established order of which, as Emperor, he was the personification and titular head. The Franciscans also ultimately became his bitter enemies, because they were employed by the Church as agents provocateurs to raise the faithful against him—the excommunicated Emperor.

The spring, and the return of the fighting season, brought an unpleasant surprise for Frederick. The forces left in the island of Sicily under Henry of Malta had apparently been insufficient to overawe the Moslems. The latter had risen, retaken Giato, and kindled an insurrection which spread so rapidly that Henry of Malta was unable to regain control of the situation; he was temporarily disgraced and deprived of the island of Malta. Evidently Frederick now realised that only a radical solution could dispose of the Moslem problem, and at a meeting with the Pope in the little mountain town of Veroli, near Frosinone, in April 1222 he succeeded in delaying his departure on the Crusade until the Moslems in Sicily should be defeated. It is probable that it was on this occasion that Frederick obtained the Pope's assent to his son Henry's coronation as King of the Romans at Aix-la-Chapelle later in the year.

Frederick took the opportunity of visiting about this time the celebrated Cistercian Abbey of Casamari, which was not far away from Veroli. He had first come into contact with the Cistercian Order during his stay in Germany, where he had been profoundly impressed by the rule which forbade them to take rents. This meant they had to cultivate their own lands, and they had in consequence become the foremost farming experts of the day. Now he humbly asked to be admitted to the brotherhood of Casamari, presumably as a tertiary, and to take part in the good works of the monastery, which had also been protected by his father and mother. It is possible that this family connection of Frederick's was commemorated in the construction of the beautiful cloister that was being built about this time, as the capitals of three of the columns bear the crowned heads of two men, one clean-shaven and one bearded—as were Frederick and Henry VI—and the veiled head of what appears to be a woman.

This gesture of Frederick's, and the subsequent gifts and honours which he accorded to the abbey—culminating in the appointment of its Abbot, John, as custodian of the great seal of the realm—were also a subtle form of flattery to the Pope, who, ever since the days when he was Cardinal Cencio Savelli, had been the patron of Casamari. The beautiful church and monastic buildings owe their existence to Honorius's munificence and either shortly before or after his meeting with Frederick at Veroli, he came to Casamari to consecrate the altar of the Conversi, the brothers whose agricultural labours made it impossible for them to celebrate the offices at the usual times, and who were therefore accorded a special altar for their own use.

Not long after the meeting at Veroli, while Frederick was still absent on the mainland, his wife Constance died on the 23rd of June at Catania. She was in her mid-thirties, and considerably younger than his own mother had been when Frederick was born. Although the stormy years of widowhood, after the death of her first husband and the loss of their son, had already made a mature woman of this princess of Aragon when she came to marry the boy-King of Sicily, after the first alarms and excursions of the early years of her marriage with Frederick Constance's life since 1216 had from a material point of view been tranquil. When she died, she still possessed the long fair tresses which had been one of her chief graces in youth.

Constance was buried in Palermo Cathedral near Frederick's father and mother, her body was covered with jewels and splendidly wrapped in a robe of crimson, embroidered with gold and pearls. A curious diadem was placed in a casket by her side, enriched with jewels which were incised with dolphins and Cufic characters, and from whose sides depended long jewelled chains in the Byzantine style, familiar from the mosaic portrait of the Empress Theodora at Ravenna.

Starting with all the disadvantages of an unwilling bride-groom, ten years the junior of his prospective wife, this first marriage of Frederick's seems to have been his most successful; and Constance lived longer than his two subsequent wives who were many years younger. Unlike them she was actually crowned Empress, and her husband seems to have treated her with a respect that he never showed to any other woman. As long as she lived, indeed, Constance was accorded all the honours of an Empress, but it appears unlikely that she received much attention as a wife after she rejoined her husband in Germany in 1216. There is no record of her, and she was only in her late twenties, ever having borne any other children after Henry, whereas not only Enzio, but several other ille-gitimate children are known to have been fathered by Frederick in the years succeeding 1216. Two of these were Frederick of Antioch and Richard of Theate. According to popular legend Frederick of Antioch was the son of a Syrian girl, and was born at the time of his father's Crusade in 1228; but he was married and lord of considerable lands in 1240, which points to his not having been very much younger than Enzio. Richard of Theate was Vicar-General of a province in 1247, and though Frederick entrusted his sons with responsible positions when very young, this was a fighting command which seems to indicate that Richard must have been born in the mid-twenties. Three of Frederick's illegitimate daughters—Selvaggia, Vio-lante, and Margaret—were married about 1238-9, which makes it probable that they were all born about the early twenties.

Given the high incidence of infant mortality in mediaeval times—six illegitimate children who lived to maturity, and apparently born of different mothers within a period of some-thing less than ten years—seems to indicate that the number of Frederick's mistresses increased as the years went by. This in itself was nothing scandalous, or even out of the ordinary, in mediaeval eyes; it was only later when the Emperor, after his return from the Crusade, quite openly kept a harem of Oriental odalisques who accompanied him upon his travels, that Frederick's sex life began to be regarded as an open scandal by the Guelf faction.

In the summer of 1222 the Moslem war was pursued in real earnest and Giato fell after a siege of three months. Frederick then gained possession of the person of the Moslem leader, the Emir Ibn 'Abs, and of his own former admiral, William Porco, and a Marseillais pirate, Hugues de Fer. Both of the latter had apparently been assisting the Moslem forces, probably by bringing them reinforcements from the African coast. The Emir Ibn 'Abs was shown none of the clemency which Frederick in the past had accorded to the rebellious Duke Thibault of Lorraine; rebellion in the Realm of Sicily always seems to have incensed the Emperor in a manner which makes it evident that he regarded it as a deliberate insult to his royal dignity, and the unfortunate Ibn 'Abs had at one time apparently also laid his hands upon some of Frederick's messengers. He paid for his temerity on the gibbet, beside William Porco and Hugues de Fer—though these two were only accorded their just deserts, as some years previously they had made a small fortune by selling the luckless participants in the Children's Crusade in the slave markets of North Africa.

Frederick returned to the mainland for the winter. In January and February he held court at Capua and later he went to San Germano (the modern Cassino) and was joined by Hermann von Salza who had returned from a mission to the Pope with a proposal to put before his Emperor which was very near to von Salza's heart. This was that Frederick should marry the hereditary Queen of Jerusalem, Yolanda de Brienne, then a child of twelve.

Yolanda's right to the crown of Jerusalem was inherited from her dead mother, Maria of Monferrat. Her father, Jean de Brienne, who had been crowned king consort upon his marriage in 1212, had acted as regent since his wife's death. The previous year he had returned to Europe in search of a husband for his daughter and had gone first to Rome. His visit coincided with von Salza's and the idea of Yolanda's marriage to Frederick probably originated with the latter. The Pope was enthusiastic. Both he and von Salza saw that, if it could be accomplished, it would provide a powerful incentive to per- suade that tardy Crusader Frederick to go and convert his wife's high-sounding title into a concrete addition to his own domains. The Crusade would be under way at last.

Frederick was not enthusiastic; the Kingdom of Jerusalem was practically reduced to a mere name, and the title was all that the twelve-year-old Yolanda could bring as a dower. Hermann von Salza needed all his diplomacy to get Frederick to agree to the marriage. No records have survived to give any idea of what arguments he used, but von Salza had now been an intimate friend of Frederick's for seven years and he knew the Emperor's sceptical turn of mind too well to use arguments of a religious kind. It is more than probable that he played on the Hohenstaufen side of Frederick's character, with its almost visionary conception of the meaning of empire. Frederick's father, Henry VI, had been planning a Crusade as a means of extending the Empire to the East when he died—perhaps von Salza managed to instil something of the same idea into Frederick. Whatever he did, it was a remarkable coup to persuade the Emperor to agree to marry a dowerless Queen.

Von Salza's original purpose in visiting the Pope had been to complete arrangements for a meeting between him and Frederick at Ferentino to discuss plans for the Crusade. Honorius fell ill, and Frederick had to wait some weeks before the meeting could be held. He welcomed this respite, for not only was he heavily burdened already with the Moslem war and his reorganisation of the realm; it became increasingly clear that the whole weight of the Crusade was going to fall upon his shoulders, for, although they were expected, none of the German princes put in an appearance for the Ferentino meeting.

Nevertheless when, on the 23rd of March, the Pope was sufficiently recovered for the discussions to begin, it became plain that this time he meant to pin the elusive Emperor down to a business-like agreement. Jean de Brienne, Raoul de Merencourt, Patriarch of Jerusalem, the King and Archbishop of Thessalonica, and the Grand Masters of the Hospital and the Teutonic Orders, and Preceptor of the Templars were all there. In their presence Frederick formally agreed to marry Yolanda and to depart for the Crusade on St. John's Day in 1225.

With another two years' grace before him, Frederick returned to prosecute the war against the Saracens in the island of Sicily. This time it was an all-out campaign planned on a large scale, employing new tactics. Simultaneous attacks were made at several points and as the Saracens yielded and gave ground, seeking the protection of higher mountains, they were divided into separate groups and eventually forced to surrender piecemeal. The new tactics had proved their worth, but it was a slow struggle, and it is estimated that the Moslems could count as many as twenty-five thousand determined warriors who fought desperately because they knew that their only other alternative was death, or life as a serf working the land for a Christian overlord. Moreover they were fighting on a terrain that they knew well, which was particularly suited to defensive action.

By July, Frederick had achieved sufficient success to warrant his writing to the Bishop of Hildesheim describing his victories over the Saracens in glowing terms. In actual fact the end was nowhere near, but already large numbers of Moslems had surrendered and agreed to live in the plain. More impressive in fact than Frederick's military successes at this stage was the idea which he had conceived for the final settlement of the Moslem question in Sicily.

He was well aware that ever since the death of William II these turbulent tribesmen had been a recurrent source of unrest and that, whenever the strong hand of a central government was relaxed or otherwise engaged, the Moslems had promptly reverted to brigandage and lawlessness, seizing the lands which now belonged to the Christians, because they felt that they belonged to them, whose ancestors had in the past been undisputed lords of Sicily for nearly two centuries.

The Emperor's departure on Crusade, let alone his premature death, would have brought these lately defeated foes up in arms again, marauding from the inaccessible mountain fastnesses in which he had just defeated them. The only practical solution to this recurring problem was their removal— but in mediaeval times, unlike the present, it was not practical politics to slaughter, out of hand, what would in the end have amounted to several hundred thousand people, who were moreover skilled artisans and agriculturists when they were not campaigning as singularly fearless soldiers.

Frederick hit upon the only solution which would at the same

time remove the Saracens from access to the mountain fastnesses of Sicily, and preserve their skilled labour for the prosperity of the realm. As they surrendered, he had them transported wholesale to the barren vastness of the plains of Apulia,
where they were grouped into agricultural settlements round
the ruined and deserted town of Lucera, which had once been a
Roman military centre.

Even after the death of the redoubtable William Porco and
Hugues de Fer the Moslems in Sicily were still receiving help
and reinforcements from North Africa and Frederick organised a
punitive expedition to the island of Djerba, which was a stronghold of the Barbary corsairs. The possession of what was
already a considerable fleet enabled him to wipe out this hor-
nets' nest and to bring into captivity the inhabitants of the entire island, to be transported in their turn to Lucera. This
savage raid scotched once and for all the possibility of any
further foreign aid reaching Moslems in Sicily.

Contrary to the usual practice of the times, Frederick continued the war against the Saracens during the winter. He took
up residence in Catania and imposed a special tax upon the
entire realm in order to raise the money with which to continue
the war. He called up the Counts of Aquila, Caserta, and San
Severino, and the son of the Count of Tricarico, all of whom
owed him military service under the feudal system, and of whose
fidelity he was not at all certain. His suspicions proved to be
well-founded; the counts presented themselves with only a
few armed vassals instead of the considerable force which,
between them, they should have put into the field. They were
arrested, and Frederick confiscated their possessions.

In January of 1224 Hermann von Salza arrived from Germany with an urgent summons from the princes of the Empire
for the Emperor to return to Germany. He found Frederick
so engrossed in the Saracen war and the plans for the reorganisation of Sicily that he soon realised that any hopes
which he might have entertained of getting Frederick to go in
person to Germany to enlist recruits for the Crusade there
were hopeless. The chief caids of the Moslems obligingly
chose this particular moment to sue for terms and, with the
pretext that Frederick's absence from Sicily at this crucial time
might endanger the results of the whole of a difficult cam-

paign—as the Saracens had succumbed to famine rather than military force and the reaping of the harvest before the summer heat would have given them fresh courage with which to continue the war—von Salza had to return to Germany to continue his efforts for the Crusade alone.

Frederick wrote in the same strain to the Pope in March, and his description of the difficulties which he was encountering was no specious excuse. Another special tax or "collecta" had to be imposed upon the realm in August, and as late as April 1225 the Sicilian barons were still mobilised for war against the Moslems. It was only in the following year that the war finally came to an end. Some 16,000 Moslems had by then been transported to Lucera.

In his letter to the Pope of March 1224, Frederick had been able to give a report on the progress of his preparations for the Crusade, which illustrates perhaps better than anything else how effectively he had already brought order out of the chaos in which he had found the realm upon his arrival a little more than three years before.

Already he had a fleet of a hundred galleys ready to put to sea, and fifty transports capable of carrying 2,000 knights and 10,000 men-at-arms were in the course of construction. The design of these transports was extraordinarily modern; they were built so that the knights could disembark directly, armed and mounted on their chargers, ready to repel hostile action and surprise attacks—they were in fact the prototype of the modern tank-landing craft.

The ability to create a fleet from scratch affords evidence, in any historical period, of sound organisation and financial resources. Already Frederick had been experimenting with financial export controls on the foodstuffs that were Sicily's main stock-in-trade, experiments which were later to lead to an immensely profitable Crown trading organisation in wheat. Now in 1224, mainly with the aim of depriving the Genoese and Pisan traders of their monopoly of the Sicilian corn trade, Frederick forbade for a while the export of all foodstuffs. The prices dropped to rock bottom, Frederick bought up large stocks and at the same time imposed a new rule which allowed the foreign traders to buy only from the Crown, with the result that he netted a handsome profit for the state.

D

This is only an isolated example of one of Frederick's commercial transactions of which documentary evidence happens to
have survived. Of much of the rest of his activities in this
field we know nothing, though the country had evidently been
making a rapid financial recovery, and Frederick had already
issued a new coinage of silver pieces called Imperials. He had
come a very long way indeed since the days when, to defray
the cost of the court and for waging war, he had been forced to
borrow 7,000 gold tari from the Bishop of Girgenti, or to
melt down the gold and silver plate of the church of Santa
Maria dell' Amiraglio—both of these old debts had since been
paid off by rewarding the parties concerned with grants of
farming land recaptured from the Saracens.

Gradually the framework for the new Sicilian state was
beginning to take shape from the plan outlined at Capua in
1220. It was a new model state where the central power was
ousting that of the barons, and its administration was to become
increasingly the province of laymen. It had its roots in the old
Norman kingdom, and was therefore somewhat akin to England,
but it was something new in the mediaeval world of the
Continent. The creation of the navy and department of defence,
the royal courts of justice, and the administration of the
country generally, called for a new type of man to fill the posts
which the new order had created. To fulfil this need, Frederick
founded the first state university in Naples in the spring of
1224. It outshone the ancient medical school of Salerno, without whose degree it was still however illegal to practise medicine in the Kingdom of Sicily. In Naples itself a law school and
Studium Generale was founded, whose graduates were to furnish
the candidates for the courts of justice and the nascent civil
service. Typical of this new class was the enterprising young
lawyer, Pietro della Vigna of Capua, who, thanks to his
impeccable Latin style and the patronage of Archbishop
Berard of Palermo, had lately joined the Sicilian Chancery as a
notary.

The benevolent despot, so familiar in Europe of the eighteenth
century, was already evident in Frederick's planning of the
new university. The teaching staff, headed by Roffredo of
Benevento, was the most eminent that money could buy. In his
letters of patent Frederick dwelt upon the charms and natural

beauty of Naples. All the practical advantages of cheap lodgings, food and special loans of money for needy scholars were provided by the Emperor's benevolence—the despot decreed that in future no Sicilian might study at any other university.

As a result of the meeting at Ferentino, Jean de Brienne, Hermann von Salza, and a Papal Legate Conrad von Urach, the Cardinal Bishop of Porto, had been sent on a tour through Europe to arouse the interest of the Western powers in the Crusade. Jean de Brienne found little enthusiasm in France, whose king was busily engaged in war with the English. Hermann von Salza and the Cardinal of Porto were barely more successful in Germany, which was even more vital to the success of the Crusade, as Frederick's undertakings for the Empire, made at Ferentino, could not become operative unless they were ratified by the princes of the Empire and King Henry.

Both Jean de Brienne and Hermann von Salza were well aware from long experience of the Near East, and from the failure of the last Crusade at Damietta, that only a carefully planned and amply financed military expedition, organised on a large scale, could have any chance of success. They warned the Pope of this, and he redoubled his efforts to urge concerted action upon the leaders of the Western world—but he met with no response, and the war between France and England continued.

In July the Cardinal Legate and Hermann von Salza met in Nuremberg. By superhuman efforts and with the moral weight of their joint missions, as representatives of the Pope and the Emperor, they had finally coerced the unwilling German princes into ratifying Frederick's agreement with the Pope at Ferentino. They even managed to rope in the Danish King, Waldemar, as a prospective Crusader, as a result of the settlement reached over Holstein and the Danish border question. It was a short-lived triumph, as shortly afterwards the Danish King backed out of the agreement, though to his credit he did eventually fulfil his vow to go on Crusade.

In March 1225 Hermann von Salza joined Frederick in Palermo. The account which he had to give the Emperor of his mission was depressing in the extreme, and he was forced to advise Frederick to try and obtain a further delay for the starting date of the Crusade. It must have been a bitter blow for von Salza personally, as the whole *raison d'être* of the order of which he was chief was the liberation of the Holy Places, but he was too sound a soldier and politician to wish to embark upon an ill-prepared expedition which would inevitably end in failure. In April von Salza reported to the Pope the results of his mission, which must have been a great deal less palatable to Honorius than to Frederick, busy as he was with the concerns of the realm. Hermann von Salza's findings were backed by other experienced men, and the Pope was also probably aware that they largely coincided with the views of Jean de Brienne.

Frederick had called for a meeting of German prelates at Foggia in June, and at the same time he requested the prelates and barons of the realm to send in written reports of the activities, and failings, of the royal officials in their areas by the end of May, and to come in person to the meeting in June, for their various claims and reports to be investigated. The reforms laid down by the Capuan edicts had now been in operation for over four years, and Frederick evidently wanted first-hand information about any abuses and complaints which they had inevitably provoked among the feudal and more conservative element in the country.

Although he intended to rule Sicily by an authoritarian centralised government, Frederick was sufficiently far-sighted to be aware that a successful government cannot always be imposed on everyone from above. In order to make it work, and to carry the country with him, it was also necessary to take into account the feelings and suggestions of others. As he was an eminently practical man he probably also wanted to know how the new organisation which he had worked out in theory stood up to actual practice. He was willing when circumstances really demanded it to modify, or go back on, some of his own ordinances. For instance, the castle of San Germano had been built within the period prescribed by the Capuan edicts, and in accordance with the law should have been pulled down. It was represented to Frederick that its walls constituted the only means of defence for the inhabitants of this frontier town, and he allowed it to stand.

It must have required considerable courage to complain to Frederick of the behaviour of his officials, or of the diffi-

culties provoked by his laws, and it may be assumed that anyone
who did so was very sure of his ground. If the complaint was
justified, and Frederick was sure of the fidelity of the claimant,
he would accept criticism even of his own actions, but he was
merciless to any official who abused his authority or was found
guilty of peculation. This aspect of Frederick's character made
it possible for such upright men as Hermann von Salza and the
Archbishop Berard of Palermo to remain firm friends with him
for the duration of their lives, in spite of the admitted craftiness
of his diplomatic dealings.

Aware that the progress of the preparations for the Crusade
had not encountered the plain sailing which he had hoped for,
the Pope also sent a legate to Foggia to work out a new agreement. Von Salza seems to have conducted the main part of the
negotiations on Frederick's behalf, and although the obliga-
tions which Frederick took upon himself as a result were, as
will be seen, onerous in the extreme, they resulted in his being
allowed a further two years' delay. Proof of von Salza's remarkable diplomatic capacity lies in the fact that the relations between the two august personages remained excellent in spite
of the further delay and hard conditions imposed, because
both Pope and Emperor felt they had scored a diplomatic
victory, each thinking that he had got what he wanted at the
expense of the other.

During July in the church of San Germano in the presence
of two cardinals Frederick swore upon his soul, and under pain
of excommunication, to fulfil his vow to go on Crusade in the
summer of 1227. It was almost exactly ten years to the day
since his coronation as King of the Romans at Aix-la-Chapelle,
when in the first flush of his youthful triumph he had taken the
Cross; to what extent at that time he had been actuated by
political motives relevant to his son's election it is not possible
to say. But it is at least probable that once Henry was safely
established in Germany his father must have often bitterly rued
the day when he had committed himself to such a hazardous
undertaking.

Now again, however, Frederick felt that he had reason to be
satisfied with the diplomatic victory which he thought that he
had achieved by obtaining a further delay, and in getting the
control of the Crusade entirely into his own hands. But once

again there would come the day when he would have cause to regret the present apparent success.

For the conditions which Frederick had accepted were onerous indeed. On the Kingdom of Sicily was to fall a tremendous burden. Frederick had undertaken to transport and to maintain in the Holy Land for two years at his personal expense one thousand knights, or to pay into a special fund for the Crusade fifty silver marks for each knight falling short of this number. He was also to provide transport for another two thousand knights, each with three horses and his own following. A hundred galleys and fifty transports were to be kept on a war footing and at the disposal of the Crusaders. As a guarantee of his good faith in this tremendous undertaking, Frederick had agreed to pay a hundred thousand ounces of gold (about a quarter of a million sterling) in five instalments into a Crusading fund, of which Hermann von Salza was to be the chief trustee. The money was to be given back to the Emperor upon his arrival in the Holy Land; if he failed in his engagement it was to become forfeit and to be used for Jesus Christ, in other words to finance another Crusade.

Chapter IV

PRELUDE TO THE CRUSADE

1225

THE first irrevocable step in preparation for the Crusade had been the agreement of San Germano; the second was Frederick's marriage to Yolanda. The circumstances of this his second marriage could not have been in greater contrast to the first. Then a widowed queen had brought to the obscure boy-King of Sicily the support of the powerful house of Aragon. Now the resplendent Emperor was about to marry if not exactly a beggar-maid at least a dowerless girl. At this time Frederick was a handsome man of thirty-one, formed in his ways, who was beginning to put on weight in spite of abstemious diet and athletic pursuits. His predilection for women was well known and, like the polished courtier that he now was, Frederick had led the fashion at his court of writing love lyrics in the Provençal style in the Sicilian dialect, which was his mother-tongue. These were addressed to the objects—there had already been at least five—of his admiration.[6] This sophisticated man of the world and absolute ruler of a vast empire was now to wed for political reasons an inexperienced girl of fourteen.

In August fourteen galleys of the imperial fleet, under the command of Count Henry of Malta, came to Acre to bring the prospective bride to the Realm of Sicily for her marriage. Upon their arrival Yolanda was married to the Emperor by proxy; the Archbishop-elect of Capua as Frederick's representative placed his ring upon her finger in the church of the Holy Cross at Acre. Apparently marriage by proxy was not common in Outremer, and the chroniclers related that there was general astonishment that a man and woman could wed when separated by half the Mediterranean. After this ceremony Yolanda, who was not officially of age until she was sixteen, was, amid great

103

rejoicing, crowned Queen of Jerusalem at Tyre, receiving the homage of the barons of her kingdom. Accompanied by the Archbishop of Tyre, Simon de Maugastel, who was also Chancellor of the Realm of Jerusalem, her cousin Balian of Sidon, and the Sicilian notables that Frederick had sent to fetch her, she embarked upon a journey which seemed to hold in store for the young heiress to a kingdom which was little more than a name the promise of a brilliant future as Empress.

Yolanda was not accompanied only by bishops and grave statesmen; among her train of ladies was a cousin who was probably several years her senior. According to some accounts this cousin was the daughter of the Walter de Brienne who had married Alberia the heiress of Tancred, the illegitimate Hauteville pretender who had been elected King of Sicily by the barons in Henry VI's day. In this case the girl was a distant cousin of Frederick, but in spite of their blood relationship, the very name of Hohenstaufen would have brought with it a memory of brutality to any descendant of Tancred, after the vindictive savagery with which Henry VI had treated his family.

Even allowing for the custom of the time, when it was nothing out of the way for a girl of fourteen to marry a man more than twice her age whom she had never seen, contemplation of her approaching marriage does not seem to have filled Yolanda with unmixed joy, and the company of a cousin whose family had suffered so grievously from Hohenstaufen cruelty cannot have been very reassuring. The chroniclers relate that when Yolanda and her ladies made a brief call on her aunt, Queen Alice of Cyprus, during the voyage, they all wept bitterly upon parting, and Yolanda could be heard, between her sobs, taking a sad farewell of the sweet land of Syria, which she was never to see again.

Frederick and her father were at Brindisi to meet the bride upon her arrival and the marriage took place with great splendour in the cathedral there, on the 9th of November. From the moment of its celebration there was trouble. The accounts of what took place are several and varied, but it appears to be fairly certain that Frederick left Brindisi abruptly the day after the ceremony, without informing his father-in-law of his intention. When the irate Jean de Brienne caught up with his new son-in-law, he found not only that Frederick had immediately assumed the style and title of King of Jerusalem, which de Brienne had expected to keep for himself at least until his daughter came of age in two years' time, but that the bride was in tears because her husband had paid her scant attention—he had fallen passionately in love with her cousin. Some chroniclers even go so far as to assert that Frederick had caused the girl to be abducted, had forcibly seduced her, and had never even appeared in the bridal chamber on the night of his marriage with Yolanda.

This story may be an exaggeration of what actually occurred, but the accounts of Frederick's passion for Yolanda's cousin come from contemporary sources which cannot lightly be disregarded, and Walter de Brienne IV, her brother, is known to have preserved a vindictive hatred for the Emperor throughout his life. On the face of it, it does not sound improbable that, Frederick's character and tastes being what they were, he might well have preferred a beautiful young woman in her twenties to an unsophisticated child of fourteen. If the tradition is correct, which had associated this sudden overwhelming passion with the "flower of Soria" to whom one of Frederick's most charming love poems was addressed, there seems to be no doubt as to the intensity of his feeling. After seven centuries, even allowing for poetic licence and the conventions of courtly love, the poem, which begins with the words "Oh, do not let me think", represents in appealingly human fashion the unhappiness of a lover about to be separated from his lady in a manner which still rings true today.

There was certainly a violent scene between the Emperor and Jean de Brienne, for which a good deal of the blame must be attributed to Frederick's undiplomatic if not actually disingenuous handling of the situation. It seems to be possible that there was a genuine misunderstanding, and that in his eagerness to bring off the marriage Hermann von Salza had promised verbally on Frederick's behalf, without consulting his master, that de Brienne would keep the title of King of Jerusalem either for his lifetime or at least until Yolanda was of age. On Frederick's side it can be argued that he, the Emperor, had married a penniless girl simply in order to add the Kingdom of Jerusalem to his domains, and that he could hardly have been expected to do so if he was not free to assume the title upon his marriage but was required to leave it to his father-in-law, who was in any case only regent as guardian for his daughter. The barons of Outremer present at the imperial court took the oath of fealty to Frederick without demur, and those who had remained in the Near East did the same to his representative, the Bishop of Melfi, who had been sent there for the purpose.

Jean de Brienne departed to Rome to lay his complaint before the Pope, who took his side and refused to recognise Frederick's assumption of the title of King of Jerusalem, which now figured upon imperial documents immediately after that of *Romanorum Imperator* and appeared on the great seal, inscribed on either side of the seated figure of the Emperor.

In Rome, Jean de Brienne found himself one of a company of malcontents from the Realm of Sicily—bishops who had been suspended by Frederick; Thomas, Count of Molise, and the Counts of Aquila and San Severino, all of whom Frederick had deprived of their lands, were also there; and their adverse influence as devil's advocates upon the Roman Curia must not be discounted in the troubles which were to arise between Pope and Emperor.

That hardy annual of contention between the popes and the kings of Sicily—the election of the Sicilian bishops—had flourished with increasing vigour during the last few years. By 1225 matters had reached an impasse in which it sufficed for the Pope or Frederick to give his backing to a candidate for the other to oppose it. The trouble lay in the fact that the approval of both the Pope and the King of Sicily was necessary before a bishop's election by the chapter could be confirmed. These terms had been laid down in the Concordat which Frederick's mother Constance had been forced to negotiate before Innocent III would agree to her infant son's coronation. They were a drastic curtailment of the rights which the previous kings of Sicily had enjoyed, but Frederick had also been compelled to ratify them before he went to Germany.

The Holy See now sought to diminish the King's rights even further by giving fresh impetus to the old "right of devolution" which entitled the Pope to fill immediately, without reference to the King or chapter, any see which had been vacant for more than six months. The Roman Curia was a past master in the art of procrastination, and a mere six months was child's play to it. Frederick retaliated by threatening to deny access to their sees to bishops appointed by the Pope in this fashion, and, though he later relented, in fact upon at least one occasion he did so.

Like the mutter of an approaching storm over these already troubled waters came the news that the Emperor, on his way to preside at the diet of the German princes which he had called at Cremona for Easter 1226, had entered the Duchy of Spoleto and insisted that the men of the duchy should provide him with an armed guard upon his progress through their territory. That he should have entered the duchy, which formed part of the Papal States, without asking the Pope's permission was in itself serious enough, but the insistence on the armed guard was a direct assertion of sovereign rights.

It is probable that Frederick's action was deliberate as, if he had wished, he could have made the journey by sea. But now that the reorganisation of Sicily was well under way, he had apparently decided to deal with the question of the imperial rights in central Italy before leaving the country to go on the Crusade, which was understandable as the route that the German Crusaders would have to follow passed through it. Whereas he was prepared to accept the Pope as titular suzerain of Sicily, Frederick, like his predecessor Otto I, regarded Central Italy as imperial territory and the ancient donations to the Patrimony of St. Peter as imperial concessions which he had the power to revoke. Accordingly he considered the Pope's exercise of the political power in this region as subordinate to his own as imperial suzerain. Needless to say this was not the papal view, which held that the whole of the Papal States belonged to the Church in perpetuity.

In 1219 and 1220 Frederick had agreed to renew the donations to the Patrimony of St. Peter, and had even given the Pope military assistance in order that he might recover the territories over which the Church had lost effective control during the troubled times through which Italy had been passing. In 1221 the Pope had thanked Frederick for the satisfactory fashion in which these reconquests had been carried out, but even at that time Frederick had insisted upon the ancient right of the *Fodrum Imperiale* (this entitled the Emperor, on his way to his coronation in Rome, to exact a kind of subsistence allowance for himself and his train when passing through the Papal States, and was, therefore, a form of sovereign right).

In 1222 the imperial legate in Tuscany had revoked the appointment of the papal representatives in the Duchy of Spoleto and the March of Ancona. The Pope had protested, and Frederick had reprimanded his legate, but the incident had served as a warning to the Roman Curia, who were only too well aware that their hold upon these two vital territories blocked all communication by land between the Empire and the Realm of Sicily. It was, therefore, to be expected that the Roman Curia should be extremely sensitive to any imperial assertion of sovereign rights in this area.

The storm broke with an indignant letter from the Pope, in which he protested against Frederick's passage across papal territory, and reproached him with ingratitude towards the Church. In his reply Frederick's pent-up irritation with the Pope found its outlet and, among other things, the long-standing grievances of the Sicilian bishops and the presence in Rome of exiles from the realm found expression. Hermann von Salza, whose difficult mission in life it seemed to be to provide a buffer between the Emperor and the Pope, had come hurrying up to join Frederick, because he rightly feared that the situation had all the makings of an open breach between the two leaders of Christendom upon the eve of the Crusade. He had evidently caught up with Frederick by the time the Emperor was in Rimini, and once again his signal services were recognised by extensive privileges being granted to the Teutonic Knights. By the famous Golden Bull of Rimini the task of converting the Prussian heathen was handed over to the Teutonic Order.

Meanwhile the situation in Northern Italy had become critical. On the 6th of March Milan and many of the Lombard cities, as well as those in the Venetian Marches—Padua, Vicenza and Treviso—had concluded an offensive and defensive league of twenty-five years' duration. What was even more serious, they were later joined by others including the strategically important city of Verona, which commanded the Brenner and the direct route that King Henry and the German princes would have to use if they were to attend the Diet of

Cremona in full force. The Emperor's decision to hold an imperial diet in Lombardy had evidently inspired the cities with the fear that the freedom that they had enjoyed since 1183 was at an end. In the intervening forty-three years they had to all practical intents and purposes become self-governing republics, and the phrase "Restoration of Imperial rights in Italy" which had featured together with the Crusade and eradication of heresy on the agenda of the invitation to the German princes to attend the diet, appeared to confirm their worst fears.

News of Frederick's suppression of the civic rights of the Sicilian cities by the ordinances promulgated at Capua must have long before reached Northern Italy, and the Lombards had evidently decided to forestall any similar action by the Emperor in their territory. Accordingly they refused to allow King Henry and the princes to cross the Brenner unless the Emperor was prepared to agree to the most humiliating conditions: not to put the cities under the ban of the Empire while he was in Lombardy, Romagna, or the Marches; not to bring more than twelve hundred horsemen; to send away all his own forces before his son's arrival; not to make any provision of food for himself for the duration of the diet (which would make him dependent upon Lombardy for his very means of subsistence); that both the Emperor and the King should accept the jurisdiction of the papal legate during their stay in Northern Italy; and that the legate should be empowered to place an interdict upon their lands and to excommunicate their persons if they took judicial action against the league or its members.

The sheer effrontery of such demands addressed to an Emperor and King who were to meet in solemn conclave to discuss preparations for a Crusade so shocked the German and Italian prelates who were with Frederick that they demanded that the Bishop of Hildesheim should, by virtue of the powers vested in him by the Pope, excommunicate the offending members of the league. As the prospective leader of the Crusade Frederick had been taken under the protection of the Pope, and the Bishop of Hildesheim had been empowered to place under ecclesiastical censure, after due warning, anyone who threatened the rights or honour of the Empire.

The action of the Lombard cities was all the more reprehensible in mediaeval eyes because they were preventing the reunion of a father and son who had not seen each other for six years. Afterwards, when relations between father and son had degenerated into an open breach, the Emperor in his bitterness laid much of the blame at the door of the Milanese for having prevented this meeting. But already Frederick had good reason to wish to see Henry; disquieting reports had already reached him and the wise *Gubernator*, Engelbert, Archbishop of Cologne, to whom he had entrusted his son and the regency of Germany, had been murdered in the previous year.

At Easter, which fell that year in the middle of April, the Emperor, who should have been presiding over the Diet of Cremona, was halted at Ravenna and King Henry and the princes were blocked at Trent. Frederick was still in Ravenna in June, having summoned the representatives of the Lombard cities to appear before him on the 24th of that month. Their failure to comply raised indignation at the imperial court to fever-heat, and the prelates, lords and jurists assembled there tried to persuade the Emperor to deprive the offenders of all the rights accorded to them by Barbarossa at the Treaty of Constance.

No doubt Frederick inwardly endorsed their views but he was only too well aware that he had no army which would enable him to support such drastic sanctions. Stifling the fury to which he could give no expression in the presence of the papal legate, Frederick tried to temporise and arrange some sort of compromise which might induce the Lombards to send their representatives to treat with him.

This last pacific effort failed. On the 11th of July, at Borgo San Donnino, the Bishop of Hildesheim placed the Lombard cities under an interdict, while Frederick imposed upon them the ban of Empire. The cities were declared rebels, guilty of *lèse-majesté*; all their inhabitants were shorn of their political rights and their schools and universities, especially that of Bologna, were suppressed. It was but empty thunder for the Emperor had no military backing with which to convert these terrible threats into reality. He was forced to ask the Pope to arbitrate, although he was well aware that much of the Lombard cities' effrontery was due to their knowledge that their action in defying the Emperor was not displeasing to the Pope. This tacit support of the Lombard cities by Honorius was dictated by political expediency, for they were the only weapon which he could use to counterbalance the Emperor's preponderance in the Italian peninsula, but in supporting them the Pope was also aiding centres where the Patarene heresy was known to be rife. It was an action that Frederick had every justification for resenting and it added fuel to the fires of his pent-up indignation and mistrust of the Pope and the Roman Curia.

The projected Diet of Cremona was a complete fiasco, but there was nothing that the Emperor could do to retrieve the situation. The Pope was still writing him long and indignant letters about the violation of papal territory, and the route for Frederick's return to Sicily was menaced. It was an equally critical position from both the political and military points of view and Frederick's judgement had been seriously at fault in allowing himself to be manœuvred into such an impasse. He extricated himself with some dexterity, however. In a letter to the Pope he laid the entire responsibility for the failure of the diet fairly and squarely upon the shoulders of the Lombards. Attributing his own clemency to the fact that he was now dedicated to Christ's cause, and stressing the damage they had done to the preparations for the Crusade, he stated that he now left their richly merited chastisement in the Pope's hands. Hermann von Salza was sent as the leader of an embassy to the Pope, an astute action on Frederick's part as the Grand Master of the Teutonic Order could safely be relied upon not only to bring home to Honorius the indignation of the German lay and ecclesiastical princes but to convey to the Pope his own anxiety that after so many years of unremitting personal effort the Crusade might now be seriously hampered by the Lombards' action, or at least that the Emperor had very good grounds for maintaining this was so.

The practical difficulties of Frederick's return to Sicily were solved by the Pisans sending a supporting force to bring him to their city. Here, with the characteristic detachment which enabled him to live at a speed and pressure which exhausted his entourage, Frederick appeared to cast his political cares from him and plunged with enthusiasm into the studies that he loved.

Leonardo Fibonacci, the greatest mathematician of the time and for centuries to come, who introduced to Europe the system of Arabic numerals which we use today, was Pisan by birth, though he had studied mainly in Oriental countries and Spain. He was then resident in Pisa and he dedicated his treatise, the *Liber Quadratorum* on squared numbers, to Frederick, with the words "I have heard from the Podesta of Pisa that it pleases you from time to time to hear subtle reasoning in Geometry and Arithmetic."

The Emperor returned the compliment by setting Fibonacci a series of problems in higher mathematics which he solved successfully. No doubt Frederick enlisted the assistance of one of the scholars of the court, probably John of Palermo, in setting these conundrums, but he was not the man to let another ghost for him in matters of this kind, and they show Frederick to be a mathematician worthy to be judged by high standards.

In this aspect of his character Frederick was more akin to his Moslem contemporaries than to Christian kings. Mathematics and the natural sciences were his preferred studies, and one of his favourite forms of recreation was to debate their mysteries and the Oriental subtleties of dialectic among the intimate circle of philosophers and men of learning who surrounded him, by now the lodestar attracting the most brilliant men of the day. Already his court formed the pattern which was to be repeated by the princes of the Renaissance—with this difference: Frederick was not content simply to play Maecenas; the scholars, philosophers and poets who surrounded him earned their scot by serving as imperial officials and civil servants as well. Though the financial rewards were far from princely, as the letters complaining of dunning creditors sent home by more than one ambitious young clerk of the Imperial Chancery bear witness, the competition was tremendous. The life of a courtier in Frederick's entourage was no sinecure; experts might surpass him on their own subjects, none of them could equal the extraordinary versatility of his genius.

Frederick now returned to Sicily to continue with the preparations for the Crusade, leaving to the Pope the arbitration of the Lombard question with a request that the Lombards should also participate in the expedition to the Holy Land. In December von Salza came to Foggia to report on the negotiations, which appear to have gone ahead with remarkable rapidity considering the slowness of communications and the Lombard propensity for delay and subterfuge. It is probable that the Pope, alarmed in real earnest for the progress of the Crusade, had brought as much pressure to bear on the Lombards as was consonant with his overriding determination to support them as a counterweight to Frederick's power.

The settlement which was finally arrived at, however, was practically a return to the position as it had been before Frederick's ill-fated expedition to the North of Italy. Pope and Emperor lifted the interdict and ban of Empire, and the rebellious Lombard cities agreed to keep the peace with the Ghibelline towns such as Cremona. The only sanction which the offenders suffered was that they were required to furnish four hundred knights for the Crusade. No apology or restitution was made to the Emperor for the insult which he had suffered or for the failure of the Diet of Cremona.

Frederick accepted this one-sided arrangement with astonishing good grace. He had now embarked upon the last stage of the preparations for the Crusade, and evidently had made up his mind to go through with it. If he had not, the Lombard action in preventing the Diet of Cremona would have been the perfect excuse ready to his hand for yet another postponement. Nevertheless the Pope's settlement, which amounted practically to condonation of the Lombards' action, touched Frederick in his most sensitive spot—the honour and prestige of the Empire. His feelings upon the subject were all the more bitter because for the present they had to be concealed, but when they finally burst forth in all their fury he was to describe as "incestuous" the papal support of the rebel Lombard communes, known centres of the Patarene heresy.

In June 1226, Thomas Count of Acerra had been sent to Outremer as Frederick's regent, and in the autumn Hermann von Salza returned to Germany armed with the Pope's blessing and Sicilian gold to recruit princes and knights for the Crusade. The great surge of faith and religious enthusiasm which had launched the first Crusades, more than a century before, had spent itself, killed by the corrupting influences of plunder, the jealousies of the Latin and the Oriental Churches, and the debilitating effects of the Oriental ways of life in Outremer itself. The shock of the fall of Jerusalem had given it a fresh impetus in the Third Crusade when Barbarossa lost his life, but the distressing spectacle of the armies of the Fourth Crusade attacking Christian cities such as Zara, and the final indignity of their sack of Constantinople, were blows from which the crusading spirit was destined never to recover except in the saintly mind of King Louis of France.

So now Hermann von Salza's best allies in his campaign for recruits were the money and the privileges which his imperial master had to offer. Among the princes and nobles who at that time were thronging to Aix-la-Chapelle for the coronation of King Henry's wife, Margaret of Austria, he found two powerful candidates—the Landgrave of Thuringia and Henry of Limburg. The promise of the revenues of the March of Misnia (Meissen) prompted the Crusading zeal of the Landgrave, and the Duke of Limburg was inspired in a like fashion by promises and money. Seven hundred of the thousand knights who were to form the Emperor's personal contribution, who according to his instructions must be of "proved bravery and experience", were recruited by lavish payments of Sicilian gold. Hermann von Salza had reason to be satisfied with his efforts, and he began to worry whether Frederick's ship-building programme would provide sufficient transport for them all.

Pope Honorius III died on the 18th of March 1227 and in a conclave of remarkably short duration the cardinals elected in his place Cardinal Hugo of Ostia, from whose hands Frederick had taken the Cross at his coronation. He was a Conti of Segni, the same family from which Innocent III had sprung, and like Innocent he was a proud and energetic man. He had also the highly trained brain of a great authority on canon law. Even in his old age he had an impressive presence and magnificent mien, and his determination to uphold the prestige of the Church was evident from the start, in his choice of the name of Gregory, in memory of his great predecessor who had brought the Emperor Henry IV to Canossa.

Although his previous relations with Frederick had been of the friendliest nature, Gregory IX made haste to leave him in no doubt that the Keys of St. Peter were now in the grasp of a firm hand. Shortly after his accession to the Holy See he wrote

to the Emperor: "God has bestowed upon you the gift of knowledge and of perfect imagination, and all Christendom follows
you. Take heed that you do not place your intellect, which
you have in common with the angels, below your senses, which
you have in common with brutes and plants. Your intellect is
weakened if you are slave of your senses."

This warning was the first overt indication of the Church's
disapproval of Frederick's morals, that were to provide the
popes with a convenient weapon wherewith to attack the
Emperor in future. The line of attack is significant, just because
it was to achieve considerable success. Had Frederick not
excelled in debauchery, as in so much else, it would, in an age
of brutal licentiousness such as the thirteenth century, have
carried little weight with public opinion; for propaganda to be
effective at any period it must have some basis of truth.

Hermann von Salza had now returned from Germany; he
had probably seen the new Pope on his journey south, before he
joined Frederick in Apulia. It was now midsummer and the
Crusaders were swarming down the pilgrim roads to the plains
of Apulia, where in vast encampments others were ready waiting
to embark for the Holy Land. Even with modern means of
transport and the organised methods of the twentieth century
the dispatch of an expeditionary force overseas calls for an
enormous effort in order to prevent confusion. How much
greater were the complications 700 years ago. The number of
Crusaders on this occasion had exceeded all expectations, and
food began to run short. In the blazing heat of an Apulian
August an epidemic broke out. It spread like wildfire, and the
Crusaders died in hundreds. Many fled from the camps, carrying the infection with them along the pilgrim roads and into the
towns where the late arrivals lodged on their way to Brindisi,
the port of embarkation. Frederick and his suite had left
Melfi in August, and accompanied Yolanda, who was in the
early stages of pregnancy, to the comparative safety of Otranto
in the extreme heel of Italy. They returned north to Brindisi
and went to live on the island of Sant' Andrea to escape infection
while superintending the embarkation. The precaution was in
vain; both Frederick and the Landgrave of Thuringia had
caught the dreaded illness, but in spite of this they embarked
on the 9th of September, hoping that the sea air would effect a

cure. The Landgrave grew steadily worse and in his delirium he thought that he was surrounded by white doves. The imperial galley put into Otranto where, after receiving the last sacrament from the Patriarch of Jerusalem, he died.

It was a serious blow to Frederick, whose chief deputy in the leadership of the Crusade he was to have been. The Emperor himself was still ill, and no doubt the tragic end of the Landgrave weighed heavily in the decision which had now to be taken—whether Frederick should continue his journey to the Holy Land, with the risk that he might also die upon the high seas, leaving the expedition leaderless. In the council of the "familiars" which followed, Hermann von Salza, who knew better than anyone else the state of mind of the Pope, seems to have envisaged the possibility of himself leading a mission to the Holy See to explain the situation, but apparently he did not even broach the idea to the Emperor who was set upon von Salza's continuing with the rest of the expedition to Outremer. In the end it was decided that the command of the Crusaders should be handed over to the Duke of Limburg who had already left in mid-August with a large detachment, and that twenty of the fifty galleys which had been standing by to accompany the Emperor should sail under the leadership of Hermann von Salza and the new Patriarch of Jerusalem, Gerold of Lausanne.

They left in mid-September and, upon their arrival in Cyprus, found the barons of the island and some of those from Outremer waiting to accompany the Emperor on the Crusade. The Cypriot barons now decided to remain at home, and Hermann von Salza continued the journey accompanied only by Balian of Sidon, Odo of Montbeilard, Bohemund of Antioch, and their followers from Outremer. Frederick's absence created profound dismay among the Crusaders who had been waiting impatiently in the Holy Land, and many of them now returned to Europe. There was considerable division of opinion among those who remained upon what action to take. The truce that had followed upon the fall of Damietta was still in force, but the Duke of Limburg decided to break it, not with the intention of provoking an all-out struggle to regain the Holy Places, but as a means of seizing, if possible, certain strategic cities which would serve as bases for more extended operations in future. Accordingly Jaffa and Caesarea were besieged, and later Sidon.

After the Crusaders' departure, Frederick went to the baths of Pozzuoli to regain his health. Famous since ancient times, these baths were probably the most highly esteemed in all Italy during the thirteenth century. They were the subject of what is probably one of the earliest "blurbs" in medical history on the curative effects of their waters and vapour baths. It was written about this time by Petrus de Ebulo, and graphically illustrated with drawings of patients undergoing treatment. Perhaps the baths' vicinity to the famous medical school of Salerno had something to do with their fame, which was no doubt increased by the Emperor's visit. They were certainly very much in vogue at Frederick's court, and later he built a hospital there for the poor.

While he was undergoing his cure, Frederick dispatched an embassy to the Pope to explain his failure to depart on Crusade. The outcome was a shock to him; his representatives returned with the news that Gregory had refused even to receive them. Eleven years of dealing with the conciliatory Honorius had not prepared Frederick for a man of the calibre of Ugo Conti. Another, and more impressive, mission composed of the Archbishops of Bari and Reggio Calabria, the Duke of Spoleto and Henry of Malta was now dispatched to Rome; they were received only by the Synod and for all the good they did they might have remained at home.

In spite of papal assertions that Frederick's illness was yet another pretext, the last of a long series, for not going on Crusade, there can be little doubt that the Emperor had really fallen victim to the epidemic, and that he was fortunate not to meet the same end as the Landgrave of Thuringia. Two of the most reliable contemporary chroniclers vouch for this and the known facts apparently support the contention that Frederick fully intended to sail for the Holy Land when he embarked at Brindisi. Vast sums had been expended in persuading German princes and knights to join the Crusade, apart from the promised special fund of a hundred thousand ounces of gold of which eighty thousand had already been paid up, and the remaining twenty thousand had been stowed aboard the Emperor's galley. The figures involved were enormous for the period, and although Frederick had been very free with his largesse during his early days in Germany, he watched the finances of his Kingdom of Sicily with all the careful niggardliness of an astute business man; no detail was too small to escape his eagle eye, or too insignificant to be turned to profit for the state revenues. He had inherited much from his grandfather King Roger who used to make periodic visits to the royal counting houses and tot up the accounts himself. It would have been most unlike the Emperor to set in motion the expenditure of these vast sums from his laboriously acquired financial reserves if he did not intend personally to oversee their use, and to ensure the success of the venture upon which they were being expended.

There is one fact, however, which indicates that although Frederick had previously been firmly fixed in his intention to go to the Holy Land, a delay at the last moment might not have been unwelcome to him. The Sultan of Egypt, al-Kamil, had in the autumn of 1226 sent an embassy to the imperial court. The ambassador who led this mission from a Moslem sultan to the leader of the Christian world on the eve of a Crusade was the Emir Fakhr ad-Din ibn as-Shaikh. He was the intimate counsellor and friend of al-Kamil and what was more important —his personality made an instant appeal to Frederick. Possibly the court at Cairo had contact through secret channels with its co-religionists who formed part of Frederick's personal household; Richard—there is no record of any patronym—who was chamberlain from 1215 to 1234 and who had his master's entire confidence, is thought to have been a Christian convert of Moslem extraction.

In any event the Sultan and his court were evidently well informed as to Frederick's interests, and aware that his tastes were closely akin to those of al-Kamil himself. Fakhr ad-Din had all the cultivated Moslem's love of dialectic and long discussions upon the mysteries of the universe, combined with prowess in the arts of war, a truly Arab knowledge of horseflesh, and expertise in the art of falconry. No other qualities could have provided him with a better passport to the good graces of the Emperor, who had spoken Arabic since his childhood.

Such was the man who came to enlist the support of the Christian Emperor for his master al-Kamil. The empire of the

Great Saladin was by now divided between three Ayubite brothers, al-Kamil, al-Ashraf, commonly known as the Sultan of Babylon, and al-Mu'azzam, Sultan of Damascus (and in control of Jerusalem and the Holy Places). Al-Mu'azzam entertained a well-justified fear that the other two intended to unite against him, and he allied himself with their common enemy Jelal ad-Din of the Khwarismian Empire. Caught between the two fires of al-Mu'azzam's and the Khwarismian armies, al-Ashraf was besieged in his capital, and al-Kamil saw that he might be left alone in the field to contend with the victors after they had defeated al-Ashraf. He therefore resorted to the desperate measure of asking the Christian Emperor for help. Frederick received Fakhr ad-Din with honour and listened to his appeals on behalf of his master with sympathy, but would commit himself to nothing.

It is difficult to judge what lay behind this temporising attitude. Was the Emperor so conscious of his strength and so sure of the ultimate issue of the Crusade by the force of his arms that he felt no steps were necessary to ensure the benevolent neutrality of even one of the Ayubite brothers while he was fighting the other, al-Mu'azzam of Damascus? Or was his non-committal attitude simply dictated by his knowledge of the bargaining methods of the Orient, and his hope that an apparent lack of interest might bring forth a better bid from al-Kamil?

The next move was to Frederick. In 1227 Berard the Archbishop of Palermo left for the Holy Land and with the regent, Count Thomas of Acerra, proceeded to Cairo bearing messages and princely gifts. These included the Emperor's own charger equipped with a golden saddle covered with gems, magnificent horses, falcons, robes and golden and other precious objects. They were overwhelmed with honours, and al-Kamil protested that he would willingly restore Jerusalem to the Emperor, but unfortunately it was at present in the possession of his brother al-Mu'azzam. His protestations of goodwill rang entirely true, and the imperial envoys must have been well aware of the reason —Frederick's presence in Outremer, at the head of the Crusading army, would please no one better than the Sultan of Egypt, who would then be free from the threat of his brother al-Mu'azzam and his Khwarismian allies.

Possibly some news of the difficulties which their imperial master was encountering in Europe had reached his ambassadors, for the Archbishop of Palermo now travelled to Damascus to find out what sort of offer he could get for the Emperor from the Sultan al-Mu'azzam. Perhaps the Archbishop hoped that he might be able to play the brother Sultans off one against the other, trading on their mutual fear and hatred. If this was the case, he found that he had misjudged this man at any rate. Here was no polished Oriental prince, so versed in subtleties that he thought it no shame to intrigue with the Christians against his brother Moslems. Al-Mu'azzam had but one answer to make to any suggestions—he was no pacifist, he still used his sword!

With polite protestations from the brother who did not own Jerusalem, and a flat refusal from the one who did, Archbishop Berard returned to report on the result of his missions to the Emperor. He was back in Apulia in January 1228, and either then, or shortly afterwards, the Emir Fakhr ad-Din followed him to the Sicilian court. The Emir made a prolonged sojourn there during which the sympathy that already existed between himself and the Emperor was transformed into a lasting friendship which finally culminated in Frederick's making him a knight and allowing him to bear the Hohenstaufen coat of arms.

The Emperor now had need of all the friends he could make. At the end of September 1227, after a secret Consistory, in which he reinforced his links with the Lombards by making several of them cardinals, the Pope pronounced the sentence of excommunication against Frederick. This was later made public at a synod of Italian prelates held on the 17th of November. In the interval Gregory launched an attack of unprecedented violence against the Emperor in an encyclical, which was dispatched from Anagni on the 10th of October.

The Pope was perfectly within his rights in excommunicating the Emperor; it was the penalty that had been agreed upon at San Germano if he failed to lead the Crusade during the summer of 1227, and there were no let-out clauses. Frederick always recognised Gregory's right in this matter; excommunication was not an unusual sanction against a tardy Crusader but normally after the performance of the required penances the sentence was rescinded.

In this instance, however, the Pope did not limit his accusations to the case in point, but tracing the whole history of the relationship between Frederick and the popes from the days when he was the ward of Innocent III, he resuscitated all the old quarrels about the Sicilian bishops and the Sicilian émigrés. He went on to lay upon the Emperor the blame for every setback experienced by the Christians in the Near East. From the Crusaders' failure to exchange Damietta for the Holy Places to the actual tragedy of its loss, which was due to the impetuosity and incompetence of leaders who had paid no attention to Frederick's injunctions to take no offensive action until the arrival of the Sicilian fleet with reinforcements; all the responsibility for these failures Gregory now laid upon the Emperor's shoulders. The Pope went even further, he stated that Frederick had not kept to his undertakings made at Ferentino or San Germano—the thousand knights had not been sent, the hundred thousand ounces of gold were not delivered, the promised shipping had not been forthcoming; finally there were even insinuations that Frederick had by his incompetence, or deliberately, chosen the unhealthy port of Brindisi and failed to supply the Crusaders with food.

Gregory's allegations as to Frederick's failure to keep the stipulations of Ferentino and San Germano were as unfounded as those which sought to make the Emperor responsible for the fall of Damietta, and the imperial representatives were able to demonstrate that they were palpable untruths. The only fact that the Pope had reported correctly was the shortage of food, which Frederick had never undertaken to supply. Brindisi was one of the normal ports of embarkation for the Crusades. Moreover Gregory in his fulminations against the Emperor had made no mention whatsoever of the Lombards' failure to send the four hundred knights, whose contribution to the Crusade was the only satisfaction that the papal arbitration of the Lombard quarrel had afforded to the Emperor after the fiasco of the Diet of Cremona.

While admitting his responsibility in failing to start, and the justification of the excommunciation upon these grounds alone —for which he offered to make any penance required—Frederick renewed his promise to start on Crusade in the following May. His offers fell upon deaf ears. The Pope's intransigence made the situation clear; it was not the belated Crusade that he cared about; he was solely animated by the desire to encompass the discredit and defeat of the Emperor. No normal religious penance of bread and water, of hair-shirts or processions with lighted tapers would he accept as the price of the lifting of the ban of excommunication. Frederick could only be freed by accepting the Pope's tutelage in his Realm of Sicily.

No ruler could accept such a condition—least of all the Emperor—and by its imposition the Pope evidently hoped to render the prosecution of the Crusade impossible and thus discredit Frederick in the eyes of the world. Perspicacious far beyond his contemporaries Gregory alone at this period seems to have recognised in Frederick the embodiment, in a far more dangerous form than those of the heretical sects such as the Patarenes and the Albigenses, of those forces which were sweeping Europe in the thirteenth century, and which challenged and ultimately reduced the powers of the Roman Catholic Church and so made possible the creation of the lay state and its religious counterpart, the Reformation. Behind Gregory's intransigence and vindictiveness, therefore, lay his fear of Frederick as the brain which had already begun to lay the foundations of a lay state in Sicily, and possibly a suspicion that in spite of the Emperor's persecution of heretics his own opinions upon Church reform might not be far removed from those of the Waldensians and Patarenes.

One of the reasons that probably accounts for Gregory's insight in this matter is the fact that he had been the intimate friend and protector of St. Francis of Assisi. He it was who as Cardinal of Ostia had assisted in drafting the Rule of St. Francis in the final form in which it had been accepted and endorsed by Pope Honorius. Many of the reforming aspects of St. Francis's beliefs, especially that of poverty, were closely akin to those of the sects who had been branded heretical and it was only the saint's acceptance of the discipline of the Church that saved him and his followers from the same stigma; and in this acceptance Gregory had played an important part. The Pope, therefore, through his friendship with St. Francis and the widespread practical experience gained in assisting in the foundation and organisation of the brotherhood, was in a far better position to know, and to judge, the reforming currents of his

time than other highly placed members of the ecclesiastical
hierarchy.

Gregory, therefore, with his insight into these dangerous
currents, was justified in his own mind in adopting any means,
or any subterfuge, in attempting to bring the Emperor low.
But he had reckoned without the audacity of his adversary. He
had assumed that excommunication would mean the end of any
talk of a Crusade. Instead, Frederick saw at once the blow he
could strike at papal prestige if he, an excommunicate, regained
the Holy Places for Christendom. He pressed on his plans
for departure with renewed vigour. Nor would he bow down
before the Pope's displeasure. He struck back in a series of
circulars to the kings and princes of the Christian world.

In these documents the Emperor applied upon a European
scale the same principle of a clear exposition of the facts of the
case, which he had used before to the nobles of the realm in the
first troubled years after taking over the reins of government
in Sicily. He reiterated his solemn vow to depart on Crusade the
following spring; he described the tragedy of the plague at
Brindisi and the Pope's subsequent refusal to accept any penance; he dwelt upon the Pope's favour to the Lombards who
had impeded the prosecution of the Crusade by preventing the
Diet of Cremona, and alluded to the further obstacles which
Gregory was now putting in the way of the Crusade by for-
bidding the clergy of the realm to assist him (Frederick had
imposed a special tax of eight ounces of gold on all fief-holders,
who were also to be responsible for the eighth part of the cost
of maintaining a soldier on Crusade while the Emperor was
overseas). These appeals did not fall on deaf ears; in Rome
itself the Senate and people insisted that the first letter should
be read aloud upon the Capitol.

According to the English chronicler, Matthew Paris, at this
stage Gregory's interference in the realm and continual obstruc-
tions stung Frederick out of the tone of measured calm that he
adopted into voicing his bitter feelings in a letter to the King
of England in which he described the Church of Rome as the
stepmother, not the mother, of believers, and priests as wolves
in sheep's clothing, instruments of a court no less proud than
wicked, bloodsuckers of Christian people. He accused the
ecclesiastical power, which owed its greatness to the secular

power, of turning against the giver the benefits which it had received, of having reduced to vassalage the Count of Toulouse and the King of England, and of now trying to make the empire its slave. He concluded with the words: "Upon poverty and simplicity the early Church was founded, and in those days she was the fertile mother of all those men whose names are inscribed in the catalogue of saints. . . . Now she wallows in riches, and it is to be feared that riches will overthrow her. . . . Unite yourselves then, and overturn this unheard-of tyranny; this danger is common to all. Remember that when your neighbour's wall is on fire your own property is at stake."[7]

Even before his excommunication Frederick had shown considerable independence and daring in his attitude to the Church over Henry's election. With his declaration that he intended to carry out the Crusade in spite of it, he had thrown down the gauntlet, but he was now to be pushed further in his defiance of the Church by Gregory's threat to release his subjects from their oath of allegiance as a reprisal for what the Pope regarded as his refusal to bow to the sentence of excommunication. The Emperor retaliated by attacking those prelates who upheld it, by refusing to perform the Holy Offices. He ordered the confiscation of their lands and belongings, also those of the Templars and Hospitallers. On Maundy Thursday the Pope repeated in public the sentence of excommunication against the Emperor with the accompaniment of all the awful ritual.

But Gregory was to learn that the hand of his enemy could reach out to strike him even in Rome. On Easter Monday he was mobbed by the populace while he was saying Mass; they barked like dogs as he elevated the Host. Frederick's friends and allies, the Frangipani family, had succeeded in alienating a section of the aristocracy from the Pope, and between them they raised the populace. The situation became so violent that Gregory had to flee from the Lateran Palace, and eventually even from Rome, taking refuge in Rieti.

When in April the Emperor held a court at Barletta, the crowd was so immense that the proceedings took place in the open air. After Frederick had seated himself upon his throne, a proclamation was read out to the assembled prelates and nobles. It was, in effect, his will prepared against the possibility of his meeting his death while he was on Crusade.

Rainald of Urslingen, Duke of Spoleto, was declared Governor of the realm during Frederick's absence. In the event of Frederick's death, his son Henry was to succeed him. If Henry died without issue, Conrad the newly born son of Yolanda was to be the heir. The declaration also decreed that there should be no increase in taxes, except in a case of great necessity, during the sovereign's absence. There was no mention whatsoever of the Pope.

On the 1st of May Yolanda died; she was only sixteen, and she had never been Empress in anything but name. Too young to have had any influence upon the brilliantly intellectual husband who was more than twice her own age, she is perhaps the most pathetic of all the figures associated with him. From the stormy beginning of their marriage, with the violent quarrel between her husband and father, Frederick appears to have treated her in the Oriental fashion which he also meted out to her successor. At first the castle of Terracina was reserved for her use; then he took her with him to Sicily and she seems to have lived for some time in the Royal Palace of Palermo. She was again with him in Apulia in the months which immediately preceded the abortive Crusade of 1227, and it must have been at this time that Conrad was conceived. Her husband was careful to see then that she was installed at Otranto, which was far to the south, and should have been away from fear of the infection brought along the pilgrim roads by the fleeing Crusaders. But it is probable that he was inspired more by his desire to safeguard the mother of a future heir than by any deep sentiment of affection for Yolanda. She lived in luxury and state as his wife and her wealth was safeguarded, but that a young girl who was used to the companionship of her relations and friends, and the gay life of Outremer, should pine in what amounted to the Oriental seclusion of a harem, either did not occur to Frederick, or if it did, he dismissed the matter as of no importance.

Yolanda's premature death, however, did affect Frederick's position with regard to her Kingdom of Jerusalem. He was now no longer the consort of the reigning sovereign, but simply the guardian of the infant King. In the eyes of the barons of Outremer the Emperor was now legally in the same position as Jean de Brienne had been before him. Though Frederick might not see things in this light, his son Conrad's subjects in Outremer did, and they would have been well within their rights in refusing to accept him as regent if they so desired. This fact was not calculated to make the problems which now confronted Frederick in the Near East any easier.

One of the Emperor's last actions before he finally sailed was to send another embassy to the Pope, led this time by the aged Archbishop Albert of Magdeburg. Again Gregory proved adamant, he would not even inform Frederick's ambassador of the nature of the penance which might cause him to lift the ban of excommunication from the Crusading Emperor, let alone give him the customary blessing. Instead the Pope told the world: "We do not know whose foolish counsel he hearkened to, or better, what devilish cunning betrayed him into secretly quitting the harbour of Brindisi without penance and without absolution, without anyone knowing that for certain he had sailed."

Chapter V

THE CRUSADE OF THE EXCOMMUNICATED

1228–1230

ON the 28th of June 1228, nearly thirteen years after Frederick had originally taken the Cross, the forty galleys of the imperial convoy slipped out of Brindisi harbour, bound for the Holy Land. If ever indeed his original vow had been inspired by religious or superstitious motives, few shreds of any pious sentiment could have been left to the Emperor now. His was to be a political Crusade, both in its planning and its ultimate aims. He was not prompted by a desire for military glory or even plunder, as had been many of his predecessors, and even less by religious belief. But what distinguished Frederick even more from previous leaders of Crusades was not only that he was departing upon this sacred mission with the anathema of the Church upon his head, but that he must succeed at all costs. The magnificent failure of a forlorn hope would avail him nothing. If he was to be able to face the Pope and the rest of Europe upon his return, he had to get Jerusalem. Nothing less would suffice.

Frederick was well aware that in embarking upon the Crusade as he had done, he was risking everything that he possessed, his prestige, and with it his hold upon the Empire, and even his realm. All had expected him to give way under the terrible blow of the excommunication; an excommunicate could not lead a Crusade—such a thing had never happened—he would be forced to make his peace with the Pope first, and not until then could he redeem his vow to liberate the Holy Places. The very idea that the Emperor should continue on his course, without first seeking absolution, was so daring that no one ever seems to have entertained it for a moment—except Frederick. Now, as in the moment of crisis in 1212 when he was offered the Empire, he decided to take the boldest course of action. Then he had been convinced that if he succeeded in what appeared to be—upon the face of it—an almost impossible venture, the lesser problems would find their own solution. So now again he calculated that the prosecution of the Crusade as an excommunicate was the only course to follow; but it was to be all or nothing—once embarked upon this perilous course he could neither fail nor turn back, success was essential, and any obstacles which stood in his way must be ruthlessly brushed aside. The Pope had made use of every means upon which he could lay his hands in initiating his struggle with the Emperor, and the Emperor could not afford to do less if he was to hold his own.

The great decision had been taken. As the anchors weighed and the sails of the galleys bellied in the wind, gradually leaving the coast of Italy behind in the heat haze of a burning Adriatic summer morning, the Emperor and his court must have experienced a sense of release, almost of exhilaration. It was an adventure as great and as dangerous as the now almost legendary ride to Germany, and it was the first time after so many patient years given to its creation that Frederick had actually taken part in one of the expeditions of his fleet. Underneath the scepticism and sophistication of an Emperor and a world statesman did something of the boy who read tales of adventure at sea still exist? Or did any atavistic memories of his ancestors, the Norman sea-rovers, stir in his mind?

The Emperor was accompanied on his voyage by at least two people who had known him intimately since his boyhood. One was Archbishop Berard of Palermo; the other was the faithful Richard who had also accompanied his master to Germany, and been imperial chamberlain for the last fifteen years. Other members of Frederick's curiously assorted retinue were Archbishop James of Capua, and Ibn-el-Gwasi, a Moslem from Palermo, who was the Emperor's teacher of dialectic. There were also a number of Saracen pages and a whole detachment of Moslem troops from Lucera. What the reverend archbishops made of a Crusading army which included among its ranks Mohammedans who practised their religion by free consent of the Emperor who led it is difficult to imagine. But it must be admitted that the Pope had quite considerable grounds for the allegation which he was later to make—that Frederick preferred "the servants of Mohammed to those of Christ".

The presence of the "servants of Mohammed" in the ranks of the Crusading army was a calculated act upon the Emperor's part. His fighting force was small—fifteen hundred knights, five hundred of whom had been sent on in advance under the command of Marshal Richard Filangieri, and some ten thousand infantry. Even with the assistance of the barons of Outremer, the Emperor could not possibly envisage a full-dress military campaign for the reconquest of the Kingdom of Jerusalem. He counted upon the arts of diplomacy to win what military force had failed to do since the disaster of Hattin. Ibn-el-Gwasi, the Saracen pages, and the religious freedom of the Moslems from Lucera were all part of the *mise en scène* for the coming battle of wits between the Christian Emperor and the Sultan of Egypt. With almost incredible daring Frederick was staking his all upon his knowledge of the Oriental mind and his own ability to negotiate a diplomatic solution.

It was a course of action calling for the utmost in daring and finesse. Frederick was condemned by his contemporaries, and has been through succeeding centuries, for his duplicity, his cruelty, his cynicism, and his lechery, but his intelligence and courage cannot be called in question. Never in his life had he greater need of these qualities. Not only was he the cynosure of the political world at this moment, but in his own entourage, and among his own household, he could never escape the watchful eyes that would have noted any lack of confidence, any sign of weakening. Frederick stood apart from his contemporaries by reason of his mental outlook as much as by the isolated splendour of his position as Emperor and the innate suspicion implanted in him by the events of his early years. In place of the more normal pursuits of other men he sought his relaxations in the study of science and mathematics, in the intricacies of philosophy and dialectic, in the violent exercise of the chase and in an unrestrained abandonment to sensual pleasures. By making use of these means of escape from the stresses of his life Frederick managed to preserve that outward calm and appearance of detachment which masked his passionate nature, and he described as his ideal in the words:

E

"Repress even the righteous impulses of the spirit, and by a virtuous self-discipline remain calm like a Caesar."

In preserving this attitude in the face of all his difficulties the Emperor did not spare himself, and he was certainly not prepared to spare others. The stakes for which he was playing were the peace and security of most of Europe, let alone his own fortunes and those of his dynasty, possibly even his life—and the ruthlessness of his dealings must be judged in this light.

The difficulties of the political situation which now faced Frederick in the Near East were far greater than they had been in the preceding year. Al-Mu'azzam had died on the 11th of November 1227, leaving a young son an-Nasir Dawid to succeed him, but news of this event did not reach the imperial court until Easter 1228. The demise of his warlike brother had strengthened al-Kamil's position as he now no longer had to fear the immediate danger of the alliance between the Sultan of Damascus and the Khwarismians. Al-Kamil lost no time in taking the offensive against his young nephew an-Nasir, and Jerusalem and Nablus were soon in his hands. Al-Ashraf was not to be outdone; in answer to an appeal from his nephew for aid, he advanced into Palestine, announcing, as al-Kamil had done, that he was coming to protect it from the Christians. The two brothers met near Gaza and they agreed in secret to divide their nephew's lands between them. They then proceeded to lay siege to Damascus, where an-Nasir had taken refuge. Instead of being able to profit by the jealousies of three brothers, rivals for the control of the Ayubite Empire, Frederick was now confronted with al-Kamil firmly ensconced in his possession of Jerusalem, acting in concert with his brother al-Ashraf, with the Khwarismians apparently assuming the role of disinterested spectators.

Meanwhile the Emperor had arrived in Cyprus on the 21st of July 1228. Cyprus had been an imperial fief since Almeric of Lusignan had done homage to Henry VI and received in return the title of King, but the link had become somewhat tenuous during the troubled period through which the empire had since passed. John of Lusignan, who was King of Cyprus at the time of Frederick's arrival, was a minor and his mother, Alice of Jerusalem, was regent. The government of the island had until 1227 been in the hands of the queen's *bailli* Philip of

Ibelin, who was also her uncle. There had been continuous quarrels, however, and the Queen had tried to replace Philip by Almeric Barlais (who was hostile to the powerful Ibelin family), but without success as the council of barons refused to accept Barlais. Upon Philip's death the High Court had made his elder brother John *bailli* in his stead.

Frederick was well aware that John of Ibelin was the most powerful man with whom he would have to deal among the barons of Outremer. His great personal wealth as Lord of Beirut, and that of his wife Melisande who was heiress of Arsuf, and his family connections—he was uncle of the Queen Regent of Cyprus and of the dead Yolanda—would alone have placed him in a position of importance, but he was also a man of outstanding character and learning—a born leader of men. Friends of Almeric Barlais who had been at Frederick's court in Apulia had no doubt done their best to prejudice the Emperor against John of Ibelin, but it is more likely that Frederick's hostility to him arose from the fact that he foresaw that any resistance which he might encounter in Outremer would probably revolve round him.

With all the difficulties that he knew to be before him, it seems strange that Frederick did not try to make friends with, or at least propitiate, the powerful faction which was constituted by the Ibelin family and their adherents. He treated them from the outset in the same autocratic fashion which he was accustomed to use in Sicily. It was a great mistake, for the diplomatic manner which he had assumed in winning over the German princes would have been much better suited to the constitutional position in which he found himself in Outremer. He was now only regent for his son Conrad but, even if he had still been King, the King of Jerusalem was in effect only *primus inter pares*, leader in war and president of the High Court but not an autocratic ruler. Moreover Frederick was a foreigner, coming to exercise an unwelcome control over Frankish barons.

The reasons for the Emperor's assumption of a high-handed manner from the outset are probably to be ascribed to his conception of himself as the leader of an expedition which would perform for the barons of Outremer the service of liberating Jerusalem and the Holy Places, that by their military weakness and internal dissensions they were unable to do for themselves.

This attitude would have coincided with Frederick's conception of his imperial function as the dispenser of law and order—he had already achieved great success along these lines in Sicily—and no doubt he felt that an initial sharp lesson would be the best way in which to impress these facts upon the barons.

Nevertheless Frederick had misjudged his man in John of Ibelin, and there is no doubt that, though Frederick succeeded in obtaining the material advantages which he sought in his dealings with him, the latter emerged the moral victor from their first encounter.

Upon his arrival at Limassol the Emperor summoned John of Ibelin to his presence, inviting him to bring with him the young King and his own sons. Ibelin appeared clad in mourning for his brother. He was most graciously received; Frederick addressed him as uncle, gave him magnificent presents, which included ceremonial robes of scarlet, and told him to wear them because his joy at seeing the Emperor must overcome his sorrow for his brother. Ibelin was then invited to a banquet which was to be held in his honour. His friends were alarmed, for it seemed evident that the Emperor was making use of this time-honoured ruse to get John and his sons into his power, but John of Ibelin courageously refused to heed their warnings. He was right; failure to accept the invitation of the suzerain of Cyprus would have been an act of gross discourtesy which would have put him in the wrong from the start.

The banquet was magnificent; Ibelin was seated in the place of honour upon the Emperor's right hand and his sons served as pages. But in the midst of the revelry armed men came silently into the room and took up their position, drawn sword in hand, behind each of the guests. Frederick then turned to his guest of honour and demanded that he relinquish his fief of Beirut and the revenues of Cyprus which had come in since the accession of the young King. Ibelin's reply was firm and courageous; his fief, he said, had been given to him by his step-sister, Queen Isabella of Jerusalem, and he was perfectly prepared to substantiate his claim before the High Court. The revenues of the island of Cyprus had been handed over, both by his brother and himself, to the regent Queen Alice. Neither threats nor the presence of the Emperor's men-at-arms would move him; and in these dramatic circumstances Ibelin delivered a proud and magnificent speech with as much sang-froid as if he had been making an oration before the High Court. He said that he was still prepared to assist the Emperor on the Crusade, but that at the risk of life itself he would not break the law.

Swayed either by Ibelin's firm stand or by the fact that his own forces were too small to risk a military engagement, Frederick did not press home his demands, but had to satisfy himself with taking Ibelin's sons and some of the Cypriot nobles as hostages, and with the recognition of himself as suzerain of the island and regent of the Kingdom of Jerusalem. Ibelin and the Cypriot barons also agreed to accompany the Emperor on Crusade. Apart from the taking of the hostages, it was a poor return for having antagonised the most powerful man in the Near East and for having transgressed the laws of hospitality in a manner which ill-became an Emperor. In the long run indeed it only exacerbated Frederick's relations with the barons of Outremer.

But repulsive as Frederick's treatment of John of Ibelin must necessarily appear to modern eyes, it was, for the moment, apparently accepted as part of the political game which the Emperor was playing in order to enforce his power upon the Latin kingdoms of the Near East by crushing the complete independence which, like the Lombard Communes, they had enjoyed since the death of Henry VI. The other barons of Outremer, who now came to Cyprus in answer to the Emperor's summons, had no compunction in backing him against the Ibelin faction. Balian of Sidon, Guy Embriaco, and later Bohemund of Antioch, joined Frederick in his march upon Nicosia, to which John of Ibelin had withdrawn, and Guy Embriaco lent the Emperor thirty thousand bezants, a considerable sum of money. Possibly the lack of ready cash had been one of the reasons which had prompted Frederick to his high-handed action in demanding the revenues of Cyprus from John of Ibelin.

Confronted with the united forces of the Emperor and the rival lords of Outremer, John of Ibelin withdrew to one of the strongest points in the island, the almost inaccessible castle called Dieu d'Amour (now St. Hilarion). A prolonged siege would have been the only means capable of dislodging Ibelin from this fastness, and Frederick could not spare the time. Finally a settlement was reached; the young King and his subjects should do homage to the Emperor as suzerain, an imperial *bailli* was to be appointed for the island, the Queen Mother was recognised by Frederick as regent, and John of Ibelin would appear before the High Court to substantiate his claim to his fief of Beirut. The hostages were released.

On the 3rd of September Frederick embarked for the Holy Land, taking with him, no doubt as a precaution, the boy-King, John of Ibelin, and most of the Cypriot barons. Almeric Barlais was appointed *bailli* of Cyprus and he and his friends were left in control of the island.

After the inauspicious beginning in Cyprus, Frederick's arrival in Acre, on the 7th of September, was a triumph. The Crusading forces, numbering about eleven thousand, were encamped near the city, and they joined with the inhabitants and the civil and religious dignitaries in welcoming the Emperor with an ovation. Although all those present were aware of the fact that Frederick had been excommunicated, no doubt they felt that now that he had fulfilled his vow and actually arrived in the Holy Land the ban would be removed. They gave full rein to their joy in the thought that at last, after so many delays and months of patient waiting, the hour of the delivery of Jerusalem was at hand.

Gerold the Patriarch of Jerusalem and the bishops of Out-remer, the leaders of the great Military Orders—the Hospitallers and the Teutonic Order, and even the Templars—seem to have forgotten their jealousies on this occasion, and joined in the enthusiastic welcome. Even the religious leaders appear to have believed that once the Pope was really convinced that Frederick had arrived in the Holy Land and intended to pursue the Crusade in all seriousness, he would withdraw the ban of excommunication. Accordingly they intimated tactfully to the Emperor that their full collaboration with an excommunicated man would be difficult, and suggested that he send an embassy to the Pope. The embassy, which was led by Henry of Malta and the Archbishop of Bari, was accordingly dispatched in haste to inform Gregory that Frederick and his army had now arrived in the Holy Land, that he did not intend to quit it until he had regained for the Christians all the territory which was now occupied by the Moslems, and to ask the Pope to open negotiations with the Emperor's representative in Italy, the Duke of Spoleto.

Having once again tried to make his peace with the Christian world, the Emperor took up his residence in a castle near Acre and devoted his energies to the main task which lay ahead— the negotiations with al-Kamil. Although the whole burden of this delicate and dangerous diplomatic game was to rest upon Frederick's own shoulders, he had at least one wise counsellor in whom he could place his trust. Hermann von Salza had a profound knowledge of the tangled web of Near Eastern politics and of the internal rivalries of Outremer. Moreover the aims and aspirations of the Teutonic Order and those of the Emperor in the prosecution of the Crusade were to all intents and purposes identical, and if it could be brought to a successful conclusion the power and prestige of the Order as the Emperor's chief supporters would also be correspondingly advanced. This was in all likelihood the reason why Frederick had been so determined that Hermann von Salza should go to the Holy Land in 1227, so that he would be fully informed about the latest developments of the situation when his sovereign arrived.

Thomas of Acerra and Balian of Sidon were dispatched with princely gifts of horses, jewels, and gold and silver vessels as ambassadors to the court of al-Kamil, who was then at Nablus. They informed him of the Emperor's arrival and delivered a diplomatically phrased message to the effect that Frederick had not come to make war or to take lands which did not belong to him, and that he wanted only the Holy Places that had belonged to the ancestors of his son Conrad. This was the opening gambit of the diplomatic game of chess in which the Emperor and the Sultan now indulged. In spite of the perils and difficulties that it involved for both sides, it is difficult to believe that the two contestants did not derive considerable satisfaction, if not actual entertainment, from their battle of wits.

Frederick and al-Kamil were an extraordinarily well-matched pair, and the basically Oriental characteristics of Frederick's character were at no time in his life so evident as in his dealings with the Sultan of Egypt. Al-Kamil's tastes, and even his habits, were very similar to those of his adversary and it is sad to think that they never met. Like Frederick, al-Kamil delighted in learned discussions which lasted late into the night when "fifty scholars reclined on divans round his throne to provide his evening conversation". He was a patron of scholars and himself a poet and particularly interested in jurisprudence and grammar. Like Frederick he was an excellent administrator who realised that the basis of efficient government lies in a sound economy and he took a personal interest in the financial administration of his country. In common with some of the great Arab scholars of his time, such as Ibn Sabin, al-Kamil was so little of a bigot that if he had not been a great Sultan he might well have suffered for his lack of orthodoxy.

Inevitably such a man must have felt himself drawn into sympathy with the Emperor of the Franks who also if he had not worn a crown might well have perished at the stake for his heretical views. To the two main adversaries in this struggle, therefore, the Holy City of Jerusalem which is equally sacred to true believers, both Christian and Moslem, really meant nothing more than an agglomeration of old churches and mosques, which both of them for political reasons had to pretend to value more dearly than life itself, though neither of them really wished to shed blood for them.

Al-Kamil dispatched Fakhr-ad-Din with an embassy in return. They came bringing Frederick magnificent presents of jewels, an elephant, ten camels of the famous Mehari breed, Arab mares of impeccable lineage, bears and monkeys, but a most unsatisfactory reply to the Emperor's message—the Sultan could not accede to the Emperor's request to give up Jerusalem, as it would bring down upon him the wrath of the Moslems. Frederick was probably not unduly dismayed; a straight answer was not to be expected at this early stage.

The Sultan on the other hand would not commit himself because he hoped that the fall of Damascus would shortly put him in an even stronger position in his bargaining with the Emperor. Moreover the difficulty of Frederick's situation as an excommunicate was also known by now in the Moslem camp. The Emperor's last embassy to the Pope had failed dismally, and two Franciscans had arrived with Gregory's admonition to the Crusaders that they should acknowledge no allegiance to the excommunicated Emperor.

The Patriarch of Jerusalem and the Military Orders were also told to give no assistance to the Emperor, and to beware of maintaining any relations with such an unbeliever. Not content with giving instructions to the ecclesiastical authorities and the Orders, who owed him allegiance, the Pope had even sent envoys to the Genoese to try and prevent them also from supporting Frederick. Gregory was evidently determined to wreck the Crusade by all the means in his power.

The division in the Crusaders' camp caused by the Pope's messengers was disastrous for Frederick, and the small army which he had at his disposal was now rent by dissension. He took a bold decision and renounced the command of the army; perhaps it was at Hermann von Salza's diplomatic suggestion that thenceforth the orders of the day were given in the name of Jesus Christ.

Fortunately for the Emperor, al-Kamil had not encountered plain sailing either. Young an-Nasir had found an energetic champion in a renegade Christian who had once been a Hospitaller and had become converted to the Moslem faith. This man had since married an-Nasir's widowed mother. An-Nasir's army now made a sortie out of Damascus to intercept his uncle's supply lines near Nablus. At the same time Frederick made a display of martial force by marching the army to Jaffa and setting to work on the fortifications; even the Templars followed him at a distance.

This military energy on the Emperor's part was prompted by the fact that it was now November, negotiations had been dragging on for months and al-Kamil was proving, if anything, less and less accommodating. Frederick believed that this was due not only to the Sultan's desire to gain time, but also that secret emissaries of the Pope were responsible for the hardening of his adversary's attitude. The Emperor's show of force brought no sign of weakening in al-Kamil, however. He broke off negotiations altogether and demanded that Frederick pay compensation for the damage done by his troops. Worse was to follow, for a galley arrived from Apulia with the news that the Duke of Spoleto, the governor of the realm, had attacked the March of Ancona and had been beaten by the papal army, that the Pope was stirring up trouble in the realm and that his forces had actually invaded the Terra di Lavoro. Frederick's position was grave in the extreme; a storm at sea had destroyed the supply ships which brought food from Sicily; the army was nearly starving; months of bargaining with al-Kamil had brought no result; the Emperor could only rely upon a small portion of an army of eleven thousand men, which even in its entirety was not strong enough to try for a military conclusion, and his realm might well already be in the Pope's hands.

Fakhr ad-Din now repaid something of the confidence which the Emperor reposed in him. It was upon his advice that Frederick at this desperate moment again dispatched Thomas of Acerra and Balian of Sidon upon an embassy to al-Kamil. In prompting the Emperor to take diplomatic action at this particular time, Fakhr ad-Din was probably acting upon the knowledge that his own master was also in difficulties, and perhaps he felt that without dividing his loyalties he could best serve al-Kamil by pressing for the conclusion of a treaty of compromise, which would also help his friend the Emperor of the Franks.

Al-Kamil had not been successful in his siege of Damascus; the city showed no sign of weakening and it was already February. Worse still the Khwarismians seemed to be taking a renewed interest in events in Syria and Palestine and in the fate of the son of their old ally al-Mu'azzam. It looked to al-Kamil as if the situation was going to revert to the highly dangerous one which had first prompted his appeal for help to the Christian Emperor with the added threat of the Emperor's presence in Palestine with a Crusading army. On the 11th of February Frederick's ambassadors returned at last with concrete proposals for a treaty with the Sultan of Egypt.

The treaty was in effect a ten years' truce, and by its terms the Christians were to receive Jerusalem, with a corridor to the sea at Jaffa, Nazareth and the surrounding country, which included two of the great Crusader strongholds of Montfort and Toron, and some land which was still held by the Moslems near Sidon. In Jerusalem itself the two places which were most sacred to the Mohammedan world—the Dome of the Rock and Mosque of al-Aqsa—remained in Moslem hands and their pilgrims had right of access and freedom to practise their religion. This particular clause not unnaturally roused the ire of the Templars, because the two mosques lie within the area of the Temple of Solomon whose restitution was thus denied to them, but the conclusion of the treaty would have been impossible without it, as according to the Moslem belief Mohammed began from there his flight to heaven.

In spite of this provision, which was a face-saver for al-Kamil, the treaty aroused tremendous opposition in the Moslem world; his nephew an-Nasir refused to ratify it, the Caliph of Baghdad protested, and the imams were furious. Al-Kamil's self-justification that he had kept the Moslem Holy Places and had only given up to the Christians their ruined churches was not well received. Frederick's beliefs in his own powers of bargaining had been well-founded; al-Kamil had gone to the utmost limit that he could in his concessions to the Emperor, and his only return was Frederick's personal guarantee of a truce of ten years, which made another Crusade unlikely during that period. Frederick himself told Fakhr ad-Din that he would never have asked the Sultan for so much if his whole prestige in the Christian world had not depended upon it.

Even more fierce was the opposition aroused in Christendom. The Emperor indeed was almost alone in his satisfaction with what he had achieved. The barons of Outremer were furious that the negotiations had taken place without their participation (Frederick only consulted four of them at the last minute before he signed the actual terms), and it is significant that none of their signatures appeared on the document as witnesses; Hermann von Salza and two English Bishops, Peter of Winchester and William of Exeter, served in this capacity.

The dissatisfaction of the barons had a good deal of justification, for Frederick was only regent for his son, and when he returned to Europe they would be left to try and defend a territory which was in fact quite indefensible. At the time of the fifth Crusade one of the reasons for turning down al-Kamil's offer of an exchange of Jerusalem, Bethlehem, and Nazareth for Damietta had been the strategic weakness of the territories that the Sultan was prepared to cede to the Christians which were materially the same as those they now received. But Frederick had got Jerusalem without giving anything in exchange. To Frederick, Jerusalem was simply a pawn in the world of European politics. He had to have Jerusalem in order to be able to return and confront the Pope with the fact that he had ultimately kept his word, in spite of all the obstacles placed in his way. He had got Jerusalem, and the secrecy which had been the essence of his personal negotiations with al-Kamil had enabled him to present the world with a *fait accompli*, his only chance of success.

The barons' discontent, which they expressed diplomatically by making their approval of the treaty subject to that of the papal legate, paled in comparison with the fury of Gerold, the Patriarch of Jerusalem. He described it as being an act without any value, that did not guarantee Frankish interests in Palestine. He stressed that the Sultan of Damascus had refused to participate in the truce or to ratify the cession of Jerusalem. Naturally enough the Moslems' retention of their Holy Places came in for his special censure, and he maintained that the fact that they had access to Jerusalem at all made it indefensible because the numbers of their pilgrims would always be in excess of those of the Christians. The clause which provided that Christians could only enter the temple if they respected the Moslem faith was a further cause for annoyance, because the Moslems had right of free access to Bethlehem.

There was undoubtedly a great deal of truth in the Patriarch's assertions, but what he failed to point out was that Frederick's treaty with al-Kamil had produced a result which the third, fourth and fifth Crusades had failed to achieve—the return of the Holy Places to the Christians without their giving up any territory in exchange. The barons of Outremer might inveigh against the treaty for its strategical weaknesses, and the fury of the churchmen, egged on by the Pope, at what they termed the shame of concluding any agreement at all with the infidel, though it rings somewhat hollow in view of the fact that Cœur de Lion in the third and the Legate Pelagius in the fifth Crusade had done exactly the same thing, can still be understood. But all that mattered to the ordinary pilgrims and Crusaders was that at long last they could again visit the Holy Places as they had done in the glorious days of Godfrey de Bouillon, when the Crusading fervour of all Europe had won the Holy Land for Christianity.

Accompanied by the Sicilian bishops, the Bishops of Exeter and Winchester, Hermann von Salza and the knights of the Teutonic Order, and a crowd of German pilgrims, the excommunicated Emperor made his state entry into Jerusalem on Saturday, the 17th of March. The Patriarch Gerold had not only refused to accompany him, but had announced that he would place the Holy City under an interdict if the Emperor entered it, because the Moslems had retained their shrines there. The scene was surely one of the strangest in the history of Christianity—the anointed Emperor, the bearer of the temporal sword, who had succeeded in gaining the freedom of Jerusalem for Christianity arrived at its gates as an excommunicate, with the added threat of the interdict hanging over him. He was met there by the Sultan's representative, the Qadi of Nablus, who handed over to him the keys of the city. In spite of all the ecclesiastical censures the German pilgrims could not contain their joy; they acclaimed the Emperor and illuminated the city, which was practically deserted because the Moslem population had fled and the local Christians, who had never shown much enthusiasm for Latin rule, remained indoors.

The following day Frederick proceeded from the old Hospital building, where he had taken up residence, to the Church of the Holy Sepulchre. His announcement that he intended to be crowned there as King of Jerusalem had further enraged the barons of Outremer, because in actual fact he was only regent. Some hotheads in the Emperor's entourage tried to persuade him to insist upon a religious ceremony, but on Hermann von Salza's advice he wisely refrained, and when the court arrived at the church no priest was to be seen except those in the Emperor's entourage which included the faithful Berard of Palermo and the Archbishop of Capua.

The Church of the Holy Sepulchre was filled with soldiers and pilgrims, the long white cloaks of the Teutonic Knights providing relief to the gloom which filled the old church, and accentuated by the absence of the gorgeous vestments of the clergy who had officiated at previous and happier coronations of the Kings of Jerusalem. A royal crown was laid upon the altar, and the Emperor himself lifted it and placed it upon his own head. Frederick then made a speech to the assembly. In it he outlined the whole story of his actions which led up to the Crusade, right from the day when he first took the Cross at Aix-la-Chapelle, through the various delays and agreements with the popes, his own excommunication and decision upon his subsequent course of action. Instead of inveighing against the Pope, he said that Gregory could not have acted differently without raising murmurs and discontent in the Christian world, and that if he had written to Outremer letters hostile to Frederick it was because he did not know of the Emperor's real intentions, and that he would probably grieve at having put so many difficulties in the way of the Crusade. Frederick ended by stating that he wished to put an end to all disagreements with the Church, and to attain this he was ready to do all that the honour of the Church and the Empire required and to repair any damages that the Church claimed, and that if God had exalted him, he wished to humiliate himself before the Most High and, because of Him, also before His representative upon earth. Hermann von Salza then translated the speech into French and German.

The conciliatory and even humble tone of the Emperor's speech was greeted with great satisfaction. It is one of the few recorded occasions upon which Frederick unbent in public from his attitude of imperial detachment; usually some representative spoke for him while he sat silently upon his throne. This fact, and the temper of the speech itself, show how seriously Frederick desired to come to terms with the Pope. He clearly realised the difficulties of his position if he could not, but it is characteristic that even while publicly offering his personal humility to the Pope as God's representative upon earth, the "Honour of the Empire" was still stressed.

After the ceremony the Emperor called a conference to discuss the rebuilding of the defences of Jerusalem which had been largely demolished when al-Kamil had offered it in exchange for Damietta during the fifth Crusade. The Grand Master of the Hospitallers and the Preceptor of the Templars, who had hitherto held aloof, agreed to participate. As a result of their discussions Frederick gave orders for the Tower of David and the Gate of St. Stephen to be repaired.

The Emperor then went to visit the Moslem Holy Places, which for a man of his mentality must have presented an interest equal to that of the Christian shrines. Here he deliberately put on an act of disparaging Christianity before the Moslems, evidently with the idea that by so doing he would ingratiate himself in their good graces. He could not have made a greater mistake, for a devout Moslem, then and now, can understand and respect a practising Christian, but for a man who believes in nothing he has only disdain. The questioning of the eternal verities, the splitting of hairs in dialectic, was all very well for Fakhr ad-Din and the sophisticates of al-Kamil's and Frederick's own intimate circles, but in the age in which he lived it could have no appeal at all for the ordinary man whether he was Christian or Moslem. Frederick's failure to understand this, his lack in fact of the common touch, explain why, for all his brilliance, he never attained the hold upon any of the peoples over whom he reigned that his grandfather Barbarossa had done.

As he was conducted around the Dome of the Rock and the Mosque of al-Aqsa by the Moslem notables, Frederick questioned them as to why he had not heard the muezzins calling (al-Kamil out of respect for him had ordered them to refrain), and his statement that one of the reasons for his coming to Jerusalem was to hear them won him no favour, but only caused suspicion among the Moslems. They were even more disconcerted by his laying hands upon a Christian priest who was following them and declaring that on pain of death no Christian should be allowed to enter the Moslem sanctuaries without their express permission, and he shocked them profoundly when, in answer to his question as to why the windows had gratings, they replied that it was to keep out the sparrows, and he retorted "Yet Allah has brought the swine amongst you after all", using the most vulgar Arabic term of contempt for the Christians.

This denigration of the Christians went hand in hand with Frederick's very real interest and admiration for all that Arab civilisation had to offer. The Moslem world was the repository of the learning of the ancient Greeks; they kept it alive, and in the fields of mathematics and medicine they had even added to it. It was inevitable that a scholar such as Frederick should hold them in reverence for this. With that inquiring mind which had already been one of his salient characteristics when he was a boy of thirteen, Frederick questioned the Arabs whom he met about every aspect of their life and thought. On one occasion when he had no more valuable presents to send with one of his embassies to al-Kamil, he dispatched his ambassadors with a set of mathematical problems and he asked the Sultan to send Arab astronomers to his court.

Once in conversation with Fakhr ad-Din Frederick asked him to explain the Caliphate, and upon hearing that the Abbasids traced an unbroken blood relationship with Mohammed, through his uncle, Frederick expressed his approval of a religious system whose head was hereditary, going on to say, "Those fools, the Christians, choose as their spiritual head any fellow they will, without the smallest relationship to the Messiah, and they make him the Messiah's representative. That Pope there has no claim to such a position, whereas your Caliph is the descendant of Mohammed's uncle." In spite of the fact that many of the men in Frederick's entourage had been chosen by him for their brains rather than their aristocratic descent, pride of race played an important part in his own make-up, and the boy of seven who had been enraged by Markward of Anweiler's soldiers laying their hands upon his royal person, when he was a man of forty-five wrote to the College of Cardinals, after his second excommunication by Gregory IX, that he could not "exercise as equal to equal a private vengeance" upon the Pope and his family "as neither he nor his race are worthy that the Imperial dignity should condescend to attack them".

In his curiosity about all that was Oriental, Frederick even made contact with some of the Assassins, the strange sect whose chief, the "Old Man of the Mountain", trained his followers to be professional murderers in return for the glimpses which he showed them of a terrestrial paradise between copious doses of hashish. This action of Frederick's was embroidered upon by his enemies until it was believed that he either employed the Assassins themselves or trained others of his own to make away with his enemies.

The impressions of his few months' sojourn in the Near East certainly remained with the Emperor for the rest of his life. He was particularly interested in Moslem architecture and is known to have made a study of the Dome of the Rock. Some art historians believe that the octagonal form of its walls served as the inspiration for what is thought to have been the Emperor's own design for the most famous of his pleasure houses—Castel del Monte, which rears its vast bulk like an octagonal diadem crowning the slopes of the Apulian Murge. The use of the hood in falconry was unknown in Europe in the thirteenth century until Frederick introduced it, as a result of his experience with Arab falconers. He also learnt of the old Egyptian use of incubators, and had men sent specially from Egypt to demonstrate their skill in this practical field in Apulia.

But perhaps the Emperor's most notorious adoption of Oriental customs was his creation of travelling harems which accompanied him on his constant journeys. Frederick's ancestors, the Norman kings of Sicily, are known to have had harems in their palaces, but there was no mention by his con-temporaries of the ladies in curtained palanquins guarded by eunuchs, which certainly formed part of Frederick's retinue in his later years, until after his return from the Near East.

Strangely enough, although the Emperor had such an admira-tion for all things Oriental, he does not seem to have made a great impression upon the ordinary Moslems with whom he came into contact, who did not know him intimately like Fakhr ad-Din, or appreciate his intellect as did al-Kamil. His physical appearance had much to do with this; a clean-shaven man with-out a beard is still only half a man to the inhabitants of the desert fastnesses of Arabia today, and Frederick's shortness of stature and his reddish hair, already inclining to baldness, would have appeared ugly in the extreme to the Oriental taste. The Moslems noted all this and his short-sightedness, and one of them summed him up as not being worth two hundred dirhems if he had been exposed for sale in a slave market.

His expedition to the Moslem shrines had been in the nature of a rest for the Emperor, but on the following day he was brought back abruptly to the troubles which confronted him, for the Archbishop of Caesarea arrived and placed the Holy City under an interdict in obedience to the orders of the Patriarch. It was the last straw; in a rage Frederick called his forces to-gether and left Jerusalem; even the reconstruction of its defences was stopped. Passing by way of Jaffa, he arrived at Acre on the 23rd of the month. On the way there he had narrowly escaped from an ambush by the Templars, and in later years he stated that the incident took place at the instigation of the Pope.

Acre was in a ferment, feeling between the Emperor's sup-porters and his enemies was at fever-heat, and Frederick him-self was in no mood for gentle measures. He ordered the town

to be surrounded by his troops, and would allow no one to
enter or leave the city without his permission. It was rumoured
that he contemplated draconian measures against the Templars,
and the Grand Master of the Temple and John of Ibelin remained invisible in their heavily guarded houses.

The Emperor's fury knew no bounds; he had priests who
preached against him beaten with rods, and removed to his
own galleys the engines of war which had been intended for the
defence of Ptolemais; he was even said to have sent some of
them to al-Kamil. News had meanwhile arrived from Italy of
the successful invasion of the realm by the papal armies under
the command of Jean de Brienne, and the Emperor was faced
with a yet more urgent reason for leaving what undoubtedly
seemed to him to be an ungrateful country. He decided to
embark for Europe on the 1st of May. The Patriarch, under the
pretext that the treaty with al-Kamil was not valid because it
had been made personally with the Emperor and had not been
ratified by an-Nasir, tried to retain some of the army in Palestine,
declaring that it would be paid out of the Crusading fund provided for by Philip Augustus's will. Frederick replied that no
one but himself would pay an army in his Realm of Jerusalem.

Before his departure Frederick appointed Balian of Sidon
and Garnier the German as his representatives. Odo of Montbeliard was to be Constable and Commander of the Army. It
was a conciliatory choice, as although Balian had supported him
from the beginning against John of Ibelin he was a native of
Outremer and had family connections with the Ibelins, while
Garnier had served with Jean de Brienne. Even this moderate
course of action did not prevent hostility and insult following
the Emperor to the end. As he made his way down to the
harbour at dawn, he was pelted with offal and filth, and could
only curse when John of Ibelin and Odo of Montbeliard came to
bid him farewell.

Frederick stopped for a few days in Cyprus. He had brought
the young King back with him, and he confirmed in the government of the island the *baillis* whom he had previously appointed.
Then the imperial galleys set sail, departing in haste, and
outstripping the rest of the convoy the Emperor arrived in
Brindisi on the 10th of June.

That it was led by an excommunicate must have seemed to

the mediaeval world to foredoom Frederick's Crusade to failure from the start. The mere fact that, in spite of the thunders of the Church, of all that the Pope could do to frustrate him, he had won Jerusalem made a profound impression upon men's minds. The Patriarch of Jerusalem might point out the weaknesses of the treaty, the military leaders of the Orders and of Outremer might dwell upon the very real strategic difficulties, but the world in general could not fail to know that once again pilgrims were able to travel to the Holy Land and visit the scene of Christ's Passion and Resurrection, thanks to the efforts of the man whom the head of the Church had condemned.

Perhaps the most commonsense summing up of the treaty, though admittedly from a source favourable to Frederick, was expressed in a letter which Hermann von Salza wrote to a friendly cardinal who was at that time in Rome.

Von Salza summed up the situation in the following words: "We know that the Patriarch has put Jerusalem under an interdict because the Saracens retain the Temple of the Lord [the Dome of the Rock] and the Temple of Solomon. But they have only a few aged priests there, who are unarmed, to perform purifications and prayers. The men of the Emperor hold all the outer gates and can prevent the passage, if they so wish, of the Saracens or anyone else. This in truth is what we have seen and understood, and what was arranged during our presence there. It is the Christians who receive the offerings made at the Temple of our Lord, which are laid on the stone upon which Christ was offered up. Do not let us forget that of old, before the loss of the Holy Land, in nearly all the cities which belonged to the Christians the Saracens were free to practise their own religion, as still today the Christians in Damascus and in other Mohammedan lands freely practise their religion. We do not wish to say that this pleases our Lord the Emperor, and that he would not have preferred to do differently, if he could. But God knows that otherwise he could not have arrived at the conclusion of the truce."

Hamstrung as he was by an army made dissident by the papal envoys, lacking the support of the two principal Military Orders—the Templars and the Hospitallers—by reason of their obedience to the Pope, Frederick had only his own skill as a diplomatist to thank for the remarkable success which he did achieve, and no small portion of the blame for his failures must be laid at the door of the Pope.

The Emperor returned to Europe to face a situation of extreme gravity both in the Empire and the realm. Whereas the Pope's efforts to stir up trouble in Germany, that went as far as trying to set up Otto of Luneburg (the head of the house of Guelf) as a pretender to the throne, had only resulted in sporadic uprisings, in Italy the position was far more serious. The imperial armies, whose main forces were concentrated in the Abruzzi and around Capua, were fighting desperately to hold their own against the invading Soldiers of the Keys—as the papal levies were called—led by Jean de Brienne and Pelagius, Bishop of Alba. Several of the chief towns of Apulia had re-volted, expelling the royal officials and murdering the Justiciar. The Pope's agents had put about a rumour that the Emperor was dead, which circulated rapidly, gathering credence as it went, so that the news of Frederick's return was greeted with astonishment and unbelief, until he showed himself publicly in Brindisi.

The onus for beginning hostilities during the Emperor's absence does, strangely enough, seem to have lain with his own representative, Rainald, Duke of Spoleto, who had invaded the March of Ancona. This offensive, while Frederick was en-countering such difficulties in the Near East and when the Pope had threatened to release the subjects of the realm from their oath of fidelity to their absent sovereign, appears to have been the height of foolhardiness, for which the only justifiable excuse could be that Rainald knew that a heavy attack on the realm was in preparation by the papal forces and hoped by taking the initiative to create a diversion.

In his efforts to conquer the Realm of Sicily during its sovereign's absence, the Pope had attempted to mobilise all Western Europe against him by appealing to kings and princes to send both men and money to prosecute a "Crusade" against the Crusading Emperor. Even allowing for the realism of Gregory's policy, this action of his presented so unedifying a spectacle that there was little response. The Lombard cities sent money and some of the French bishops a band of knights, but the Pope's appeals to England, Spain, and Portugal fell on deaf ears.

After landing Frederick went to Barletta, and from there issued a proclamation announcing his return. His adherents flocked to join him. Among them were a company of Teutonic Knights returning from the Holy Land, whose ships had been forced to seek shelter in Apulian harbours owing to a storm. With these welcome reinforcements Frederick was able immediately to send a considerable body of troops to relieve Capua under the command of Thomas of Aquino, with the promise that he himself would shortly follow in person. Frederick arrived there on the 8th of September and received a tremendous welcome.

Suddenly, with one of those extraordinary turns of the wheel of fortune by which the fate of empires seems to change overnight, the whole situation altered and, from being menaced in the very possession of his realm, the Emperor found that his armies were pushing the fleeing Soldiers of the Keys on all fronts. Even that seasoned campaigner, Jean de Brienne, joined in the general rout. The only man to stand firm was Pelagius, who garrisoned the impregnable heights of Monte Cassino, seizing the treasury of the abbey to pay his soldiers, and defied all comers. The Abbey proved to be as impregnable in the thirteenth century as it was in the twentieth, and when all else had surrendered or fled into papal territory, Pelagius and his valiant garrison were permitted to march out with all honours of war.

By the 28th of October Frederick was in full possession of his realm. Sora which alone, apart from Cassino, had resisted his advance had been taken by storm by forces led by the Emperor in person. The inhabitants were put to the sword, and its walls and houses destroyed so that, like Carthage, the plough could pass over the site of the faithless city. With the terrible example of Sora before them, the Apulian cities of Foggia, Casal Nove, and Santo Severo surrendered and waited in fear and trembling to hear the verdict of the Emperor, but for the moment he contented himself with ordering the destruction of their walls.

Frederick's apparent clemency to the Apulian towns, and the fact that he stopped the pursuit of the fleeing Soldiers of the Keys at the frontiers of the Papal States, when he could have driven them before him to the walls of Rome, were actions that had but one aim in mind—the conclusion of peace with the

Pope. With this same end in view Frederick dispatched a circular letter explaining his actions in the Holy Land to the
princes of Christendom, as conciliatory in tone as his speech in
the Church of the Holy Sepulchre.

Inevitably it fell to Hermann von Salza to lead the many
diplomatic missions which for several weary months now
shuttled to and fro between the imperial and papal courts.
The victorious Emperor was trying with humble moderation
and infinite patience to extract from the defeated but unwilling
Pope the terms of a settlement in which ironically enough the
Emperor was forced to give way upon almost every point. A
general amnesty for the papal supporters in Sicily was proclaimed, the Sicilian clergy were exempted from taxes and
secular law, and Frederick even seems to have made some
further concessions over the election of the Sicilian bishops,
that perennial bone of contention between Emperor and Pope.
Confiscated Church property was restored, including even that
of the Hospitallers and the Templars. This last must have
been a very bitter pill for Frederick to swallow after his
experiences in Outremer.

Concession after concession was wrung from the Emperor
by the relentless old Pope, who still refused to come to an
agreement. In his moderation and submissiveness in this
moment of military triumph Frederick displayed true statesmanship, and by his conciliatory attitude in the eyes of the world
placed the onus of the continued discord in the heart of Christendom upon the shoulders of the Pope. The mere fact that the
victorious Emperor was compelled to sue so humbly for peace
demonstrates, nevertheless, the enormous moral power of the
mediaeval Church, which lifted it above mere military defeats.
As an excommunicate it would have been impossible for
Frederick to restore order in the realm and to keep his hold
upon the vast possessions of the Empire. The whole of Europe
wished that the quarrel might be settled; the princes of the
Empire went to intercede with the Pope and personally guaran-
teed Frederick's good faith; several members of the College
of Cardinals were opposed to the Pope's intransigence and in the
end the indomitable old man gave way and condescended to
accept the wholesale concessions that his victor was humbly
prepared to offer.

At last, in the middle of July of the year 1230, the Pope's emissary, a Dominican monk called Gualo, brought Gregory's terms for the settlement to the Emperor; they were dutifully accepted, and peace was at last concluded by the Pope's ratification. While the final arrangements for the formal signing of the treaty were being made, Frederick waited at Rocca d'Arce, on his side of the Garigliano river which formed the frontier between the realm and the Papal States. He kept Hermann von Salza with him, while he sent his emissaries, the Bishops of Reggio, Modena, Mantua, and Winchester, down to Ceprano where the peace was to be signed. With them went a young court notary, Pietro della Vigna, who in a minor role had played quite an active part in the prolonged drama of the peace negotiations.

On the 28th of August the stage was set for the final act and the ban of excommunication was lifted from the Emperor in the little chapel in the camp at Ceprano.

With an impetuosity reminiscent of his youth, Frederick then set out with a small band of followers for Anagni, where the Pope was living at the time. They encamped in the valley below the grey-walled town which had already given to the Holy See three of its most forceful popes—Alexander III, Innocent III and Gregory IX. It was a place of ill-omen to the Hohenstaufen, its walls had resounded to the sonorous periods of the awful sentence of excommunication declared against two of them—the Emperor Barbarossa and his grandson Frederick II. But today all was amity, the Pope invited the Emperor, who was now the "beloved son of the Church", into the town to come and see him. They dined together in the papal palace, that seventy years later was to be the scene of the most terrible affront endured by any pope—when Sciarra Colonna struck Boniface VIII.

It was an intimate occasion, this meeting of the Pope and Emperor who had hitherto heaped the most unpardonable insults upon each other's heads. Afterwards Gregory, with a naïveté surprising in the holder of the world's most reverend title, wrote to a friend describing how Frederick had come without any imperial pomp to visit him in his home. Though in his spiritual capacity Gregory might defy the Emperor, evidently Hugo Conti as the descendant of a family of small provincial nobles was somewhat in awe of the personage who was the holder of the vast heritage of the Hohenstaufen and the Haute-villes. The Pope and the Emperor had a long talk in private; Hermann von Salza was the only person present at this tête-à-tête, with which both the august participants afterwards declared themselves to be profoundly satisfied.

The meeting at Anagni put an end to the first and last Crusade of an excommunicant, and the dispute that had threatened to wreck the peace of Europe was finally settled with the kiss of peace. The Pope now ordered the Patriarch of Jerusalem to ratify the treaty concluded with the Sultan al-Kamil, and dispatched a letter couched in severe terms to the Grand Master of the Templars, warning him that his Order should not by any act of hostility break the truce which was so necessary to the security of the Holy Land. The interdict was solemnly lifted from the Holy Places in the presence of the Patriarchs of Antioch and Aquileia, and of four bishops representing the Emperor.

The epilogue to the drama was finally accomplished in the following year, when on the 12th of August 1231 the Pope at last formally recognised Frederick as King of Jerusalem. The human motives which lay behind the prolonged delay in this last recognition were mentioned in the papal bull. Somewhat cryptically the Pope excused himself for not having accorded the recognition earlier "for reasons whose value the Emperor himself will appreciate"—in other words the Pope no longer needed to support Jean de Brienne in his claim to Jerusalem, because the wily Jean had done much better for himself. He had married another of his daughters—Maria this time—to the child-Emperor Baldwin II of Constantinople, with the careful proviso that the title of Emperor should be his until his death. This time he was taking no risks.

PART III

The Creative Years
1230-*circa* 1237

Chapter VI

THE CONSTITUTIONS OF MELFI

WITH the Peace of Ceprano came a period of tranquillity. The years between Frederick's return from Germany in 1220 and his departure on Crusade had been beset with troubles—the problems of the Lombard cities and of the Moslems in Sicily, the quarrel with the papacy, the efforts needed to finance the Crusade itself. But now, for a while at least, Frederick could confidently expect that his ship of state would sail in calmer waters. For a while only—for it is doubtful whether Emperor or Pope believed that their fundamental differences could be permanently resolved. But at least the Peace of Ceprano would afford some years of respite.

It is characteristic of Frederick that once the realm was pacified after its invasion by the papal armies, and order finally restored, his first thought was not to visit Germany, where he had not been for eleven years, nor yet to embrace the son whom he had not seen either for more than a decade—but to devote himself with all the daemonic energy that he possessed to the further perfectioning of the administration of the kingdom, whose foundations he had laid in Capua eleven years before.

Frederick had one love in his life to whom he remained consistently faithful and from which even his brief experience of, and susceptibility to, the glamour of the East did not seduce him, his beloved realm. Sicily was the "apple of his eye" to her King and his letters while he was abroad on the Empire's business were filled with phrases, sometimes Oriental in their imagery, that speak of his love and longing for his native land. "We have chosen our domain of Sicily for our own amongst all other lands, and taken the whole kingdom as the place of our abiding, for we—radiant with the glory of the title of the Caesars— yet feel it no ignoble thing to be called 'a man from Apulia'. Borne hither and thither as we are on imperial floods far from the havens and harbours of Sicily, we feel ourselves a pilgrim and a wanderer from home." It is strange to find a polyglot, most of whose life was spent in constant journeying and who was the reverse of sentimental, employing such phrases, but cynic though he might be in all else Frederick lavished on his native land the love which most men feel for their family and friends.

To the mediaeval mind the supreme duties of a ruler were to dispense justice and to keep the peace. The ancient coronation ceremonies of the Kings of the Romans at Aix-la-Chapelle laid particular stress upon the King's sacred obligation to "make justice flower during his reign". The formula was repeated three times—first in the prayers, then again when, after the actual anointing, the bishops gave back to the sovereign the sword and sceptre, enjoining him to "love justice", and finally in the coronation oath itself, when the King promised to keep the peace, respect the rights of the Church, not to diminish the Empire, and *to give the people justice*.

To Frederick, with his love of order and his admiration for the classical world, this aspect of his royal functions was one of the most important, he really felt himself to be *lex animata in terris*. When he was once again able to take up the reins of government in the realm his first thought was to investigate the legal system, or rather the complicated welter of the various systems that Byzantine, Lombard, Moslem and Norman conquerors had left behind them. In 1230 he called for a general survey of all laws that existed in the kingdom. The ancient constitutions were examined, the wise old men versed in the law of time-honoured custom and usage were questioned, and their statements noted down by scribes. The upshot of these researches was that the Emperor decided to promulgate a new properly co-ordinated legal system—a truly herculean task which had not been attempted since the days of Justinian—but which resulted in the production of Frederick's *Liber Augustalis* or the Constitutions of Melfi (as with later additions the code is more popularly known) which achieved fame rivalling that of the *Codex Justinianus* of the Byzantine Emperor.

King Roger II had in 1140, in the Assizes of Ariano, to a certain extent co-ordinated the various legal systems that existed in Sicily, and in its essence his Norman laws had been a return to those of Justinian, some vestiges of which had survived in the old Byzantine provinces of Southern Italy. In his desire to give legal form to the Hautevilles' conquest of Sicily, whose only legitimate justification was the Pope's investiture based on the donations of Constantine and Charlemagne, Roger borrowed much from the Byzantine conception that the king's right came from God alone, and that it was sacrilegious to oppose him. Apart from these high-falutin sentiments, called in to bolster his own authority, Roger's Norman shrewdness had not attempted to impose alien laws, but to take what was best suited to his purposes from the existing Roman, Byzantine and Canon law. In 1140, however, the Norman conquest was too recent, and the diversity of races in the territories which he governed too great, for the king to attempt to reform anything but public law. He was careful to state that "The laws newly promulgated by our authority are to apply to all—but they bring no change in the customs and laws of the subject peoples."

Frederick in creating the Constitutions of Melfi drew much of his inspiration from his grandfather, both in the concept of the source of the royal power and in the actual laws themselves. During the period of nearly a century which had elapsed since the Assizes of Ariano, Sicily, in spite of the troublous times through which she had passed, had remained nominally at least a single sovereign state, and the passage of time had done much to weld together the diverse peoples of the realm. Frederick was now able to go far further than King Roger, and to produce the first great legal code of the Middle Ages.

In later years Pietro della Vigna became so much Frederick's right-hand man that succeeding generations attributed entirely to him the preparation of the Constitutions of Melfi. In actual fact he was probably only one of a team of jurists which included Archbishop James of Capua, who may well have been the directing brain. Pope Gregory certainly regarded the archbishop as one of those principally responsible for the framing of the new code, which he viewed with profound misgiving. He wrote in fact to the Archbishop accusing him of serving as the Emperor's instrument in preparing laws which "renounced salvation and conjured up immeasurable ill".

Not content simply with admonishing a churchman, the Pope

wrote to the Emperor himself: "It has reached our ears that thou hast it in mind to promulgate new laws, either of thine own impulse or led astray by the pernicious counsels of abandoned men. From this it follows that men call thee a persecutor of the Church, an overthrower of the freedom of the State." During the nine months which were given to the preparation of this the first Constitution of Melfi, rumours of something of the revolution that it was to create in mediaeval ways of thought must have reached Gregory's ears. The insight which had enabled the Pope to recognise in Frederick a disruptive force of far greater danger to the mediaeval conception of life than his most warlike forebears put Gregory instantly on the alert. But the Pope was in no position to renew hostilities with the Emperor at this time, and Frederick had been careful to sugar the pill of the constitutions with many measures that would be pleasing to the Church, so that the danger of a renewed rift was averted.

The Constitutions of Melfi were indited in the rolling periods of sonorous Latin prose for which the Imperial Chancery was famous. Although the code was only intended for use in the realm, not the empire, the full style and titles of the Emperor were given in all their august grandeur.

IMPERATOR FRIDERICUS SECUNDUS
ROMANORUM CAESAR SEMPER AUGUSTUS
ITALICUS SICULUS HIEROSOLYMITANUS ARELATENSIS
FELIX VICTOR AC TRIUMPHATOR.

The introduction traced the origin of human law from the fall of Adam and Eve, who had violated the divine law, and were banned from Eden (the ban of empire was the most terrible penalty which civil law could inflict in mediaeval times). Thus the anarchy resulting from the Fall had brought about the need for the state and the rule of princes to restore order; thus rulers were responsible to God.

Frederick's conception of the sources of his power to rule and legislate were drawn from theories (very similar to those of King Roger) expounded by his legal adviser, the celebrated authority on Roman law, Roffredo of Benevento, according to whom "the Emperor bases his right on a gift of grace bestowed by heaven" and "receives his impulse from heavenly reflection".

This divine mandate the Emperor must carry out by defending
the Church, keeping the peace, and giving justice to the peoples
over whom he was called upon to rule.

The first laws in the code dealt with heresy, their provisions
being the same as those of Canon law. The precedence given
to these laws, and their actual content, were no doubt intended
as a sop to the Pope, but they also served to support Frederick's
theory of the sanctity of the state, as the crime of *lèse-majesté*
was formally placed on a par with sacrilege, in confirmation of
various laws of his predecessors. Article 17 of Roger's Assize
had already established that it was sacrilege to dispute the royal
judgements, acts or dispositions, or to question whether he
whom the King had chosen or appointed was worthy. A man
who questioned the sentence of one of the King's judges could
be tried for sacrilege, as the Count of Molise was in 1168,
after accusing one of Roger's judges of having given false
judgement against him. Frederick carried this concept even
further and equated rebellion against the imperial power with
heresy both in Sicily in 1232 and later in Lombardy.

Of more interest to modern eyes is Frederick's concept that
all were equal before the law. "We who hold the balance of
justice for the rights of all, do not wish to make distinctions
but to achieve equality in our judgements. Be plaintiff or defen-
dant Frank, Roman or Lombard, we wish that he should be
awarded justice." The sovereign, although he was the divinely
ordained fount of all justice, was himself subject to the law
because "Although the supreme imperial dignity, to whom it
is given to promulgate laws, is free of the law, we will take
care however that as a matter of convenience in the observation
of laws, and in the inflexibility of justice, we also will
follow the law common to others, and as we wish to preserve
the principles of justice, we will not make use of the royal prerogatives against the law to the damage of our faithful subjects,
because we consider damage to our faithful subjects damage to
ourselves, and their gains our gains."

Advanced as Frederick's views were upon legislation, his
Liber Augustalis appears to modern eyes to have been a curious
mixture of actual law and rules that laid down the foundations
of the administrative system under which the country was to
be governed, and for this reason it has been called the "Constitu-

tion of the Bureaucracy". Frederick's lay state was only in its infancy and the separation of these different functions was not yet envisaged. Private law was scarcely touched upon.

The first Constitution of Melfi continued, and elaborated, the policy laid down at Capua of concentrating all the reins of power in the Emperor's own hands, though the laws enacted to achieve this end were again to a very large extent derived from those of King Roger. At Capua the old Norman principle that criminal justice was a right reserved to the Crown had been restated; in practice in Norman times this had applied mainly to the island of Sicily and to Calabria, in the rest of the mainland provinces it had actually usually been exercised by the counts. After Capua the Emperor had set about recovering these rights throughout the realm, and now at Melfi their inalienably royal character was underlined by laws which threatened any prelate, count or baron who usurped them with the confiscation of his land; though this was also apparently a revival in a modified form of a previous Norman law. From now on criminal jurisdiction was, with insignificant exceptions, to be administered by the Emperor's justiciars, who were in fact usually nobles, but were paid for their services by the state. The last court of appeal was the High Court presided over by the Grand Master Justiciar who had four judges to assist him. Written records had to be kept of all judgements. For certain crimes a state prosecution, akin to our modern system, was instituted. Trial by ordeal was abolished.

Concentration of military power under the crown followed the same lines as the centralisation of criminal justice. The Capuan edicts had paved the way for this by the confiscation of the castles and limitation of nobles' movements outside their castles with armed bands. The onus of keeping the peace lay with the Emperor, and his instruments in doing so were the network of state fortresses and his army of mercenaries, which provided an effective counterbalance to the feudal power of the nobles. Restrictions of the right to carry arms, already noted at Capua, were reinforced; and as in the days of Roger private war or personal vengeance was prohibited. The old feudal custom whereby if a man was attacked he could invoke the name of his feudal overlord as a *defensa* (defence) was now transferred to the Crown, and if after the invocation of the Emperor's name the aggressor did not withdraw, he was liable to be called before the High Court for judgement of his crime.

The last relics of autonomous government in the cities were suppressed, and limitations were placed even upon the right of churches and religious orders to acquire fiefs or freehold land. These last were again a revival of Norman laws, which in effect meant that no fiefs might be given to the Church without the sovereign's permission, or freehold land to churches or orders who did not owe feudal service to the King; if land was left to them in a will it had to be sold within a year, the Church retaining the purchase money. This last provision fell heavily upon the Military Orders such as the Templars, Hospitallers, and Teutonic Knights, who were exempt from feudal service; its aim was to prevent all the freehold land falling into the hands of the Church. The restriction upon giving fiefs to the Church was due to the fact that there was an early Norman tradition that it could hold land without giving feudal service in return, and in his efforts to recuperate all rights which belonged to the Crown, Frederick was not going to allow one jot or tittle of them to escape if it was humanly possible to do so.

To the foundations of the modern state that had been laid at Capua, the Constitutions of Melfi added the framework upon which it could be further developed in future. For parallel to the process of centralisation that deprived the feudal lords of many of their privileges, there ran the concept that all men were equal before the law, which brought with it new ideas of human dignity and liberty that made a very real contribution towards bettering the lot of the common man. Frederick himself once said that "nothing is more odious than the oppression of the poor by the rich", and if for economic reasons he was unable to dispense with the servitude to the glebe, and in fact was obliged to enforce the return of the villeins to the royal demesne, he mitigated the penalties against those who had left, and they were given three months in which to return if they were still living in the same province, or six months if they were further away. Legal advice was free for widows and orphans, and the High Court was specially instructed to look after the cases of the weak and unprotected who might be subjected to intimidation in local courts.

The status of women has always been a fair barometer by

F

which the enlightenment of any society or civilisation may be gauged, and the provisions of the Constitutions of Melfi with regard to them, owing again much to the Code of Justinian, were truly remarkable for the mediaeval world. Women could inherit property, to kidnap them was a very serious offence, rape, even of a prostitute, was a capital offence, though there must be evidence that the woman had put up a serious resistance. The pimp was sentenced to slavery or forced labour, a mother who prostituted her daughter was liable to heavy penalties, though these were mitigated if it could be proved that she was forced to do so by poverty that made it impossible for her to provide a marriage portion or even food for the child. Today these laws appear to be elemental, but it should be borne in mind that in Cologne during the thirteenth century the law inflicted no penalty upon a man who raped a woman if she was found alone in the street at night.

A case could not be brought against a minor, or against a homicidal maniac. The death sentence was inflicted upon any-one who kidnapped or committed an offence against the sur-vivors of a shipwreck; failure to give assistance to the victims of shipwreck was punished by a heavy fine. Usury was forbidden to all except the Jews, and they were protected by the fact that they were juridically considered to be the serfs of the Emperor. Weights and measures were controlled by the state, which also enacted laws against the sale of bad food, and laid down that for reasons of hygiene all butchering was to take place well outside the confines of the towns.

The laws which governed the civil service and the adminis-tration of justice probably contributed more than any others to ensure that impartial justice was done, and that the ordinary citizen was not subject to the tyranny of overbearing officials. All officials were appointed by the Emperor, to whom they were responsible, and their term of office was for one year only, though renewable. The great officials, known as justiciars, were governors of provinces, subject to two master justiciars who governed half the realm; these two men in their turn were responsible to the grand master justiciar who presided over the High Court. Here again was a revision and tightening up of the system prevalent in Norman times.

The justiciars could not be natives of the province which they administered, neither they nor their children might own land there, nor could they buy land or make any contract, marry or become betrothed to a native. No hospitality might be accepted by them other than that which was necessary in the exercise of their official functions. Officials might not be accompanied by their wives. Bribery was strictly forbidden, and the penalties inflicted upon corrupt officials were extremely severe—a judge giving an unfair judgement on a capital offence was himself subject to the death sentence.

Roughly speaking the justiciar corresponded to the prefect of a French department today, with this difference, that his main task was the speeding up of the administration of justice. The Emperor did not like justice to lag, and cases were required to be settled within three months. The justiciar was mostly concerned with penal law, but appeals in civil law also came within his jurisdiction and he was required to proclaim the tax requirements. The justiciars' and other officials' pay was far from princely, and they were called upon to answer for any damage suffered by the state with their own possessions, even their own lives. Each official was expected to act as a check upon others, and subjects had the right to present complaints against them twice yearly.

Apart from his normal official duties the justiciar might be called upon to perform all manner of personal services for the Emperor: to oversee the care of any of his precious falcons which might have been sent to rest in his area, provide cranes or other game birds for the training of the same falcons, provide hounds for the Emperor's hunting, or even make investigations into the realms of natural history on his behalf. The life of a justiciar in Frederick's service was far from being a sinecure.

In their functions the justiciars were assisted by professional judges and legal counsellors, notaries and clerks, all of whom were paid servants of the Emperor. For minor judicial duties there were also the bajuli, who were responsible to the chamberlain. From the very great number of bajuli which existed—in the province of the Abruzzi alone there were nearly two thousand—it is evident that they were officials of a very minor order. Whereas the justiciars proclaimed what the taxes were to be, to the master chamberlain's office fell the task of actually collecting the money. Previously the master chamberlain had also been responsible for the administration of the royal demesne, but under Frederick the expansion of the civil service caused the master chamberlain's office to lose some of its importance, and the demesne was administered by the *Magistri Procuratores Demanii*, or master proctors, who, with their subordinate proctors, were specially concerned with the revocation of the demesne rights.

The master chamberlain was nevertheless a man of great influence. He had the ear of the Emperor and was his intimate councillor, and he was also intendant of his finances. In Angevin times, after the fall of the Hohenstaufens, the master chamberlain was responsible for the administration of the king's private treasure, the guard and upkeep of the royal palaces and pleasure houses, the administration of the royal hunting enclosures, and the control of the pasturage of the demesne.

It is probable that these functions were much the same as they had been in Frederick's time, and from them it is evident that the master chamberlain must have known more about the Emperor's private life and habits than most of the other royal officials. Frederick had two chamberlains during his reign, the first, Richard, a Sicilian born and the owner of large estates in the island, who had known Frederick from his youth. He is thought to have come of Moslem stock, and possibly to have been the chief eunuch. His successor, who was appointed about a year after his death, was certainly a Moslem; he was known as Giovanni il Moro, and was the son of a Saracen slave and a negro. It was through him that Frederick sent his instructions for the care of the women of the harem at Lucera where Giovanni il Moro frequently lived.

In Norman times the same man, known as the admiral, had been commander-in-chief of both the army and the fleet. Under Frederick the army came under the marshal. The Emperor also had a very effective secret police service. About the details of this organisation very little is actually known, but its efficiency may be judged by results—the Emperor, even when he was abroad, often knew more of what went on in a province than the justiciar himself. One of the functions of this force was the preparation of dossiers upon the activities of subjects suspected of hostility to the state, such as a secret relationship with the papal curia or exiles, or heresy. These were prepared in note form in a small book, which even gave the sources of the information which it contained. This was then presented to the unfortunate object of suspicion whose reactions, in view of the Emperor's well-known implacable cruelty towards all traitors, can well be imagined.

For administrative purposes the realm was divided into nine provinces which remained substantially the same until the unification of Italy during the last century. They were the Abruzzi on the north-eastern border, the Terra di Lavoro and Molise on the west, and in the centre the principality of Benevento, to the south of the Molise the Capitanata which is the vast plain in the north of the modern province of Apulia, Apulia which was roughly the southern half of the modern province including Bari and Otranto, the Basilicata that fills the "instep" of Italy and reaches north to Melfi, and Calabria. Sicily was divided into two provinces to the east and west of the river Salso. The only land frontier of the realm ran roughly in the form of an S from the river Tronto in the north-east to Terracina on the Tyrrhenian coast of Italy. It was, at the time of the unification of Italy, the oldest-established frontier in Europe.

No state administration can work efficiently without the basis of a sound financial system. Frederick had a lively appreciation of this fact and in his first Constitution of Melfi he laid down the basic rules which governed the financial policy of the realm. With all its faults, and they were many, this system nevertheless enabled him to engage upon the titanic struggle with the papacy that lasted for thirteen years, and only ended with his death. Perhaps the most telling comment on its success was the letter addressed by Pope Clement IV to Charles of Anjou in 1267, after the Angevin conquest of the realm. To all popes the name of Hohenstaufen was anathema, nevertheless Clement wrote to his protégé as follows: "It is strange that you should complain of the poverty of a Realm from which that noble man Frederick, in spite of his having incurred greater expenses than your own, enriched enormously both himself and his family and satisfied as well Lombardy, Tuscany, the March of Ancona, the Trevisan March, and Germany." For a Pope to hold up Frederick, the most deadly of that "brood of vipers" the Hohenstaufen, as an example to that faithful son of the Church,

Charles of Anjou, was eloquent testimony indeed of the efficiency, ruthless though it was, of Frederick's financial administration.

Financially speaking Sicily's two great assets were her enormous wheat production, which had made her one of the granaries of the Empire in Roman times, and her geographical position as the meeting place of all the seaborne trade routes which traversed the Mediterranean from east to west. This last was of particular importance in an age when coastal navigation was the rule, and where many of what we would today call luxury goods came almost exclusively from the Orient. It was the reason why two of the greatest maritime powers of the Middle Ages—Genoa and Pisa—had engaged in such furious rivalry to secure a foothold in the island of Sicily, and had played such an important part in the politics of the island during Frederick's minority.

Frederick's financial policy was primarily aimed at gaining state control of these two basic assets, and as a corollary, at introducing the production of Oriental goods into his own realm, both for export and to render their importation unnecessary. The means which he used to gain his ends was a ruthless system of state control and monopolies—the monopolies were also extended in some cases to include such basic necessities as salt, which is still a government monopoly in Italy today.

One feature that renders any analysis of Frederick's finances particularly difficult is the inextricable manner in which his personal finances were mixed up with those of the state. As heir to the Norman kings he was the greatest landowner in the country, he also had a personal interest in the demesne, that was bound to give him an annual tribute of one-twelfth of all its produce in kind. This immense personal fortune provided the hard core of the Emperor's finances, and we have seen that from the moment that he attained his majority, and through successive reforms, his basic policy was to ensure the return of all that part of the demesne and those privately owned lands which had belonged to the crown, and had been usurped during his minority and absence abroad.

The main products of the royal lands were wheat and wool (the rights of pasturage for sheep remained a very valuable Crown prerogative in the Kingdom of Sicily right through

Bourbon times). Frederick himself was the greatest wheat producer in the country, and all cereals, vegetables, flax and hemp produced in the demesne had to be handed over to the state store-houses. Thus the state and Frederick between them, apart from their enormous purchasing power, controlled so much of the country's wheat supply as to result in their enjoying a controlling interest, if not a practical monopoly. The Crown control of the wheat trade was rendered even greater by the existence of a large state merchant fleet, created by Frederick, and the fact that no ships exporting grain after the harvest could leave Sicilian harbours until the imperial grain ships had already sailed. Documentary evidence has survived to show that the Emperor, on two occasions at least, made use of his control of the wheat market, combined with his unlimited powers, to make a very handsome profit for the government. The first occurred during the Moslem wars, after his return from Germany, the second later in his reign when he was absent in Northern Italy. On this occasion he learnt that Genoese traders were planning to turn a famine in Tunisia to good account by buying up stocks of Sicilian wheat and selling them in North Africa. Frederick gave orders for the closure of the Sicilian ports and, after negotiation with the Tunisian government, ordered the imperial fleet to sail with 50,000 loads of corn.

A steady state income was ensured by Frederick's organisation of the customs services. With an extraordinarily modern conception of free trading within the kingdom, he abolished internal tolls as far as possible, and concentrated his attention upon collecting revenues instead from the import and export trade. State warehouses were built in all ports and upon the main land routes into the kingdom, and all imported goods had to be deposited in them, a customs fee of 3 per cent of the selling price being paid by the buyer, while the seller paid the storage fee. For exports the same rules applied, though the customs fee varied according to the state's need of the goods exported, and in cases of national emergency the export of the strategic materials of the day—weapons, war horses, and cattle—might be forbidden.

The warehouses, that were known by the Arabic name of *fondachi*, had inns attached in which the foreign traders lodged, and where the government could keep an eye upon them. The fee for their board and lodging was included in the storage fees. In spite of his state monopolies and control of trade, the Emperor clearly recognised the great value of foreign trade to the country's finances, and traders were treated with consideration, even to the extent that the traders of an enemy country were considered as neutrals in time of war. Trade was also encouraged by commercial agreements with foreign countries, and embassies to the sovereigns, Christian and Moslem, whose realms bordered upon the Mediterranean were frequent.

In his efforts to better his country's trade Frederick was constantly on the look-out for new crops which might be introduced into the country—the cultivation of henna and indigo were two of his innovations. He also encouraged industries based on the introduction of Oriental raw materials into the realm, the refining of sugar being a case in point.

Frederick's admiration for the Cistercian Order had been prompted by their knowledge of farming and husbandry, that judged even by modern standards was remarkable. For instance they had been responsible for the invention of a system of overhead irrigation of fields in which fodder was grown, enabling cattle to be fed on green crops for all but the two coldest winter months in the frigid winters of Northern Italy— these fields, known as marcite, are still in use today. The Emperor himself was a farming expert of no mean order, the royal farms were run on modern lines, and horse and stock breeding were the subject of scientific study and care. The Emperor's breeding establishment for horses at Palazzo San Gervasio in Apulia was famous. The Master of the Horse at the imperial court, Giordano Ruffo, was the author of a book on the management and care of horses called *De Medicina Equorum* which was a standard work for centuries, some of the remedies it contains bearing comparison with those that are in use today. Near Syracuse there was at least one royal farm which specialised in horse breeding, and another given over to the breeding of cattle. Frederick also created artificial fish-ponds, the remains of one of which can still be seen near Lentini in Sicily, and, like any mediaeval monarch whose favourite sport was hunting, his game preserves were dotted about the length and breadth of the country.

The chief state monopolies were salt, iron, dyeing, silk, and hemp. The latter was probably instituted with the welfare of the all-important navy in mind—Sicily has always been noted for its production of hemp of which the Royal Navy is today a purchaser. The prices of salt and iron were fixed by the state, and the organisation of these industries was handed over to four men. The growth and manufacture of silk had been introduced into Sicily by King Roger, and the high quality of the products of the Sicilian industry may still be judged by the magnificent examples of its production that are to be found in the museums of the world—the famous coronation mantle of King Roger, which later became that of the Holy Roman emperors, is a notable example. The manufacture of this precious product Frederick handed over to the Jews of Trani. The royal monopoly of dyeing was also handed over to the Jews, in the first instance to those of Naples and Capua, but later this industry seems to have been extended.

The Emperor also realised that a basic essential of financial administration is a sound currency. Already during his first period of reform in the realm, at the time of the Moslem wars, new silver coins called imperiales had been issued, and Frederick, for the first time in centuries, minted a golden coinage known as Augustales. The coins themselves were a deliberate imitation of those of the great Roman Caesar Augustus. Frederick's head was portrayed on them in the guise of a Roman emperor crowned with laurels or a diadem of sunlike rays, his shoulders wrapped in the imperial mantle. Around his portrait was the legend IMP/ROM/CESAR/AUG, on the other side was the imperial Roman eagle and his name—Fredericus. Beautiful though they were, probably the finest example of the numismatist's art in all the Middle Ages, these coins do not seem to have been popular, perhaps because like other of Frederick's innovations they were too far in advance of the standards of the times.

Taxation was defeudalised, and became increasingly heavy as the reign advanced. The imperial officials and tax collectors had to keep carefully recorded accounts in writing to be forwarded to the central government. The most onerous tax was the *Collecta* which had originally been imposed only in times of great financial stringency, and was in effect a capital levy upon land. This tax was now levied with increasing regularity until it became an annual event. The amounts collected varied according to the needs of the imperial finances; in 1248, at the height of Frederick's titanic struggle with the papacy, it came to as much as a hundred and thirty thousand ounces of gold, well over a quarter of a million sterling.

As Pope Clement had said in his letter to Charles of Anjou, the unfortunate Realm of Sicily was called upon to satisfy the financial needs of the Emperor in his attempts to dominate the whole of Italy and Germany, and moreover, though the Pope forebore to mention this, to provide the wherewithal for the payment, equipment and supply of armies fighting against the Lombard communes and the rebellious forces which papal agents had raised against the excommunicated Emperor in Germany. No country, no matter how rich or how well organised, could be expected to bear so heavy a financial burden without disastrous results, and that Sicily was beggared by it is not surprising. But that she did not break down completely under the strain was due to the extraordinary efficiency with which the administration of the country had been established during the few years of tranquillity which her dynamic sovereign had enjoyed.

Melfi, the town from which the constitutions took their name, stands almost precisely in the centre of the "foot" of Italy in the north-eastern border of Lucania. It had been an important administrative centre since Norman times. Its castle stands high, about one thousand five hundred feet above sea-level, and is situated among the great beech and chestnut forests that still cover the slopes of the great extinct volcano, the Monte Vulture—the Vulture mountain. The blazing heat of the summer on the Apulian plain is tempered here by cool breezes and the shade of the great forests, and Melfi became a favourite place of summer residence for the imperial court, though Frederick himself often withdrew to the greater seclusion of his hunting box at Lagopesole, which is in the highlands not far away.

It was to Melfi that in the summer of 1231 the Emperor summoned the ecclesiastics, barons, justiciars, and the great officials of the state, to the court which was held for the promulgation of the first Constitution of Melfi. It was a magnificent occasion, upon which the Emperor appeared in state, seated high upon his gem-encrusted throne, while his officials read out the decrees.

The court was a long one, lasting through August and September, and the Emperor had been in residence at Melfi since May; evidently he must have supervised closely the final composition of the new constitution and its presentation to the authorities of the kingdom. Some say that the representatives of the Third Estate were even called to this momentous ceremony, but it appears to be more likely that they were officially called for the first time in the following year, when the Emperor had returned to the realm after the Diets of Ravenna and Aquileia.

The calling of the Third Estate, which was begun in 1232, later became a regular institution throughout the realm. In a decree given at Messina in 1233, the Emperor declared that meetings of the representatives of the people, or *colloquia* as they were called, were to be summoned twice a year in each province so that the people might be informed about taxation and air their grievances. The decree stated that a special representative of the Emperor must be present at the meetings, and he was required to make a written report of proceedings to the imperial government. These meetings were held on the 1st of May and the 1st of November, and continued for from eight days to a fortnight. The larger towns sent four representatives and the smaller towns and castles two.

The date of this decree is particularly significant. 1233 was the year after the risings in Messina and the other Sicilian towns, when the Emperor went personally to investigate the situation on the spot. Evidently he was convinced that some form of popular representation was necessary to fill the gap created by his suppression of the civic liberties of the towns and thus, autocrat though he was, Frederick may be said to be the first monarch of mediaeval times to call the Third Estate and, albeit unconsciously, to take the first hesitant steps towards democratic practice.

Frederick's calling of the Third Estate was not for any consultative purpose—they were to come and hear the Emperor's will and to take back his command—but nevertheless the fact that they were summoned was a remarkable portent, and who can tell what part they might not have played in the future of the realm if in the centuries to come it had developed on the basis of the Constitutions of Melfi into a closely knit national entity under the rule of native kings, instead of falling as it did under the dominion of foreign conquerors and absentee rulers. As it was, the tragic end of the house of Hohenstaufen brought with it the centuries of neglect and decay that reduced the Kingdom of Sicily, which in their day had been one of the richest kingdoms in Europe, to the condition of a distressed area that still represents a major problem to the Italian government of today.

Chapter VII

" OUR PLACES OF SOLACE "

THE Castle of Melfi, where the constitution had been promulgated, had been founded by Frederick's Norman ancestors of the house of Hauteville; and there in 1073 Pope Gregory VII had recognised Robert Guiscard as *Dux Apuliae*. Guiscard had built four great stone towers which were probably connected by a defensive wall; this nucleus was converted into a keep by the Emperor, who also enlarged the castle in all directions, surrounding the whole with a curtain wall of irregular outline strengthened at intervals by massive polygonal towers.

It is probable that the work of enlarging Melfi Castle was begun shortly after the Emperor's return from Germany, and was well advanced if not completed by the time he left for the Crusade, as he was in residence there shortly beforehand.

Melfi Castle has suffered from grievous earthquakes and many subsequent reconstructions, but the enormous room known as the "Sala delle tre scodelle", from its triple-domed roof, is still referred to by local inhabitants as the room in which the Emperor promulgated the Constitutions of Melfi. Linked to it by an ante-room is a large room (with a beautiful view over the mountains) which contains a spacious alcove. In one corner of this room there is a secret doorway that gives access to a narrow passage leading to a staircase in a tower, that descends to the stables and one of the castle gates. This room is said to have been the Emperor's bedroom and, although it is impossible to say whether the tradition is founded upon fact, a detailed study of the castle by the architect who was responsible for its repair after the earthquake of 1851 has shown that these architectural features are of very early origin.

Melfi is a less orderly construction than most of the Frederician castles, but the Emperor was in need at this time of a royal

173

residence and an administrative centre for this remote portion of his kingdom, which he had never seen until his return from Germany. Apulia had always been a trouble centre of the Realm of Sicily under the Norman kings; many of the barons were of Norman stock, descendants of the adventurers who had come to Southern Italy at the same time as the Hautevilles, and these bold and warlike men considered themselves the equals of the Hautevilles, whom in the first place they had raised to the position of leadership by election. Robert Guiscard and his brother Roger had become *primus inter pares* among their fellow Normans by sheer force of character and military prowess, and their descendants had to maintain their assumption of royal state by keeping a strong hand upon the reins of government and their Norman compatriots. During Frederick's minority and absence in Germany the barons of Apulia enjoyed, if possible, even greater freedom and licence than the rest of the realm as, with the exception of the Abruzzi, they were the furthest removed from the centre of government in Palermo.

Frederick was quick to perceive the strategic importance of Apulia as a link in his lines of communication between the Empire and the realm—for one thing its excellent harbours and the friendship of Venice gave his galleys the freedom of the Adriatic. This alone would have sufficed to make Frederick determined to keep a tight hold upon the province, but to this was added something of a more personal nature—Apulia appealed to him more than any other portion of his vast domains. It is significant in this respect that he styled himself not a man of the Marches after Jesi where he was born, nor yet a Sicilian after the island where he was brought up, but "A man of Apulia". The vast horizons of the great plains of the Tavoliere, the open rolling country of the Murge hills, and the lonely forests of the Monte Vulture held some magic for him that made him yearn for them when he was forced by reasons of state to spend long years abroad. The civilised beauty of Tuscany and the verdant fertility of Northern Italy held no such appeal for him. His letters written while he was there are filled with his longing for Apulia, and to Apulia he would return whenever he was able to snatch a period of rest and repose.

Frederick first visited the province during the winter of 1221–2, and in the following year he began to build himself a palace at Foggia, a town which lies in the centre of the great plain. It was the first of the many royal residences that he was to build in the realm. Nothing but the arch of the principal gateway now remains, but from the descriptions which have come down to us the palace appears to have retained some of the characteristics of the mauresque pleasure houses of Palermo where he was brought up. It was rich in marbles; pillars of verd-antique lined its colonnades, marble lions adorned basins where fountains splashed in courtyards filled with the golden sunlight of the deep south. On frosty winter nights when the stars seem to hang like lanterns in the clear air over the vast expanses of the plain, the Emperor and his huntsmen would ride in by the great gate, flanked by imperial eagles, to sup before blazing fires of olive wood, and to discuss the day's chase.

The Crusade put a temporary stop to the Emperor's building activities, but no sooner was the realm pacified anew than they began again in real earnest, and it was to his favourite province of Apulia that Frederick first turned his attention. Unlike the majority of his contemporaries, the Emperor concentrated upon building for the practical necessities of government and for his own pleasure; in later years the Church was to reproach him with having created no pious foundations such as churches and monasteries and, with the exception of the Cathedral of Altamura, which was begun early in his reign, this was true. The monuments that Frederick left behind him were almost entirely lay in character and from this fact, which was so unusual at that time, springs their unique interest.

Little trace has survived of the smaller buildings, but the massive solidity of the castles has withstood the shock of earthquakes, wars and the usurping Angevins' desire to erase all trace of the hated house of Hohenstaufen.

The Apulian castles were the earliest of the Emperor's creations. Primarily they were designed for coast defence, the control of strategic roads, and other military purposes. Most of them served as royal residences as well and some were designed purely for what Frederick termed *loca solatiorum nostrum*—our places of solace—and of these the famous hunting box of Castel del Monte is the supreme example.

The year 1230 saw the beginnings of this vast building plan, and two of the coastal defence castles which were initiated about this time have survived in recognisable Frederician form until today. No longer a heterogeneous group of buildings as at Melfi, but skilfully designed, they stand foursquare, built of massive rusticated blocks of Apulian stone, guarding the harbours of Bari and Trani. Their square corner towers which still frown down upon the blue waters of the Adriatic are pierced by lancets at the lower levels, but higher up arched and rose-shaped windows give some hint that their purpose was not purely defensive. Inside, in spite of subsequent centuries of maltreatment as prisons or barracks, some vestiges of their former grandeur still remain.

At Bari Frederick built upon the foundations of a Norman castle, and some of the towers probably date from that period, but the vaulted, pillared entrance hall with its mixture of romanesque and saracenic styles was certainly of his own creation, as was the graceful loggia leading into the central court. The capitals of the columns are carved with acanthus leaves, with hawks and other birds, and fine geometric designs. One corbel which supports the vaulting is sculptured with a row of steel-helmeted soldiers' heads, who smile or frown down upon the observer with extraordinary liveliness. Some of these carvings are signed by Melis da Stigliano, a noted sculptor of the time whose work is to be seen in other of Frederick's castles as well as in Bari Cathedral. An open staircase led from the courtyard to the royal appartments of the *piano nobile*, in one of whose vast halls there still stands a column adorned with the imperial eagles. The castle is thought to have been built under the direction of Giovanni di Cicala by Riccardo di Barberia and Bartolomeo di Foggia; this last was also employed to build the Foggia Palace.

Trani Castle faces the magnificent romanesque cathedral across the waters of a small bay. Use as a prison has shorn it of all exterior adornment, but restoration might reveal many hidden treasures. Even in its present sad state the interior is rich in romanesque windows whose surrounds are sculptured with birds and flowers. The remains of a regal staircase, whose vaulted canopy rested upon sculptured corbels, can still be clearly seen. Some curious cantilevered stone steps leading to the battlements are also intact, though smothered by subsequent buildings. An inscription on the sea wall records that the castle was finally completed in 1249 by Philippe Chinard, Stefano di Trani and Romoaldo di Bari.

Of the military castles that of Oria was the earliest. It was begun prior to the Crusade and finished in 1233. It controls the important route between the ports of Brindisi and Taranto, and is in an excellent state of preservation, but its early origin and purely military character make it the least typically Frederician among the Apulian castles. Like the fortress of Lucera, which was begun in the year that Oria was finished, this castle consists of an immense walled enclosure guarded at intervals by towers. Both these military castles were built upon a classical site. Here, however, the resemblance ends; whereas Oria was simply a castle garrisoned by a small force, Lucera was the centre of the imperial Moslem army.

Between 1222 and 1226 Frederick had transported some sixteen thousand Moslems from Sicily to the great rolling plains of the Tovaliere that surround the steep sides of the rocky outcrop upon which Lucera stands. To begin with these exiles were engaged upon agricultural work—the reclamation and farming of the barren plains—then, possibly as a result of the warlike prowess of the Saracen contingent which he took with him on Crusade, the Emperor decided to recruit his former enemies into his own army. To provide an administrative centre for this foreign legion the Emperor built upon the ruins of the Roman *castrum* an immense fortress which covers the entire summit of the hill. The formidable brick walls were reinforced at regular intervals by square and polygonal towers and, in what is now a desert, there arose an entire Saracen town complete with mosques and dwellings for a population of many thousand souls.

Here dwelt the dreaded companies of Saracen cross-bowmen, and here Moslem craftsmen forged weapons of the world-famous damascened steel. These followers of Mohammed who had eaten the salt of the Catholic Emperor prepared for use against his Christian enemies the poisoned arrows and the hellish brew known as "Greek Fire" whose raw materials—sulphur and crude oil—existed in quantities in the Realm of Sicily. They were experts too in the construction of engines of war; those huge catapults, mangonels, and trebuchets, which could in time destroy even the massive walls of mediaeval castles. No wonder Frederick turned a deaf ear to ecclesiastical requests for the conversion of this redoubtable army for whom interdict and excommunication held no terrors. It is difficult to imagine a modern parallel to these Saracen legions of the Emperor, or to realise the terror they inspired in the Christian world.

In the centre of this strange fortress the Emperor built himself a castle. This took the form of an immense tower-like keep whose scarped rectangular base was heavily fortified, and above this rose an octagonal tower, in whose centre was a paved courtyard with a fountain or well. Its vaulted rooms were furnished with great luxury, and we know that it contained classical statues of bronze—the figure of a man and a cow which had adorned a fountain at the ancient Basilean monastery of Grottaferrata—and that antique works of art were brought overland from Naples for its embellishment. From the windows of his great tower the Emperor could enjoy magnificent views over the endless spaces of the Apulian plain, that even today impresses the observer with its solitary grandeur, and which in this area still retains its ancient Byzantine appellation of the Capitanata.

Within the fastnesses of this keep was stored part of the imperial treasure watched over by the Saracens of the royal bodyguard; here too were hidden the most intimate secrets of Frederick's personal life. In the secluded chambers of this tower lived the beautiful Saracen dancing girls for whom, in November 1239, Frederick wrote from far away Lodi to order robes lined with marten fur, linen underclothes and capes of silk. They had women servants to wait upon them and were guarded by eunuchs; some of them usually accompanied the Emperor upon his constant journeys. They travelled in considerable luxury with numerous possessions, and at the siege of Parma some of them fell into the hands of Frederick's enemies because they refused to jettison their baggage in order to make good their escape.

According to Frederick these women were simply troupes of entertainers whom he kept for his amusement and that of his court; and that he delighted in the skill and grace of Arab dancing girls is well known. But there is little reason to doubt the stories put about by the Guelf faction that they were members of an extensive harem in which the Emperor indulged his taste for erotic pleasures. In fact he was so attached to these dancing girls that although their presence at his court was regarded as prima facie evidence for the charges of heresy and immorality which were brought against him by Innocent IV at the Council of Lyons in 1245, and although in his eagerness at that time to make peace with the Pope Frederick promised to dismiss them, some of them were still in camp with him at the siege of Parma in 1248. It is true that the drawings of these dancers to be found in the margins of Matthew Paris's manuscript which were based on the description of Richard of Cornwall, who had actually seen them, are chaste indeed. But, given Frederick's extreme partiality for women—he had some eleven illegitimate children, mostly by different mothers—it seems unlikely that his relations with these constant travelling companions were in any sense platonic. He was an epicure and a sensualist, brought up in a semi-Oriental country, and had a marked preference for many aspects of Eastern life; to such a man it would not seem strange to live as his Norman predecessors, the "baptised Sultans", had done in the midst of a harem.

Only the vast rectangular base of this mysterious Lucera tower now remains, where the ruined galleries for the Saracen archers of the guard and the water cisterns can still be traced; the courtyard, fountain, and the luxurious chambers of the imperial apartment have all long since disappeared. Contemporary with Lucera and the other Apulian castles, but not entirely of Frederick's construction, is the castle of Gioia del Colle—the earliest of his Apulian hunting boxes to have survived. Much of Gioia is Norman, and it may originally have been built to guard the road from Bari to Taranto, but for Frederick it was pre-eminently a pleasure house, with no other defences than those afforded by its great towers of rusticated stone and the marshy land that lay to the north. The site was certainly chosen for the good hunting for the Emperor's falcons which was to be had over the open rolling downland of the surrounding Murge hills.

Gioia is among the smallest and most intimate of Frederick's castles to have survived, and owing to the comparative absence of subsequent alterations it is possible to arrive at a very clear idea of what it must have been like in the Emperor's own day. Its modernity is really surprising; the external doors and windows are framed by arches of finely wrought rusticated stone, and are more reminiscent of a Florentine Renaissance palace than a castle of the thirteenth century. The central courtyard is light and airy, and has an open staircase and loggia also in the style of a Florentine palace. This leads into the rooms of the *piano nobile* which are well lit by graceful Gothic windows, adorned with stone tracery and sculptured with flowers and birds; above some of them the imperial eagle is still to be seen. Stone seats flank the embrasures of the windows and surround the walls of the principal hall—known as the throne room, from a throne lately reconstructed from ancient fragments discovered in the castle. Unlike modern houses in the area, all the principal rooms of Gioia Castle are furnished with commodious fireplaces, and indeed this imperial suite is much more habitable by modern standards than many local palaces of later periods. These were no vast mediaeval halls but well-lit, well-ventilated rooms of a reasonable size, with beamed wooden ceilings in the Norman style, excepting in the tower rooms which have fine vaulted stone roofs.

The castle evokes a picture of a fortified country house built for the gatherings of a small court, a group of intimates, who for a time cast court etiquette aside in the enjoyment of pleasures shared—a long day's hunting in the sun and wind of a southern Italian winter day, then music and good conversation around the fire at night.

It is a castle, however, which is unlikely to have known the drunken revelry of boon companions, for Frederick was both fastidious and abstemious. He, himself, ate only one main meal a day, but in food as in the other comforts of life he liked the best. His cook, Berard, was famous for the preparation of *scapece*—a dish that is said to have originated with Apicius, the Brillat Savarin of classical times—and which is still eaten in southern Apulia on feast days. *Scapece* consists of fish or vegetables, such as young marrows or aubergines, fried and then marinaded in a sauce prepared with saffron and wine vinegar.

Frederick also seems to have been particularly fond of the delicately cured ham known as *prosciutto* in Italy, and Jambon de Parme abroad, for a letter is still extant, written from Sarzano in 1239, ordering "good prosciutti for our court". Cheeses mentioned in documents of the Hohenstaufen court are still renowned in Italy today. In his book on falconry Frederick describes one—a kind of cottage cheese still made from ewe's or cow's milk—which he recommended for feeding falcons. He also noted that dogs are particularly fond of cheese, a piece of personal observation this, culled no doubt from scraps welcomed under the supper table by his favourite hounds.

The vegetables cultivated in Italian kitchen gardens of the thirteenth century included asparagus, spinach, cucumbers, marrows, cauliflowers, leeks, turnips, scallions, salads such as endive and cresses, and an immense range of herbs—basil, thyme, parsley, hyssop, marjoram and several varieties of mint. The Realm of Sicily was also renowned for its many varieties of fruit. Grapes, melons, pears, damsons, citrus fruits, figs, dates, and almonds abounded there in a period when many of them were unknown or rare delicacies in Northern Europe. Raisins and other dried fruits and nuts were already a family dessert. Sugar had been grown in Sicily since the time of the Norman kings and was used in the preparation of medicinal sirops as well as for puddings. Aspics of some kind evidently also featured upon the royal menus, as a chancery note is still extant ordering good fish from the lake of Lesina, near Foggia, for the famous *scapece* and for making *gelatinum* that was probably a variety of aspic akin to that which is still called *gelatina* in Southern Italy today. Another chancery note orders "real pepper", a very great luxury at the time, for the Emperor's table. Orders for wine are frequent in the court registers; among them occurs one special order for Greek wine, and another for the wine of Gallipoli, in Apulia, which is still famous. Thus it is evident that viands that appeared upon the Emperor's table must have presented a far greater variety than was possible for his contemporaries in Northern Europe, and their very character suggests a much lighter diet than the haunches of venison and barons of salt beef which the rigours of northern winters imposed even upon the kings and nobility of other countries.

The promulgation of the first Constitution of Melfi, in 1231, with its centralisation of the governmental power and supres-

sion of the civic rights that had previously been enjoyed by
many of the Sicilian towns, resulted in a series of risings in the
island, so serious as to call for the personal presence of the
Emperor. Frederick was forced to return to the island and
evidently made a more detailed study of conditions than at any
period since 1221, which resulted, among other things, in his
decision to build a series of castles. With the exception of those
built at Enna and Caltagirone, both important inland centres of
communication, these Sicilian castles were designed primarily
for coast defence but also to provide convenient bases for the
royal administration and garrisons. At Caltagirone, Trapani,
Termini, Lentini and Milazzo, Frederick appears to have been
content to enlarge and reinforce existing castles, but at Syracuse,
Catania and Enna he embarked upon entirely new constructions,
though previous castles or fortifications were already in existence. At Augusta he built a castle and founded an entirely
new town.

These last four, which are by far the best preserved of the
Frederician castles in Sicily, were, like those of Apulia, evidently intended to serve as palaces as well, for they too were
furnished and decorated with very considerable luxury. Earthquakes and other hazards have robbed all but the Castello Ursino
at Catania of their *piani nobili*, where the royal apartments were
usually situated, but even in their present truncated state the
Sicilian castles impress the observer not only with their massive
strength, but also with the fine workmanship of their architectural details.

The castle at Syracuse, still called the Castello Maniace after
the Greek fortress which originally stood upon the site, was the
first to be built. Already in this prototype the strong French
Gothic influence, which is evident in all the Sicilian castles,
makes its presence felt. The castle is square, built of finely dressed
stone blocks, and has an immensely strong round tower at each
corner. The main gate is in the form of a Gothic arch and
flanked by pillars of red Breccia marble surmounted by lions.
High on the wall on either side are stone corbels that were
built to hold two magnificent bronze rams of ancient Greek
workmanship; one of these has survived and is now one of the
chief treasures of Palermo Museum. On the sea wall opposite
the main gate are the remains of a large window which must

have commanded magnificent views over the reaches of the blue Mediterranean. Inside, the castle is today a complete ruin, but it is still possible to recognise some traces of its former amenities: the huge stone fireplace is also flanked by consoles which once held what long-lost treasures of classical antiquity? The capitals of the pilasters are sculptured to resemble ferns or palm fronds adorned with flowers, and stone couches surround the walls in the same manner as in the throne room of Gioia del Colle. In the now ruined corner towers were rooms with vaulted stone ceilings supported by sculptured corbels; some of these are carved with lions; and on one of them is the head of a clean-shaven young man, whose long wavy hair is surmounted by a crown. This is thought by some to be a portrait of the Emperor, but until it is cleaned of its present encrustations of soot and grime any serious attempt at identification is impossible.

The Castello Ursino at Catania though smaller is built upon the same lines as Castel Maniace and its better state of preservation enables the observer to form a very clear idea of what the castle was originally like. Much of the thirteenth-century system of plumbing has survived and the lavatories are of an efficiency remarkable for the period, being furnished not only with the usual commodities but also with a small alcove cut into the wall to contain the chamber-pot. In one of the larger rooms the ancient classical method of vault construction employing terra-cotta jars, to lighten the load, was evidently employed.

Like the castles of Syracuse and Catania, that of Augusta is rectangular in shape, enclosing a central courtyard. It is the largest of the Sicilian castles, and in its massive strength in some respects it recalls the castles of Apulia, for like them some of its square and polygonal towers are built of great blocks of rusticated stone. Augusta Castle is at present used as a prison, and access to it is difficult in consequence, but the existence of cisterns and water conduits in its towers suggests that in Frederician times some of them may have been furnished with the exceptional luxury of bathrooms.

At Enna (Castrogiovanni in mediaeval times) there already existed in the thirteenth century a large fortress, known as the Castle of the Lombards, a very necessary defence in the case of a town which was the strategically important communications centre of the island. The massive octagonal tower which stands on a small hill to the west of Enna was for long considered to have been built by Frederick II of Aragon, whose favourite place of residence Enna was. More recent research has, however, shown that the tower was in fact built by Frederick II of Hohenstaufen, and that in spite of later external alterations it still shares certain architectural features with the famous Castel del Monte. The tower now contains only two octagonal chambers, one above the other, linked by a spiral stair built in the thickness of the wall. Originally, however, there were probably a third storey and external balconies; moreover, the tower was surrounded by an octagonal curtain wall six feet thick, within whose defensive encirclement there would have been additional buildings for housing attendants and stabling. In the documents of the Aragonese kings of the next century the Enna tower is referred to as a "Regia Domus" or "Regium Solacium", and, in spite of its fortified aspect, it was probably designed by Frederick as a small pleasure house and refuge from the torrid heat of the Sicilian summer (Enna stands at a height of about three thousand feet, and the nights are cool there even in August), for the Emperor was partial to the town, and the wild beauty and classical associations of the surrounding countryside would have held a special appeal for him.

With the exception of the Enna tower, these Sicilian castles of the Emperor were all part of his plan for the centralised control and government of the island part of his realm; their functions as fortresses and administrative centres are clear in this respect. The Castellans were imperial officials recruited, almost certainly, from another area of the realm; sometimes even they were foreigners, as was the case in Cefalu in 1239 where the castle was handed over to the care of "our prudent and faithful Hugo the Englishman". What does seem to betoken an unwarranted extravagance to modern eyes, however, is the luxury of their appointments as royal residences as well, for these castles were situated at a distance of from twenty to forty miles from each other in the eastern province of Sicily, and the island was already well provided with royal palaces.

Moreover it is evident from the documents in the imperial archives that a permanent domestic staff was maintained in them at the royal expense; though this aspect of the matter evidently aroused Frederick's concern as a canny administrator, for in 1240 we find him writing from Foligno to his administrator in the castle of Messina with instructions to set the maids "to spinning or some other useful work so that they do not eat their bread in idleness".

Why, then, did a sovereign who kept such careful personal control upon the purse strings of his budget expend large sums to provide himself with what seems to have been such a superfluity of residences? The answer lies in the need for personal control if Frederick's intention of defeudalising and centralising the state was to be carried through in an age when the administrative services were in their infancy, and posts and telegraphs non-existent; and when, of necessity, a ruler depended upon his own observation or that of his trusted representatives. Thus Frederick with his far-flung domains and world-wide interests travelled constantly, and the courtiers and statesmen in his service unceasingly. Men like Hermann von Salza and Pietro della Vigna must have spent half their lives in the saddle, riding day after weary day along the atrocious roads of mediaeval Europe, which were rivers of mud in winter and dust bowls during the summer. The strain imposed by the hardships of this kind of travel were tremendous, and it is not surprising to find that so capable an organiser as the Emperor, with the vast means that he had at his disposal, arranged matters so that as often as possible these journeys could be broken for himself and his entourage by a period of comfort and ease while staying in one of his castles or *loca solatiorum*.

Many of the contemporary chroniclers have preserved for us eyewitness accounts of the imperial caravan upon the march, a spectacle of unparalleled pageantry and colour. First came the advance guard of horsemen or Saracen light cavalry whose Arab steeds and unfamiliar garb struck an exotic note, the atmosphere of "apes and ivory", of Oriental glamour, with which the name of Frederick has been associated down the ages. In the midst of them padded silently along the swift-pacing camels of the famous Mehari breed—the gifts of the Emperor's friends the Sultans of Babylon and Egypt—and behind the bright-coloured curtains of the palanquins mounted upon their backs there lounged those veiled and mysterious beauties whose presence, imaginary or otherwise, added to the caravan that magnetic aura which J. Addington Symonds in another context described as "the hoofmark of illustrious crime". The palanquins were guarded by towering black men of hideous aspect—the eunuchs—at whose castration the Emperor himself was supposed to have officiated, at least according to the papal adherents, who appear to have possessed a gift for salacious gossip which might well be envied by the modern Sunday Press.

After an interval, to allow the dust to settle, would follow the court itself, and among the cavalcade of brilliantly attired knights and courtiers the watching crowds would anxiously seek to identify the Emperor himself—that terrifying personage whose titles awarded him the right to be addressed as "sacred" and "divine". There can have been little difficulty in picking out the auburn-red hair, the calm countenance, and the piercing, almost hypnotic, glance of eyes which have been variously described as blue, or "green, like a snake". The well-knit form, attired as like as not in huntsman's clothes and mounted upon the famous black charger Dragon, would have been marked out by the deference with which the trotting horsemen made a way for his passage.

Then would follow the seemingly endless train of pages and attendants attired in brightly striped tunics and ochre-coloured hose, carrying on their wrists, protected by the tasselled falconers' gloves, the precious falcons which were among the Emperor's most prized possessions. Ranging the road beside them, or coupled in pairs and led by grooms on scarlet collars and leashes would follow the imperial hounds, lean and rangy, built for speed, but shining from careful grooming and attention. Then, stranger still, the hunting leopards, the swift cheetahs, sitting with their eyes hooded like the falcons upon specially cushioned seats mounted on the crupper of the Saracen grooms who were in charge of their training.

If the journey was a long one, involving the transference of the whole court, the entire imperial menagerie would follow on. The elephant with a wooden tower upon his back in which was seated the mahout and some Saracen cross-bowmen; the giraffe whose very existence had been unknown until the Emperor imported this the first of its species ever to be brought to

Europe. Then came the lynxes, the lions, the exotic birds, and a whole train of cursing and sweating muleteers and pack-horses, upon whose backs in sacks and chests and coffers were carried the imperial treasures, the baggage, the books, the registers and documents of the imperial chancery, which had to follow wherever its royal master led. The poor scribes and notaries, responsible for producing order out of chaos at the journey's end, riding to and fro in the dust to ensure that none of the precious packages slipped, or if a beast went lame, that another was there to take its place so that everything should be ready for the Emperor's requirements at the end of the long day's march.

In 1233, with the Peace of Ceprano only three years behind him, Frederick could already look back upon some remarkable achievements—the reorganisation of the legal and adminis-trative system of the realm by the Constitutions of Melfi, the assurance of its sea and land communications by the network of Apulian and Sicilian fortresses, the foundation of new towns, notably Augusta and Lucera, and the resettlement of the hostile Moslem tribesmen as docile farmworkers, or obedient legion-aries, in Apulia.

In the creation of the Apulian and Sicilian castles the Emperor had already shown himself to be, like most great rulers, a liberal patron of the master builders and artists of his kingdom. The architects of the Sicilian castles are unknown, but in Apulia the craftsmen and sculptors whose skill had hitherto been chiefly devoted to the creation of churches and cathedrals had been diverted to the building of castles and palaces, which were the material expression in stones and marble of the lay state whose creation was the Emperor's goal.

Hitherto, apart from demanding far higher standards of domestic comfort, superior to anything known in Christian Europe since classical times, Frederick had apparently been content to leave the actual design and style of the castles to the men who built them, taking a personal hand only in the matter of their furnishing and adornment. Before his time, builders, churchmen and princes had made use of the ruins of antiquity only as quarries for stone and pillars or to provide richly coloured marble fragments for the creation of those splendid church pavements which we know as "opus alexandrum"; a few had robbed classical burial grounds of their sculptured sarcophagi to be used afresh as tombs. Until Frederick came upon the scene, however, no one appears to have regarded sculptures of the ancient world as works of art for the adornment of their own homes.

Some faint stirrings of interest in the ruins of classical Rome itself had found expression in the last half of the twelfth century in the earliest guide book to the city ever to be written—the *Mirabilia Urbis Romae*—in which for the first time some attention was paid to the monuments themselves and not simply to their religious significance as the scene of early Christian martyrdoms.

Love of the learning and wisdom of the ancient world Frederick had somehow acquired during his troubled childhood, and now in his maturity he was the first, not only of his generation but for another century and a half, to recognise and appreciate the glories of classical sculpture, and to cherish it and try to reproduce its perfection in his own time. The first hint of Frederick's remarkable artistic insight, which marks him out so clearly as the earliest protagonist of the Renaissance in Italy, was the design of the gold coinage—the Augustales.

In the spring of 1234, the Emperor visited the town of Capua with his son Conrad. For two years past a great work of clearance had been in progress in the northern suburb, in preparation for the erection of new fortifications to guard the bridge across the Garigliano river, whose meanderings rendered the city wellnigh impregnable and can still create a very formidable barrier, as the Allied armies discovered in the autumn of 1944.

The importance of these new fortifications was not to be limited to the military field. They were to create a revolution in the world of art, for the defences of the Capuan bridge were to be the first herald of the Renaissance—the first glimmerings of a light which was not to dawn for more than a hundred years but which if Frederick's vision had triumphed might well have illuminated the Realm of Sicily in the first half of the thirteenth century.

It is significant that for the creation of this revolutionary design the Emperor did not employ an architect or master builder but drew it "with his own hand"; for this we have the authority of Riccardo di San Germano, one of the most reliable of mediaeval chroniclers and one, moreover, who was particularly well-informed upon all the doings of the Emperor because he was a member of the court circle.[8]

Frederick is known to have been well-versed in the mechanical arts, and in the fortified gate which was to defend the Garigliano bridge, he wished to re-create after his own fashion the triumphal arches of the Roman Caesars, whom he regarded as his predecessors. The gate consisted of two massive polygonal bases surmounted by two round towers that flanked the roadway leading to the bridge. These towers were joined by the triumphal arch which was adorned with sumptuous marbles and sculptured busts and trophies. The gate was probably only finally completed about 1247, and became the wonder and admiration of the surrounding countryside. When in 1557 all but its foundations were destroyed to make way for fortifications adapted to the use of cannon, the people of Capua wept to see their beloved triumphal gate destroyed. But its memory was perpetuated in the triumphal arch of the Aragonese victors over the usurping Angevins in Naples, and Frederick's design served ultimately as a source of inspiration for this monument which is one of the glories of the Italian Renaissance.[9]

Some rough pen and ink drawings conserved in the imperial archives of Vienna enable us to form an idea of what the Capuan gate must have looked like during its period of glory; and the patient excavations and researches of modern scholars have added to this small sum of knowledge. In the construction of the towers Frederick revived the ancient classical art of stone cutting, in the rare style known as chamfer and fillet, of which original examples were close to hand for copying in the ruins of the ancient Capuan amphitheatre. The angles of the tower bases were surmounted by a series of terms sculptured in the form of human heads; and the diversity of feature and expression of these sculptures indicates that they were probably portraits of members of the court. They were of both sexes and varying ages; the heads of two women and an elderly man, with deep-set eyes, are of outstanding vigour and liveliness. The sculptures are now preserved in Capua Museum, together with the more important ones which adorned the central triumphal arch itself.

Travellers who saw the gate before its destruction describe it as being surmounted by antique statues taken from the ruins of classical Capua, while further down was placed the sculptured figure of the Emperor wearing his crown, and flanked by busts of his statesmen. Below this was the bust of a woman wearing upon her breast the imperial eagle, personifying the Imperial Justice or faithfulness of Capua to the Emperor's cause. The gate itself was formed of purest white marble, and surrounded by trophies of Frederick's victories. How many of these sculptures were genuinely antique and how many were the work of Frederick's "Imperial" school of Capua will probably never now be known, for only some of them have survived.

Though seriously damaged, enough exists of the most important sculptures of this group to prove that in them Frederick did indeed seek to revive sculpture in the classical style of ancient Rome. Apart from the portrait of himself portrayed full-length seated upon his throne and draped in the robes of Caesar, the other surviving sculptures include portraits of two of his most famous statesmen who were natives of the Capuan province, and allegorical heads in the style of classical deities.

The figure of the Emperor, though sadly mutilated and lacking head, feet and hands, was evidently executed by a sculptor of considerable ability, inspired by the statues of antiquity, who in his treatment of the draperies has caught much of the classical feeling. The busts of the two statesmen—Pietro della Vigna and Thaddeus of Sessa—are executed in the same style, with classical robes knotted up on their chests and wreaths of laurel leaves encircling their heads; their curling hair and beards were evidently modelled upon those of some classical sage or philosopher. But there the resemblance with the antique model ceases, the faces themselves have great individuality and animation and for all their solemnity there is a suggestion of the enigmatic smile of Gothic sculpture completely alien to the classical world. Small details of the workmanship, too, betray the fact that these busts, which at the first cursory glance might appear to be classical, could never in fact have come from the hand of an antique sculptor. The wreaths of laurel leaves, though finely worked, stand away from the heads as a solid entity on their own, in a manner which was unknown in antique times, and the heads themselves are too flat and round to be mistaken for classical work.

The other surviving sculptural fragments—the head of the bust representing the fidelity of Capua and another of Jupiter—bear stronger resemblance to their classical prototypes. The Capua head was evidently inspired by some ancient representation of the goddess Juno, possibly the famous Farnese Juno which is now in Naples Museum. Mutilation has been powerless to rob this really remarkable work of art of its capacity to impress us still. The serenity of the expression, the ghost of a smile, and the straying locks which escape from the confinement of a garland of vine tendrils show that the inspiration of the Emperor's will had awakened that which could inform the spirit of the antique world with new life, and this is the true measure of Frederick's achievement.

In his dream of reviving the Roman Empire in his own time Frederick was not inspired by visions of unlimited imperial power, but with the conception of a whole new world based upon the wisdom and learning of classical times, in which the arts and sciences would flourish as they had of old. It was to be a renaissance of the spirit of man, not in the ecclesiastical sense, but in that which blossomed in Florence during the next century. The real significance of these Capuan sculptures lies in the fact that when so much else has been swept away, they have survived—poor mutilated fragments that they are—as a monument to what might have been. They were the fruit of the few years of tranquillity which Frederick enjoyed after the Peace of Ceprano. What might he not have achieved if he had reigned in one of the more tranquil periods of Europe's history?

Who were these sculptors of the "Imperial school" of Capua? What were their origins and what other works did they achieve? These questions are likely to remain unanswered for so little of their work has survived. One thing only is certain—they owed the inspiration, which led them to revive the classical art of Rome, entirely to their patron the Emperor. Southern Italy had produced nothing like these sculptures since the fall of the Roman Empire, and would not again for more than a hundred years, though the seeds which they sowed were transplanted to another soil and in Niccolò Pisano produced the first budding of the Renaissance.

Some other examples of the work of this school have survived in Southern Italy, most famous among them being the head of a woman that stands upon the pulpit of Ravello Cathedral. Its provenance is unknown, though it is likely that the model was a member of the Rufolo family. Its creation is variously attributed to the artist who created the pulpit itself—Nicola, son of Bartolomeo da Foggia, who worked upon Frederick's castles, or to the great Niccolò Pisano himself. Another head of a woman of a slightly later period, which was discovered in the neighbouring village of Scala, is now in the Berlin Museum.

A very important addition to this meagre list of survivals has recently been made by the discovery in Barletta of a portrait bust of the Emperor himself. It has been severely damaged— the nose is missing and the forehead and mouth are badly scarred—but enough remains to convince the beholder that this is a consummate portrait of the man. Humour is written clearly upon the face, and great vivacity is evident in the speaking attitude in which it is portrayed. The profile reveals a firm chin, and the deep-set eyes convey an underlying impression of a capacity for ruthlessness and cruelty that is concealed by the irresistible charm of the expression of the head when seen full face. The genius of the sculptor enabled him to portray at one and the same time these conflicting aspects of Frederick's character described by so many of his contemporaries.

The style of the bust is similar to that of the Capuan sculptures. The shoulders are swathed in classical draperies, held at one side by a fibula inscribed with the letters S.P.Q.R.; the head is crowned with laurels; and a much-mutilated inscription on the base may be interpreted as DIVI FRI CAE—signifying in abbreviated Latin form the Emperor's style and titles DIVI FRIDERICI CAESARIS—Divine Frederick Caesar's, to which it was probably intended to add the word IMAGO—image or portrait. The classicism is limited, however, to the dress and laurel crown; the portrayal of the man himself is clearly mediaeval— the long "page boy" cut of the hair curling at the ends; the pronounced naturalism of the portraiture which candidly discloses the lined forehead, the wrinkles round the eyes, the deep furrows from nostril to jaw; the dryness of the flesh, hollowed under the cheekbones; and the slightly crooked smile.

Thirteenth-century fresco in the church of San Pellegrino at Bominaco, near Aquila

A southern Italian lady of the thirteenth century

Castel del Monte

The somatic characteristics of the face correspond to those of the Augustales, and the dry fleshlessness would be explained by the fact that the Emperor is represented here shortly before his death, when the plumpness of earlier years had given way to the emaciating effects of a stomach complaint from which he ultimately died.

The last two castles that Frederick built in Apulia contain sculptured decorations which are also the work of artists of the "Imperial school" of Capua. With the exception of a headless bust, these are mere architectural details that give a luxurious finish to the main lines of the buildings, but for all that they were evidently the work of highly skilled craftsmen and are imbued with the same striking admixture of classical feeling and personal vivacity. Of these two castles, one—Castel del Monte—is so closely associated with the Emperor's name that it, rather than the porphyry tomb in Palermo Cathedral, should be considered as his monument. The other—Castel Lagopesole—lost in a remote valley on the borders of Apulia, is practically unknown to the outside world and during the last century was described, by an otherwise eminent authority, as being a heap of ruins.

Golden as the limestone hills upon which it stands, and from whose heart its great blocks were hewn, Castel del Monte crowns the summit of the Murge like an imperial diadem. The castle is formed of two concentric octagons (the inner one is a courtyard), and at each angle of the outer walls stand octagonal towers. Thus in its design it repeats ten times the mystic figure eight, which gave to the crown of the Empire its octagonal shape, symbolic of imperial unity, and it may be that in choosing this unique form for the castle, which is generally admitted to have been built to his personal design, Frederick wished to immortalise in stone the symbol of his Empire.

The windows of Castel del Monte command the furthest reaches of the great coastal plain of Apulia on one hand, and upon the other the barren country of the Murge. It is a wild, windswept place, which even on a spring day of the twentieth century conveys a feeling of limitless horizons, of isolation from the world of men, and of close affinity with that of nature. Sparrow-hawks hang balancing in the wind and the air seems to be rent by the swiftness of their passage as they stoop towards

G

their prey. Just so, seven centuries ago, must Frederick have watched his falcons hunting over the same Murge hills, when he managed to escape for a few days from the cares of state.

Castel del Monte is the finest and best preserved of the Frederician castles that have survived, and the theories as to the origins of the eclecticism of its unique style have filled volumes, but it has now come to be generally accepted that the Emperor himself was the architect. The only contemporary documentary reference to the castle occurs in a dispatch in the imperial registers of 1240, in which the Emperor instructed the Justiciar of the Capitanata to see urgently to the paving, which indicated that the building was probably very nearly complete at that time. In all likelihood work on the castle was begun during the early thirties, possibly about the same time as the Sicilian castles, and in its general outline Castel del Monte is more akin to the Gothic style of the Sicilian castles, with their round or polygonal towers of finely dressed stone, than the rectangular masses of rusticated blocks that characterise the other Apulian castles.

Here, however, the resemblance ends, for Castel del Monte with its repetition of the octagonal form is in a class by itself. The octagon, which appears to have held a particular attraction for Frederick, as the Enna tower and the imperial residence at Lucera bear witness, had for long been favoured in the Orient. The famous Dome of the Rock at Jerusalem rests upon an octagon which also appears frequently in early Georgian churches. We know that the Emperor had seen and admired the Dome of the Rock during his brief visit to Jerusalem, and in Palestine he may have seen other buildings in this same form, that had for him the added attraction of its imperial associations.

Castel del Monte had, therefore, both Gothic and Oriental roots, and to this was added a revival of the antique in the same spirit as the Capuan gate—for the main entrance of the castle was also inspired by the triumphal arches of Imperial Rome. This imposing portal is flanked by fluted pilasters surmounted by Corinthian capitals and crowned by a classical pediment in the Corinthian style, whose proportions are based upon the architectural canons of antiquity. The door is framed by pillars upon which rest couchant lions of red Breccia marble, reminiscent of those in the castle of Syracuse. The whole portal is rich in marbles, and so were the steps leading up to it, while the doors themselves, that were later removed by the Angevins, were of finely worked bronze. The headless fragment of a bust, similar to those of the Capuan gate, was found during the restoration of the castle. It is thought to have been a portrait of the Emperor, as ancient records state that the door was surmounted by his bust crowned with sun rays, as he is represented on some of the Augustales.

The interior of Castel del Monte consists of sixteen rooms, rhomboid in shape, contained upon two floors. The eight octagonal towers contain guard-rooms, store-rooms, lavatories, and bathrooms—these last are of extraordinary modernity—and on the first floor one of them was apparently arranged as a mews for the falcons. The external windows on the ground-floor rooms are placed high in the walls, and some of them are rather dark in consequence, but this is partly compensated for by the rich colouring of the interior fittings. The vaulting of the roof is supported by half-columns, in the shape of pilasters, of rosy Breccia marble and the walls were covered with the same material. A fragment of the original pavement has survived in one of the rooms, and it is of a richness in keeping with the rest—composed of coloured marbles and faience, probably of Saracen workmanship. Nearly all the ground-floor rooms have communicating doors, and three of them also open on to the central courtyard. In the middle of this, until the end of the eighteenth century, there was an octagonal bath hewn from a single block of white marble, with seats or steps inside. In summer the courtyard appears to have been shaded by an awning suspended in the same manner as in the ancient theatres and circuses.

There are traces of bas-reliefs having been let into the walls of the courtyard, and above one door it is possible to discern the sculptured outline of a nude equestrian figure with flowing chlamys, which is thought to have represented the Emperor. At first-floor level the courtyard was surrounded by a balcony (this was still in existence in the eighteenth century), and on to this opened three beautiful french windows of classical design, which are still in a remarkable state of preservation; they are rectangular, surmounted by an arch and flanked by finely carved marble pillars. These windows are unique in mediaeval architecture, resembling as they do the work of Palladio or some other great architect of the Renaissance.

The rooms of the first floor of the castle were evidently intended for the Emperor's own use and for that of his favoured friends and the great officers of the court. Even in their present denuded state they conjure up an atmosphere of luxury and intimacy that is extraordinary for the period in which they were built. Each room is lit by Gothic windows ornamented with carved marbles, and the walls above the marble cornice are constructed in the ancient Roman *opus reticulatum*; below they were covered with thin slabs of precious Greek marbles since vanished, as in the imperial palaces of old. The vaulting of the roof is supported by slender columns ranged in groups of three; they are of unique beauty—the marble is rose-coloured, veined with blue and lavender—and the capitals are carved to represent graceful fronds of foliage of a delicacy equal to the finest Greek workmanship. The keys of the vaulting vary in design from room to room—roses, groups of sea birds, in one case the head of a fawn. These sculptures are the work of sculptors of the "Imperial school" but they also bear a strong resemblance to the sculptures of the famous Niccolò Pisano—who was probably of Apulian origin.

The tower rooms, other than those occupied by spiral staircases of stone cut with mathematical precision, contain small octagonal chambers with finely vaulted ceilings, which lead to lavatories cut into the thickness of the wall, supplied with running water by lead pipes connected with rain-water cisterns situated in the roof.

Three of these first-floor rooms appear to have been designed as the imperial suite; they consist of an ante-room which has a french window that opened onto the balcony, and is also approached by a tower staircase connected to the falcons' mews. The ante-room opens into a second room whose triple Gothic window, the only one of this size in the castle, commands a magnificent view of Andria, most faithful among the cities of Apulia—the birthplace of the Emperor's son Conrad, and the place of burial of two of his wives. This room, together with another adjoining it, probably served as the actual living-rooms of the Emperor himself. The third room has a large open fireplace and access to two turret rooms. In one of these, as well as the usual lavatory, there appears to have been a bathroom also supplied with running water.

None of the rooms in the castle are large in size and there is no feeling of that outward pomp and circumstance, coupled with primitive domestic arrangements, which one is inclined to associate with the life of mediaeval monarchs. If all its plumbing were in working order Castel del Monte would be essentially habitable even today and here, even more than at Gioia del Colle, there is the impression of a house which was built for a man whose personal preference was for a life of seclusion, almost Oriental in its character. The small number of rooms, the intimacy of their size, the—for the period—almost incredible luxury of their appointments, bespeak the Oriental potentate rather than the European monarch of the thirteenth century. Nor do the bathrooms and the running water suggest a frowsty mediaeval atmosphere of layers of heavy clothes, rarely changed or cleaned. In an age when dirt was often considered to be an outward and visible sign of Christian chastity, the Emperor's daily bath, taken even on Sundays, was regarded as an open scandal; almost an impious slight to the Deity. Even the clerks of the imperial counting houses at Melfi and Venosa were provided with two changes of underlinen out of the privy purse; from which it seems that Frederick's court was pervaded by a most pagan atmosphere of cleanliness!

Unfortunately no imperial inventory has survived to tell us how Castel del Monte was furnished in Frederick's time, but from what we know of his tastes and habits it is possible perhaps to reconstruct some of the most essential features. The niches on either side of the fireplace in the Emperor's private rooms suggest the presence of some classical works of art, perhaps small bronze statues or Tanagra figurines of the ancient Greek workmanship that he admired so much, and in which the soil of Apulia, as a one-time province of Magna Graecia, is particularly rich. Books there would certainly have been in quantity, for we know that they accompanied Frederick on all his travels, and that the cupboards of the imperial library were filled with the works of classical authors, particularly on scientific subjects, all carefully arranged and classified. We can imagine some of them, exquisitely illuminated and bound, reposing upon a carved wooden lectern near the fire, with the Emperor's great throne-

like armchair, ornamented with gold and piled with bright silk
cushions, standing close beside it and perhaps a hound dozing
by the warm embers, on guard during his master's absence.

On cold winter nights the windows would have been screened
with rich silk curtains, and the room warmly lit by the glow of
candles set in crystal and enamelled bronze stands, and the
more intimate light of oil lamps, perhaps made in the form of the
Emperor's tame elephant, with a tower upon his back, whose
fame was perpetuated in this form even in Germany. The
walls would have been covered with rich hangings; Frederick
once ordered purple and gold damask for his wife's use. The
marble seats round the walls and low folding stools would have
been cushioned with the embroidered silk cushions whose manufacture was a speciality of the Saracen craftsmen of Sicily and
Lucera; while carpets from the Orient and from the looms of
the Messina workshops would have covered the floor. The bed
itself would have had a silken mattress and covers of cendal,
for the Emperor ordered such luxuries even for state prisoners
or hostages such as the nephew of the King of Tunis.

The dining-table may have been of marble, like the one which
is said to have come from Frederick's hunting box at Ferentino
that now serves as the high altar of Lucera Cathedral. The top
is made of one superb slab of polished marble, and the legs are
in the form of small romanesque columns. The covers would
have been of finest linen; all flax produced by the demesne was
an imperial perquisite, and, judging from the service that
formed part of the Princess Isabella's dowry, the plate was
magnificent—of purest silver and gold exquisitely chiselled and
wrought.[10]

Such riches and luxury were all the more remarkable when
they were enjoyed in the isolation of a remote hill-top of the
Murge, miles from the nearest town. This aspect of Frederick's
tastes shows him to have been a follower of the Roman emperors
and a precursor of the Renaissance princes, both of whom built
for themselves palatial pleasure houses in the country, where
they might enjoy the beauties of nature and study in peace the
writings of the classical authors. Frederick in fact might be
termed the first of the humanists, for in his love of the beauties
of nature (shared, it seems, among his contemporaries only by
St. Francis and by the poets of his own court) and the amazing

versatility of his cultural activities he was far closer to the complete man of the Renaissance than to the mediaeval world in which he lived.

The last of the castles which the Emperor built illustrates perhaps better even than Castel del Monte his capacity for selecting a site of incomparable natural beauty. Although Castel Lagopesole, as it is called, was in actual fact a military castle, guarding the road from Melfi to Potenza, it was built on the site of one of Frederick's hunting boxes, and in its final state was intended to serve both as a fortress and one of the *loca solatiorum*. It crowns a small hill-top at the head of a green valley nearly three thousand feet above sea-level, which is dominated by the immense forested bulk of Monte Vulture. Even today these forests are the largest in Italy outside the Alpine areas, and they are still the haunt of wolves. The sheep-dogs of the valley wear metal collars studded with sharp spikes to protect them in their affrays with the wolves that attack the flocks in cold weather, and in this remote place time does not seem to have moved very much from the days when the Emperor used to send instructions to his administrators to put out wolf powders to destroy the vermin which wrought havoc in the imperial game preserves.

Lagopesole owes its name to the Lacus Pensilis, the hanging lake now drained, in which the river Brandado had its source. Thus within easy reach of the castle there were to be found fish and the waterfowl which were a favourite prey for the imperial falcons; bear and wild boar also abounded in the forests of the Monte Vulture. It was to the cool seclusion of his *domus solatiorum* in this natural game preserve that the Emperor would withdraw with a group of intimate friends during the great heat of the summer while the main body of the court remained in its summer quarters in Melfi Castle.

Castel Lagopesole was begun in 1242 and not entirely completed at the time of the Emperor's death, but it was evidently habitable for some time before then, for Frederick spent the last summer of his life there in 1250. It is a vast rectangular mass of roughly hewn stone, towerless, but reinforced at one corner by a huge buttress reminiscent of that of Crac des Chevaliers in Syria. Lagopesole resembles neither the Apulian nor the Sicilian castles, though in some of its architectural details it is akin to Castel del Monte—two stone corbels of the donjon tower were evidently the work of the same group of sculptors. One of these takes the form of a fawn's head similar to that of Castel del Monte, the other represents a woman's head which resembles the terms of the Capuan gate.

The zigzag approach to the castle up the steep scarp of the hill ends with a sharp turn from right to left; this would force anyone approaching the castle to present his unshielded side to the archers on watch at the loopholes. Lagopesole shares this defensive feature with the fortress of Lucera, and in its vast size it is perhaps closer to the Saracen citadel than any of the other Frederician castles. The interior is divided into two courtyards, both of which were evidently mainly given over to the use of the garrison, though the whole of the north-western side of one of them was occupied by the royal residence.

This palace is now unfortunately a ruin, but in the few architectural features which have survived, the kinship, though in a rougher style, with Castel del Monte is evident. The main entrance door resembles those which open on to the courtyard of the Andria Castle, and it too was surmounted by the nude figure of a horseman with flowing chlamys. Red Breccia marble was employed for the window surrounds and for the corbels, whose sculptured fronds repeat the same designs as those of the capitals in the ground-floor rooms of Castel del Monte. Bathrooms and lavatories also exist here, cut into the thickness of the wall as in the Andria Castle, and here again there exists the complicated system of pipes and water-catchment from the roof.

It is not from these mutilated fragments of former grandeur that the castle takes its atmosphere, but from the natural splendour of its situation. The royal apartment looks out towards the Monte Vulture, and its high Gothic windows command a view of truly imperial splendour as the last rays of the setting sun etch the cone of the volcano with deep purple shadows, and it appears to erupt anew in the radiance of the dying day. The surrounding valley is already shadowed in gloom of the coming night, while the castle on its eminence is still bathed in the roseate light, and seems as if isolated from the world below. This is indeed "such stuff as dreams are made on", and who can tell what thoughts of past glories and future splendours such a scene may not have conjured up in the Emperor's mind when he chose this wild and beautiful spot as one of his "places of solace"?

Mercifully for Frederick the future, whose secrets his astrologers vainly tried to pierce, remained as inscrutable to him as for any man. He could not foresee that these magnificent palaces would one day witness the doom of his dynasty.

Chapter VIII

" POI CHE TI PIACE AMORE "

ONE of the most vivid pictures that has come down to us of life at the imperial court occurs in the famous chronicle of Fra Salimbene; in it he describes the scene outside the house in which the Emperor lived at Pisa. This was apparently surrounded by a garden with a vine loggia that threw a grateful shade, and according to Fra Salimbene's eyewitness account it presented a spectacle filled with gaiety—a crowd of young men and women in brightly coloured clothes played harps and violins, while others sang and danced to the music, and the rest stood looking on, holding on the leash leopards and other strange beasts from across the seas. Crowds from the town had gathered to witness the colourful scene which they watched in silent admiration.

In following the great events of the period—the Crusade, the wars with the Lombard communes, and the long-drawn-out struggle with the papacy—it is sometimes difficult to remember that life at the imperial court was not entirely concerned with affairs of state. There were the daily round of gossip, intrigue and love affairs, dancing, festivities and hunting, the usual diversions at any period of a rich and privileged society revolving round the person of a sovereign. All the more so, in this particular case, because the Emperor himself evidently enjoyed life and was a connoisseur of its pleasures and diversions, who even when he was older still preferred to be surrounded by young people.

Contemporary custom favoured this, for it was an essential part of the education of any young man of good family to pass some years in the household of a great prince, and the sons of Spanish kings, German princes and nobles from all over Italy were eager candidates for the great honour of serving at the court of the Emperor. This valuable experience was not the monopoly of the privileged few, however; able young men like Pietro della Vigna and other brilliant jurists, while not born in the purple, climbed the ladder of promotion and fame by way of the imperial chancery, and took part in the gaieties of this brilliant court which attracted gifted men from all over Europe and even the Near East. Needless to say this type of life was very expensive, and one or two letters of these young men have survived to tell the familiar tale of the financial difficulties of keeping up with the current of fashionable life, where the need of fine clothes and horses, probably of expensive falcons and hounds as well, could land their purchaser up to his ears in debt, with his horses and his chattels impounded by dunning creditors. Fine clothes then, even more than now, were an expensive essential to court life, and we can imagine these ambitious young courtiers disporting themselves clad in the latest fashion of the time—long ample robes that reached to the ankle, but were shortened to knee length for hunting, and exchanged for armour in time of war. In summer their clothes might be made of cendal or some other light silk, dyed in brilliant primary colours and enriched at throat and wrist with fine embroidery, girt at the waist with a jewelled belt from which hung an ornamental dagger. In winter those who could afford them wore voluminous cloaks lined with rich furs, sometimes with a small shoulder cape of the same material. Their hair was worn in a long bob curled at the ends which is known to modern feminine fashion as the "page-boy cut"; when out hunting these long locks were confined by a close-fitting cap that fastened with a strap under the chin; though for riding a felt hat with a turned-up brim, prolonged into a narrow peak in front—such as Italian university students still wear today—was also much in favour.

The women's clothes were more ample, and probably even more expensive; they swept the ground in graceful folds, of wool trimmed with rich furs in winter, and in summer of cendal or other silks, embroidered at the hem with gold and silk threads, and at the neck and the borders of the flowing sleeves with gold thread and pearls, and for ladies of great wealth were ornamented with small jewelled or enamelled plaques; the dress was gathered in at the waist by a girdle similarly worked. The loose sleeves of this outer robe would fall back to show the long fitting ones of an under-dress, but young girls or serving maids might reveal their forearms bare to the elbow. Usually these clothes relied for their effect upon the jewel-like primary colours, which we can still admire in the miniatures of mediaeval manuscripts, but in the case of ladies of high position they were sometimes embroidered with an all-over pattern—a criss-cross diamond effect seems to have been particularly favoured. We know that the English Princess Isabella brought with her to Italy a London embroideress skilled in *Opus Anglicanum*, and upon great occasions she probably wore robes embroidered with this wonderful work, that looked as if it was woven of fine gold ornamented with scenes in miniature embroidered in silk thread.

Women's hair was usually parted in the middle and drawn back loosely framing the face; the lady of the famous Ravello head wears hers in this fashion surmounted by a high jewelled coronet, from which long pendants of pearls hang down on either side to her shoulders. A head-dress of similar style was buried with Frederick's first wife, Constance of Aragon, and the chronicler's description of the first court held by Charles of Anjou, after his conquest of the realm in 1266, states that matrons and even unmarried girls wore crowns adorned with pearls and other jewels like that of the Queen, from which it appears likely that this was a fashion general to ladies of rank in the Sicilian realm.

Women's slippers were made of cloth or very fine leather, elaborately embroidered and sometimes even ornamented with pearls. Their cloaks were embroidered at the edges and fastened on the breast with a jewelled brooch; in winter they were fur-lined, frequently with what appears to have been squirrel lock. When a lady went out of doors she was usually hooded and veiled, even when riding. Princess Isabella won the hearts of the matrons of Cologne by throwing hers back so that they could see her face when she rode in state through the city on her way to be married; a gesture which it is unlikely that she was ever able to repeat in the strict seclusion of her married life.

In spite of the Oriental jealousy that apparently prompted Frederick to keep his wives hidden from sight, women were certainly not banished from the court; the popularity of dancing, which is so often mentioned in the poetry of the period, affords evidence of this, but it is also confirmed by Salimbene's description of the scene at Pisa. The enjoyment of music and dancing in a garden appears to have been one of the favourite diversions of the court and even from the chancery documents it is evident that Frederick was fond of gardens. In 1239 he sent orders from Sarzana for a garden to be made at his castle at Cosenza; it was to be planted with vines—no doubt for the creation of a trellis such as Salimbene described at Pisa—for this was a feature common to gardens of the period. The Royal Palace at Syracuse also had a garden, so had two of the smaller Sicilian *loca solatiorum*, and one of them contained a grove of sweet-smelling myrtles, a large grassy meadow and fish-ponds. The art of gardening was evidently far more advanced in the Realm of Sicily than elsewhere in Europe. In 1494 Charles VIII of France wrote home a rapturous description of Neapolitan gardens and brought two Neapolitan gardeners back with him.

In his famous treatise on agriculture, written at the end of the thirteenth century, when he was nearly ninety, Pietro de Crescenzii described his ideal garden designed for a King or nobleman. This included so many of the things which are known to have existed in the pleasure gardens of Palermo and Frederick's other palaces that it is probable that their fame had spread through Italy and that they served the author as a model. This is all the more likely in view of the fact that Pietro de Crescenzii's family belonged to the Ghibelline faction in Bologna and he was exiled from the city for his political sympathies, spending most of his life in the Ghibelline cities of Central and North Italy where the imperial influence was still strong even after Frederick's death.

Pietro de Crescenzii's garden had a wood planted to the north of the palace, where wild animals could roam; to the south was a shady garden with fish-ponds, the home of deer, rabbits and birds of all kinds, especially singing birds and nightingales. It had a topiary room of clipped trees for hot days, green arbours covered with vines, and its walks were bordered with fruit trees. This garden was planted with pines, cypresses, palms and citrus fruits, and in the flower garden a fountain was situated in the midst of a grassy lawn bordered with roses, violets, lilies and sweet-smelling herbs.

This plan for Pietro de Crescenzii's royal garden might have been written to describe the background of one of those scenes of courtly life that are familiar to us from the French Gothic tapestries of a later period. The same idyllic scene lives on in the poetry of the imperial court; its lilting rhythms were designed to be set to music, often for dancing, and its words repeat with infinite variety the eternal theme of courtly love.

"Poi che ti piace Amore" are the words of the first line of a poem which is attributed to "Lo imperadore federico" in a manuscript collection of thirteenth-century poems. It sets the theme that was taken up and repeated by the song-writers of the whole court who naturally imitated an Emperor who "loved to sing, to create verses and to compose". Dante himself regarded Frederick as the father of Italian poetry, not only because the Emperor was one of the first poets to write in the Italian language, but as he says in his *De Vulgare Eloquio*: "The illustrious heroes Frederick Caesar and his noble son Manfred, followed after elegance and scorned what was mean; so that all the best compositions of the time came from their court. Thus because their royal throne was in Sicily, all the poems of our predecessors in the vulgar tongue were called Sicilian."

In the thirteenth century, Latin was still the official language of diplomacy, of court documents, and of great occasions; and poets too continued to write Latin verses, but already in daily usage among the common people it had evolved into many different dialects. Today eminent authorities advance conflicting arguments as to just why Italian poetry was born at Frederick's court; some attribute it to the heritage of the Moslem poets of the Saracen emirs of Sicily, others to the influence of the Provençal troubadors. Probably the poets of the Sicilian school owed something to both these sources, but Dante's explanation seems to be the most convincing; it was the atmosphere of the court itself that produced this sudden uprush of poetic inspiration, which found its natural means of expression in the flexibility of nascent Italian rather than in the sonorous flow of Latin.

For it was a court of youth and wit, filled with the surging currents of a new conception of life, of wider horizons, that attracted the most brilliant men and, one suspects, the most beautiful women of half the known world. Nothing like it exists in our own day or indeed since the era of the benevolent despots of the eighteenth century and the courts of the Renaissance princes which arose like phoenixes from the ashes of this imperial court's destruction. If it is possible to imagine an environment that combined the centre of world power with the elegance of Paris, the gaiety of old imperial Vienna, the erudition of the Royal Society, and the zest for life of our own Elizabethans, all brought together by the magnetic power of a dynamic personality, then it is possible to gauge the stimulating atmosphere of life as it was lived at Frederick's court.

It is unlikely that these courtier-poets set any great store by the poems which they wrote; and they would have been astounded if they could have looked into the future and seen that this elegant diversion of their leisure hours was to create a literary revolution. It was the fashionable thing to do to address love sonnets to some fair lady, whose beauty was praised above emeralds, and whose indifference, feigned or real, cast the ardent lover into the depths of despair.

The sonnet was invented by one of these poets of the Sicilian school, and its originator is believed to have been Giacomo da Lentini, who was at court in 1233, but who usually lived and worked as a notary at Catania. His poetry was admired by Dante, and he is generally conceded to have been the greatest of the Sicilian poets. Forty of his poems have survived, and many of them display an intimate love of nature which was a distinguishing characteristic of the Sicilian school. In one of his poems he compares his love to a ship tossed upon a stormy sea and a similar metaphor occurs in the verses of Pietro della Vigna.

These similes drawn from nature are one of the most surprising attributes of Sicilian poetry in a period when natural beauty was usually ignored, and they may well represent a reflection of what is known to have been the personal taste of the Emperor. One of his intimate personal friends, Percival Doria, a member of the great Ghibelline family of Genoa who was also a noted poet, wrote a beautiful poem that opens with the description of a clear morning with the birds singing, which gradually clouds over into a heavy, overcast day compared, inevitably, with the changeability of his mistress.[11] But the most striking simile of all comes in a poem by Rinaldo d'Aquino, one of three brothers, all poets, who were relations of St. Thomas Aquinas. In it he describes his unrequited love as a fire burning in the midst of snow and ice. The picture is so vivid that the rise and fall of the metre seems to repeat the lambent movement of the flames, and one is tempted to think that the poet drew upon some memory of a camp-fire burning in the midst of a snowy landscape during one of his campaigns.

Rinaldo d'Aquino was evidently more fortunate in another of his loves, and in a gay song he relates how he lost his heart to a lady at a dance. The song itself was evidently intended to be set to dance music, for the rapid repeated rhyme of the lines is of the type that was sung by the leader of the dance while the rest danced in a ring or in a long chain, joining into the chorus as they swayed together to the music of the refrain.

These dance songs, filled with allusions to roses, nightingales and the beauty of the ladies who partnered the poets, are by far the most numerous among the poems of the Sicilian school that have come down to us. But there are others in which passion flings aside the mask of pretence and lighthearted flirtation. Of these, Giacomo Pugliese's "La dolce ciera piacente" ("The sweet pleasing face") is the most famous. In it the poet entirely forsakes the usual conventions of courtly love, and in lines which vibrate with sensual feeling, he describes a passion that was quite evidently amply requited. Some legacy of the Arabic love songs of Saracen Sicily is still to be found in these poems of passionate love—the amber-scented breath and lips of the beloved are still there, perfumed now like the rose or some other flower.

Two other poems of the Sicilian school exist that are filled with passionate longing of a very different kind. They were written by one of the most renowned younger poets of the court —King Enzio, Frederick's oldest illegitimate son—when he was a prisoner in Bologna, enclosed within the high stone walls of the Guelf city, from which he was destined never to escape. One of these poems, of which only a fragment remains, contains what are the most often quoted lines of all poetry of the imperial court—

Va Cansonetta mia a salute messere
dilli lo mal ch'i' aggio
Quelli che m'a'n balia—si distretto mi tene,
ch'eo viver non poraggio.
Salutemi Toscana-quella ched è sovrana,
in cui regna tutta cortezia
e vanne in Puglia piana-la magna Capitana
là dov'è lo mio core notte' e dia. . . . [12]

These lines were written shortly after Enzio's capture by the
Bolognese in 1249 when his father was still alive in Apulia, and
he had hopes of ransom or rescue and a chance of seeing again
the "Puglia piana-la magna Capitana" which Frederick and his
sons loved so well; no wonder that it is related of Enzio in
prison that "in the morning he sang, in the evening he wept".

The second poem is infinitely more sad, written evidently
when many of Enzio's twenty long years of imprisonemt had
dragged by. It was probably composed for a poetical contest,
as the first line taken from a passage in Ecclesiastes occurs in
two other poems written by his friends. Whereas these others
pass on to different topics, Enzio devotes his whole poem to the
passage of time, repeating the word at the beginning of each
line of the first verse:

Tempo vene che sale a che discende
Tempo da parlare a d'attacare
Tempo d'ascoltare e da imprendere,
Tempo di minacce non temere,
Tempo di ubbidire chitti riprende
Tempo di molte cose provedere
Tempo di negghiare che t'affende,
Tempo d'infingere di non udire. . . . [13]

The conclusion is inevitable that it was his own life as a prisoner
that Enzio was describing, with time hanging endlessly on his
hands as year after weary year dragged by, with hope gradually
fading.

Tragic as Enzio's fate was, it played an important part in
the evolution of Italian poetry. During his twenty years of
imprisonment in Bologna he was treated with great honour and
his bravery, beauty and charm made him an outstanding figure.
The palace where he was imprisoned is still known as the Palazzo

di Re Enzio, and in it he held court to a circle of poets who were influential in transplanting the poetry of the Sicilian school to Central Italy. It is significant in this connection that, apart from Bologna, the cities where the new art of Italian poetry first blossomed outside the Realm of Sicily were Pisa, Arezzo, Lucca, Siena, and Florence, all of which had enjoyed the closest relations with the imperial court. The subsequent rise to supremacy of the *Lingua Toscana* in the realms of Italian poetry undoubtedly owes a debt to the prolonged presence of the court in Central Italy.

King Enzio's poems were not the only ones of the Sicilian school in which the shadows of life were reflected; very many of them dwelt upon the sorrow of lovers' partings, and from what we know of the continual journeys of the court in times of peace this is not surprising. To these transient peace-time separations were later added tragic farewells brought about by the rising tide of war. In some of these poems of lovers' partings the sentiment is plainly but a convenient device upon which to build a graceful tribute to the lady's charms in recognised courtly form, in others the words are imbued with a depth of human feeling, and it is surprising to find that two of the four poems which are with fair certainty considered to be the work of Frederick himself, fall into this category.

The poems, known from their opening words as "Dolze meo drudo" and "Oi lasso, nom pensai", both of which are attributed to the Emperor, are filled with the sorrow of lovers' farewells; so much so that reference in the second to the "power of others" responsible for their parting has caused some critics to doubt whether the all-powerful Emperor could possibly have been the author, as no one would have been in a position to separate him from the object of his affections. Others maintain that in writing these poems Frederick was simply paying lip-service to the literary conventions of his time which decreed that lovers' partings were a fashionable subject for poetic invention. In both of them, however, there is a certain amount of circumstantial evidence to show that the poems were inspired by a genuine leave-taking from an actual person. In "Dolze meo drudo" the author blames Tuscany for taking away his heart, and in "Oi lasso, nom pensai", which is addressed to the "flower of Soria", the poet states that he feels that he will die when he boards the ship that is to carry him away; and affairs of state, which were the cause of Frederick's continual journeying, could well have separated him from his mistress.

If this is so, then it shows that sensual and inconstant as he was the Emperor was still capable of genuine sentimental feeling even if only for a short period. A curious phrase that supports this view occurs in a long letter filled with scientific questions which the Emperor addressed to Michael Scott, his court philosopher and astrologist. In a question dealing with the survival of the soul, Frederick asked "And how is it that the soul of a living man which has passed away to another life than ours cannot be induced to return by *first love* or even by hate, just as if it had been nothing, nor does it seem to care at all for what it has left behind?" The introduction of such human passions as love and hate into a scientific discussion begs the question—was the Emperor capable of them himself? Of hate he certainly was, and his rating its power on a plane equal to that of first love seems to indicate that even he knew from personal experience something of the power of love.

Apart from his three wives, whom he married for reasons of state without ever having seen them previously, it is a remarkable fact that of all the women who were associated with Frederick, including even the mothers of his illegitimate children, the name of only one is known to history. She was the mother of Manfred and Constance (who married the Nicean Emperor John Vatatzes), and her name was Bianca Lancia.

The Lancias were a noble Piedmontese family which had long been associated with the house of Hohenstaufen. Three Lancia brothers, Henry, Hugo and Manfred, were at the court of Frederick Barbarossa. This Manfred died in 1215, leaving two sons and a daughter—Manfred, Giordanino and Bianca. He appears to have been a hopelessly bad business man, for although he inherited large estates he was continually selling property and in the end his family were reduced to the verge of poverty. Apart from his improvidence, this first Manfred was a man of parts; he was quite a gifted *trovatore*, writing poems in Provençal, and a friend of the Marquis of Monferrat, whose court was renowned in Northern Italy for its distinguished manners and culture in the Provençal style.

His son, Manfred, who was a youth of about seventeen in 1212, seems to have met Frederick and formed a friendship with him at the time of the latter's momentous journey to Germany. In 1216, Manfred acted on one occasion at least as representative of Frederick in Northern Italy. In a document of 1218 Frederick referred to Manfred as "Fidelis noster", and in 1226 he was at the Emperor's court at Sarzana. About 1230, the whole of Manfred Lancia's family appears to have emigrated to the Sicilian Kingdom where he already occupied a position of sufficient importance at court to be asked to witness state documents, for his signature as a witness is on one dated from San Germano shortly prior to the signing of the famous Peace of Ceprano. During the years 1231 and 1232 Manfred Lancia was constantly at court, and his position was evidently one of great influence, for his signature appears frequently upon state documents as a witness among those of officers of the highest rank in the Sicilian realm.

Frederick was at this time a widower. He was an active man of forty-seven, at the very height of all his extraordinary powers of mind and body (when he was fifty-four he was still capable of spending twenty-four hours on horseback), and with the trials of excommunication and the Crusade behind him he was on the crest of the wave, already reaping the rewards brought by the reorganisation of his beloved Kingdom of Sicily. It was at this time, probably in the summer of 1232, at Venosa, that Manfred, his son by Bianca Lancia, was born. The court was at Melfi and, as was his custom, Frederick seems to have withdrawn with a small circle of intimate friends to the greater seclusion of one of his hunting boxes situated in the surrounding wild hill country, the beauty of whose woods and springs was praised in the odes of Horace, whose birthplace Venosa was. There can be no question of Frederick having been attracted to Bianca for political reasons; her family had been desperately poor and owed their present prosperous position entirely to Frederick's patronage. On the contrary it seems likely that Manfred Lancia's sudden rise to an important position at court was not altogether unconnected with the Emperor's passion for a woman of his family.

About Bianca we know very little, not even if she was the sister or niece of Manfred Lancia. Partly in consideration of the fact that Manfred was about the same age as Frederick, she is thought to have been his niece—the daughter of his sister Bianca. Of her appearance we know nothing, no indiscretions of courtiers or chroniclers have survived to tell us if she was tall or short, dark or fair, though it is permissible to assume that she was a woman of great beauty and considerable gifts. All his life her son was renowned for his good looks, his gifts as a poet and his love of beauty, and the mere fact that her name is remembered when those of the mothers of Enzio, Frederick of Antioch and all the rest of Frederick's illegitimate children are forgotten is significant. Moreover, Bianca evidently retained some influence over the inconstant Emperor during a period of sixteen years or more for after the death of his third wife Isabella in 1241, Frederick endowed her with vast lands and possessions—the counties of Gravina, Tricarico and Monte Scaglioso, and the honour of Monte St. Angelo. This last is of particular interest because it had always formed part of the dower of the queens of Sicily, settled upon them at the time of their marriage.

The majority of historians have little doubt that Frederick actually married Bianca Lancia, probably after the death of the Empress Isabella. His gift to her of the honour of Monte St. Angelo, and the fact that at the time of her son Manfred's marriage to Beatrice of Savoy in 1248 Manfred Lancia, her brother or uncle, was referred to in imperial documents as "dilectis affinis noster" (our well-beloved relation), and took precedence over the bride's father, Thomas of Savoy, are regarded as evidence of this. Moreover, Bianca's estates were later made over to her son. Frederick confirmed this donation in his will and it is significant that Manfred is the only one of his illegitimate children who was mentioned in this official state document, though all the sons held important positions and the daughters had married into the greatest families in Italy or abroad.

The evidence that this marriage actually took place certainly appears to be well-founded, that it was kept quiet and neither officially recognised nor made public may be attributed to the fact that the Emperor was an excommunicate at the time. That Bianca was not of royal blood would have prevented her being regarded as anything more than a morganatic wife.

The particular interest of the marriage lies in the fact that it is the only occasion upon which the Emperor is believed to have made any attempt to legalise the position of any of his mistresses and it would have been the only one he ever contracted by reason of his own inclination and not as a matter of state policy. That he did so, and in addition gave Bianca vast estates more than ten years after the birth of Manfred, seems to provide definite proof that in the case of this one woman Frederick was actuated by something more than mere sensual attraction. His marriage to Isabella and the existence of other mistresses, as well as the famous odalisques, do not seem to have affected their relationship. Unlike his feeling for the other women in his life, the sentiment which he entertained for Bianca was no mere passing fancy, and if his attentions wandered, they do seem to have returned to the mother of his favourite son.

Manfred was certainly the nearest and dearest to Frederick of all his children; chroniclers say that he loved Manfred "as the eyes of his own head". The Emperor's book on falconry—*De Arte Venandi cum Avibus*—was dedicated to Manfred, who prepared a new edition of it with loving care after his father's death. Infinite pains were lavished on the boy's education; in later years Manfred himself said that during his childhood at his father's court he was taught by "many great doctors of theology and philosophy".

Although Frederick seems to have entertained an almost Oriental affection for most of his children, with some of the others he was a spartan father in certain respects—he loaded them with honours, but he left his sons to shoulder heavy responsibilities when young, the daughters he married off advantageously when they were almost children. Manfred also bore his share of responsibility early, but he appears to have been brought up in much closer domestic propinquity to his father than the others, and he alone among them was at his father's bedside when the Emperor lay dying. This marked affection seems to afford added evidence that a close tie had linked father and son since Manfred's earliest childhood, and to indicate that a different kind of relationship had existed between the Emperor and his mother—putting her on a different plane from his other mistresses. Moreover, Frederick's friendship with the boy's uncle, Manfred Lancia, continued to be of the closest right up to the end of his life—during the winter of 1248-9 the Emperor lived for some months in the Lancias' house at Vercelli.

With the ferocious jealousy that characterised Frederick's relationships with women, it is unlikely that Bianca saw much of the gay life of the court after she had become Frederick's mistress, but beforehand we can imagine her as a member of that bright company of young people dancing in the gardens of one of the imperial palaces on a summer day, and the Emperor like any other of his courtiers addressing his love poems to her. Perhaps she was the lady to whom he wrote "Poi che ti piace Amore", that he wished to enthrone when she was his, or whose thoughts he so gracefully interpreted in "Dela mia disianza" where the lady hesitates to admit her love for fear of man's inconstancy—as well she might if Frederick was the man.

The autumn and midwinter after Manfred's birth Frederick spent in one of his favourite hunting boxes at Apricena, near where the forest of the Incoronata joined the marshes and lakes that fringe that northern coast of the wild promontory of the Gargano; Manfred Lancia was with him, and perhaps Bianca and his newly born son as well. On later visits the boy must have been initiated into his father's favourite sport, for the marshes and lakes were filled with the waterfowl that were the prey of his beloved falcons, to which he devoted the study of a lifetime. It was indeed as a result of Manfred's insistent requests when he was a boy growing up at his father's side that Frederick turned to authorship as well as poetry and wrote his famous book on falconry, *De Arte Venandi cum Avibus* ("Of the Art of Hunting with Birds").

Treatises upon falconry were not uncommon in the Middle Ages both in Europe and the Orient, but the European ones at least were merely handbooks on the training and care of falcons. The Emperor's book stands apart as something of far wider scope—a scientific study of ornithology as well as a most minute and detailed disquisition upon falconry as an art rather than as a sport; and certainly it has withstood the test of time. It was regarded as the standard authority on the subject of falconry right up to the eighteenth century, during which a critical commentary on it recognised its scientific value; and two editions of an English translation have been published during the last twenty years.

In certain aspects *De Arte Venandi cum Avibus* was something quite new in the Middle Ages; the scientific treatment of the subject, the clarity and order of its arrangement, the scholarly refusal to accept anything but facts proved by the Emperor's personal observation or that of his trusted representatives, and the terse and trenchant style, single it out from among the writings of the time. No doubt it owed much to the *Zoology of Aristotle,* which had been translated by Michael Scott earlier in the century; but Frederick on several occasions had fault to find with Aristotle's descriptions of birds and their habits. He wrote: "We have followed Aristotle when it was opportune, but in many cases, especially in that which regards the nature of some birds, he appears to have departed from the truth. That is why we have not always followed the prince of the philosophers, because rarely, or never, had he experience of hunting which we have loved and practised always." The Emperor also firmly rejected the widely held mediaeval belief that barnacle geese were hatched from trees or barnacles—he had barnacles brought south to prove it—neither would he accept the legendary existence of certain species of birds, such as the phoenix, of which only one couple was believed to exist at a time.

But the rare quality that chiefly distinguishes *De Arte Venandi cum Avibus* is the Emperor's capacity for minute and exact observation and the clarity with which this is transferred to paper. If he could not discover the reason for any particular phenomenon he said so; if the facts were not available he drew no conclusions but left the question open, and if he advanced a theory he did so with great caution. This clear thinking and orderly habit of mind is all the more remarkable in the superstition-ridden age in which Frederick lived, but examples of the same type of mental training can be found in earlier periods in Sicily. The Admiral Eugenius, sometimes called Eugene the Emir, who was in charge of the financial administration of William I and one of the most noted translators at the Norman court (among other things he translated Ptolemy's *Optics*), had the same habit of mind, and his poetic description of a water-lily illustrates this same capacity for minute factual observation. Where did this particular type of mental training come from? It is tempting to ascribe it to Arab influence, for the same characteristic is to be found in the clinical exactitude of the Arabian doctor's observation of diseases. If this were so, it would afford added evidence of the Moslem influence in Frederick's education.

The facts which reveal the Emperor's capacity for observation are all the more remarkable because they are of the kind that could not be read up in books, or learnt during comfortable hours of leisure spent in one of his hunting boxes—they could have only been known to a man of infinite patience who had spent an immense amount of time watching birds in their natural habitat. There can be no doubt that Frederick really loved birds and animals, for only a passionate interest would have enabled a man with the cares of governing a vast empire to find the time to accumulate the profound personal knowledge of birds and their habits which informed every page of his book.

De Arte Venandi cum Avibus, in the incomplete form in which it has survived—the section that dealt with the diseases of falcons is missing—is divided into six books. The opening chapter of the first book is devoted to falconry as the noblest of arts, and continues with a general treatise upon the structure, flight and habits of birds; the descriptions of structure and flight reveal that the author had a sound understanding of the laws of mechanics. The second book deals with the birds of prey, their capture and training; the third with the different kinds of lures for inducing the falcons to return to the huntsman; the fourth with the hunting of cranes with Ger falcons; the fifth with the hunting of herons with the sacred "sakker" falcon; and the last with the use of smaller types of falcons for hunting water birds.

The last four books are of so technical a nature that their appeal is really limited to experts in falconry, but the first two are of absorbing interest to any student of nature. The Emperor begins by dividing birds into three categories: land birds, water birds, and amphibious birds, which spend their lives between the two elements. It is here in his study of their anatomy and habits that Frederick's profound knowledge of bird life is revealed. For instance he observed that birds who obtain their food by scratching the earth have the inner face of the claw on the middle toe of each foot serrated for the purpose: that cranes have the inner front toe of each foot curved like those of birds of prey, and that in order to preserve their sharpness these toes lie sideways on the ground. He advances a theory that vultures have no feathers on their necks because he has watched them thrusting their heads right into the carcases of dead animals while they are feeding. He it was, too, who discovered the nesting habits of cuckoos; he noticed a strange chick in a nest and brought it home to be reared with great care and found that it grew up into a cuckoo.

Perhaps the most interesting passages in the whole book are those devoted to the migration of birds. Apulia is still one of the areas of Italy that is richest in bird life and one of the main migration routes. These facts probably influenced the Emperor's predilection for the province, which he mentions in connection with the migrating habits of cranes—this is one of the rare topographical references in *De Arte Venandi cum Avibus*. In emphasising the extraordinary weather sense of birds and their instinctive knowledge of the perils of exhaustion, Frederick describes how his Ger falcons had taken migrating cranes in the Capitanata in an exhausted state, with their feathers covered with blood. While advancing his theory with due scientific caution, he states that in his opinion this was due to exhaustion having caused blood to flow from their nostrils. In another passage he notes how in adverse winds migrating birds will come to rest tamely upon a ship, and stay there until a favourable wind springs up, when they take wing immediately. Then not even an abundance of food offered to them will make migrating birds feed or rest.

Frederick displayed a remarkable familiarity with types and habits of birds all over the world. For instance, he describes a humming-bird's flight, and the characteristics of pelicans, parrots, and hoopoes; some of these, no doubt, he had the opportunity of studying in his private menagerie, for the sultans of the Orient were well aware that a rare bird or animal was more acceptable to the Emperor as a gift than the usual treasures or jewels. Other information about exotic species he evidently gleaned from his correspondence with his Oriental friends and from members of the embassies which were accredited to his court. But on his own admission he, like his grand-father King Roger, spent large sums of money in collecting this information by means of special agents. He also made use of his administrative machine for gathering such information, as is evident from the court registers; and in 1239 he wrote to thank his superintendent of buildings in Sicily for notes upon the haunts and nests of herons.

The enormous expense involved in the practice of falconry upon a royal scale is also evident in the second book, in which were enumerated the various kinds of falcons and their capture and training. Frederick considered Ger falcons "the lord and chief of falcons", and described their natural habitat as the snowy island between Norway and Greenland, called Yslandia in the German tongue. The capture of Ger falcons is a major under-taking in the twentieth century, and their transport today even to England is a problem. Imagination boggles at the diffi-culties which it must have presented in the thirteenth century to far-away Apulia.

The Emperor was solicitous about the care of Ger falcons upon their long journey, and advised that they should be allowed to rest for a winter, or even a whole year, after their arrival. It is in his directions for the care and training of these birds that Frederick's love and understanding of them is most plainly displayed. He evidently felt a deep sympathy for their very wildness and their desire for the boundless freedom of flight, and viewed man's capacity to train them as a privilege: "The birds of prey are mere instruments in the hands of a master . . . yet the skilled falconer should give his entire atten-tion to them and their equipment. . . . The falconer's primary aspiration should be to possess hunting birds that he has trained through his own ingenuity to capture the quarry he desires in the manner he prefers. The actual taking of the prey should be a secondary consideration."

The falcon's training began by accustoming her to the proxi-mity of man. In order to conquer her fear and to prevent her from damaging herself by wild fluttering, bating as it was called, her eyes were seeled or blindfolded by passing a thread through the lower lid and drawing it up to cover her eyeball. It was Frederick who introduced from the Orient the use of the hood, which in Europe has now superseded this practice, but he advocated the use of both systems for temporarily depriving the bird of its vision, and thereby of strange sights that would alarm it. Most terrifying of all, he warned, is the face of man. After the seeling was accomplished the bird had to be carried continuously on the wrist of relays of falconers in a dark room for twenty-four hours—this same system is still used in central Asia. On the second day the falcon was fed for the first time. The Emperor advised a good-sized chicken's leg as a suitable meal, but eggs carefully cooked in milk or sheep's-milk cheese were also considered acceptable. The falconer was to see that his hands were carefully washed and scrupulous cleanliness was to be observed in preparing the falcon's food.

While the falcon was feeding, the falconer was instructed to sing a little song to her, which would gradually be associated by the bird with her food. He was also told to touch and caress her, always with clean hands, and she was to be indulged each day with a regular gentle petting and stroking. No wonder that Frederick wrote that a good falconer must love his calling and be diligent and persevering. A falconer employed by the Emperor was required to possess sagacity, a good memory, and good sight, hearing, and a pleasant voice. He had to know how to swim, be daring, not too young, not a heavy sleeper, as he had to inspect the birds during the night and rise at dawn to take them out. Neither must he be greedy nor a drunkard, bad-tempered or erratic, nor even absent-minded. It must have been a most exacting calling.

The falcon's first outing was hedged about with tremendous precautions. It must take place at dawn, in solitude, with no distracting sights and sounds to alarm her. Gradually her training began and from tackling smaller birds the falcon worked her way up until, if she was temperamentally suited, she learnt to work in casts in unison with other birds for capturing such large prey as cranes and herons. In her training the falcon had to become accustomed to working with dogs. To ensure a good working partnership Frederick instructed the falconers to feed dogs with cheese and other food under the falcon's feet. It was a slow, intricate process, and it is interesting to note that in Oriental countries at any rate the whole of this complicated process has changed little with the centuries. The training of the imperial falcons for the Mikado of Japan was, until the last war, exactly the same as that which the Emperor advocated in Europe seven hundred years before.

With characteristically scientific caution Frederick examined the various systems of luring in use in different countries before advocating his own preference for one of cranes' wings accompanied by a cry of recall. He noticed that British falconers (he seems to have known both Scotch and English ones) remained silent when throwing the lure into the air to summon their falcons to return. He questioned them about this "and they could only reply that it was their customary practice". Frederick evidently considered it a very poor explanation, and attributed this typically British preference for silence to the fact that our falconers hunted cranes and herons more than any other birds, and that in order to flush them the falconers had to shout, which might have become confused by the falcon with the luring call; nevertheless the Emperor did not approve.

Several manuscript copies of *De Arte Venandi cum Avibus* still exist in the famous libraries of Europe. Some contain only the first two books, others all six, but even so they are thought to be incomplete. About the year 1265 William Bottatus of Milan wrote to Charles of Anjou offering to sell him two volumes sumptuously adorned with gold and silver which had been taken as loot among Frederick's baggage at the battle of Vittoria in 1248. From the description it is evident that these volumes were not only a de luxe edition of *De Arte Venandi cum Avibus* as we know it, but with further additions upon the diseases and cure of falcons and another whole book on the different breeds of dogs, their feeding, care and training. These books, which were magnificently illustrated, are thought to have been the Emperor's own master copy, but unhappily no further trace of them has survived. The earliest manuscript that does exist is owned by the Vatican Library; it dates from the middle of the thirteenth century, probably during Manfred's reign, as it contains his additions and comments.

This copy of *De Arte Venandi cum Avibus* is one of the most treasured manuscripts of the Vatican Library by reason of the beauty and originality of its miniatures, which illustrate with great fidelity the text of the book: the right and wrong way to hold a falcon; the right and wrong way to mount a horse holding a falcon; the caution with which the falcon must be taken for her first airing; spraying the falcon from the mouth with water to calm her and prevent her from bating (the Emperor instructed falconers to rinse their mouths out three times before doing so!).

The great beauty of the book, however, lies in the pictures of the birds themselves; here the artist has managed to combine scientific veracity of presentation with an extraordinary feeling for the grace and movement of birds in flight. This mediaeval Peter Scott has also caught something of the impressionism of Japanese prints, and it is not surprising to find that his particular style is attributed to the fact that he himself is thought to have been either of Oriental origin or subject to Oriental influences.

In spite of the scientific treatment of the subject and the terseness of the style, which allows for little local colour or personal comment, *De Arte Venandi cum Avibus* nevertheless gives us some insight into its author's character and personal views. Frederick was most emphatically a sportsman; the big bag to be boasted of after the chase was evidently abhorrent to him. The art which enables man to train wild creatures was what appealed to him—cruelty or force can play no part in the training of a falcon—it is labour of infinite understanding and patience, and evidently in Frederick's case of love as well. The Emperor summed up his point of view in describing the aims of good falconers—who should "aspire to have fine falcons, better trained than those of others, that have gained honour and pre-eminence in the chase. When these aspirations are satisfied they feel they have been fully repaid for their trouble."

Chapter IX

SCIENCE AND PHILOSOPHY

THE Emperor's scientific approach to his subject in *De Arte Venandi cum Avibus* was reflected in another zoological work which was written by a member of his court. This was the *De Medicina Equorum* of Giordano Ruffo—a study in the care of horses, their diseases and curative treatment, that was undertaken at Frederick's command by his Master of Horse, but only completed after the Emperor's death. It is a book of more specialised interest than the Emperor's own as the subject-matter is mainly concerned with diseases and their treatment, but it was a standard work for centuries and some of the remedies which the author recommends are still in use today.

Like the Emperor, Giordano Ruffo divided his treatise into six books entitled "Of the Conception and Birth of Horses", "Of the Catching and Breaking of Horses", "Of the Keeping and Training of Horses", "On how to Recognise the Corporal Beauties of Horses, and the Function and Members of their Bodies", "Of Illnesses Natural and Accidental", "Of Medicines and Remedies for Curing Horses". These last two books form the most important part of the whole work; in them fifty-seven diseases are listed, and their symptoms observed and described with minute care. It is this power of careful factual observation, so similar to that of the Emperor himself, that constitutes the chief interest of the book today, as an example of the habit of mind which was general to all the scientific activities of the court.

Science and mathematics were the preferred studies of the Emperor, and his personal tastes naturally influenced those of his court. But even outside his own circle Frederick encouraged learning assiduously, both because it was his natural instinct to do so and as a deliberate matter of policy; for he clearly realised that a wider diffusion of knowledge was one of the basic necessities of the lay state that he was striving to create. His foundation of the University of Naples was one step in this direction, and by this and other means he did achieve much for the diffusion of education, even to a certain extent among the poorer classes. When his son Manfred was King a chronicler said that when Frederick succeeded to the throne few people in the realm could read or write, but that in his own day many children knew the elements of grammar.

Frederick did not limit his efforts to the realm. In 1232 he sent a gift of books, including works of Aristotle on logic and physics which he had specially translated from Arabic and Greek, to the professors of Bologna University. The gift was accompanied by a letter in which the Emperor described how as a boy he had loved learning, and how still, whenever he could snatch time from the affairs of state, he would spend it in pleasurable reading in his library where manuscripts of all kinds "classified in order, enrich our cupboards". Frederick subsidised and encouraged with his patronage a whole circle of translators and scientific writers. Some of the most notable among these were Jews—Jacob Anatoli of Marseilles, and Jehuda ben Salomon Cohen—and it is an interesting revelation of the lack of prejudice of his age that the Emperor had evidently made a profound study of Jewish beliefs and customs. This knowledge once stood him in good stead in Germany in dealing with an alleged case of ritual murder of a Christian boy by the Jews, which produced anti-Semitic outbreaks that endangered the public peace. Upon another occasion Frederick asked a learned Jew why one of their writers had not explained the origins of the Mosaic rite of purification with the ashes of a red cow that according to him stemmed from an ancient Indian rite mentioned in the *Book of the Indian Sages*. The Emperor was evidently held in great esteem for his learning by the Jews and his sayings were quoted together with those of Aristotle and Alexander the Great in *The Mirror of Manners*, a Jewish treatise of the period.

Frederick was also deeply interested in medicine. He is said to have prescribed personally for his friends and family, and in the British Museum there is still extant a manuscript that gives a recipe for the treatment of wounds which is attributed to "the Emperor Frederick". The Sicilian realm

Castel Lagopesole. The view from the gate looking towards Monte
Vulture at sunset

Three illustrations from the Emperor's book on falconry, *De Arte Venandi cum Avibus*, showing the right and wrong ways of holding a falcon, and the structure of birds

was the home of the greatest medical school of mediaeval times, the School of Salerno, whose fame was widespread throughout the whole Latin world. Although the school declined in influence at the time of the Angevin conquest of Sicily and by the beginning of the fourteenth century had become a nonentity, its renown lingered on into the time of our own Queen Elizabeth whose godson, Sir John Harington, translated its *Regimen Sanitatis* into English. Long without influence, it was finally suppressed by Napoleon in 1811.

In his Constitutions of Melfi the Emperor laid down, as King Roger had before him, that no doctor could practise medicine in the realm without taking a degree at the School of Salerno. The training was rigorous, beginning with a course in logic, and continuing with five years' study of surgery (which included the use of anaesthetics of a kind—the soporific sponge is specially mentioned), of which the last year had to be passed in gaining practical experience—the student working as assistant to a practising surgeon. The Emperor instituted at Salerno the first school of anatomy in Europe, and his laws governed with minute precision the whole exercise of the medical profession— free treatment of the poor, the number of daily and nightly calls a doctor should make, the fees he was allowed to charge, and his relations with the pharmacists, who had also to take an oath to dispense their medicines correctly. Both doctors and pharmacists were subject to rigid controls and supervision by imperial officials, and for transgressions of the law they were liable to have their goods confiscated.

Numerous medical treatises were composed for the Emperor. One of the earliest, which was written by Adam Charter of Cremona, laid down the hygienic regulations to be observed by armies and large bands of pilgrims—evidently the epidemic among the Crusaders in 1227 had taught Frederick a lesson. One of his court philosophers, Master Theodore, also wrote a treatise on hygiene and at Frederick's request he composed for him a special diet sheet. One of Theodore's pupils, Petrus Hispanus, also dedicated a treatise on hygiene to the Emperor, and another court doctor, Zaccaria, compiled from Greek sources a treatise on ophthalmology of particular interest to Frederick who suffered from bad sight.

All this medical research and knowledge was put to practical

H

purpose by the Emperor, both in the laws which he promulgated that aimed at bettering the hygienic conditions of the cities of the realm, and in his own personal life. The modernity of the plumbing in his castles shows his recognition of the importance of hygiene and personal cleanliness; his practice of taking a daily bath gives the lie to the description of the Middle Ages as "a thousand years without a bath!" Frederick observed a very strict health regime, with frequent blood-lettings, and although he was evidently something of an epicure in the matter of food, he was abstemious in eating and drinking and kept to a strict diet, fasting during the day and only eating a meal in the evening.

The outstanding character in the scientific life of the court was the man who was for many years the official resident philosopher and astrologer, Michael Scott. So many legends have grown up around his mysterious person that it is almost surprising to find that he really did exist. Michael was born about 1175, and may have been a member of the Scott family of Balwearie in Fifeshire. As a young man he studied philosophy and mathematics at Oxford and Paris. During the second decade of the thirteenth century he was an active member of that group of translators who worked at the University of Toledo, and it was here that he accomplished his most important work, translating al-Bitruji's *Astronomy* and the *Zoology* of Aristotle, together with Averroes's commentaries upon other Aristotelian works. Thus he was responsible for introducing to the Latin world three works which were to have a revolutionary effect upon the scientific thought of Europe.

Michael Scott was a man of about fifty when he first met Frederick. He was a typical example of the polyglot wandering scholar of the Middle Ages—a churchman who knew Latin, Arabic and Hebrew—who gravitated from one centre of learning to another, always with a weather-eye open for a wealthy patron, for he was evidently a man of considerable ambition and certainly of much guile. He gracefully evaded Henry III of England's offer of a remote Irish bishopric with the excuse that he knew no Erse—the office of imperial astrologer was far better suited to his undeniable talents.

Michael Scott was without doubt a serious scholar and the works that he chose to translate broke new ground in the

Western world of learning of his time. He was, moreover, capable of objective and precise descriptions of natural phenomena, such as the volcanoes and medicinal springs of southern Italy, which he undertook to examine at the Emperor's request. But from his own writings it is evident that he lacked the critical faculty and penetrating mind that the Emperor could bring to bear upon the subjects which he knew from personal experience. Unlike his greater contemporary Fibonacci, the greatest mathematician Europe produced until the eighteenth century, Michael Scott was, in fact, something of a charlatan, and in answering other questions that Frederick put to him it emerges that both he, and in certain respects the Emperor himself, were true children of the mediaeval world in which they lived.

In justice to Michael Scott, it must be borne in mind that astrological writings and predictions were the pot-boilers by which many mediaeval scholars kept the wolf from the door. Though a man such as Leonardo Fibonacci never stooped to such facile means to fame and prosperity—after his travels in Moslem countries he remained quietly living in his native town of Pisa—by using them Michael, and many others like him, enjoyed the luxury and excitement of life at princely courts. Fibonacci's fame was known mostly to the select world of scholars, whereas Michael Scott has left behind him a popular legend which is widely diffused not only in Italy but in his native Scotland.

In a note in the *Lay of the Last Minstrel* Sir Walter Scott described the extraordinary exploits which popular tradition still ascribed to Michael Scott in the nineteenth century. He noted that "in the south of Scotland any work of great labour and antiquity is ascribed either to Auld Michael, Sir William Wallace, or the Devil". If Michael Scott was inclined to be boastful about his own powers, as a showman at any rate he cannot be underrated. It is not given to many men to take such a hold upon popular imagination that they are not only remembered by the generations immediately succeeding their own, but that a poet living six centuries afterwards should still draw inspiration for one of his most telling scenes from their legend, as Sir Walter Scott did in the moonlight scene in Melrose Abbey where Michael Scott's grave is rifled of his magic books.

In view of this Frederick may perhaps be forgiven for being so impressed by his "philosopher's" undoubted achievements as to be hoodwinked by his less reputable activities such as the casting of augurs and horoscopes. His gullibility here in fact shows that the Emperor could at times be a typical representative of his own era rather than, as he usually was, far in advance of it. And in justice to Michael Scott it must be stated that, apart from his translation of Greek and Arabic works of science, he wrote three treatises upon astrology and general science which were not only popular during his lifetime, but survived in general use right up to the advent of printing, and even into the sixteenth century. The first two were the *Liber Introductorius* and the *Liber Particularis* and if much of their subject-matter was of the "eye of newt and toe of frog" variety, well calculated to appeal to a superstitious public, there was also a considerable amount of genuine scientific and medical observation in all three books, of which the third, the *Liber Physionomia*, was in some respects an early study in psychology.

According to Michael Scott's account subsequently published in his *Liber Particularis* the Emperor addressed a confidential letter to him (probably at the time when he was undergoing a cure at Pozzuoli after his abortive start on the Crusade in 1227). This letter begins "My dearest Master" and goes on to say: "We have often in divers ways listened to questions and solutions from one another concerning the heavenly bodies, that is the sun, moon and fixed stars, the elements, and the soul of the world, peoples pagan and Christian, and other creatures above and on the earth, such as plants and metals; yet we have heard nothing respecting those secrets which pertain to the delight of the spirit and the wisdom thereof, such as paradise, purgatory, and hell and the foundations and marvels of the earth. Wherefore we pray of you, by your love of knowledge and the reverence you bear our crown, explain to us the foundations of the earth, that is to say how it is established over the abyss and how the abyss stands beneath the earth, and whether it stands of itself or rests on the heavens beneath it. Also, how many heavens there are and who are the rulers and principal inhabitants, and exactly how far one heaven is from the other, and by how much one is greater than the other, and what is beyond the last heaven, if there are several; and in

which heaven God is in person of his divine majesty and how he
sits on his throne and how he is accompanied by angels and
saints, and what they do continually before God. Tell us also
how many abysses there are and the names of the spirits that
dwell therein, and just where are hell and purgatory, and the
heavenly paradise, whether under or above the earth." One
manuscript copy continued: "or above or in the abysses, and
that is the difference between the souls who are daily borne
thither and the spirits which fell from heaven; and whether one
soul in the next world knows another and whether we can return
to this life and speak and show oneself; and how many are the
pains of hell".

Another manuscript copy of Michael Scott's account phrases
the last question in a different fashion: "and how is it that the
soul of living man which has passed away to another life than
ours cannot be induced to return by first love or even by hate,
just as if it had been nothing, nor does it seem to care for all it
has left behind"; the letter then goes on to ask questions
about the size and construction of the world itself, the nature
of volcanoes and the various types of waters, rivers, seas and
volcanic springs. They are a revealing set of questions under-
lining once again that Frederick was a man of the Middle Ages
as well as the forerunner of the Renaissance, both in his belief
that any living man could provide him with answers to such
questions and in his framing of the questions themselves, particularly in his preoccupation with the immortality of the soul.

Michael Scott was not at a loss to produce answers to these
questions but whether they proved satisfying to the Emperor
may be doubted. At a later date Pope Gregory IX accused
Frederick of saying that he would only believe what was proved
by force of reason and nature, and Michael Scott would have
encountered some difficulty in justifying his answers upon these
grounds. An amusing illustration of the nature of the relationship which existed between the Emperor and his philosopher is
recounted by the chronicler Fra Salimbene. In making his
calculations for measuring the distance of the heavens from the
earth, Michael Scott mounted a church tower, and when they
were completed presented them to Frederick, who professed to
be much impressed. The Emperor was aware, however, of how
Michael had set about his experiments, and had the roof of the

tower lowered slightly. Casually one day in passing he asked the philosopher to repeat his calculations. Michael was evidently quite a match for his master in tricks of this sort, for he solemnly repeated the performance and afterwards announced that either the heavens were further away or the tower had sunk into the ground, whereupon Frederick embraced him.

According to contemporary hearsay, scientific experiments were very much a feature of life at the imperial court; Fra Salimbene in his chronicle gives a list of those which were said to have been carried out by Frederick himself. According to Salimbene, in an effort to establish what is the mother tongue of the human race, the Emperor had some children brought up from birth in complete silence, in order to ascertain what language they would speak. The experiment was a failure, and all the children died. The chronicler relates how on another occasion Frederick in his eagerness to know about the life of fish and marine plants, ordered Nicholas the diver to plunge deeper and yet deeper into the waters of the Straits of Messina, until he failed to return. Further evidence of Frederick's curiosity about the life of fish appears to have turned up in unexpected fashion two and a half centuries after his death. In 1497 a pike was caught and given to the Elector Palatine, which had fixed to its gills a copper ring with a Greek inscription that read—"I am the fish that the Emperor Frederick II put in the lake with his own hands on the 5th October 1230."[14]

Fra Salimbene gives other examples of carelessness of human life in this connection. The friar, admittedly a notorious gossip, relates how once Frederick had two prisoners given the same meal, afterwards one of them was made to rest and the other to take exercise, then their stomachs were cut open (it is to be hoped after their execution) in order that their processes of digestion might be observed, to establish whether exercise or rest was better for the digestive system. Again according to Salimbene, in another experiment, which would have been infinitely more shocking to the mediaeval mind, Frederick had a condemned man shut up in a barrel to see if his spirit emerged from it when he died. When nothing did, the Emperor declared that this was evidence that the soul did not survive death, but he had to change his verdict to "non proven" when some of the court pointed out that the man's cries had been heard through the barrel, though no visible sign of them was seen to escape.

There is no valid authority for the truth of these stories, though Salimbene knew one man who was in touch with the Emperor and shared his interest in science—Brother Elias of Cortona, who was for a time Minister-General of the Franciscan Order and after his deposition by the Pope took up residence at the Emperor's court. But certainly they reflect what his contemporaries thought of Frederick and contain as well an undercurrent of truth. That the Emperor did conduct experiments, if only of the kind that enabled him to discover the nesting habits of cuckoos, is not open to doubt. His passionate desire for knowledge which drove him on to seek an explanation of the mysteries of the universe caused him also to question everything, no matter how sacred, and equally caused him on occasions to be taken in by the charlatanry of men like Michael Scott. He is even reported to have denied the doctrine of transubstantiation and to have said that he did not believe that simply by the act of Elevation the priest created a God; pointing to a field of ripening corn he asked: "How many Gods will be raised out of this during my lifetime?"

In 1239 Frederick was formally accused by Pope Gregory IX of having denied the Virgin Birth and of having declared that the world had been deceived by three impostors—Moses, Mohammed, and Jesus Christ. It would have been difficult to ascertain the truth of these allegations even in Frederick's lifetime, and no Pope was ever to repeat the charge, but from what we know of the intellectual climate which prevailed at the imperial court we cannot confidently dismiss them as false. However the story of the three impostors did not originate with Frederick; it was already circulating at the end of the previous century, and the blasphemous parodies of the Goliardic poets of that period show that even then the abuse of power and overbearing behaviour of the Roman Curia and some of the higher clergy had already produced a cynical reaction to what has perhaps too often been called "the age of faith".

It is certain that in the privacy of his own intimate circle Frederick's behaviour was very different from the almost hieratic pose of a remote and godlike Emperor which characterised his public appearances. Fra Salimbene, who was an acute observer of the contemporary scene, and as a member of the Franciscan Order definitely not a Ghibelline sympathiser, gives in his chronicle an eyewitness account of an evening passed at the Emperor's dinner table, which was retailed to him by a reliable observer who was present with the Cremonese ambassadors. Cremona was the most faithful to the imperial cause of all the cities in Northern Italy, and its accredited representatives at Frederick's court would most likely have been friends well known to him, not foreign ambassadors in the ordinary sense.

At first in general conversation everyone lauded the Emperor, saying how noble, wise and powerful he was, then gradually they started to laugh and make jokes about him, chaffing him to his face; and Frederick, who was sitting at the head of the table, frequently pretended not to hear what they were saying so that he should not feel called upon to reprimand or punish them. This freedom which reigned in what Salimbene called "the heart of domesticity" of Frederick's circle, that allowed his friends to joke in his presence even about the sacred person of the Emperor, may well have been even less restrained when it came to the discussion of the scientific topics in which he himself was so deeply interested. It is probable that in these nightly conversations no hold was barred—no theory too daring, and no subject too sacred, to be analysed, criticised, and even held up to ridicule. There would have been nothing singular in this as similar discussions were raging in the intellectual climate of Paris at the same time.

In public Frederick always conformed of necessity to the role of a Catholic prince—the eldest son of the Church—but there is little doubt that in private his views were very different. He may not have subscribed personally to the story of the three impostors, but with his far-ranging mind he would probably have found nothing shocking in discussing it—or indeed any aspect of the Christian religion. With his scientific outlook he detested shams and shibboleths and he was not prepared to accept any legend or theory at its face value, as witness his corrections of Aristotle, "the prince of philosophers", in *De Arte Venandi cum Avibus*. Even when he was ostensibly on friendly terms with it, Frederick was well aware that the Church, and all that it stood for, was the enemy of his conception of the lay state and the new world that he was trying to create. If the reports of his irreverent denial of the doctrine of transubstantiation are founded upon fact, his attitude may be partly explained by his fear of the power of the priesthood. The doctrine was very much a matter of actuality in his day. It had only received formal statement in 1215, at the fourth Lateran Congress—and it was inevitable that it should become a topic of discussion in the philosophical circles in which the Emperor moved and that, hostile to the Church as they were, they should have feared the immense power which it gave into the hands of the priesthood.

What were the Emperor's own religious beliefs? Now, as in his own lifetime, it is almost impossible to arrive at a satisfactory answer, because it seems likely that even in the secret recesses of his own mind they fluctuated. Certainly he was not an orthodox Catholic nor probably did he subscribe to any heretical Christian creed or to the Moslem faith, as his enemies alleged. But it is difficult to believe, either, that he was a complete materialist; his interest in the various forms of religion, as his knowledge of Jewish and Indian rites bears witness, seems to show that he was continually searching for the eternal truths which lie behind all religions. But above all it is in his constant preoccupation with the immortality of the soul that Frederick's fundamental spiritual belief is most clearly seen— a complete materialist would have denied its very existence, and not interested himself, as Frederick did throughout his life, in its powers of survival.

Manfred cast a very interesting light upon the spiritual aspects of his education at his father's court in the introduction which he wrote to his translation of the pseudo-Aristotelian *De Pomo*. In it he described how during a serious illness he was believed to be dying, and how his friends pitied him because they thought that he must be in terror at the imminent prospect of death. "But", he says, "we had firmly in our mind the theological and philosophical doctrines taught to us by many great doctors of theology and philosophy in the imperial palace of the divine Augustus, the most serene Emperor our lord father, upon the nature of the world, the dissolution of bodies, the creation of the soul, on its eternity and perfectibility, and upon the mutability of matter and all that which does not follow it into decay and corruption. Thus we did not grieve at our death as they imagined, as in what concerned the future reward of our perfection we did not confide in the merits of justice, but in the grace of the Creator."

Manfred goes on to explain that it was at this time that he chanced upon this book that "Aristotle wrote at the end of his life, in which it is shown that the sages do not grieve over the destruction of their earthly shell, but with joy hasten towards the prize of perfection, to whose attainment they have spared neither time nor labour, and immersed in profound studies shunned the cares of a material life. And we told our kindly attendants to read this book, because there they would learn why we did not fear to pass out of this life. And not finding it among the Christian tongues, but having read it in Hebrew translated from Arabic, upon regaining our health we translated it, for the benefit of many, from Hebrew into Latin." One cannot help contrasting the enlightened courage of Manfred's attitude in the face of death with the mediaeval barbarity of the deathbed of his father's predecessor, the Emperor Otto, who lay moaning the *Miserere* upon the floor while calling upon the attendant priests to lay on the stripes as a sign of his penitence.

A man who had educated his son to hold such views cannot be called a materialist. But the spiritual independence evinced by this attitude of mind must have appeared suspect to the mediaeval priesthood, robbing them as it did of their power to dominate through fear; even Manfred's entourage were amazed at his point of view. Manfred, it is clear, had no doubt as to the soul's immortality, and one is tempted to think that his father in his constant searching and questioning was inspired not so much by disbelief of the soul's survival, as his desire for what he conceived to be "proof by force of reason and nature". One has the impression that Frederick, no matter how wily and dissimulating he may have been with others when he considered that policy demanded it, was at least honest with himself. He would accept no makeshift or muddled thinking, no comfortable panaceas; he wanted to know the truth if it was possible for the intellect of man to divine it. This intimate struggle within himself, which derived from his basic honesty in regard to the things that he felt really mattered, is reflected in his apparent indecision, his inability to make up his own mind as to what he really believed.

Until the beginning of the thirteenth century the philosophy of the West was mainly Augustinian and Platonic. St. Augustin and the early Christian fathers had recourse to Plato, whom they considered closer to Christianity than any of the other classical philosophers, in relating the Christian revelation to the world of reality—in trying to reconcile the natural with the supernatural. From the Arab world, by the work of translators such as Gerard of Cremona and, in Frederick's day, Michael Scott, the rationalist philosophy of Aristotle was suddenly pitched like a stone into the still waters of the established order of things, creating more and more ripples as its disturbing influence spread. It is true that some of these works had been translated during the preceding century, both in Sicily and in Spain, but they did not achieve a wider circulation until the beginning of the thirteenth century, and it was in this atmosphere of intellectual turmoil (Innocent III had forbidden the study of Aristotle in 1209) that Frederick grew up. The controversy for and against Aristotle raged throughout the century, and it was only due to the influence of St. Thomas Aquinas, who had first studied his works at Naples University and later at Paris, that the Aristotelian philosophy was finally officially accepted by the Catholic Church in 1366.

Michael Scott, as we have seen, was largely responsible for introducing the works of Averroes, the greatest commentator on Aristotle, into the Western world. Many of the "Aristotelian" books which had been previously translated were in fact by other authors, and contained an admixture of neo-platonism; Averroes reintroduced Aristotelian philosophy in its original purity. He lived and worked in Spain during the twelfth century, so that his commentaries were of comparatively recent date when they reached the imperial court with Michael Scott. It is now increasingly believed that it was the impact of this new-old conception of Aristotle which prompted Frederick to take the daring step of addressing to the scholars of the Moslem world a series of philosophical conundrums known as "The Sicilian Questions".

This custom of posing scientific and mathematical questions to learned men was repeated several times by Frederick during his lifetime. We have it on record that he did so to Leonardo Fibonacci in 1226, in his letter to Michael Scott in 1227, to the Sultan of Egypt during the Crusade, and at some later date to Jehuda ben Salomon Cohen, and there may well have been other questionnaires of which the record has been lost. But these earlier questions were more in the nature of private discussions between the Emperor and members of his court or friendly rivals, undertaken for their mutual intellectual amusement and entertainment. The famous Sicilian Questions were something far more ambitious. They were sent out by the Emperor about 1240; first to Egypt, Syria, Iraq, Dubub, and the Yemen; and when he did not get what he considered to be satisfactory replies from these, to the Almohad Calif al-Raschid of Morocco. They caused a tremendous stir in the world. Frederick had already been excommunicated for the second time when they were sent, and in broadcasting them thus throughout the Oriental world he must have been well aware of the extent of the publicity they would receive. Their content, even when regarded in the light of scientific inquiry, was scarcely of the nature which one would expect to find a Christian discussing publicly with the Infidel.

The only answers to these questions to have survived are those of Abd al-Haqq Ibn Sab'in, to whom they were sent by the Almohad Calif through the Governor of Ceuta. Ibn Sab'in was one of the greatest scholars of the Moslem world of his time, but he was far from orthodox, and he had already been persecuted by his co-religionists for his nonconformity. In his replies to the Christian Emperor's questions, however, he displayed an impeccable Moslem orthodoxy, though he added that he would like to speak with Frederick "mouth to mouth". It is fascinating to speculate what the two of them would really have said to each other if they had ever met—the unorthodox Emperor who, like many apparent Christians of his time, used the philosophy of Aristotle as a cloak for his own unbelief, and the unorthodox Mohammedan savant whose failure to believe that "there is no God but God" brought him in the end to a suicide's death.

The burning topics of the day among the Moslem philosophers were the relationship between God and the world, and the relationship between the intellect and the other faculties

of the spirit, and these are the basic ideas which lie behind the
Sicilian Questions. The first was: "The Philosopher [Aristotle]
in all his works expressly says that the world exists in eternity,
and he certainly thought so. If he demonstrated it what were
the proofs, or if not, in what manner does he discuss it?" The
second question was as follows: "What is the scope of theological science; what are its primary postulates, if postulates it
has?" The third: "What are the categories and how are the
ten that we know used in all manner of sciences? But are there
really ten, and why cannot we add or subtract some? How is
all this proved?" There is no full text of the fourth question,
but it opens with the words: "What proof have we of the
immortality of the soul?", and goes on to discuss the apparent
contradictions upon the subject contained in the works of
Aristotle and Alexander of Aphrodisias. The fifth question is
phrased thus: "How are the words of Mohammed explained—
'The heart of the believer is between the two fingers of [God]
the Merciful'?"

These were remarkable questions for a Christian Emperor
to address to unbelievers. To discuss the eternity of the world,
when the Bible describes its creation and foretells its end, was
daring in the extreme. The second and third and fifth questions
were probably prompted by Frederick's desire to know the
opinion of Moslem scholars and philosophers upon the problems
posed by the philosophy of Aristotle and their interpretation
according to reason or faith. Taken in conjunction with his
fourth question upon the immortality of the soul, they seem to
reveal the nature of the struggle that was going on in the intimate depths not only of the Emperor's own mind, but in those
of many contemporary philosophers.

Ibn Sab'in's replies were couched in a highly disdainful
style, probably prompted by his desire to reinstate himself in
the eyes of orthodox Moslems, and in this he succeeded; his
replies were regarded by them as a triumphant vindication of
the superiority of Mohammedan scholarship. In his replies
Ibn Sab'in made a tremendous display of erudition, quoting from
the Koran, the Pentateuch, the Gospels, the Psalms, the Sohof,
Plato, Socrates and Aristotle. Throughout he followed the
orthodox Mohammedan view, rejecting Aristotle where he did
not conform to it, asserting the immortality of the soul, and

supporting his arguments from Moslem, Christian and classical sources. But in his answer to the question on theological science, he expressed his desire to discuss the question with Frederick personally, which might be taken as a hint that in his replies he had not completely revealed his opinion upon the subject. It is interesting to note that when, in 1243, Ibn Sab'in's brother, Abd Allah, was sent on an embassy to Innocent IV, the Pope was already aware of the nature of the questions and of Ibn Sab'in's replies to them, and there can be little doubt that they must have confirmed the Roman Curia in their estimate of the Emperor's dangerously heretical leanings.

Fra Salimbene, for one, had no doubts as to Frederick's scepticism. In his estimate of the Emperor's character, which appears in his chronicle after his description of Frederick's death, he begins with the phrase: "Of faith in God he had none" and goes on to say: "he was crafty, wily, avaricious, lustful, malicious and wrathful. . . . Yet he was a gallant man at times, when he wished to show kindness and courtesy he could be friendly, cheerful and gracious. He was industrious, knew how to read, write and sing, how to make songs and music. He was a comely man and well made, though of medium stature. I saw him and he pleased me much. He knew how to speak many languages . . . and if he had been a good Catholic and loved God and the Church and his own soul he would have had few Emperors to equal him in the world."

Even when reviewed in the light of the centuries of research which scholars have devoted to studying the Emperor's enigmatic character and personal beliefs, with all the added advantages at their disposal of access to the secret documents of his chancery and his private letters, Salimbene's summing up still appears to have been a very fair estimate of an extraordinarily complex character. It must certainly have been based on the first-hand knowledge of his fellow Franciscan, Brother Elias, who as we have seen was in a position, denied to all modern scholars, to give Salimbene an inside view of life at court, of Frederick's appearance, manners, and behaviour in his own intimate circle, and in a position to form a very shrewd estimate of what Frederick's thoughts and beliefs really were.

Frederick's character was an enigma and a source of wonder

to his contemporaries, even more than it is to us today. Just how much he astonished them and fired their imagination may be judged by Matthew Paris's description of him as "Stupor Mundi". Frederick moved men to wonder, to love or to hate, but he never left them, or succeeding generations, indifferent to his extraordinary character. More than most men, the paradoxes of that character were created by his upbringing. From the Hohenstaufen side of his family he inherited his mystical conception of the Empire. In all else he was the heir of his other grandfather, King Roger, and all the influence of his upbringing and experience during his most formative years went to accentuate this side of his character. If he had received the education which his father intended for him, as the scion of a German princely house, it is doubtful if the Norman side of Frederick's character would have had so much the upper hand, and it is unlikely that he would have created the stir in the world that he did.

It was the hothouse atmosphere of Palermo, with its currents of advanced Oriental thought, its admixture of Moslem, Greek and Latin civilisation, that gave to Frederick's character its curious twist. This and the fact that during the most formative years of his life—from seven to twelve—he ran wild among the population of this polyglot city. Left to his own devices by a succession of tough soldiers of fortune who exercised power in his name, he educated himself at first-hand from the seamy side of life itself and, according to a Moslem chronicler, received instruction from the Kaid of the Saracens. It was only before and after this period, and possibly at broken intervals during it, that Frederick received a more orthodox education at the hands of Catholic priests.

It is scarcely to be wondered at that his inheritance and this extraordinary childhood produced a strange and complex man. If Frederick had not been naturally gifted with great intelligence and an innate love of learning; if in fact he had not possessed tremendous spiritual qualities, though not in the religious sense, his early life and surroundings might well have transformed him into a brutal and licentious sot, who, once he had reached his majority, would have given free rein to his inherent vices, living, in his sadly reduced royal estates, as a petty princeling unable to establish his authority in his own kingdom, and perishing in all probability ignominiously in some palace revolution organised by rival claimants for the exercise of power.

What saved Frederick were his intellectual capacities and his profound inward consciousness of his own royalty, which was already a well-established feature of his character at the age of seven, as his tutor was aware.

Suddenly, at a most crucial juncture in his life, and at the early age of eighteen, came the tremendous challenge of the offer of the Empire, with its promise of apparently unlimited power. Then followed the almost fairy-tale succession of good fortune that placed Frederick on the imperial throne at the age of twenty, without his having had to pass through the years of struggle and of bloodshed which had preceded his uncle Philip's accession, or his having known the years of apprenticeship under the tutelage of a parent of outstanding character as his own father Henry VI had done.

His early accession to power, and the lack of any discipline during childhood and adolescence excepting that which he imposed upon himself, were probably responsible for many of Frederick's unattractive qualities—for his cruelty, his sudden ungovernable attacks of rage, his complete abandonment to physical lust. The very nature of the absolute power he wielded made his own self-control the only brake upon his will or instincts. Frederick was accustomed to being referred to as "divine", to hearing his dwelling called the "Sacred Palace", to being surrounded by obsequious courtiers who referred to him even in their private correspondence in terms which were not far removed from those normally reserved for the Deity. That he did not succumb utterly to this atmosphere, but was capable of taking jokes and criticisms against himself in good part, if he was convinced of the affection and sincerity of the person concerned, shows that in other and more fortunate circumstances Frederick might have revealed much more of the very human side of his character which undoubtedly existed.

The inability to endear himself to a wider circle, when he had such ability to charm by personal contact, as witness his fascination for Fakhr ad-Din and his attraction for Salimbene, is one of the many curious contradictions in Frederick's character. He seems to have been completely lacking in the common

touch which so endeared his grandfather the Emperor Barbarossa to the soldiers of his armies and to the people of Germany. It was really only in the circumstances of intimacy with
people whom he knew well, or with whom he had actual personal contact, that he could exercise his charm. When confronted with a mass of strangers he lost this power and we have
seen how dismally he failed in this respect with the barons of
Outremer.

Another factor that contributed to Frederick's isolation was
his very intellectual brilliance—which has never been a quality
calculated to appeal to the crowd at any period, whether its
possessor is a sovereign or a common man. In collecting around
him, as he inevitably did, a court who shared his intellectual tastes
and pursuits, Frederick cut himself off from the life of his time and
created yet another barrier between himself and the life of the
people. He lived in an esoteric world of his own, whose rarefied
atmosphere was only shared by savants of international renown and the most brilliant brains of his time. The mathematical problems which he set Leonardo Fibonacci and the
Sicilian Questions are a fair sample of the type of subject
that constituted the principal topics of conversation at the
imperial court, and were regarded as a relaxation from affairs
of state. They were the Emperor's chief interest—the poetry,
the dancing, the music and the love affairs were sheer pastimes.

If this aspect of Frederick's character has aroused the admiration of scholars of succeeding generations it is because it is
more akin to their own outlook, and for that very reason it was
out of tune with the thought of all but a very small minority in
his own time. This is why the Angevins, after their defeat of
Manfred, found it possible to put the clock back, and apparently
to sweep away all traces of the Hohenstaufen. Frederick's
innovations, and the ways of thought which he handed on to his
son, were too far in advance of their time to be generally understood or appreciated. In fact they did not entirely disappear,
but lay quiescent wherever they had been sown, like seeds
beneath the snow, waiting for the proper season, when they
burst into fresh life in the glorious spring of the Renaissance.

Another curious contradiction in Frederick's character was
the recklessness which alternated with his usual prudence—he
was indeed erratic, capable of great enthusiasms and equal

cynicism. His belief in the superstitious notions of Michael
Scott on the one hand and his distrust of Christianity on the other,
reveal this inconsistency in his private life, but it affected in a
much more serious fashion his political and military activities
as an Emperor. In general, Frederick displayed considerable
political adroitness, and his astuteness as a diplomat is well
illustrated by his bargaining, in very adverse circumstances,
with al-Kamil. But when everything seemed to be going well
he was apt to be carried away and, abandoning his habitual
caution, to embark upon a reckless course, from whose consequences his great ability was not always sufficient to extricate
him. Three outstanding examples of this fatal characteristic
are to be found in his abortive expedition to Northern Italy in
1226, his premature abandonment of the siege of Brescia in
1237, and his lack of continued vigilance at the siege of Parma
in 1248. These later events were to show that his recklessness
was not just a youthful failing. It was coupled with an intellectual arrogance that frequently led him to underestimate his
opponents. Frederick was also gifted with an inborn optimism
—contemporary references to his gaiety and cheerfulness are
frequent; it was a natural characteristic in a man who had always
enjoyed superbly good health, and excelled from childhood in
the sports which were admired in his own circle—he was a
magnificent horseman; a champion in the exercise of arms,
that played such an important part in the education of a
gentleman; a renowned huntsman, and he was notoriously
successful with women.

It is not surprising that such a man, when he felt himself
to be borne up on the tide of success, should forsake the habits
of caution and dissimulation which had been superimposed upon
his passionate nature by the adverse circumstances of his childhood, and give full rein to his basically sanguine temperament.
What is astonishing is that he continued to do so for so long,
and that this optimism only seems to have deserted him at the
very end when cynicism and suspicion gained the upper hand
after years of fruitless struggle. It is sad to think that this
characteristic which revealed the human and appealing side of
Frederick's character should have been responsible for so many
of his failures; if he had been more consistently scheming and
cautious he might have achieved far greater success, within the

limits of his fatal inheritance. He might have judged better too who in the closing years of his life were his real and who only his fair-weather friends. As it was the genius which could have achieved so much was destined to bring ruin upon himself, his dynasty, his realm and his Empire.

PART IV
The Struggle Joined

Chapter X

THE ZENITH

1231–1237

THE Peace of Ceprano which had set Frederick free to give full rein to his creative capacities also permitted him to return his attention to the problems of the Empire, that he had been forced to abandon at an inconclusive stage before the more pressing necessities of the Crusade and the aftermath of his excommunication.

Significantly it was the claims of the Empire in Italy, not Germany, that primarily engaged his notice. The peace was barely concluded when, with the inevitability of some Greek tragedy, events made inevitable by Frederick's fatal double inheritance of the Kingdom of Sicily and the Hohenstaufen dreams of imperial expansion began to unfold towards the final climax of the long struggle between the mediaeval popes and emperors. It was a struggle which was not only to destroy the Emperor but ultimately to bring the papacy down as well in the ruins of the great interregnum and the papal captivity of Avignon; thus ringing down the final curtain upon the Middle Ages.

In the century that preceded Frederick's reign the power of the Empire had markedly declined, and the two previous Hohenstaufen emperors had been aware that in spite of all their high-sounding titles, their position lacked a solid basis of power of the kind which the hereditary monarchies of England and France were already beginning to build up. This was the reason for their coveting the Kingdom of Sicily. The possession of Sicilian resources would fulfil their need for the financial backing for the immensely rich personal possessions which were necessary to maintain their power within the Empire. The situation was even more acute in Frederick's time. His succession to an impoverished ancestral Duchy of Swabia and a greatly weakened imperial power dictated his policy of concessions to the ecclesiastical princes—just how successful this policy was in attaching Germany to him personally may be judged in the light of later events—but he paid for it by an increasing dependence upon his Sicilian resources.

If he had been content to play a lesser role, Frederick might, by concentrating his extraordinary energies upon Germany, have succeeded in building up the imperial power again, but to do so he would have had to relinquish Sicily to his son; unhappily for the peace of the world, to a man of Frederick's temperament and tastes such a course of action was unthinkable. To keep both Germany and Sicily firmly within his grasp, geographical reasons made it essential that the imperial power should be renewed over Lombardy and some part of the papal states, in order to provide a safe overland line of communication between them. To achieve this the primary essential was the subjugation of Lombardy, which would deprive the Pope of his last effective ally in the Italian peninsula and inevitably bring about the weakening of the temporal power, thus facilitating the imperial recovery of part or all of the Patrimony of St. Peter.

The political and military necessity of this course of action was reinforced by the Emperor's own personal inclinations. He nourished an implacable hatred of the Milanese for their defeat of Barbarossa at Legnano, for their hostility to himself at the time of his accession to the Empire, and for their refusal to accord him the iron crown of Lombardy; moreover he was strongly opposed to the form of municipal self-government which was the pride of the Lombard communes. Their subjugation would, therefore, not only satisfy his desire for revenge, but also pave the way for his ultimate aim—the removal of the seat of Empire from Germany to Italy and the reinstatement of Rome as the imperial capital.

All the complicated influences of inheritance and environment—Hohenstaufen ambition, Italian upbringing, classical culture and polyglot tastes—merged to make this the ideal of Frederick's life. Based upon Rome he felt that the Empire would once more become universal, illuminated by the international prestige of the city of the Caesars; territorially it would be united and the power of its one great rival—the papacy

—would be limited to its proper spiritual sphere, under the protection of the temporal sword of the Emperor.

The history of the whole world would have been changed if Frederick had achieved his grandiose scheme, whose repercussions would still be felt today. All that apparently stood in his path were the obstinate inhabitants of a few bourgeois communes and the indomitable courage, and hatred, of a nonagenarian. Twice Frederick seemed to be within an ace of success, but the odds against him were in reality too great; ranged behind his principal foe was the incalculable power of the mediaeval Church, which had guided the thoughts of men since the fall of the Roman Empire. It was not only the papacy he was fighting, though that was formidable enough, but the mentality of his own age, and his weapons were insufficient.

The overture to this tremendous drama took the apparently innocuous form of the Emperor issuing invitations to an imperial diet. Beginning again where he had been forced to leave off in 1227, Frederick summoned his son, King Henry, the German princes, and the representatives of the cities of Northern Italy to meet him at Ravenna on All Saints' Day, 1231. The diet was to be devoted to "the honour of God, of the Church and of the Empire, and the prosperity of Lombardy". As a result of the Pope's counsels of moderation and advice that more would be obtained by peaceful means in Lombardy than by a show of force, the Emperor once again set out to hold his diet in this unruly province with only a small personal following. Gregory had promised to exercise his good offices in obtaining a conciliatory attitude on the part of the Lombards and free access to the Brenner for the German delegates.

But from the Lombard point of view the situation was even more threatening than in 1227. The apparent amity of the Emperor and Pope had already resuscitated the waning friendships of the cities of the league, who had recently re-cemented their alliance. The news of the impending diet galvanised them into immediate action; defensive measures were hastily undertaken and the Alpine passes were closed to the German delegates. The Pope's good offices, if indeed they were ever employed, were evidently of no avail, and the Diet of Ravenna looked like becoming as great a fiasco in 1231 as the Diet of Cremona had been in 1226.

Biding his time with apparent calm, Frederick delayed the opening day until Christmas and once again, as in 1227 in Pisa, he turned to the pursuit of his personal interests to distract him from the failure of his political ones. In the treasure house of the Byzantine emperors and Gothic kings, Frederick filled his days with archaeological activities, excavating the tomb of Galla Placidia that had been buried in a heap of rubble, and in the selection of rare marbles and antique statues which he dispatched to Sicily for the adornment of his own castles, thus showing himself yet once again as a precursor of the Renaissance even in this unamiable habit of plundering ancient monuments.

By Christmas-time quite a large number of the German princes had succeeded in making their way across the Alps by various means, but the Lombards' action in closing the passes forced them to adopt all manner of shifts and subterfuges in order to be able to answer the imperial summons to a diet in a province of the Empire. It is, therefore, scarcely surprising to find that the ban of Empire was placed upon the offending cities, and that the imperial sanctions against heretics were renewed with awful solemnity, no doubt with one eye upon the Pope, as a reminder of their prevalence among the citizens of Milan. Otherwise the diet was celebrated in an atmosphere of high festivity. It was a meeting of old friends such as Hermann von Salza, Archbishop Berard of Palermo, and Gebhard von Arnstein, who took part in the round of feasting, jousting, and hunting which was arranged for the entertainment of the court; while the populace was regaled with shows by mimers, acrobats and tumblers and the sight of the famous imperial menagerie—the elephant, the lions, the panthers and a host of other strange animals and birds that in mediaeval eyes contributed in no small part to the glamour of the imperial court.

In spite of the festive atmosphere a shadow more grave than the hostile attitude of the Lombard communes marred the rejoicings of the Diet of Ravenna; it was caused by the absence of the most important delegate of all—the Emperor's son, King Henry. Admittedly the closure of the passes represented a greater obstacle in his case than in that of his subjects the princes, but ways and means could have been found for him to rejoin his father by the Friuli route which so many others had followed, had he possessed the will to do so.

Unsatisfactory as it was, the Diet of Ravenna at least cleared the air in proving to the world at large that the Pope's good offices had not been enough or, possibly, that they had not been pressed home with sufficient energy to enable the Emperor to rely upon them in his future dealings with the communes. This second fiasco amply demonstrated the fact that force was the only language that an emperor could employ in order to make himself understood by his Lombard subjects. The Pope again offered himself as mediator and sent two cardinals north as his representatives, but from his choice of Lombard cardinals and their subsequent action in going first to see the rebellious towns, instead of waiting upon the Emperor to hear his views, it was painfully evident where Gregory's sympathies lay, and equally patent that any mediatory action undertaken by him would be heavily biased in favour of the Lombards.

In any event Frederick did not wait for the appearance of the Pope's envoys. Early in March he rode out of Ravenna and boarded a galley which had been kept secretly in waiting. He had given no indication of his future plans other than instructing the German princes to hold themselves in readiness for a further session of the diet in Aquileia at Easter. The closure of the Brenner and his son's non-appearance at Ravenna had decided the Emperor upon a double course of action. The first was a state visit as a gesture of friendship to Venice, whose benevolent neutrality must be assured as a means of keeping the Friuli–Styria route open, as the only alternative to the Brenner. The second was a direct command to his son to present himself at Aquileia at Easter.

The Patriarchs of Aquileia had exercised temporal power in their diocese since Carolingian times. In the eleventh century this had been extended to cover almost all of the province of Friuli, which they held as an imperial principality, deriving their power directly from the Emperor himself. The strategic importance of the province, as the back door to the Empire, was the reason for this privileged position. Successive emperors had been careful to see that the office of Patriarch was traditionally filled by one of their co-nationals who was usually to be counted upon as their supporter in any difference of opinion that might arise between them and the popes. A Patriarch of Aquileia it was who had assisted at the marriage of Frederick's mother and father and crowned them with the iron crown of Lombardy, thus incurring a papal interdict for his presumption.

The Most Serene Republic did not view the Emperor's proffered hand of friendship with any great enthusiasm, but they could scarcely refuse his devout request to pay homage to their national shrine of St. Mark, and the Grand Council gave their consent to his entering Venetian territory. Frederick stayed for a few days in Venice, made an offering of rich gifts to the sanctuary of St. Mark, and received in return a splinter of the True Cross, which he subsequently gave to Hermann von Salza, who was no doubt a more appreciative recipient of this signal honour. Towards the end of March, Frederick sailed for Aquileia, there to await the arrival of Henry. Some idea of the state of tension which now existed between father and son may be judged from the fact that the Emperor designated the neighbouring town of Cividale as Henry's place of residence, almost as if it were some foreign potentate with whom he was about to treat.

This coldness on the part of Frederick towards his son was something entirely foreign to his nature for, in spite of all his other faults, he really does seem to have been an affectionate father both to his legitimate and illegitimate offspring. His pride in his children made him expect great things of them, and he may be reproached with having laid too heavy burdens upon them while they were still too young. In this, however, he was not really singling them out for markedly differential treatment from that which he accorded to the many young nobles who flocked to his court. The younger generation of the Aquino family, his kinsmen the Hohenburg brothers, and at least one of the Caraccioli, were all entrusted with positions of grave responsibility while they were still in their twenties; and the Emperor's illegitimate sons, Enzio, Richard of Teate, and Frederick of Antioch and even Manfred, shouldered greater burdens when they were younger still.

Whereas these other young men seem to have acquitted themselves satisfactorily, Henry, the eldest son, displayed the Hohenstaufen liking for the good things of life without showing any sign of having inherited his ancestors' force of character and talent for statesmanship. Like his father he had matured at an early age, and like Frederick at the age of fourteen he was impatient of all restraint, a fatal characteristic in a young man who lacked his father's clarity of vision and steadfastness of purpose. The pleasures which were to Frederick the frivolous accessories of life were his son's ruling passion, and what was worse, he drew his advisers for the affairs of state from among his boon companions.

Poor Henry was not only foolish but unfortunate. Engelbert, the statesmanlike Archbishop of Cologne, whom his father had appointed as his *gubernator* when he was left in Germany as a child, was assassinated when the boy was only thirteen, and the other guardians who subsequently had charge of him until he came of age at eighteen do not seem to have been able to exercise the same moderating influence upon this difficult youth as their predecessor; while his father's prolonged absence from Germany encouraged Henry in his aspirations for complete independence. Ten years' separation inevitably reduced Frederick to a very shadowy figure in his son's mind, both as father and as Emperor, and no sooner had Henry reached his majority than he began to run counter to his father's policy.

From the first Frederick had based his government of Germany upon obtaining the support of the princes. Initially this policy had been dictated by the weakness of his own position, it was also the prime requisite for obtaining Henry's election that set him free to return to Sicily, and as a long-term policy the loyalty of the princes was the basic essential which would enable Frederick to absent himself from Germany in the pursuance of his vast scheme. To obtain this end, he had lavished upon them all his charm and diplomacy, distributing favours and large sums in cash, and to the ecclesiastical princes in particular he had relinquished many of the royal prerogatives and privileges. By way of return the princes had more or less kept the peace in Germany, supported him solidly on the Crusade and in his troubles with the Pope, and had materially assisted him in the negotiations which led up to the Peace of Ceprano.

Thus from Frederick's point of view his policy had achieved its end; but it was not in the best interests of Germany. Even if he had been successful in his plan for uniting Germany to Italy in one vast empire, Germany would have been relegated to a secondary position; his failure to do so loosed upon the country all the horrors of civil war in which the princes, who by his act almost achieved the status of petty sovereigns during his lifetime, vied with one another, reducing the unhappy country to a state of anarchy.

Archbishop Engelbert had evidently summed up Frederick's intentions at an early stage, and he concentrated upon educating Henry as a purely German King, preventing him from forming foreign attachments or contracting a foreign marriage. If the young King had been blessed with a fraction of his father's ability the outcome might have been a happy one, but as it was he felt that he knew more about Germany than Frederick and was entitled to take his own line of action. The arrogance of the princes, whom Henry had neither the prestige nor the character to control, antagonised him as it had done many of his predecessors, and he turned for support to their inferiors—the lesser nobility, the knights, the ministeriales, and even the burghers of the towns—surrounding himself with the least desirable representatives of these classes. The tragedy lay in the fact that if Henry had been a greater man, these were precisely the elements upon which the strength of a united Germany might in future have been built, but he was incapable of such vision, and in any case his character was not of the type to attract the serious men among them.

The princes were well aware of this, and when in 1230 Henry took the part of the citizens of Liège against their bishop, they united against him and succeeded in intimidating him to such an extent that they forced him to make a complete volte-face. At the Diet of Worms in the spring of 1231 they wrung from him privileges that made the lay princes as independent in their own domains as the ecclesiastical ones had been since Frederick had accorded them the "Privilegium in favorem principum ecclesiasticum" in 1220. The King relinquished the imperial rights of coining money, exacting tolls and customs, and building fortifications in the princes' lands. Frederick had only made similar concessions to the ecclesiastical princes— who by the non-hereditary nature of their office constituted a lesser threat to the Emperor than the princely families—in exchange for the election as his successor of his son and heir. Now Henry by his foolishness had weakened the imperial power and surrendered rights of inestimable value for nothing.

From motives of policy Frederick was compelled to put a good face upon the matter for he knew he could not retract what Henry had already given. Certainly he counted upon some very plain speaking to his son at Ravenna, but Henry's failure to put in an appearance changed the whole aspect of the matter from that of culpable stupidity to wilful disobedience; and disobedience was to Frederick the most unforgivable of crimes, striking at the basis of what he held most sacred—the imperial authority.

The full measure of Henry's foolishness may be judged from the fact that he was unwilling, either through fear or self-satisfaction, even to obey his father's summons to come to Friuli. In the end the imperial Chancellor, Bishop Sifrid of Ratisbon, who knew Frederick well, having assisted him in the negotiations for the Peace of Ceprano, succeeded in getting Henry to Cividale.

The King had to agree to accept the Emperor's conditions before he was received into his father's presence, and the conditions were humiliating, particularly for a young man of Henry's temperament. They amounted to putting him on probation, with the hated princes acting as watchdogs for his good behaviour and implicit obedience to the Emperor. A document was even drawn up which stated that the Patriarch of Aquileia, the Archbishops of Magdeburg and Salzburg, and the Dukes of Saxony, Meran and Carinthia, would be responsible for Henry's maintaining his promises and would take up arms against him if he did not. Henry was also forced to write to the Pope to say that he would be prepared to accept his own excommunication if he did not obey his father.

This was harsh treatment indeed, but Frederick had no other alternative, unless he was to reassume the direction of German affairs himself, for the pursuance of Henry's policy would have forced the princes into league against the Crown, thus constituting a threat of civil war in Germany and seriously endangering the whole fabric of the Empire. In the circumstances Frederick could not be expected to show fatherly indulgence, nor was he the man to put personal considerations before those of state.

The problems of Henry's making having been dealt with, Frederick agreed to confirm his son's concessions to the lay princes and settled down to discussing the plans for the reduction of Lombardy. The upshot was that the German delegates promised to raise an army for this purpose the following spring, and upon this understanding they were dismissed with lavish presents while the Emperor set about further preparing the ground for the expedition which he hoped would settle once and for all the thorny Lombard question. To this end Frederick entered into negotiations with the brothers Ezzelino and Alberico da Romano, who were a rising power in the Trevisan March, and they soon repaid his friendship in good earnest by gaining control of the vitally important city of Verona which laid the Brenner open to the German army.

The early months of 1232, that had opened so disappointingly for Frederick, concluded in a blaze of splendour. In Pordenone he had renewed the treaty of alliance with France, and the ambassadors of the Old Man of the Mountain and the Sultan of Damascus waited upon him with magnificent presents. The Sultan's included the famous planetarium made in the form of a tent in which astral bodies, worked in gold and jewels, moved in their circuits by hidden mechanism. Frederick declared that he prized this gift more than anything else in the world except his young son Conrad, and sent in return a white peacock and a white bear; this last created a great sensation upon its arrival in Syria because it would jump into the sea to catch fish; it must presumably have been a polar bear and its existence in the imperial menagerie casts an interesting light upon Frederick's connections with northern countries. The Emperor entertained his guests to a great banquet at Melfi after his return to Apulia in May. This celebration was held in honour of the Moslem feast on the anniversary of the Hegira; at it, to the astonishment of many, Christian bishops and German nobles sat down at table with the representatives of the Mohammedan potentates. Such an entertainment could have taken place at no other European court in the thirteenth century.

The Pope meanwhile was having trouble with the Romans, an endemic situation from which all mediaeval Popes suffered but Gregory more than any other, and affairs finally reached such a crisis that he was forced to call upon his good friend the Emperor for aid. The situation might have become embarrassing for Frederick, as it was plain that Gregory expected his personal intervention at the head of an army—the last thing that would have suited the Emperor's book—but fortunately for him Messina and several of the towns of eastern Sicily chose this particular moment to revolt against the suppression of municipal liberties brought about by the Constitution of Melfi. This situation provided a justifiable excuse for the Emperor to absent himself, while giving instructions to German, Provençal and Burgundian knights to go to the Pope's assistance.

There was trouble too in Outremer. Under the leadership of John of Ibelin the barons had defeated Frederick's representative Richard Filangieri, and Hermann von Salza was dispatched to investigate the situation. With the assistance of the papal legates, von Salza succeeded in patching up some sort of peace, but local hostility to Frederick and Filangieri was too strong for it to be of a lasting nature. In spite of the Pope's deposition of the intransigent Patriarch Gerold, the situation degenerated, and within a year Cyprus was lost.

By this time Frederick had again agreed to accept the Pope's offer to mediate in the Lombard dispute, and in order to discuss this, and the Emperor's aid to the harassed Pontiff, a new embassy was required. Hermann von Salza's absence in the Near East had deprived Frederick of his usual ambassador, and in his stead he dispatched the Grand Justiciar, Henry of Morra, and a rising star at court, Pietro della Vigna. This brilliant Capuan jurist, who was a little older than his imperial master, had first been brought to court by Archbishop Berard of Palermo, who had been struck by the polished Latin style of a letter which this enterprising young man had addressed to him as long ago as 1220.

For the last twelve years Pietro della Vigna had worked in the imperial chancery in various minor capacities, later making his début in a small way in the diplomatic world at the time of the Peace of Ceprano; this new mission was to launch him upon his great career—Pietro della Vigna was to become the outstanding example of the new type of civil servant which was brought into being by Frederick's creation of the Sicilian prototype of the modern lay state. Hitherto mediaeval statesmen had been nobles or churchmen, but Pietro della Vigna came of an impoverished middle-class family and he had never taken holy orders, which until then had provided the only means to a successful career for young men who lacked noble birth and

I

influence. In spite of his poverty Pietro had apparently studied at Bologna University, but it was to his birthplace that he owed the training which brought him to the fore.

Capua had long been famous for its school of *ars dictandi*— the formal style of Latin prose writing that was so much admired at this period, and of which Pietro della Vigna was to become the most renowned exponent. To us today his letters and dispatches appear to be so heavily overloaded with hyperbole and biblical and classical allusions that they resemble in the literary field the florid baroque architecture of the south, but for centuries his writings were cherished by the chanceries of Europe as models of style.

This gift of Pietro's was a sure passport to the Emperor's favour as, in common with the other arts, Frederick considered that the correspondence of the imperial chancery should be the mirror of style. He carried this idea to such extremes that, according to Fra Selimbene, he once had the thumb of a scribe cut off for having wrongly spelt his imperial master's name. Questions of style apart, it was supremely important to the Emperor to have at his disposal a man who excelled in the art of drafting the letters and manifestos which, from the earliest days of his reign, played such an important part in Frederick's political activity. As the rivalry with the Papal Curia increased, so did the importance of this form of propaganda, in which the Church had the advantage of the experience of centuries, to such an extent that in comparison all the other European rulers were mere tyros.

We do not know if Pietro della Vigna had any hand in drafting the circular letters which Frederick sent out before the Crusade, but it is possible that this was so, as he already occupied a position of sufficient eminence in 1230 to take an important, if not the principal, part in the drafting of the Constitution of Melfi. During the summer of 1232 he prepared the Emperor's letters to the Pope; it was natural, therefore, that he should be chosen to accompany Henry of Morra on his mission. This proved to be inconclusive; the Emperor's demands for satisfaction for the closure of the Brenner were not met, and the situation was further complicated by his understandable refusal to recognise the Lombard League as such; to him they were simply so many cities of one of the provinces of his Empire who opposed his legal authority. Even in the midst of his difficulties with the Romans the Pope could not afford to put too much pressure upon this his one powerful Italian ally, and, aided by the Emperor's apparent preoccupation with other things, he diplomatically allowed the negotiations to fizzle out.

In the following year the Pope's position was unexpectedly reinforced by the most untoward happening—Northern and Central Italy were swept by a wave of revivalist religious frenzy, which has gone down in history as the "Great Halleluja". Fanatical preachers toured all Northern and Central Italy exhorting the people to penance and proclaiming a universal peace. Thousands fell under their sway, and so great was their influence that even a hardened sinner like Ezzelino da Romano was forced to swear obedience to the most powerful of them all—Fra Giovanni di Vicenza—who was popularly proclaimed Duke of Verona. As suddenly as it had fallen the spell was broken. After some four hundred thousand persons had attended a peace meeting near Vicenza the whole artificial fabric broke up and the internecine warfare of the northern cities broke out again in full force, restoring the *status quo*.

This orgy of repentance passed by the Sicilian realm, and its monarch was so much occupied with his own affairs that for the moment Lombardy appeared to be forgotten, though Frederick had now obviously realised that the quarrel could only be settled by force of arms. The rebellion in Sicily was put down with savage cruelty. Frederick's conduct on this occasion was one of the darkest stains upon his character, for he teacherously broke his promise of pardon. Any form of rebellion against the imperial power always brought out the worst in him, for, believing that it was divinely inspired, he regarded opposition to it as a form of sacrilege. So now in suppressing the Messina rebellion, Frederick invoked the anti-heretical laws of the Constitution of Melfi, consigning the rebels to the stake. The ring-leaders were fortunate in escaping to Malta where they were caught and merely hanged, but many of the luckless citizens of Messina, who had taken refuge in a church and subsequently surrendered upon being promised pardon, were seized and put to death. Similar massacres took place in Catania, Syracuse and Nicosia; and Centorbe, which put up some sort of resistance, was destroyed, such of its inhabitants as survived being forcibly transported to the newly founded city of Augusta.

In December of 1233 the Emperor held a court at Syracuse, and again in January of the new year at Messina. After crushing the rebellion without pity he made a thorough investigation of the situation in the island of Sicily. He was too intelligent a man to believe that it would be to his own advantage to rule by oppressive methods indefinitely, and after six years' absence he wished to be informed personally of the conditions reigning in the island which had given rise to such an outbreak. At Syracuse a law was promulgated that forbade his Sicilian subjects to marry foreign nationals. It was a curious provision for a man of such polyglot origins and tastes as Frederick to have made, and who, moreover, ruled an empire that embraced so many different nationalities. It would almost seem as if the Emperor were convinced that some foreign element had been at work in stirring up trouble. Another result of his investigations into the state of Sicily was the institution of provincial courts for the reform of abuses in the administrative machine, and the creation of numerous trade fairs and markets in the realm. It was at this time too that the Emperor began building the Sicilian castles.

While Frederick was wintering in the clement climate of the island of Sicily, Italy was devastated by the rigid cold of one of the worst winters of historical times. Rivers were frozen and Venice was linked by sheets of ice to the mainland, there was starvation and misery everywhere, and famine even in Rome. Driven by hunger the mob sacked the palaces of the cardinals and even the Lateran; the Pope fled to Rieti and appealed to the kings of Christendom to come to his aid. Even the habitually cynical Romans had been affected by the Great Halleluja, but now that they had reverted to their hostility to the Pope they elected an anti-papal senator who claimed in their name part of the territories of the Patrimony of St. Peter— the Campagna and Tuscany.

It was an ill wind for the Pope but most convenient for Frederick, for the news from Germany had been disquieting. All the reports indicated that Henry was alienating his father's greatest friends, and that gradually disorder was spreading through the country. Looking ahead Frederick saw that his son's incapacity would soon provoke a crisis in Germany, and in that event the Pope's support might well be essential to him. The time was propitious. If at some future date he might need papal support, the Pope himself was in urgent present need of the Emperor's aid. Taking his young son Conrad with him, Frederick paid a surprise visit to Gregory in his refuge at Rieti. Superficially at any rate, it was a friendly meeting, and it was probably upon this occasion that the Pope suggested to the Emperor that he should take an English wife—Henry III's sister the Princess Isabella—for not long afterwards Pietro della Vigna was dispatched to London to undertake the preliminary negotiations for the match.

It was a serious step for Frederick to take, as inevitably an English marriage would, to a greater or less extent, estrange the French who had always been loyal allies of the Hohenstaufen. But Henry's behaviour in Germany had brought the question of a possible change in the succession to the fore, and the Emperor had only one other legitimate child, the seven-year-old Conrad. Then there was the further advantage that an English alliance would deprive the hostile Guelf faction in Germany of English support, an important consideration in the event of further trouble with Henry, which now appeared to be unavoidable It was in anticipation of this that Frederick now extracted from the Pope an agreement for Henry's excommunication.

On his side the Emperor promised immediate intervention on the Pope's behalf against the insurgent Romans. Frederick had a sizeable force of German soldiers with him in Italy at the time, under the able command of Richard Cœur de Lion's old comrade-in-arms, the Bishop of Winchester, and the Count of Toulouse. Nevertheless the Emperor went in person to the assistance of the papal forces who were being attacked by the Romans at Viterbo, and succeeded in relieving the town though, after devastating the surrounding countryside, he failed to take the fortress of Raspampani near the modern Tuscania.

This active intervention of the Emperor's on the Pope's behalf and their apparent friendliness again aroused the suspicions of the Milanese, but Gregory sent word to them in secret that in spite of his need for Frederick's support against the Romans, he would do nothing to prejudice the Lombards' position. After the failure of Raspampani Frederick appears to have tired of fighting the Pope's battles for him, and returned to Apulia, though he left his army behind to continue the offensive, and with this backing Gregory finally negotiated a peace with the Romans.

The Emperor's prescience in going to see Gregory was rewarded sooner, probably, than even he had anticipated. As it turned out Frederick had ensured papal support for his future actions in Germany only in the nick of time, for at the same moment that his father was besieging Raspampani, Henry had thrown down the gauntlet to the princes. In defiance of his father's most solemn injunctions and in violation of his own oaths, the King sided with the inhabitants of the Rhineland cities and freed them from their allegiance to their bishops. Unrest, which until then had been latent, rapidly developed into civil war and Henry and his brother-in-law the Duke of Austria made a concerted attack upon one of the Emperor's warmest supporters, the Duke of Bavaria. When the news reached the Emperor, he at once invalidated his son's freeing of the Rhineland cities and threatened the disturbers of the peace; meanwhile the terrible blow of excommunication fell upon the unfilial son who had dared to turn against his father and Emperor.

The full depth of Henry's treachery was not known until the end of 1234 when it emerged that during the autumn the young King's agents, Anselm of Justingen and Walter of Tannenburg, had secretly negotiated an agreement between him and the Milanese. It was an offensive and defensive alliance which was to be renewed in perpetuity every ten years, and as an outward and visible sign of this astonishing pact of friendship between a member of the house of Hohenstaufen and its most inveterate enemies, Henry was offered the iron crown of Lombardy which had been refused to his imperial father for the past fifteen years. Thus to treachery was added insult—it would have been impossible for a son of Frederick to have taken any action better calculated to enrage and wound his father.

The Emperor passed Easter 1235 in seclusion at his hunting box at Precina near Foggia; then he set out for Germany. On his way north Frederick held court at Fano to arrange for the administration of the realm during his absence which, given the state of affairs in Germany, might well be expected to be of long duration. The next lap of the journey from Rimini to the coast of Friuli was accomplished by sea.

It says much for the Emperor's personal prestige that he set out for Germany after so many years' absence, and upon such a serious undertaking as quelling his own son's rebellion, with only a small personal following. It is a curious fact that Frederick seems to have been far better able to take the measure of his German subjects, with whom he had so little in common, than that of the Italians whom he preferred. Evidently his previous experience had convinced him that plentiful largesse, combined with the glamour of his own personality, were the best means with which to subjugate his northern kingdom. Accordingly he set forth armed only with the riches that the *collecta* recently imposed upon his Sicilian subjects had provided him, and all the panoply of Oriental splendour with which he knew so well how to dazzle the Germans—the imperial menagerie accompanied him to play its part in the game of imperial politics.

If, by persuading Gregory to excommunicate King Henry, the Emperor had prepared the ground well in advance for his unhappy mission, the Pope was not in such a fortunate position. Gregory had landed himself in a quandary—his Lombard friends had allied themselves to the man whom he had been forced to excommunicate, and furthermore they had been guilty of encouraging a son to rebel against his father. In the circumstances the Pope had no other alternative but to support Frederick, the justly outraged father, though it must have been a bitter pill for him to swallow. It was too late to produce some face-saving formula for mediaeval consciences, that might have enabled him to support, even clandestinely, Henry's alliance with the Lombards, which would have suited his book so much better; the best that Gregory could do was to support Frederick in Germany, and to soft-pedal as much as he could the part which the Lombards had played in the whole affair.

Many of the German princes had travelled to Aquileia to greet their Emperor, and more flocked to join him during his journey across Styria and Bavaria, where they witnessed the Duke's reward for his fidelity to Frederick in the betrothal of his seven-year-old daughter Margaret to the young Prince Conrad.

The Emperor's arrival in Germany was sufficient to cause

his son's supporters to desert and to flee for refuge to their own strongholds. Abandoned by all Henry begged Hermann von Salza to intercede with the Emperor on his behalf; apparently he still cherished the hope that he would be forgiven and reinstated and in the mistaken idea of strengthening his position he made the crucial error of retaining Trifels and other fortresses—he is even said to have attempted flight. But his father was adamant—nothing but unconditional surrender would suffice.

Finally in the first week of July, in Worms, the wretched youth flung himself at the Emperor's feet and lay, sobbing, on the ground as with a voice broken with misery he begged his father's pardon. A dreadful silence descended upon the whole court as Frederick made no move or sign of recognition of his son's presence; at last, as if unable to bear the strain, several of the princes interceded upon Henry's behalf, and he was allowed to rise. But there and then he was forced to renounce in the presence of the whole court all his titles and possessions, and to throw himself unreservedly upon his father's mercy.

Henry was sentenced to be exiled from the Emperor's presence for ever, and was imprisoned in Heidelberg castle, with the Duke of Bavaria, his deadly enemy, for gaoler. His life was spared, but that availed him little. The rest of it was to be spent immured in the imperial fortresses of Sicily, for he was handed over shortly afterwards to the Marquis Lancia, who conducted him to the Castle of San Felice (now San Fele) near Melfi, where he languished for years. Later he was transferred to Nicastro, and was on his way to yet another prison when he committed suicide at the age of thirty by riding his horse over a cliff.

If Frederick was pitiless to his own son, it is difficult to conceive of any other course of action that was open to him. In the thirteenth century to set Henry at liberty would have been to invite every malcontent or enemy to rally to him, or to make use of him as a pawn in their hostility to the Emperor; and Henry had already given overwhelming proof of not only criminal foolishness but outright treachery. There was no alternative to making him a prisoner of state, other than his execution, but for all his bitterness and rage Frederick never seems to have envisaged such a step.

Henry had been solely to blame for the troubles which had arisen in Germany, and with a fine sense of justice and diplomacy the Emperor dealt lightly with his son's adherents. He even released the Milanese envoys who were found hiding in Trifels, and ultimately forgave the Bishop of Worms and the rest of Henry's more eminent supporters, nor is there any record of Frederick's having, as might have been expected of even the most clement mediaeval sovereign, exacted a toll of blood among the smaller fry for the rebellion against his authority.

While the last act of the unhappy drama of Henry's rebellion was taking place, the whole of Germany was preparing for an event of a very different character—the Emperor's marriage to the English princess Isabella. Even in the gloomy depths of his prison poor Henry must have heard some distant rumour of the approaching celebrations, and meditated upon the tragic irony of events that found him now a prisoner while his father was preparing to marry the beautiful girl who had been proposed as a bride for himself ten years earlier. The negotiations for the wedding had been in progress since the previous August, when Pietro della Vigna was first dispatched to London; he had returned later with plenary powers to negotiate the marriage contract, and it was this onerous mission that really brought Pietro to the foremost rank among the imperial diplomatists. He was empowered to swear upon the Emperor's soul that he was willing to wed the princess and, what was most important of all, to negotiate the amount of the dowry. In this last Pietro seems to have driven a shrewd bargain, for the future Empress brought with her a dot of thirty thousand marks sterling, half as much again as her predecessor, the princess Joan, had been given when she married William the Good, the last Norman king of Sicily.

Pietro della Vigna was also fortunate in the fact that Isabella really seems to have been beautiful—when at last he was allowed to see her, after her brother, King Henry, and the English barons had debated for three days the pros and cons of this momentous match, the chroniclers relate that Pietro gazed upon her with delight; relieved, no doubt, that in contracting this marriage of state for his imperial master, he was not to be responsible for introducing a plain princess into the bed of such a connoisseur of feminine charms as Frederick.

When Isabella was brought from the Tower to the Court of Westminster for the betrothal ceremony, which took place at the end of February, Pietro della Vigna renewed his master's offer of marriage to her personally, swearing upon the Emperor's soul and offering her his ring. After the princess had given a graceful acquiescence, Pietro placed Frederick's ring upon her finger, and amid great acclamations saluted her as Empress of the Romans.

Isabella was twenty-one at the time. She had been brought up in a highly civilised court; in spite of his deficiencies as a sovereign Henry III was a great patron of the arts and his sister's gracious manner and distinguished speech impressed even Frederick. Henry seems to have been fond of Isabella, for the Close Rolls of the time contain several records of his presents to her. One was a packet of a hundred almonds—a great luxury in the England of those days—and there are other entries which describe objects as varied as luxurious furnishings for her private chapel—a silver chalice and stole and maniple of gold embroidery—and saddles for her use. If Henry was extravagant on his own account he was evidently not niggardly over his sister's wardrobe—even before she made this splendid match her clothes were magnificent; scarlet robes furred with doeskin, a scarlet skirt furred with grey squirrel, and blue and green dresses of fine French stuffs, trimmed with ermine, figure among the items listed in the Close Rolls.

When it came to Isabella's trousseau its splendour was the talk of London. Her crown of purest gold was beautifully worked with the images of four English martyr kings; she had a magnificent necklace, and coffers full of other jewels; a whole service of gold and silver plate was sumptuously worked. Even the cooking-pots were of silver—though this was, justifiably, considered to be an unwarranted extravagance. There were magnificent robes and silken furnishings for the nuptial bed, and a train of the finest horses.

The Archbishop of Cologne and the Duke of Brabant came to fetch Isabella after Easter, and in the beauty of an English spring the princess said farewell to her native land for ever; she must have longed for it sometimes in the arid summers of Apulia, and on her deathbed her last words were spoken to recommend it and her brother to her imperial husband. But now all was gaiety and splendour, three thousand knights accompanied her, first to Canterbury where she prayed at the tomb of Thomas à Becket, then on to Sandwich where ships provisioned with the finest wines, wheat and bacon were waiting on the 11th of May to take her to Antwerp.

From Antwerp to Cologne Isabella's journey was one long triumphal procession. At Cologne itself ten thousand burghers came out to meet her and riders on Spanish horses surrounded her, indulging in mock battles and breaking their lances in her honour. The city rang with the pealing of bells, and she was received by the clergy bearing banners, and the nobles of the town. The streets were decorated with flowers, brilliant tapestries hung from the houses and meistersingers accompanied her as she rode in procession through the streets—their music pleased her so greatly that she kept them at her court for the rest of her stay. The whole town was agog to see what their Emperor's bride was really like, and when Isabella was told that the ladies watching from their windows to see her ride by had hoped to see her face, she won all their hearts by letting fall her hood and veil. A magnificent entertainment was staged for her in which galleys filled with singers, that floated upon artificial waves made of silk, were pulled through the streets by horses. This festive atmosphere continued for the six weeks that Isabella remained in Cologne, until the summons came for her to proceed to Worms for the wedding. It was a ceremony of unparalleled splendour attended by four kings, eleven dukes, thirty counts and marquesses, and prelates and knights innumerable. Four whole days were given up to feasting and jousting; the German meistersingers, French minstrels, and Provençal and Italian *trovatori* rivalled one another in providing music for the guests; though the occasion was considered to be too solemn for the lighter forms of entertainment such as those provided by tumblers and acrobats.

Isabella can have seen little of this rejoicing for she was immediately introduced to the secluded harem life which was to be her lot; on the advice of the court astrologers the marriage was not consummated until the day after the wedding. Immediately thereafter Frederick handed her over to the charge of black eunuchs, who Matthew Paris described as being "as hideous as old masks". Frederick was twenty years older than

Isabella, and it was a purely political match, but even so his treatment of her seems callous in the extreme. The princess was only allowed to keep two of her English women attendants; one was her maid Kathrein, a Londoner who was skilled as an embroideress of the famous *Opus Anglicanum*, the other was probably her old nurse Margaret Biset, who had been with her since childhood. History does not relate what Margaret Biset, that early prototype of the English nanny on the Continent, made of "the old masks" who shared her task as guardians of her young mistress.

In retaining only two of the women in his wife's service Frederick was evidently determined at the outset to ensure that there should be no foreign clique at his court. It seems probable, however, that later he may have relented a little in this respect, for eight years after Isabella's death, two English women named Agnes and Magalda, who appear to have been single, were living in houses which belonged to the Emperor at Foggia. The most reasonable explanation for the rather odd presence in the thirteenth century of these two unattached English females so far from home seems to be that at one time they may have been attached to the Empress's household.

But in Worms the Emperor dismissed all the rest of Isabella's English train, loading them with costly presents, and sending in their care three leopards as a gift to his brother-in-law King Henry. These living symbols of the English royal arms were destined to become foundation members of the Tower of London Zoo—Frederick seems to have led the fashion for royal menageries, which in conservative England survived for another six centuries.

The junketings of the imperial marriage over, Frederick settled down to the serious business of restoring order in the German political world. He called a diet in Mainz for August, which continued there through September and October, and was completed in November in Augsburg. It was the most important political event of Frederick's reign in Germany, and influenced the history of the country for centuries to come. The German princes were present almost to a man, and the proceedings were conducted in an atmosphere of such stateliness and splendour as to recall the golden days of Barbarossa.

The primary aim of the diet was to give legal form to Henry's deposition, and this was done by the enactment of a new law which laid down that whoever took arms against his father, allied himself with his enemies, or threatened his life and liberty, lost all right to his paternal and maternal inheritance, and was condemned to be handed over to imperial justice. Henry was thus definitely disposed of, and his father armed with added legal means with which to attack his son's former supporters if necessary. The Emperor went one step further in his fury against Henry and recognised the princes' right not only to elect but also to depose the sovereign—a very perilous precedent and contrary to the policy of his ancestors, though he had already accepted it *de facto* by his own accession after the deposition of Otto.

The lay princes' rights accorded to them by Henry at the Diet of Worms in 1231, and confirmed by Frederick at Aquileia, were examined in detail and embodied in a code of laws which were promulgated for the first time in German. Some of the Sicilian laws were now introduced into Germany— such as the suppression of trial by combat and the payment of blood money—an imperial grand justiciar on the Sicilian model was also instituted, though without jurisdiction over the princes. This new code was not an all-embracing constitution like that of Melfi but if time had allowed it could have paved the way towards a more ordered legal system.

The last really important event of this momentous diet was the termination of the feud that had for generations divided the houses of Guelf and Hohenstaufen. Frederick had by now regained all the hereditary lands of his own family, which had been dispersed during the life of his uncle Philip, and he had added to them by purchasing outright the lands of Brunswick. These last he made over as a gift to Otto Guelf, creating him Duke of Brunswick-Lüneburg—and so an alliance based on friendship replaced the vendetta that had caused so much bloodshed in Germany. The diet closed with a high mass sung in Augsburg Cathedral which the Emperor attended in the full glory of the imperial regalia. Afterwards he gave an enormous banquet to which were invited all the German princes and twelve thousand knights.

Frederick now withdrew to spend Christmas and the rest of the winter season in comparative seclusion at his favourite residence of Hagenau, and there he received the ambassadors of the King of Castile and a Russian duke. The menagerie had accompanied him and the inhabitants of Colmar rushed to see the camels peacefully chewing the cud in a neighbouring field. One of them was shortly dispatched as a gift to Henry of England with a train of pack-horses loaded with gifts. It was also at this time that, from his profound knowledge of the Jewish religion, the Emperor was able to give judgement disproving a case of ritual murder of a Christian alleged to have taken place at Fulda, that had been the cause of a pogrom. Not content with simply giving judgement from his own knowledge, Frederick instituted an inquiry addressed to all the Christian kings, in which he asked them to have recent converts from the Jewish faith questioned upon the subject of Jewish rites and ritual—the result of this inquiry was a triumphal vindication of his own conclusions.

The sojourn at Hagenau was, however, more in the nature of a rest after the trials and anxieties of the preceding year, and in preparation for the campaign against the Lombards which now loomed close upon the horizon; and Frederick spent his days in hunting and in the company of his new wife. After the brief, and rather terrifying, encounter of their marriage, Isabella now appears to have succeeded in arriving at some sort of friendly relationship with her eccentric husband. She had no more influence over him than either of his other wives, less in fact that Constance, who was actually crowned Empress, nor, to her brother's annoyance, did she ever appear in public upon state occasions wearing her crown. But, within the limits of his curious attitude to women, Frederick seems to have admired her and even to have been fond of her. Isabella's good looks and witty conversation pleased him, and when her brother, Richard of Cornwall, was allowed to visit her he found her surrounded by new and "unknown toys and games and musical instruments" which the Emperor had ordered for her amusement.

Isabella appears to have been particularly fond of music— we have seen how much she enjoyed the meistersingers' performance on her wedding journey—and in the fragment of the imperial registers that survived until the last war there was an entry ordering a sackbut for her, either for her own use (both her brothers played instruments) or one of her minstrels. These same registers also contained many references to the requirements of "Our dearest consort"—servants for her household, preparations to be made for her arrival in Naples, orders for clothes, rich silks and brocades, and even slippers. These make their appearance in between dispatches of the most serious nature, and the Emperor's personal requirements which were usually concerned with falcons, hounds, and hunting leopards. If she was forced by her husband's jealousy to live a life of seclusion, the Empress was evidently maintained in the greatest luxury. But in common with any other woman of the thirteenth century, Isabella was left in no doubt that her only real function in life was to produce an heir and as many other children as she could to safeguard the succession.

Another, and more curious, interlude preceded the Emperor's return to the world of the hard realities of the Lombard quarrel. In May 1236 Frederick went in state to Marburg for the translation of the body of the recently canonized St. Elizabeth of Hungary, his own kinswoman and the widow of the Landgrave of Thuringia, who had died in the epidemic at Brindisi in 1227. When the body of this saintly princess—who in her widowhood had abjured the world in imitation of St. Francis—was lifted from the grave, the Emperor crowned her head with a golden coronet, and stood devoutly by while her mortal remains were transferred to a golden casket which was to be enshrined in the great church raised to house them. On the morrow Frederick wrote a detailed account of the proceedings to his old friend Brother Elias, now Minister-General of the Franciscan Order. In it the Emperor's pride of race, which in his younger days had rarely manifested itself, clearly emerges. He rejoices that the newly canonized saint was of royal blood, and goes on to note that only those of noble birth could touch the Ark of the Covenant and finally that Christ himself was of the royal line of David!

This sudden demonstration of piety on the part of Frederick might be partly explained by his pride of kinsmanship, and partly by the fact that St. Elizabeth could now be regarded as the patron saint of the Empress Isabella, whose christian name was a romance version of her own. But it is more likely that the solemn pomp of the occasion served above all else to present

the Emperor effectively in his role of a devout prince first among
the Christian kings. It was necessary at this precise moment
to underline this aspect of Frederick's sovereignty, for the
Pope had suddenly started to preach the imperative necessity of
an immediate Crusade.

Gregory's motives in doing this were purely political, for
Jerusalem was safe in Christian hands for another four years
until the ten years' term of Frederick's treaty with the Sultan
had expired. It was not anxiety for the Holy Places that had
prompted the Pope's sudden fervour for a Crusade, but something much nearer home—the imminent threat to the Lombard
cities. The German princes were united in their determination
to back their Emperor in the subjugation of these unruly subjects, for the Lombards had been allies of the traitor Henry
who had tried to introduce the iniquitous regime of self-governing communes into Germany by freeing the cities of the Rhine.
Henry had at least performed this one service for his father;
his actions had ranged the princes solidly behind the Emperor
in his enmity against the Lombards.

The Pope had begged for a short respite in which to pursue
peaceful negotiations with the Lombards, and Frederick had
given him until Christmas to arrange a settlement. But
Gregory seized upon even this slight relaxation on the Emperor's part as a sign of wavering, and demanded that Frederick
should agree to accept, unconditionally, any terms he might
arrange, a ridiculous request that the Emperor naturally turned
down, but to preserve outward amity he dispatched Hermann
von Salza to join Pietro della Vigna, who was watching the
Emperor's interests at the papal court.

The Grand Master's mission was fruitless, as the Lombard
envoys failed to put in an appearance until after his departure
from Rome, and in spite of Gregory's insistence he refused to
return to wait upon their pleasure. Thus Frederick had proved
his point by his diplomacy in sending von Salza at the eleventh
hour to negotiate. The world could now judge that the crafty
communes were prepared to play fast and loose with Emperor
and Pope alike, because they were fully confident that in the last
resort they would have Gregory's support. Such behaviour
aroused a protest even from the King of Hungary who wrote to
the Pope warning him against supporting the Lombards.

The time for diplomatic caution was past, it had served its purpose, and it had furnished repeated proofs—if that were necessary—that nothing would serve but the military defeat of the Lombard communes. Just as there was no mistaking the Emperor's deeds, when he collected his German army ready to descend through the Alpine passes, so now his words made his intentions equally plain—Lombardy was but the first step, Italy was the goal, and he proclaimed it for all to hear when he stated "Italy is my heritage as all the world knows". The gauntlet had been flung down and with savage irony Frederick seized upon the Pope's pretext of the Crusade and, tearing it to pieces, revealed it for what it was—"to cross the sea to fight the infidel, when heresies pullulate around us, would be to dress the wound without extracting the iron. As it is impossible to undertake a Crusade without great treasure and the aid of a large army, and my resources are not sufficient, I propose to consecrate the riches of my enemies to the cause of God." Nor was the Emperor exaggerating when he implied that heresy was rife among the Pope's Lombard protégés—the Patarenes had risen in Mantua, and pursuing the Bishop into the cathedral, had crucified him above the altar, and committed other terrible acts of sacrilege and cruelty.

Now there was to be no turning back, the great struggle with the Lombards, that was to be the first and most important step in the battle for Italy, was joined. Frederick strained every nerve, and employed all his resources, in preparing for this campaign which was to be the crisis of his whole career. The gold of the Empress's dowry was used to hire the knights and mercenaries who would constitute the hard core of the army, another *collecta* was raised in Sicily to meet the costs of the war, and the feudal armies of the princes were called up.

But even in this supreme effort the results fell far short of the achievements of his predecessors; Frederick can never have disposed of as much as a modern division to put into the field— at the most some fifteen thousand men—a puny force when contrasted with the hundred thousand that the chroniclers attributed to Barbarossa. This was the tragedy of Frederick's life, and a prime cause of his downfall—he never possessed the military force which was the basic essential for achieving his dream of empire—but with his sanguine temperament and consciousness of his own brilliance he does not seem to have realised it. Although Frederick became an efficient general he was not a military genius; in fact he does not appear to have been as capable a soldier as either of his grandfathers.[15]

The Emperor marched south as soon as the Alps could be crossed, arriving in Verona on the 16th of August. There was desultory fighting going on over most of Northern Italy but the Milanese had prudently withdrawn to the shelter of their city walls, so that the campaign of the summer of 1236 was more in the nature of a preliminary skirmish to clear the ground for the great battles of the year to come. In company with the Romano brothers Frederick seized and sacked Vicenza. An extraordinarily circumstantial account of this event has survived among the chronicles of the times. Its paints so vividly the horror, confusion, and destruction of war, and the rivalries which existed within the cities themselves, that it might serve as a description of war in Italy as seen by a civilian of any period.

The writer described his mournful fate as follows: "I, though a most faithful subject, was seized by the Germans and bound, whereas I ought to have been honourably rewarded by Frederick. For I alone, when no one else dared do it, openly withstood the Lombard League, siding against the Marquis [of Este]. I did this out of love for the Emperor and the Lords Romano, not like others out of hatred of the Milanese. I was a most faithful trumpet in preaching loyalty, but others are rewarded and I am not. I have not ceased to preach like any Dominican, for I have seen Frederick's justice towards his subjects, his glory, and his most righteous customs. Now since I have been robbed neither Frederick nor the Lords of Romano recognise me. For three days I have walked through the city in a most mean garment; some gave me money to buy back my books and to get food and raiment. I excuse our Lord the Emperor, because I was unknown to him; and also the Lords of Romano, because of the dangers that threatened them; I was ever true to them, and so I remain sure of reward. I saw many noble ladies and people of both sexes stripped naked, one man could hardly recognise another; all were punished, the just and the unjust. ... We at Vicenza suffered for the fault of a few; although our merciful Lord Frederick might have ruined all the citizens, he pitied them, and gave them back all their real property, and ordered Ezzelino to set free the prisoners, but to detain the rebels. Many Guelfs were released, but I was thrust out at midnight by the Germans, naked and stripped of all."

Other chroniclers relate an incident curiously at variance with Ezzelino's reputation for cruelty, especially to women; they describe how he killed a man who was raping a lady of Vicenza, and turned to the Emperor saying that he would have done the same to him if he had been guilty of "so great a scandal". It was at Vicenza that Frederick is said to have demonstrated to Ezzelino the art of government by means of a symbolic act— he beheaded with his dagger the tallest grasses in the Bishop's garden. Even on a serious military expedition of this kind, the Emperor was accompanied by his astrologer; on this occasion it was probably Master Theodore, who was put to the test by being asked through which gate of the town Frederick would make his departure. The reply was given in a sealed letter, and Theodore was vindicated when, after passing through a breach which had been specially made in the walls, his master read the words "By the new gate".

When the autumn weather made campaigning in Italy impossible, the Emperor crossed the Alps to deal with the outstanding problems left in his northern kingdom—the settlement of accounts with the Duke of Austria, who had sided with Henry and failed to put in an appearance at the Diet of Mainz and Augsburg. There was another and more imperative reason for Frederick's return, but it was one that he could scarcely admit to openly—the question of the succession—which he had apparently felt it was premature to broach at Mainz. This was even more pressing because, after nearly two years of marriage, the Empress had finally given birth to a daughter, Margaret, instead of the eagerly awaited son.

After spending a quiet Christmas at Graz, in the new year of 1237 the Emperor proceeded to Vienna; his enemy Frederick of Babenburg, Duke of Austria, fled at his approach, shutting himself up in the fortress of Wiener Neustadt. At the end of January a splendid court was held in the Austrian capital, which was attended by the King of Bohemia, the Dukes of Bavaria and Carinthia, the Landgrave of Thuringia, the Patriarch of Aquileia, the Archbishops of Mainz, Treves and Salzburg, and Hermann von Salza. These august persons elected Conrad King of the

Romans, thus assuring his succession, and amid the feasting and celebrations that followed, Frederick declared Vienna an imperial city, directly dependent upon the Emperor, and appropriated to himself the Dukedoms of Austria and Styria. From Vienna he proceeded to Speyer, where at a diet held in June the rest of the princes confirmed Conrad's election.

With Germany solidly behind him and the succession assured, the Emperor returned to Lombardy, crossing the Brenner in September for the last time. The Romano brothers had not been idle during the intervening months. Padua was now in their hands, and with it the whole of Italy to the north-east of Verona and Ferrara; Mantua capitulated, and with the Ghibelline cities of Parma and Cremona, the imperial forces possessed a spearhead of land pointing straight at Milanese territory. Only the people of Piacenza had defected by accepting a Venetian podestà, and swearing at the Republic's request that they would never again elect a Ghibelline to this office. Thus Venice, which was alarmed at the strength of Frederick's forces on her borders and feared the imperial hegemony in Lombardy, by extracting this promise from Piacenza succeeded in sabotaging the negotiations with the Lombards in Rome, which in the face of the imperial might looked like being concluded at last. Piacenza, that dominates one of the most important crossings of the Po, has always been a city of strategic importance, and its control by a Ghibelline podestà was a condition of prime importance to the Emperor, who had insisted upon it in the Lombard negotiations.

All Italy held its breath to see what the Emperor's next move would be, but to armchair strategists of the period it must have been evident that his first objective would be the city of Brescia, which lies roughly between the lakes of Garda and Iseo and controls the northern route to Milan. If Cremona resembled a spearhead thrust against Milanese territory, the fortress of Brescia presented an equal threat to the imperial forces, and barred the way to their ultimate goal—the city of Milan itself. On the 21st of October the imperial forces took Montechiaro, a fortress outpost on Brescian territory, but a siege of the city itself was frustrated by the Milanese forces which had hurried to the defence of their ally and were encamped by its walls. The Milanese were about ten thousand strong, and even with his German army reinforced by six thousand Saracens from Lucera, and knightly contingents from Sicily and the Ghibelline towns of the north—some fifteen thousand men in all—the Emperor could not hope to bring them to battle in the open field with the refuge of Brescia so close at hand. His only alternative was to draw them off. With this end in mind Frederick marched south, the Milanese followed at a distance in order to intervene if he should attack another Lombard city, but nothing would induce them to join combat in the open plain.

By the end of November deadlock had been reached, with the two armies facing each other at Pontevico but separated by the marshes which surround a little tributary of the river Oglio, itself a tributary of the Po that flows roughly south from the Lake of Iseo. The Milanese would not be drawn from the safe cover of their marshes, the fighting season was fast drawing to a close, and if the Emperor could not come to a definite conclusion with them at this crucial moment they would have the whole of the winter in which to muster new reinforcements, besides causing irreparable harm to his prestige. Frederick's only hope was to lure them into the belief that he had decided to retire from the contest in disgust. Cremona, the obvious centre for his winter quarters, lay only a few hours' march away, and accordingly he made a feint in that direction, crossing the Oglio and marching south with much military noise and bustle.

Frederick did in fact send part of his forces to Cremona, but with his striking force of cavalry and the Saracen archers, he marched silently north and lay in hiding near Soncino. At last the news came that he had been waiting for—spies informed him that the Milanese had broken camp and were marching north before turning west to take route for Milan. The message arrived on the morning of the 27th of November. Making a forced march to the north, by afternoon the Emperor was in position to intercept the enemy. The Milanese were marching gaily along singing songs and were taken completely by surprise when an imperial knight rode up on a white horse, shouting to them to be ready for the Emperor was about to give battle. The imperial forces burst out from the woods where they had been hidden; and the Milanese fled to rally round their *carroccio*—the battle trophy of the commune—which was at Cortenuova, a small neighbouring town. Sending his mounted Saracen archers in hot pursuit, the Emperor followed with the heavier forces of the armoured knights. When he arrived upon the scene of battle, the Saracens had been practically decimated, but they had wrought frightful havoc among the Milanese and the ground was covered with dead and dying, though the Lombards continued to fight grimly on, grouped around their *carroccio*, in entrenched positions. The imperial knights charged with their battle-cry of "Soldiers of the Emperor! Soldiers of Rome!" and in the gathering shadows of nightfall it was plain that they had won a great victory. Darkness made it impossible for Cortenuova to be assailed that night and at dawn it was found that the defeated Milanese and the garrison of Cortenuova had slipped away under the cover of darkness; though to their shame the remnants of their *carroccio* was found abandoned with their arms and baggage.

Paeans of joy and triumph went up from the imperial armies, for they had indeed won a great victory. Thousands of Lombard dead littered the field, and there were many prisoners including no less a person than the Podestà of Milan, Pietro Tiepolo, son of the Doge of Venice. But in the triumph of the moment the Emperor, who had hitherto proved himself to be no mean strategist, failed to observe one of the first rules of warfare—he neglected to dispatch a force to follow up his success by mopping up the fleeing Milanese. Frederick may have been misinformed as to the number of the fugitives, but over-optimism had always been one of his failings, and something like half the Lombard forces survived to fight another day.

The entry of the imperial forces into jubilant Cremona was staged like the triumphs of the Caesars of old. The Emperor rode in splendour in the van with imperial banners flying. The famous elephant, bearing a wooden tower filled with trumpeters, drew the Milanese *carroccio* to which Pietro Tiepolo was bound in an ignominious position lying flat on his back, while other prisoners followed in chains. The Cremonese, who had first welcomed the Emperor when as an unknown boy he had set out to conquer the Empire, and had remained staunchly faithful ever since, welcomed him with delirious joy—at last their hero had humbled their deadly enemies the Milanese to the dust. No wonder Pietro della Vigna waxed ecstatic and poured out sonorous periods in Latin to describe the victory of the imperial arms. . . . "Caesar smote all foes with his own hand, the

Germans dyed their swords in blood and the happy knights of the kingdom fought wonderfully at the side of their prince."

The close of the year 1237 saw Frederick at the zenith of his power; to all his other achievements as a diplomat, a law-giver, a patron of learning and a great political leader, had been added the ultimate triumph of military success. It seemed as if Milan and her allies—those rebellious cities that had humbled even Barbarossa and resisted Frederick from the first—had now at last to face the imperial day of reckoning, and the ageing Pope saw his only hope of preserving his temporal power in Italy ruined at Cortenuova.

To drive this lesson home to the Bishop of Rome who had dared to say "Thou seest the necks of kings and princes bent under the knee of the priest, and Christian Emperors must subject their actions not to the Roman Pontiff alone; but they have not the right to rank him above another priest", the Emperor dispatched his greatest trophy—the Milanese *carroccio*—as a gift to the people of Rome, who set it up amidst great rejoicing upon the Capitol. The day seemed not far distant when its imperial donor would follow it in triumph to the selfsame spot, for such was his dearest ambition; at this full tide of his success the goddess fortune appeared to grant him his every wish, and before long the glad news came that the Empress had borne him a son.

Chapter XI

THE SECOND EXCOMMUNICATION
1237–1241

AFTER the victory of Cortenuova Frederick seemed to bestride the mediaeval world like a Colossus. Thirteen years later he lay dying, his dream of empire shattered. There had been victories between, and right to the last it seemed that he might triumph; but the record is of failure, and history has judged that failure to have been inevitable.

It was the tragedy of Frederick's life that the one thing to which he remained always faithful, to which all his energies and endeavours were devoted, for which he broke his word, perpetrated terrible cruelties, poured out all his treasure, and sacrificed his friends, his family, and himself, was the inevitable instrument of his destruction—his conception of empire. Materialism had no part in this, it was a mystical ideal which in Frederick's case took the place of religious belief. The seeds of this mystical belief in the sacred character of royalty, so strangely at variance with his normally materialist and sceptical outlook, were evidently inborn in Frederick from earliest childhood. In the precarious ignominy of his position as a hostage in the hands of Markward of Anweiler and William Capparone this strange child must have hugged to himself in secret his knowledge of his own royalty as a compensation for the slights he had to bear. His accession to supreme power at an early age and by such unexpected good fortune provided the psychological factors which transformed a childhood inheritance into the dominating factor of the character of the man. Frederick's consciousness of his own royalty appeared to one of his superstitious character to have received the approval of divine providence by his meteoric rise to power. It was his sacred duty to see the imperial power, which had suffered so grievously during his own childhood, restored to its rightful position of pre-eminence, and it was to this conception, not to his own advancement, that Frederick was prepared to sacrifice everything.

The mediaeval idea of empire was rooted in the Old Testament concept of the king being divinely appointed to his task—he was the Elect of God. Frederick himself attributed the origins of the imperial power to the Augustinian conception of chaos resulting from original sin, which brought in its train the rule of princes for the establishment of order. This was a traditional view. What was new in Frederick's concept, but in accordance with contemporary thought influenced by Aristotelian philosophy, was his idea that the imperial power was also derived from the laws of natural necessity that are fundamental to the creation of the state. He illustrated this view by drawing a parallel with the state of marriage, which owes its existence to the necessity of sanctioning in due order what is a basic need of man.

Thus the Empire existed for the creation of order, and it was the sacred duty of the Emperor to maintain it. His instrument in doing so was law, which viewed in this context also partook of the sacred character of his divinely appointed function. To the mediaeval world this duty of promulgating laws was one of the Emperor's most solemn attributes, he was *lex animata in terris* and his very word was law.

In his conception of Empire, which he had pledged himself by the most sacred oaths at his coronation to uphold, and to defend from any diminutions of its powers and territories, Frederick was indeed a typical representative of his time. This defence of the "honour and rights of the Empire" was the one duty that he considered to be really sacred. The phrase occurs over and over again in his letters, state documents, and manifestos; all other necessities of state were subordinate to this overruling aim. Frederick might be accommodating upon the political issues but nothing and nobody were ever allowed to offend in any way against this sacred charge to which he sacrificed everything—men, money, his own well-being and that of his subjects, and not least his own peace of mind. It was his predominant thought when he lay dying, and in his will for the last time the words appear again—the Church was to have all her rights restored to her, save only those which were "contrary to the honour and rights of the Empire". In these words lie the chief drama and ultimate tragedy of Frederick's life. For the honour and rights of the Empire could never be equated with the claims of the other "universal" force—the papacy. The Pope laid claim to similar but even greater powers which, unlike the Emperor's, did not stop at the grave. Frederick was perfectly prepared to acknowledge the Pope's authority over the souls of men both before and after death, but their bodies he considered to be his sacred charge, and his alone. He was not prepared to share what he considered to be his responsibility before God even with the Bishop of Rome. In spite of theories which have been advanced to prove it, there does not seem to be any real justification for the view that Frederick wished to found a schismatic Church. His idea was a purely political one based, admittedly, upon his divine right. Whatever his private religious views, he never publicly questioned any dogma of the Church. It was the temporal power that he tried to destroy, because he fully realised that it was incompatible with his aim of a united Empire, especially of an Empire based upon the imperial city of Rome.

However much Protestants may acclaim Frederick's view, there is no doubt that the popes were right in thinking that in an age when brute force reigned supreme, the papacy would have been reduced politically to the position of a mere cipher if it had been shorn of its territorial possessions and its great wealth, only to become a pensioner of the all-powerful Emperor. Frederick's battle with the papacy was thus inevitable. What seemed at the time to be an irresistible force was bound to clash with what was in reality an irremovable object and the result, quite apart from the fanatical courage of Gregory and the diplomatic finesse of his successor Innocent, was equally inevitable. The force that prevailed against the Emperor had still the power in 1849 of calling French soldiers successfully to its aid. What hope had Frederick of defeating it six hundred years earlier?

But for the present all went well. Within ten days of Cortenuova (December 1237), Lodi had opened its gates to him, thus bringing him to within twenty miles of Milan, and at last that stiff-necked city sent emissaries to sue humbly for peace. The mission was led by a Franciscan, Fra Leone di Perego, who was

instructed to offer the city's oath of fealty to the Emperor, their
banners to be burnt if he so willed, a large sum of money as an
indemnity, and ten thousand soldiers to fight in the Holy Land.
But Frederick would have none of it—he demanded unconditional surrender.

No doubt the Emperor was animated partly by his implacable hatred for the Milanese in giving this reply, and even if
they had surrendered it is doubtful if he would have shown the
same mercy to them as he did to other cities of the league that
sued for peace at this time. The Milanese were evidently of
this opinion, and Frederick's demand hardened their attitude.
They could surrender unconditionally at any time, but at the
moment their great city stood unscathed, its walls intact, and
the surrounding land was a network of water-courses of which
the Milanese knew well how to make use in defensive warfare.

Was Frederick drunk with success and hatred in refusing the
Milanese offer? Or had years of experience in attempted
negotiations with the wily citizens, whom Fra Salimbene had
described as being as "slippery as eels", convinced him that
only the seizure, probably the destruction, certainly the military occupation, of this turbulent city would solve the whole
Lombard question which had been a thorn in his side ever since
his accession to the Empire? In the light of after-events it is
easy to say that Frederick's judgement on this occasion was
blinded by his personal feelings, but was he really wrong in his
conviction that only the utter subjection of Milan would solve
the Lombard problem? A patched-up peace, even the institution of an imperial podestà, all these could so easily be over-
thrown once the Emperor's back was turned and his attention
was engaged elsewhere—in settling accounts with the Pope for
instance. Whether he arrived at his conclusion by uncontrolled
instinct or by mature reflection, Frederick was right in his
estimate of the situation—that the military subjection of
Milan was an essential preliminary to the achievement of his
aim of a united Italy. Where his innate optimism in success
led him astray was his failure to assess correctly the military
force, in terms of generalship and men, which would enable
him to achieve his objective.

No doubt tales of the wild disorders in the city of Milan
itself, that followed the defeat of Cortenuova, reached the

Emperor's ears, and led him to believe that the project was not
so difficult as in fact it was. The rabble of the city rose, led by
the heretical element, and broke into the churches committing
awful outrages—hanging the crucifixes upside down and piling
the altars with filth. But when order was restored, and the
citizens reviewed the situation in the sober light of reason, they
realised that they now had no alternative but to resist, and the
word went round "Better to die by the sword than from hunger,
the stake, or the rope."

In her extremity Milan was supported by only three cities of
the Lombard League—Alessandria, Piacenza, and Brescia—
and two of the cities of Romagna—Bologna and Faenza. They
were courageous indeed who then ranged themselves beside
Milan in the face of what must have appeared at the time to be
overwhelming odds; for even the Pope at this moment held his
breath, while the future of Italy for centuries to come was
decided upon the plains of Lombardy.

For that was the issue at stake; if Frederick had succeeded in
conquering those six cities, Italy was his, and the temporal power
of the papacy would have ceased to exist. The subjugation of
Lombardy would have enabled the Emperor to weld Italy into
a united kingdom on the advanced pattern of the Sicilian realm.
Whatever else his failings, there is no doubt as to Frederick's
administrative capacity, and under his shrewd guidance the
peninsula might have become one of the great European powers
instead of the patchwork of small states which she remained
until the nineteenth century.

The Lombard resistance in the name of municipal liberty in
actual fact retarded Italy's political development for centuries.
Even in Frederick's day the great jurist Roffredo of Benevento
defined the statutes of the Lombard cities as "hard, miserable,
and exceedingly oppressive, although they vaunt their enjoyment of the maximum of freedom". A century later the municipal liberty of Florence—which was governed by her citizens
—meant in actual fact that she was ruled by a small minority of
three thousand persons who enjoyed the full rights of citizen-
ship, out of a population of some ninety thousand. From the
communes arose the Signori, and in the place of a strong
centralised government, these countless petty tyrants, who
succeeded one another in bloody internecine strife, imposed upon

a luckless population a constant state of civil war and a burden of oppression heavier by far than the rule of contemporary European kings. Frederick's government might have been tyrannical at the outset, as was any other in the thirteenth century, but the unity and reign of law and order which was his aim would have developed with the centuries and have spared Italy the constant civil wars or foreign domination that was to be her lot until 1870.

Frederick was well aware of the principle for which he was fighting, and he evidently knew also that the struggle would be a hard one—even if he did not appreciate quite just how hard —for he now appealed to the rulers of the world to help him by sending military contingents to assist him in the struggle for "this matter touches you and all the kings of the earth . . . what encouragement to revolt would be given to all of them that would fain throw off the yoke of authority if the Roman Empire were to suffer loss through this kind of insurgence". Put in this light the kings realised that it was indeed a matter which touched them all closely, and England, France, Hungary, the Nicean Emperor, and even the Oriental sultans sent forces to assist the Emperor of the West in his campaign against the insurgent cities. Their forces swelled considerably the numbers of the imperial army which was drawn not only from the Empire, the Realm of Sicily, and Burgundy, but from many of the cities of Northern and Central Italy as well.

As in the previous year, Verona was the base from which the Emperor began his military operations. He passed Easter there, and was presently joined by his son—the ten-year-old King Conrad—and the German army. It was upon Ezzelino da Romano's advice that Frederick decided to open the Lombard campaign with an attack against Brescia. To leave this town unscathed when mounting an attack on Milan from Verona would have been a grave risk, exposing his flank and lines of communication. Accordingly the initial thrust against Brescia began in July, but it was not pressed home to constitute an all-out siege until the following month. During this preliminary fighting the imperial forces suffered a stroke of bad luck; Cala-mandrinus, a noted Spanish military engineer, whom Ezzelino had dispatched to make siege weapons for the Emperor, was captured by the Brescians. It was a serious blow, as Cala-mandrinus was pre-eminent in his art and his ability was now at the disposal of the besieged, who had welcomed him with open arms, presenting him with a house and wife. As the siege advanced he amply proved his worth by constructing engines that not only held the imperial army at bay, but destroyed much of their equipment.

There followed a fortnight's savage fighting, during which Brescian prisoners were tied to the imperial siege machines in the vain hope of deflecting their fellow citizens' aim, and Frederick himself was nearly taken prisoner, but was saved by a gallant action in which Henry de Troubleville and his hundred English knights took part. The Emperor was evidently surprised to find that Brescia, instead of being overawed by his large army, was proving to be a very tough nut indeed to crack, and decided to send emissaries to try and negotiate a surrender.

It is not known what terms Frederick had empowered Bernardo Rolando de Rossi, the leader of the mission, to offer. In any case they were not accepted because this member of a well-known Parmesan family, with whom the Emperor had been on friendly terms for some years, played traitor and counselled the Brescians to hold out. The reasons for de Rossi's action have never been satisfactorily explained. Contemporary chroniclers give several rather unconvincing explanations which tend to show that at some time Frederick had unwittingly offended de Rossi who afterwards nourished a hidden hatred for the Emperor. Whatever the cause, de Rossi's desire for vengeance must have been overwhelming for he took a terrible risk. In spite of preliminary setbacks Frederick disposed of a vast army and resources, and there should still have been many weeks of good fighting weather ahead, when the siege could have been brought to a successful conclusion, in which case the tale of the emissary's treachery would have been certain to emerge. But again bad luck dogged the Emperor's action, torrential rains hampered all military action in September, while a mysterious sickness broke out among the horses and cattle in the imperial camp—induced, according to one chronicler, by the Brescians having driven infected animals out of the city into their midst.

After a final unsuccessful attack Frederick decided, on the 9th of October, to call off the siege. It had lasted exactly two months and six days, but these few weeks had been enough to destroy the legend of the Emperor's invincibility. To withdraw at that stage was a grave error of judgement on Frederick's part; true he had won one great pitched battle in the field at Cortenuova, but his ultimate victory in Lombardy, by the very nature of the struggle against the embattled cities of the Lombard League, was never likely to be settled outright by fighting in the open. Siege warfare would inevitably be the final test of his ability to subdue Milan. And here at Brescia, with the vast army summoned from the ends of the known world with so many flourishes and fanfares, he had failed to take a much smaller and less highly fortified city.

Cost what it might the siege of Brescia should have been continued to the bitter end. Three years later at Faenza Frederick showed that he had learnt the lesson of Brescia, but at the moment his military sense appears to have failed. No doubt he thought he could rest comfortably upon the laurels of his victory at Cortenuova and return to the attack in the following year. He could not have made a greater mistake. Nothing succeeds like success, and this was especially true in thirteenth-century Italy; one single failure was sufficient to set the quick-sands of conflicting interests which characterised Italian politics trembling under his feet. It was just the opportunity that the Pope had been waiting for, and he was not slow to take advantage of it.

The Emperor, however, was still in a defiant mood. Enzio, the eldest of his illegitimate sons, a brave and handsome lad who seems to have borne a greater physical resemblance to his father than any of Frederick's other children, was knighted in Cremona with much ceremony and married to Adelasia, heiress of the Sardinian province of Torres and Gallura in her own right, and, by a previous marriage, of Cagliari as well. No doubt negotiations for the match had been in process for some time; but instead of treating it as a purely domestic matter, the Emperor seized the occasion to declare Enzio King, and to proclaim "We swore at our consecration to get back the pro-vinces which had been taken from our predecessors, and we will make use of all our force to keep this vow. As it is undeniable that Sardinia is a dependence of our crown, it is by legitimate right that we reunite this island to our Empire."

Enzio was immediately dispatched to occupy his new kingdom,

in spite of the fact that his father must have been well aware that the Pope also laid claim to be the suzerain of Sardinia. The weeks following immediately upon the fiasco of Brescia were scarcely a tactful moment to make gestures of this kind. Either Frederick had not yet fully realised the seriousness of the situation, or possibly he entertained the mistaken idea that the recovery of Sardinia might, to a certain extent, offset the failure of Brescia. In any case his action simply served to heap coals upon the fire of Gregory's fury, and a papal protest, couched in strong terms, was not long in coming.

The imperial military successes of the past two years had forced the Pope's activities against the Emperor into underground channels, but they had not ceased. Strange rumours began to circulate about the Emperor, the accounts of his denial of the doctrine of transubstantiation and of the three impostors date from this time, and to those were added scandalous tales of his immoral life. A bevy of Christian mistresses for a man in his position was too commonplace in those days to arouse any surprise, but the famous odalisques served as a convenient basis for these accusations, to which the papal propagandists, who were their source, added as the years went by every unnatural vice conceived by the mind of man. These rumours proved to be the first mutterings of the storm which was soon to break with unprecedented violence; already they served as an additional excuse for the Pope to bring complaints against the Emperor about the state of the Sicilian Church and certain other matters of faith. At the end of October a delegation of four bishops, two Germans and two Italians, was sent to question Frederick upon his attitude to the Sicilian Church and other matters of faith. After taking council with his nobles the Emperor submitted to the examination with apparent good grace, even humility, and succeeded in satisfying his interlocutors of his good faith.

These papal allegations about Frederick's ill-treatment of the Sicilian Church were, of course, yet another stalking-horse— just as the Crusade proposals had been in 1236—to draw attention away from the Emperor's very real grounds for complaint over Gregory's arbitration of the Lombard question during the last ten years. Nevertheless Frederick again agreed to discuss the Pope's grievances in the hope of negotiating a settlement.

A page from *De Arte Venandi cum Avibus*, with illustrations of migrating birds

The Duomo of Bitonto, built between 1175 and 1200, where the
Emperor's body lay in state on its journey to Palermo

The complaints were presented under fourteen headings, but were in fact of no importance. Once again those hardy annuals the problems of the Sicilian Church and the wrongs done to the Templars and the Knights of St. John were prominent; to this were added complaints of a like nature such as the Emperor's opposition to the conversion of a Moslem prince whom he held as a state prisoner. The Lombard question, that was the real root of the matter, was presented simply as a side issue that prevented the undertaking of a new Crusade. The unusual patience which Frederick displayed on this occasion was due to his desire to gain time—for the grim reality of what the Brescia fiasco had cost him was gradually beginning to dawn, and he had undoubtedly sensed what the stiffening in Gregory's attitude portended—an open break with the Pope—which at this difficult moment was to be avoided at all costs.

At the same time, however, Frederick had placed in the hands of the papal commissioners an exposé of the progress of the Lombard negotiations over the past ten years which was embarrassing in its truth and clarity. It ran: "With regard to the Lombard question, the Emperor has told us that several times he has submitted it to the arbitration of the Church and from it he has reaped no advantage. It is not only that the first time the Lombards were condemned to furnish four hundred knights, but the Pope allowed them to acquit themselves of this debt in such a fashion that they were sent against the Emperor in the Realm (in 1228 when he was on Crusade). The second time they were condemned to furnish five hundred knights, but the Pope decided that they would be sent to Outremer under the protection and at the disposal of the Pope and Church, who had not suffered any offence, but in any case this was never carried out. The third time, at the request of two cardinals, and with the cognisance of Master Pietro of Capua, the Lombard affair was against placed completely under the arbitration of the Church, according to the terms dictated by the Pope. But since then there has been no question of it. It was only when the Lord Pope learnt that the Emperor, seeing that he had been trifled with so many times, prepared to come down into Italy with an army, quickly asked that the affair should once more be submitted to him. The Emperor, although he had failed him several times, however consented to submit it again to the

K

Pope, but indicated a time limit, on condition that the affair should be settled to his honour and to the advantage of the Empire. This condition the Pope would not accept—as a letter of his proves—although now he says in another letter that the Church would have been disposed to decide the affair safeguarding the honour and the rights of the Empire. From which it emerges that these two letters contradict each other in the most obvious fashion."

There is no doubt that in the Lombard quarrel Frederick had not only right upon his side, but had displayed extraordinary patience in his dealings with the Pope. All that had been offered him in return was the derisory satisfaction of the four hundred Milanese knights to serve on the Crusade, after the insulting closure of the Alpine passes in 1226. Since then he had received precisely nothing for the interminable negotiations of years and repeated affronts; no wonder Gregory wished to obscure the issue by introducing red herrings like the projected Crusade and the plaints of the Sicilian Church.

Behind the smoke-screen of these pretended negotiations, both adversaries were working feverishly to prepare their positions before joining in the struggle which they were now both well aware loomed inevitably ahead. As at the time of the Crusade it was still the aged Pope who was the aggressor; by every means he could Frederick sought to gain time while trying to divide the Pope's supporters. He had good reason. Gregory was a doughty foe, as was shown by his success in engineering a secret alliance between those deadly rivals— the two great maritime powers—Genoa and Venice. Genoa had become increasingly hostile to Frederick since the loss of her Sicilian bases; but only lately had the anti-imperial party in the city seized the upper hand and installed a Milanese podestà. Venice, who had viewed the Emperor's increasing power and activity in Lombardy with considerable apprehension, had received a mortal insult in his treatment of Pietro Tiepolo, in the triumph of Cremona; and he—their Doge's son—was now held a close prisoner in Apulia. Under skilful papal persuasion the two resentful cities agreed to sink their differences and to sign an offensive alliance—it was a serious blow to Frederick both from the political and military point of view.

Frederick meanwhile had retired to spend his winter in comfort, and in considerable state, in the monastery of Santa Giustina on the outskirts of Padua. With him as his guests were Ezzelino and the Marquis of Este whom the Emperor was trying to reconcile and win over to his cause. For them he provided magnificent entertainments, and the good monks must have been sorely inconvenienced, for his household included the famous elephant—though this beast was noted for being very gentle and well behaved—twenty-four camels, five leopards, falcons, hounds and all the panoply of the imperial hunt. The abbot Arnold, however, seems to have fully appreciated the signal honour that was being paid to his monastery, especially after the Emperor had sympathised with some of his complaints against Ezzelino and confirmed him in the rights of ownership of Santa Giustina; for he presented his illustrious guest with costly tapestries, a magnificently decorated throne and footstool, two wagonloads of the best wine, thirty bushels of barley, twenty-four wainloads of hay, and huge sturgeons from Ferrara.

The Empress meanwhile lived in retirement at Noventa, a few miles to the east of Padua, and there at intervals her husband came to visit her. Were they purely duty visits paid for the sake of appearances? Or did this strange man sometimes find relaxation in the company of his young wife and year-old son Henry from the tremendous strain which he was undergoing at that time? For the hunting parties and the splendid court life at Santa Giustina were the smiling carefree mask that covered the grim reality of diplomatic intrigue and political plotting for the tremendous stakes of averting an open war with the Pope, and his own excommunication.

Relations between Emperor and Pope were still outwardly friendly, though Gregory had sent Brother Elias, then still Minister-General of the Franciscans, as his representative to protest against Enzio's marriage. (Frederick's private comment was that the Pope had wanted Enzio as a husband for his own niece.) But beneath the surface it was war to the knife. Aware that he had nothing to hope for from Gregory but the vindictive pursuance of a vendetta which sooner or later was bound to lead to his own excommunication, Frederick pushed forward with increasing energy a new policy—that of trying to split the College of Cardinals and so undermining their support of the Pope.

There was in fact a pro-imperial party among the members of the Sacred College, of which Cardinal Giovanni Colonna was the foremost exponent. This partisanship existed not so much because any personal feeling of attachment for the Emperor animated these pillars of the Church, but because they viewed with profound uneasiness the passionate hatred that drove Gregory to involve the Church in an all-out struggle against him.

In an effort to take advantage of this uneasiness, Frederick addressed a letter to the cardinals in which he stated un-equivocally that the Sacred College would bear the responsibility equally with the Pope if he was excommunicated, and that the real reason for Gregory's taking such a step was his desire to assist the heretical Lombard communes. It is a curious letter in which scarcely veiled threats of retaliation against those who injured him were allied to phrases that reveal the same sentiment of pride of royal descent that was evident in Frederick's letter to Fra Elia at the time of St. Elizabeth's canonisation. The Emperor wrote: "We would wish that it could be possible for us to exercise equal to equal a private vengeance, by obtaining satisfaction at the expense of the man [Gregory] who causes this scandal, and of his family; so the outrage which is done to us might fall back upon him and his. But as neither he nor all his race are worthy that the imperial dignity should condescend to attack them, as he draws his audacity from the authority attached to his position, and as the union of so many venerable brothers appears to encourage him in his fatal obstinacy, we are troubled to the bottom of our soul; since we have decided that to defend ourselves against our persecutor it is necessary that we also attack those who resist us."

Meanwhile the life at court continued in a gay round of hunting parties and feasting and the Emperor made sure of Ezzelino da Romano's support by giving Selvaggia, one of his six illegitimate daughters, to him in marriage. Palm Sunday was the occasion for a special celebration of a popular nature, a rare occurrence in Frederick's public life; in this moment of tension he was evidently making a very special effort to attach the people of the important city of Padua to his person. It was

an ancient custom for the citizens of Padua to meet and celebrate the feast by games and other diversions in the meadows
of Prato della Valle that lie between the city and the monastery
of Santa Giustina. The Emperor appeared in their midst clad
in robes of purple, wearing the imperial crown, and smilingly
took his place upon a raised seat or throne from which he
watched their merry-making. Nor was this all—Pietro della
Vigna pronounced an oration in which he stressed his master's
affection for the good people of the city. It was a gay scene, a
sunlit spring day at the end of March, with the nobles and great
officers of the court in their brilliant robes adding a touch of
pageantry to the crowds in holiday attire. The sinister rumours
of strife between the two leaders of the Christian world seemed
to be far removed from reality; but at precisely the same
moment at a secret consistory at the Lateran, Gregory was engaged in reading the sentence of the Emperor's excommunication to the cardinals; while in far-away Salerno Hermann von
Salza, who had devoted his life to preserving unity between
Emperor and Pope, breathed his last. A merciful fate preserved
him from the knowledge that all his efforts had been in vain and
the titanic struggle which he had laboured to prevent had
broken upon the world at last.

The excommunication was not made public until four days
later, when on Maundy Thursday, in a voice shaking with
fury, Gregory, who was approaching his hundredth year, read
out his lengthy peroration upon the reasons for the Emperor's
excommunication. The charges were varied: stirring up dis-
affection in Rome, failure to assist the Crusade, failure to return
the expropriated lands of the Templars and Hospitallers, but
above all they dwelt upon the iniquities of the Emperor to the
Sicilian Church. No mention was made of the Lombard quarrel,
which was in reality the root of all dissension between Pope
and Emperor. Gregory decreed that the sentence was to be
read afresh at each and every celebration of high mass throughout the Christian world, and he declared Frederick's subjects
loosed from their oaths of allegiance.

The news spread fast, and within a week Frederick had
definite cognisance of the fate that had befallen him. An
atmosphere of gloom descended upon Padua; the people were
silent, the court officials downcast, and already the strained

relations of the rival factions of Ezzelino and the Marquis of Este, which Frederick had been trying throughout the winter to cement with bonds of friendship, began to rise again to the surface. Even the marriage which had been arranged between the two families—of Alberico da Romano's daughter with the Marquis's son Rinaldo—had failed to heal the breach; and in the general atmosphere of suspicion and mistrust Frederick could sense that many of his supporters in the hour of success were merely waiting for the first available opportunity to desert and turn against him. He made sure of hostages from both families by demanding the custody of Rinaldo and his bride, whom he dispatched to Apulia.

The Emperor was the first to recover from the shock of his own excommunication. He called a meeting of the foremost citizens of Padua in the town hall, where Pietro della Vigna addressed them in a long speech whose "text" was drawn from Ovid. Shorn of its elaborate oratorial paraphernalia his theme was simple and even conciliatory. As good, equitable and just a prince as Frederick had not ruled the Empire since Charlemagne. He it was who was the sufferer, not the Church. If the sentence of excommunication had been justly pronounced the Emperor would have submitted to it with humility, but the ministers of the Holy See had acted with haste and imprudence. Pietro della Vigna did not attack the Pope directly but laid the burden of his master's grievance at the door of the chiefs of the Church. After his minister had finished, to the astonishment of all the Emperor himself spoke from his throne in his own defence. This, and his speech in the Church of the Holy Sepulchre on the Crusade, are two of the very rare occasions of which there is any record of Frederick's ever having made a speech in public. Now, as upon the previous occasion, he spoke to defend his own actions vis-à-vis Gregory and again he made a remarkably conciliatory speech. There is no doubt that on both occasions Frederick had good grounds for complaint; the Pope was the aggressor, and again the excommunication was prompted by Gregory's overwhelming hatred, and for very different reasons from those which were ostensibly given.

Continuing his conciliatory policy and assuming an attitude of dignified calm in the face of persecution, Frederick dispatched an embassy headed by the bishops of Sant Agata and

Calvi to the papal court. They bore a document in which the
Emperor refuted in detail the charges that had been brought
against him and asked the cardinals to call a special council
before which he was prepared to prove his innocence. But the
Pope refused to listen to them or to the four bishops who had
examined Frederick the previous autumn. In vain too were the
protests of European kings who tried to make peace between
Emperor and Pope; St. Louis sent one of his personal councillors,
the Bishop of Langres, and the King of Castile wrote a letter of
protest. The English chronicler Matthew Paris, admittedly a
spirited critic of the papacy, wrote: "The father of the faithful
tried to persuade them [the peoples] that obedience consisted
in revolt, duty in forgetting oaths."

Once the restricting bonds of prudence which the Emperor's
successes of the last few years had necessarily placed upon the
Pope's hatred were gone, Gregory gave full rein to his passion.
The Christian princes and prelates were instructed to give the
widest possible publicity to the sentence of excommunication;
and as the reports of its dissemination throughout the Christian
world—in Aragon, in Scotland, even in St. Paul's Cathedral
in his brother-in-law King Henry's capital, and throughout
his realm—began to come in to the imperial chancery, the
Emperor's fury mounted until it too burst out in a virulence
which equalled Gregory's own. He addressed letters of protest
to the Christian kings, stating openly to the King of England
that his refusal of a marriage between Enzio and one of the
Pope's nieces was one of the causes of Gregory's rage.

Gregory replied with his famous encyclical that opened with
the words "A furious beast has come out of the sea, which
with the paws of a bear, the head of a lion, is like unto a
leopard", and he went on publicly to accuse the Emperor of the
gravest of all heresies—the denial of Christ Himself—in giving
credence to the tale of the three impostors. It is interesting to
note that even in the midst of this paean of rage against his
hated foe, the Pope also alluded to the question of a marriage
project for wedding Enzio to a member of his family, which he
said that he had spurned.

The indignant denials of both parties that they had ever contemplated such a union affords strong presumptive proof that
at some time such a project had in fact existed, and the failure

to bring it to fruition had further embittered the feelings of both sides. The Pope said that the Emperor had also offered him castles; and it seems likely that Frederick had made an attempt to settle once and for all the struggles and jealousies which had divided the popes and emperors throughout the centuries. This action was not without precedent as both Barbarossa and Henry VI had done the same by offering the Pope an annual money payment in lieu of the income derived from the papal states and Church dues; probably the projected marriage between the families of Emperor and Pope had been intended to set the seal upon such an agreement.

The Emperor's reaction to the Pope's encyclical accusing him of heresy was of a violence to match Gregory's own. With an indignant rebuttal of all its accusations and a firm assertion of his own faith, Frederick described the Pope himself as Antichrist. The wordy struggle now descended into an unseemly wrangle in which the two heads of the Christian world canvassed Europe for supporters; and it must be admitted that the aged Pope emerged from the struggle with considerably less dignity than the Emperor.

When Gregory tried to stir up the German princes against their sovereign, urging them to hold a new election, he was met with a firm refusal and a clear statement as to the limits of the papal powers in this respect—the Pope could only invest an Emperor whom the princes had chosen to elect, he could in no circumstances depose him. The Pope then tried to tempt St. Louis to agree to Frederick's deposition by offering him the Imperial Kingdom of Arles for his brother Robert of Artois; only to be met with the indignant reply that it was not in this manner that one could dispose of a prince whose dignity was so high in the Christian world he had no superior—if he was unworthy he could only be deposed by a General Council.

But if in the world at large Gregory's actions aroused antipathy and scorn, nearer to home, and this constituted a more immediate threat to Frederick, the blow of the excommunication had begun its deadly work. In May Treviso was attacked by the nobles of the area under the leadership of Ezzelino's brother, Alberico da Romano. Its imperial podestà was expelled, and as the Emperor hurried to quell the insurrection an eclipse of the sun added to his troubles. Frederick himself was well aware that this phenomena was due to natural causes, but a superstition-ridden soldiery and population were not—they regarded it as a fearful omen—and in the end the enlightened Frederick, the student of astronomy, was forced to withdraw his forces from the Trevisan march.

The Emperor now decided to return to Verona, and to make it his base for an attack upon Milan. Alberico's defection had increased his suspicions of the Marquis of Este and his following, and these proved to be well founded. For when he insisted that the Marquis should accompany him to Verona, on the way the Marquis and his following made a sudden dash for the stronghold of San Bonifacio; and once within its walls not even the eloquence of Pietro della Vigna, who had been sent to parley, would induce him to emerge. Azzo d'Este left many of his friends as hostages in the Emperor's hands, and they were soon dispatched to join his son and daughter-in-law in the strongholds of Apulia. On the 13th of June, in the Piazza of San Zeno in the midst of a vast crowd, Pietro della Vigna read out the proclamation that the ban of Empire had been placed upon the Marquis of Este and the Trevisan rebels.

During the next eight months, from midsummer 1239 until January 1240, the Emperor remained in North Italy; the summer months were occupied with inconclusive military engagements in which he tried to bring the hostile Lombard armies to battle in the open field, but without success. He did not again attempt the siege of any city, although he was in secret correspondence with the Milanese nobility who tried to persuade him to make an all-out attack upon theirs, promising to raise an insurrection in his favour. Perhaps Frederick did not trust them, and probably he rightly feared Milan's military strength which was quite equal to his own, with the added advantage of fighting on home ground among the treacherous water-courses that surrounded the city. In September it looked as if an engagement might take place, but it was averted by the able generalship of the Milanese podestà, who not only diverted the Olona so as to flood the imperial camp, but dug ditches filled with the waters of the Ticinello to create a barrier between the two armies.

To bolster the resistance of Milan there had arrived in the city's midst a remarkable man, the Papal Legate, Gregory of

Montelungo. Montelungo had risen from small beginnings, he was only a sub-deacon, and, though a fanatical partisan of the Church, his aims were military rather than ecclesiastical; in Milan he himself wore armour, led and reviewed armies and permitted the members of the religious orders to bear arms. Licentious in his private life, he was possessed of great personal ambition. He was energetic and intelligent, and above all a capable diplomat and organiser. The ultimate failure of the imperial arms in Northern Italy was largely due to the activities of this one man alone. By his tireless efforts Montelungo succeeded not only in undermining Frederick's military position, but, what was far more difficult, in uniting all the dissident elements, who in spite of their enmity to Frederick were split by internecine jealousies, into one coherent body of opposition to the Emperor. From the earliest days of his mission in Lombardy Gregory, as the official representative of the Holy See, provided the rallying-point for the anti-imperial forces which had previously been lacking; and it is indicative of this process of cohesion that gradually all enemies of the Emperor came to be known by the generic name of Guelf.

Nor were Frederick's troubles limited to the military field, his financial embarrassment was considerable. For the past three years he had been forced to maintain large armies constantly on a war footing; it is true that the feudal levies were usually sent home for the winter months, as they were now in November 1239, but the Saracens had to be fed and the other mercenaries had to be both paid and fed for most of the year.

Sicily was already heavily taxed; but this was not enough, and fresh taxes were constantly being levied to meet the cost of the Lombard war. For a few years yet the realm was able, thanks to Frederick's remarkable financial organisation, to bear this constant economic strain without disintegrating completely, but already the first warning signs of the ultimate collapse were beginning to appear.

In the autumn of 1239 the Emperor's debts amounted to 24,653 ounces of gold, or some seventy thousand pounds, an enormous sum for those times, but still he was forced to go on borrowing money. The imperial registers of the period contain many references to his financial affairs; one interesting entry of the 15th of January 1240 shows that a Viennese merchant Henry Baum acted as one of his banking agents. Rates of interest were high and Frederick's financial responsibilities tremendous; this same entry shows that they even included such items as providing for the living expenses of the ambassador of the "King of Russia" who was then in Vienna.

These registers of the Imperial Curia, which cover the whole of the period from the autumn of 1239 until the summer of 1240, provide a fascinating picture of life as it was lived from day to day in this itinerant court as it travelled across northern and central Italy right down into Apulia. The chief interest of these registers lies in their revelation of how the Sicilian administration was now centred in the imperial court and directed from it. The secret alliance which the Pope had engineered between Genoa and Venice had now become public owing to its being extended to include Milan, Piacenza, and the Holy See itself. This latest development rendered Sicily open to attack from both land and sea, as the great maritime powers possessed redoubtable fleets, and Frederick knew only too well that Genoa would be thirsting to regain her Sicilian bases and that Venice also no doubt had her eye upon the harbours of the realm. In fact by a secret clause of the treaty the Pope had agreed to Genoa regaining Syracuse and to Venice being awarded Barletta and Salpi. With such a tempting bait dangling before their eyes it was easy for Gregory to persuade his allies to prepare for an immediate attack upon the realm.

This was the crisis in his affairs—of which Frederick was probably informed by his efficient intelligence service or secret sympathisers at the papal court—that prompted the Emperor for the first time since 1220, when he had agreed with Pope Honorius to keep the Sicilian realm entirely separate from the Empire, to amalgamate the entire administration of his vast possessions under one central chancery directly under his own command. Since his departure to Germany five years previously, the realm had been governed by a regency council consisting of the great officers of state and some of the bishops. Such a cumbersome committee was not adapted to the making of swift decisions, or taking the rapid action made necessary by war, and if the realm was to serve as the treasure chest and arsenal for the great struggle which lay ahead, it had also to be

put on an immediate war footing if it was to withstand the shock
of invasion.

In perusing the imperial dispatches which set all this complicated machinery in motion, the modern reader cannot but
admire the clarity and efficiency of the brain that directed the
whole process, and had built up the remarkable administrative
machine that made its execution possible. From Lombardy,
Tuscany, and the Papal States, the imperial mandates went
forth; the court was constantly on the move, and the officials and
scribes had to accompany the Emperor in all his wanderings.
Loading their documents and registers on to pack-horses and
mules in the morning, unloading them again at the end of the
day's journey, these harassed men had to labour far into the
night to keep abreast with the tremendous volume of work that
was piled upon them. The orders themselves had to be carried
by courier to the nearest port, then by fast imperial galley to
the realm and, finally, transported again by courier to the
official responsible for their execution.

The organisation required for such an undertaking was tremendous, the work itself exhausting. The letter of a scribe
addressed to Pietro della Vigna paints a very human picture of
what the life of the ambitious young official in the Imperial
Curia must have been like: "I am, as one might put it, of one
body with my pen—my own person is so confounded with my
register. I am so often hot, so often cold, hard work so often
overwhelms me, as this register, the companion of my martyrdom, bears witness . . . to the pains of this personal fatigue is
joined the modesty of my salary, which you know bears no
relation to my work."

If Frederick drove his officials and secretaries to the verge of
collapse and was sometimes impatient and even cruel over their
shortcomings, it was mainly because he himself was tireless and
endowed with a superhuman energy; but when he realised that
he had driven them too hard, or himself had made an error, he
would make his apologies in a kindly and most endearing fashion.
One of his letters to Andrea da Cicala affords a good example of
this: "The unfortunate words which caused you pain and so
suddenly upset the calm of your firm mind, sprang from a mood
of wrath and irritation. We are all the more rejoiced that thy
well-tried uprightness and good faith remained unshaken by

such idle words. . . . Need we say more . . . canst thou still find room to doubt . . . apart from the subtle signs of affection which the eyes cannot see, thou must be conscious of our trust since we leave our cares in thy hands and rely on thee as on a second self."

All the time the great work of reorganisation went on; castles were garrisoned, severe security measures were undertaken, ports were controlled, a censorship was instituted—special imperial permission was necessary to take a letter into the realm —all communication with Rome was forbidden; and any transgression of these rules was punished with draconian measures. The whole security situation was rendered infinitely more complicated by the fact that the Emperor's excommunication had converted the clergy in the realm into a potential fifth column. But Frederick found efficient, if ruthless, means to deal even with this problem. The justiciars were charged with the unenviable duty of informing the clergy in their area that Frederick wished religious services to continue in spite of the ecclesiastical ban; he could not force them to perform mass, but their failure to do so would be regarded as evidence of disloyalty. Confiscation of the property of priests unwilling to obey, and even the death sentence, became common—the former had the added advantage of helping to fill the depleted imperial coffers. Thus by gradual degrees the whole of the Sicilian Church was purged of all bishops and priests who did not put obedience to their sovereign, or at least their own personal security, before their fidelity to the Pope.

Concurrently with his reorganisation of the realm, the Emperor set about creating an Italian state on the Sicilian model. Enzio became his viceroy for the whole of Italy with the title of Imperial Legate, and individual provinces were put under the command of vicars-general, or captains-general, whose functions roughly corresponded to those of the Sicilian justiciars. The political and military situation was too fluid to allow this system ever to become really consolidated—the vicariates changed in size and shape according to the ebb and flow of the war—but if the Emperor had been ultimately successful, there is no doubt that this new administration would have provided the basis for a united government of Italy. As fluid as the areas of the vicariates were the movements of the men who held these offices; at first they included many representatives of the Sicilian nobility and imperial favourities such as Tebaldo di Francesco. But as the struggle grew more bitter, and conspiracies rendered the Emperor increasingly suspicious, the circle became more and more restricted until ultimately, with the exception of Ezzelino and the Marquis Uberto Pallavicini, the office of vicar-general was awarded only to Frederick's illegitimate sons or to men who were attached to him by ties of blood or marriage.

In spite of the ephemeral character of Frederick's Italian state, the office of the vicars or captains-general was destined to play an enduring part in subsequent Italian history. It was to provide the prototypes, the roots, from which the Signori ultimately sprang. In the first instance many of the Signori called themselves captains-general, and even continued to style themselves imperial vicars, when all but this last shadow of the imperial power had long since vanished from Italy. As the Signori became more firmly established, all pretence at the popular sources for their power vanished; the final step towards their becoming petty sovereigns in their own right was achieved when their position was regularised by the later emperors creating them dukes and marquises.

But it is not only the political power of the Signori that had its origins in Frederick. To him can be attributed too not a little of the brilliance of the Renaissance courts. For in imitation of the Emperor, his illegitimate sons and the other imperial vicars surrounded themselves with the same atmosphere of luxury— the court poets, the astrologers and even the menageries—as Frederick had created. The tradition persisted, to burst forth in full flower in the famous courts of the Viscontis in Milan, the Gonzagas in Mantua and the d'Estes in Modena and Ferrara.

Early in February 1240, in a letter to the Archbishop of Messina, Frederick announced his intention of taking the war right into the heart of the enemy camp. He wrote: "After for long having confidence in the justice of our cause; and recognising that far from remembering our services, the Roman Court has pronounced itself against us on all occasions; we believe it is now necessary to adopt a different course of action to that which we have followed until today. We shall, therefore, renounce the amity of which we have given so many proofs, and now we shall resort to force. In consequence it is our firm intention to annex to the Empire the Duchy of Spoleto, the March of Ancona, and other lands which at different periods have been taken from it." Clearly his intentions were no longer limited to the Duchy of Spoleto and the Marches, as a line of communication between Empire and realm; the whole of the Patrimony of St. Peter was now to be attached to the imperial domains—thus depriving the Pope of the temporal power and restricting his authority to the purely spiritual sphere.

The Emperor had passed Christmas at Pisa, and on his birthday had taken the extraordinary step of himself preaching a sermon from the pulpit of the cathedral after mass had been said. The burden of his discourse was that his mission was one of peace—he had come to bring peace to the world. This incident ushered in one of the most extraordinary periods of Frederick's life; his public statements, many of his proclamations, even his letters, take on a messianic turn of phrase. He had branded the Pope as Antichrist and as an infidel, and now he came perilously near to identifying himself with the Saviour of the world.

Of all the proclamations, circular letters to the princes, and propaganda of all kinds that now poured unceasingly from the imperial chancery, the most astounding is the letter which Frederick addressed to his birthplace, the little town of Jesi in the March of Ancona, which he was about to annex to the Empire. In this letter the idea of the divinity of the Emperor reached its most audacious height—"The instincts of nature compel us to turn to thee, O Jesi . . . the place of our illustrious birth, where our Divine Mother brought us into the world, where our radiant cradle stood. . . . Thou, O Bethlehem, city of the March, are not least among the cities of our race; for out of thee the leader is come!" The tone of this letter was taken up and repeated by sycophantic courtiers; examples of this trend appear in letters written to Pietro della Vigna, comparing the master of this High Court Judge to the Mystic Lamb of the Apocalypse and Pietro himself to St. Peter. Even a bishop once wrote to Pietro, excusing himself for delay in answering the Emperor's summons by saying that "walking upon the waters" he would come to see his Lord.

Phrases such as "Peter, lovest thou me?", "feed my sheep" and "Peter who bears the keys of the Empire and locks what no man may open, and opens what no man again may lock" appeared in official correspondence. It is scarcely surprising that they should have led to the supposition that Frederick intended to found a schismatic Church, with Pietro della Vigna as his high priest. But in actual fact these sacrilegious turns of phrase were in reality probably only an attempt to produce a propagandist style which would provide a counterblast to the thunders of the Church, in a world whose mental atmosphere was keyed up with prophetic sayings and the recurrent belief that the end of the world, or the coming of Antichrist, was at hand. The sudden mass movement of the year of the Great Halleluja, and the later orgy of repentance of the flagellant friars, indicate how close to the surface the currents of religious hysteria ran during the thirteenth century. References to the Emperor and members of the imperial family as divine should not be misinterpreted in this context, they were common practice in the twelfth and thirteenth centuries and were called *deius de prole deorum*; and even long afterwards, when the Emperor and all his sons were dead, descendants of the Hohenstaufen dynasty through the female line were still referred to as "divine children", or "offshoot of the divine blood".

Preceded by this extraordinary propaganda barrage, the invasion of the Papal States began, and at last the tide of fortune seemed to have turned again in the Emperor's favour. Practically without encountering any opposition he advanced, and the cities of the Campagna flocked to put themselves under his banner—Civita Castellana, Corneto, Tivoli, Orte, even the rebellious Viterbo. Sutri was taken and magnanimously pardoned—barely twenty miles now separated the imperial forces from Rome. The end seemed to be in sight; the goal of all Frederick's ambitions—the imperial city of the Caesars where he would reign as their successor—was almost within his grasp.

Rome was in an uproar, rumour followed fast upon rumour, a comet which had lately appeared was regarded as an omen of great events, of the Emperor's inevitable success. In vain did the few who still supported the Pope openly prophesy the most terrible happenings, the most awful sacrileges, if the excommunicated Emperor once entered the sacred city. Gregory had long been one of the most unpopular of Popes, and a fickle populace, ever avid for new sensations and for the glamour and splendour of the atmosphere which surrounded the approaching conqueror, were prepared to welcome Frederick with open arms. Most of his cardinals had deserted the aged Pope; what had an old man in his dotage to offer in comparison with the magnificence of an Emperor in the prime of life, and one, moreover, who was fast approaching with a formidable army?

Gregory's cause seemed hopeless, but the indomitable old man did not give up; braving the insults of the jeering crowd, he walked through the streets of Rome which re-echoed to the cries of " *Ecce Salvator, Ecce Imperator, Veniat Veniat Imperator!* " It was the 22nd of February, one of the great feasts of the Church; and the most sacred relics—the splinter of the True Cross, the heads of the Apostles, St. Peter and St. Paul—were solemnly carried in procession from the Lateran to St. Peter's. In disdainful dignity, oblivious it seemed to all that was going on around him, the majestic old man paced through the tumultuous streets. The uproar was at its height when the Pope halted; turning to the crowd, he pointed to the relics and called out for all to hear. "These are the antiquities of Rome, for whose sake your city is venerated. This the Church, these are the relics which it is your duty, Romans, to protect. I can do no more than one man may; but I do not flee, lo, here I await the mercy of the Lord." Then taking the papal tiara from his head he laid it upon the relics and exclaimed—"Do you Saints defend Rome if the men of Rome will not defend her." In a moment the Emperor and all his glory were forgotten, and with tears and lamentations the people pressed around the Pope, crying their willingness to defend Rome, taking the Cross as the sign of their sacred charge.

Gregory himself was astonished at the miracle which had been wrought by his own superb courage. For an instant the fate of the world had trembled in the balance—it was the choice between the mediaeval world and one which would have heralded the Renaissance—but in the thirteenth century Gregory and all he stood for was nearer to the hearts and minds of the Roman crowd than all the glamour of the *Stupor Mundi*.

Frederick knew that he was beaten. After Brescia he realised what the siege of even a small city with a determined garrison entailed. Even if he succeeded in gaining an entry to the capital, with the connivance of the imperial party, he would have been faced with a mediaeval Stalingrad, for the great ruins of antiquity such as the Colosseum, the theatre of Marcellus, and Hadrian's tomb had been converted into formidable fortresses, and any family of note possessed a house fortified by tall defensive towers. Rome could only be taken with the goodwill of her citizens or at an overwhelming price in blood and money.

Early in March the scribes of the imperial chancery announced that the Emperor was returning to his beloved realm.

If Rome, upon which he had set his heart, had repudiated the Emperor, his loyal subjects the princes of the Empire did not; nor did public opinion in the majority of the Christian world. One of Frederick's most telling propaganda themes against the Church had been his clear statement of the fact that, without any assistance from her, he had liberated the Holy Places—"It is my business to recall to those who govern the Church that what they have gained in the Holy Land is due to my labour, that I braved the sea and thousands of dangers for the glory of God. The Pope persecutes me because he is jealous and wishes rather to collect riches than to diffuse the Christian faith. . . . God may judge between me his soldier and the Pope his Vicar."

Especially in England, where the exactions of the papal tax gatherers were particularly resented, and Gregory's predilection for the heretical Lombard communes well known, the ban of excommunication was regarded as unjustified. Men said that the Emperor had indeed exposed himself to the perils of the Crusade on Christ's behalf and "We have not up to now observed an equal piety in the Pope."

Gregory had dispatched Albert of Behaim to try and stir up trouble in Germany but he met with a spectacular failure, as letters from the papal agents show. "Many of the princes called the Pope's agents enemies of the Christian Church, false prophets, and firebrands of discord. The most vehement ask by what right does the Bishop of Rome without our agreement meddle in the affairs of Germany . . . he can look after his flocks in Italy; as for us we know how to defend our own against these wolves in sheep's clothing." Another wrote: "A sentiment of enthusiastic patriotism is manifesting itself to such a degree in all Germany, that if before autumn you do not send, with the necessary power to have another Emperor elected, a Legate so able as to set right opinions, now so far astray, events will see the Princes and Bishops themselves descend upon Italy with a powerful army to maintain the pretensions of the enemy of the Holy See."

The upshot of the whole matter was that first the secular, then the ecclesiastical, princes, and finally all of them together, wrote letters of protest to the Pope. This last letter was brought to the papal court in April 1240 by Conrad of Thuringia—the newly elected Grand Master of the Teutonic Order—who, treading in the footsteps of his predecessor Hermann von Salza, came in person to try and bring to an end the quarrel between Pope and Emperor which was the despair of Christendom. The princes made no bones about informing the Pope directly that his espousal of the Lombard communes was the root of the whole trouble. The ecclesiastical princes admitted their obedience to the Church, but pointed out that they were also vassals of the Emperor, and as such owed obedience to him. They concluded with an offer to come personally to Rome to mediate.

Frederick's conciliatory policy towards the princes paid him ample dividends at this time; they supported him solidly, and none of the papal efforts to seduce them succeeded in raising any opposition to the Emperor, as had so often occurred in the case of his predecessors—as at the time of Otto's deposition for example. For propaganda reasons Gregory could scarcely remain intransigent in the face of the princes' frontal attack. He now declared that he was prepared to forgive the Emperor, and that he was prepared to treat with him if the Emperor's arch enemies, his rebellious Lombard subjects, were included in the negotiations. It was the one condition that Frederick could in no circumstances accept. Nothing could have been more contrary to the "rights and honour of the Empire" which he considered to be his most sacred duty, sworn upon oath at his coronation, to protect.

Gregory was well aware of this, in reality he had no desire to treat with the Emperor, but at least his offer made the position clear to all—it was the heretical Lombards, not the Sicilian

Church, which had been the cause of Frederick's excommunication. The Grand Master of the Teutonic Order died a few
weeks later. His mission had been a failure, as was inevitable
in the circumstances, nor were any of his successors destined to
succeed. Support of the Lombard communes was the corner-
stone of papal policy in Italy; it was to remain so until the day
of Frederick's death, and upon this obstacle all hope of recon-
ciliation between Pope and Emperor was destined to founder.

In the meantime Frederick had returned to the realm, going
straight to his favourite province of Apulia. At Foggia on
Palm Sunday he held a remarkable gathering—a *colloquia*—
that was in effect a parliament, to which the Third Estate was
called. There had already been a precedent for this at the time
of the Constitution of Melfi, but the preparations for this particular *colloquia* appear to have been more elaborate. The
orders summoning the representatives of the people had been
dispatched to the justiciars on the 1st of March from Viterbo,
requiring each borough to send one man, and the larger cities
two. Specially privileged cities, such as Palermo, received a
communication direct from the Emperor, instructing the Bajuli,
justices, and people to proceed to the election of a Sindaco who
should represent them at the parliament, where they would be
admitted to their sovereign's presence, as he wished to be surrounded by his faithful subjects, who would then bring back his
orders.

Within a few months of this *colloquia* the man who twenty-
five years later was to summon the Commons of England for
the first time to Parliament, passed through Apulia. Simon de
Montfort's wife, Eleanor, was a sister of the Empress and together they visited the imperial court in northern Italy. Simon
went on to Brindisi to embark for the Holy Land where he was
to join Richard of Cornwall's Crusade. As he passed through
the realm he must have heard of and surely been impressed by
Frederick's innovation.

Before leaving the realm, the Emperor instituted a special
tax upon ecclesiastical benefices, and a militia charged with
bringing about the submission of Church lands whose incum-
bents were disobedient to his orders. He also dispatched an
army to besiege Benevento which, as a papal enclave in the
territories of the realm, was a centre of Church resistance.

Frederick then set out for central Italy, taking an army with him to Terni in the Duchy of Spoleto.

The position of the imperial forces in the north had declined since Frederick had left Lombardy for Pisa at the end of 1239. Two important cities of Romagna—Ferrara and Ravenna—had fallen to the Guelf forces under the leadership of Gregory of Montelungo. Advancing up the Adriatic coast, the Emperor now laid siege to Ravenna, and after six days the town capitulated, gave up hostages, and was pardoned. Bologna was Frederick's next objective; the capture of that staunchly papal town would have laid open to him the passes into Tuscany, but to achieve it he would have to bypass another Guelf stronghold, Faenza, which would have constituted a threat to his flank and lines of communication. Accordingly Faenza was invested at the end of August.

November came, and with it the end of the campaigning season, but still the stubborn citizens held out. Frederick could not afford a repetition of Brescia, and contrary to military practice of the period he decided to go into winter quarters while still continuing the siege. Accordingly an enormous fortified camp, a city of wooden huts, was built to surround the beleaguered city. The expense of this campaign was enormous, and the treasuries of the Sicilian churches were rifled of their plate, their gold and jewels, which were collected by the imperial officials. It was probably against this security that Frederick now issued leather money—coins stamped like the augustales with the imperial eagle and his head; these were afterwards faithfully redeemed against their promissory value in gold. In spite of the tension of these weary months, with the added threat of the Venetian fleet ravaging the Apulian coast—the Emperor ordered Pietro Tiepolo to be hung in full view of their galleys outside Brindisi harbour as a reprisal—Frederick passed the winter as was his wont in learned studies and discussions, even correcting a translation of an Arabic treatise on falconry that Master Theodore had made for him.

As the winter advanced, famine stalked the streets of Faenza, and all the useless mouths—the women and children and the old men—were driven out of the city. But Frederick would show them no mercy; he said that their fathers had insulted his mother, the Empress Constance, when in an advanced stage of her pregnancy she had passed through the city. They had mutilated her palfrey, "Venting their rage upon a brute beast", and paying no respect to her royal rank or sex. Furthermore, they had once killed a knight wearing the imperial armour under the impression that it was himself.

After experiences such as these the people of Faenza had little hope of clemency when they ultimately surrendered, after eight months' siege, on the 14th of April 1241. The city was practically reduced to ruins, the walls were destroyed, and there was fighting in the centre of the town, which the imperial forces had entered by means of digging underground tunnels. To their universal astonishment, instead of wreaking his vengeance upon them, their conqueror smilingly forgave them with the words: "Thus we enter the town in our overflowing gentleness, and with the outstretched arms of inexhaustible clemency we greet the conversion of the believers . . . that they may know that nothing is juster and lighter and easier to take on them than the yoke of the Empire."

All unknowing, on the field of Faenza Frederick laid the foundation of a modern European state—Switzerland. A delegation of the men of Schwyz had crossed the Alps in midwinter, probably by the newly discovered St. Gothard pass, in order to demonstrate their fidelity to the Emperor in his battles; and they had fought valiantly at his side. They were in conflict with their seigneur, Rudolf of Hapsburg, who wished to extend his rights over Schwyz and Unterwald. In recognition of their services Frederick gave them a charter which declared them free men, under his own personal protection and that of the Empire. It was not an entirely disinterested gesture on the Emperor's part, as the territory of Schwyz, together with that of Uri—over which he had already acquired imperial rights— controlled the northern entry to the St. Gothard. From such small beginnings, cemented by the permanent alliance of the three cantons of Uri, Schwyz, and Unterwald in 1291, arose the Swiss Confederation and the modern state of Switzerland.

The Pope had not been idle in pursuing his vendetta against the Emperor during the siege of Faenza. The ban of excommunication had not been sufficient to destroy his enemy's power; accordingly, Gregory determined to call a General Council at the Lateran where, with a carefully selected list of pro-papal delegates acting under his personal direction, he could scarcely fail to achieve his aim. Immediately after his excommunication Frederick had not been averse to arbitration between himself and the Pope by a General Council; but a genuinely representative one called by the College of Cardinals, which included his own supporters as well as those of the Pope.

Frederick was quick to perceive that the General Council called by Gregory in August 1240 for Easter 1241 would by no means be the impartial tribunal which he had in mind. He therefore forbade any of his subjects to attend the council and sent letters to the European powers warning them that no safe-conducts would be allowed for any of the delegates to cross his territories; furthermore he issued orders to all his officials to arrest anyone who dared to put in an appearance. The wily Gregory, fearing that in the circumstances—the Emperor controlled all the land routes to Rome—it would be impossible to hold the council, wrote suggesting to Frederick that there should be a year's truce during which the conditions for peace could be discussed.

Frederick was not hoodwinked by this manœuvre, and replied: "Why call from far away arbiters for a council when we have wise men here, like the Bishop of Brescia, and so many other western prelates? If we agree upon a truce the Lombard confederacy, those irreconcilable enemies of the Empire, should be excluded. As for the council, as it is notorious that in the letters of convocation the Pope has not spoken of the future peace, but only mentioned the grave affairs of the Roman Church, this changes the whole question. As the Bishops who have given funds to make war against us, and Lords who have broken their fealty to us such as the Marquis of Este, the Count of Provence, Alberico da Romano, and many others are called to be judges in their own cause, while the Ghibellines will not be admitted there; we cannot recognise the competence of such a tribunal which is justly suspect."

Gregory now exhorted the delegates to come by sea; he had arranged for their passage, at very considerable cost, with the Genoese—these hard-headed merchantmen did not hesitate to drive a good bargain, Pope or no Pope! One of the clauses of this agreement was that the whole thing should be kept secret, in the hope of surprising the Emperor with a *fait*

accompli. But Frederick had too many friends among the Genoese nobility for this to be possible—the Dorias and the Spinolas
were closely attached to him and his own Admiral, Ansaldo de
Mari, was a Genoese. A regular correspondence was evidently carried on between them and the imperial court by
secret means; one letter concealed in a cake of wax was intercepted by the Genoese authorities.

In spite of the imperial ban, the ecclesiastics of the Western
world could scarcely ignore the summons of the Sovereign
Pontiff; and by April a considerable number of English, French
and Spanish ecclesiastical delegates had arrived in Genoa. The
English took one look at the overcrowded, and in some cases
unseaworthy, transports and galleys which were to run the
gauntlet of the imperial fleet, and the majority wisely decided
to remain on dry land. The others embarked on the 28th of
April in twenty-seven galleys and thirty-three transports. For
the first week all went well; but the Genoese captains, evidently
made over-bold by their success to date, unwisely made the
decision of taking the shorter route to Civitavecchia, passing
through the narrow strip of sea which lies between Corsica and
the Pisan coast. And there in the Tuscan Archipelago the
imperial fleet lay in waiting for them, between the islands of
Giglio and Monte Christo.

The battle was short and bloody; three of the Genoese
galleys went down with all hands, twenty-two others and most
of the transports were captured, only three ships of the Genoese fleet escaped, bringing the Spanish delegates to Civitavecchia to tell the tale of the disaster. Four thousand prisoners
fell into the hands of the victors, including a hundred high Church
dignitaries, two of whom were cardinals. Frederick regarded
this overwhelming naval victory as a sign that God was on his
side, and his valuable convoy of prisoners was soon hustled off
to the realm for confinement. In their sufferings, and they were
severe, they wrote to the Pope begging him to make peace;
perhaps Frederick himself thought that he might be able to use
them as a bargaining counter to obtain his release from excommunication. But even in this extremity, suffering as he was
from the agonies of an illness which betokened his fast-approach-
ing death, the proud old Pope was adamant.

Frederick, however, did not give up his attempts to reach

some sort of settlement. His brother-in-law, the returning Crusader Richard of Cornwall, had landed in Sicily in July, and on his way home he stopped to visit the Emperor in his camp near Terni. Matthew Paris gave in his chronicle a lively account of the affectionate welcome that the Emperor extended to Richard, and the care which was taken of him after the fatigues of his long journey—baths and blood-letting, and special entertainments. It was only after a few days, however, that Richard at the Emperor's express command was allowed to see his sister Isabella, who was pregnant at that time. Even in camp she was evidently kept in jealous seclusion, and had not been permitted to appear to welcome her own brother upon his arrival. But Richard found her surrounded by luxury, amusing herself with musical instruments and strange toys, that the Emperor had ordered for her diversion. Almost certainly she would not have been present at the magnificent reception which her husband gave for Richard, where troops of acrobats and dancers performed for his amusement. What particularly pleased the Earl were two Saracen dancing girls, of great beauty, who danced standing upon rolling spheres, which they kept in motion with their feet; swaying and bending the while and accompanying their graceful gestures with the music of castanets and tambourines.

Richard's sojourn was by no means wholly taken up with these diversions; he reported to the Emperor the grave state of affairs in the Holy Land where, according to all accounts, he had conducted himself with considerable sagacity, and was accorded Frederick's unqualified approval. Richard's ability as a negotiator evidently so impressed his brother-in-law that he was dispatched on a mission of peace to the Pope—Frederick was going to leave no stone unturned after his recent success had put him in an advantageous position to bargain. Richard's mission was a failure, and he returned to the imperial camp outraged at the scant respect which had been shown to him as a returned Crusader, both by the Pope and the people of Rome. Frederick told him that he was "glad that you have learnt by experience the truth of what we told you beforehand".

Frederick now decided to make an all-out attack upon Rome. He descended upon the Campagna, laying waste the countryside as he advanced; he seized and sacked Tivoli, Borgonova, and Monteforte. By mid-August he was at Grottaferrata in the Alban hills, where from his camp he could look down upon the city which he so much coveted, and which now for the second time in two years seemed to be within his grasp. Gregory was dying at last. The incredible physique that had enabled him to withstand for nearly a century the primitive conditions of life, the disease and the fevers of mediaeval Italy that laid so many men low in their prime, was failing him at last. Tortured by a disease of the kidneys, for which the baths of Viterbo, now denied to him by the Emperor's iron grasp that encircled Rome, were the only cure, he lay in terrible suffering. On the 21st of August he died. But even his death was a last gesture of defiance to the hated Emperor; now that the Pope was no more, Rome itself was but an empty shell whose conquest would have no meaning.

Events were to show, indeed, though he did not live to see them, that Pope Gregory's vindictive will to pursue the struggle had ensured the Emperor's ruin. It had pinned Frederick down in Italy; he dared not leave the peninsula when victory seemed to be almost within his grasp. His experiences while he was on Crusade had taught him that with Gregory in the Chair of St. Peter, the realm and all he possessed was in danger once his back was turned. But in 1241 a foe a thousand times more awful than the Saracens was knocking at the gates of Europe— the Mongol hordes had defeated the armies of Christendom at Liegnitz in April; in May at the diet of Esslingen King Conrad had called for a Crusade of all Germany to meet the terrible threat. While the homeland of his fathers was fighting for its bare survival, the Emperor, who should have led their armies, was absent in Italy; besieging the paltry town of Faenza, capturing Christian bishops at sea, and finally, attacking Rome itself where the Pope lay dying.

Chapter XII

THE NADIR

THE Mongol threat which had burst upon Europe at the end of 1239 was the most terrible that the Western world had been called upon to face since the coming of the Huns. The originator of the Tartar Empire—the great Genghis—had died in 1227, and it was during the Khanship of his son Ogotay that the Golden Horde conquered the whole of Russia, under the command of Genghis's old general, Subotay. The new Kahn spurred Subotay on to further conquests, and early in 1241 Hungary was overrun, its King Bela fugitive in an island of the Adriatic, and Poland, the Baltic states, Bohemia, Silesia, and Austria in deadly peril; the Mongols were at one moment within seventy-five leagues of Vienna.

These ferocious people owed their supremacy to the incredible staying power of their cavalry, able generalship, and the terror which their brutality, exercised as a matter of policy that had been dictated by Genghis himself, inspired in the whole world—one of their generals had three hundred noble Hungarian matrons massacred before his eyes. Such was the menace that now threatened to overrun the whole of a divided Europe, whose two natural leaders, Pope and Emperor, were so absorbed in their own quarrels that they had let it come upon them unawares.

The Empire stood in the direct path of the impending invasion, and the princes had sent an embassy to the Pope, demanding a Crusade in its defence, and begging him to sink his differences with the Emperor. But to Gregory the submission of his hated enemy was more important than the safety of Europe; the Emperor must first give in, he said, and the ambassadors went back empty-handed.

Frederick was to a certain extent forewarned of the gravity of the situation, as no doubt the ambassador of the "King of

Russia ", for whose maintenance he had made arrangements with Henry Baum of Vienna in January 1240, had been dispatched to enlist the assistance of the Emperor of the West for his unfortunate country. Perhaps it was from this source that Frederick obtained the intimate knowledge, which he displayed in his letters to the kings of Europe, of the physical characteristics and customs of the Tartars. These manifestos were sent to the leaders of the Christian world calling them to arms for the defence of Europe. They were stirringly phrased in the best style of the imperial chancery, but they were a psychological blunder; it would have been better to keep silent about the terror which was threatening civilisation if the Emperor was not prepared to go and fight it in person. Moreover the very knowledge that Frederick possessed of the true nature of the Mongol menace told against him; it gave rise to sinister rumours that he himself had summoned the Mongols in order, thereby, to dominate Europe and to sweep Christianity away; and his continued absence from the battle-front gave further colour to the story.

The quarrel with the Pope and the Lombard communes kept a large part of the imperial armies tied down in Italy when they should have been concentrated in Germany for its defence. The effect of this upon public opinion in Germany can well be imagined, especially when it was left to King Conrad—a thirteen-year-old boy—to take the Cross for his country's defence at Esslingen in May 1241; and to issue the imperial order that every man with an income of over three marks was obliged to take up arms in his country's defence. In this moment of crisis the princes took command themselves, and Duke Henry the Pious's gallant stand at Liegnitz, in which he and all his knights were slaughtered upon the field, although a defeat, brought a check to the Mongols' advance, as they themselves were so severely mauled as to be unprepared to fight a further battle with the forces of the King of Bohemia, who had arrived upon the field too late. The Empire owed its deliverance to them and to the opportune death of Ogotay, which recalled the Mongol forces to the East where the election of a new Great Khan and subsequent internal disorders distracted their attention from the conquest of Europe.

But the trembling peoples of the Empire were not to know

that the changed political situation on the steppes of Central Asia had brought about their salvation. The Mongols were still at their eastern gates and in occupation of the whole of Russia—where they remained for two centuries to come—and the Emperor still tarried in Italy, caught in the intricate web of that unpredictable country's politics. While Gregory was alive there was some justification for Frederick's continued presence in Italy, but when the Germans saw that even the death of his arch-enemy did not bring him back to organise their defence, they realised once and for all how little they really mattered to their Emperor, who was more preoccupied with the results of the papal election than with their own survival.

Frederick wrote letters promising to return to Germany as soon as the new Pope had been elected, but they did not serve to turn the current of opinion that was running strongly against him. Mesmerised by his grandiose dream of an empire based on Rome he could not see how disastrously his absence from Germany at this crucial time would tell against him. To this dream he sacrificed in a few months the firm hold that his dominating personality, his charm and his conciliatory attitude to the princes had enabled him to build up ever since his accession.

Meanwhile the conclave for the election of the new Pope was in progress. As might be expected there was a serious rift in the Sacred College between those of its members who had supported Gregory's policy of resistance à l'outrance to the Emperor, and those who advocated a more conciliatory attitude. Six of the ten cardinals present at the conclave adhered to the latter point of view, but they lost their numerical advantage by the death of one of their number—the English Cardinal Robert of Somercote—who died as a result of the appalling conditions in which the conclave was taking place.

The all-powerful Senator of Rome, Matthew Orsini, wished for the speedy election of a "Guelf" Pope, and he proceeded to ensure it by his appalling treatment of these defenceless old men, who were imprisoned as if they were so many criminals in the Sepizonium—a ruined relic of the palace of the Caesars on the Palatine.

The Sepizonium was the customary place in which conclaves were held, but no conclave, either before or since, can ever have taken place in conditions of such horror. The ten cardinals were shut up in a single room, whose roof and walls were damaged by recent earthquakes; they were allowed no servants or medical aid, and were left in the charge of brutal soldiers who had received their orders from Matthew Orsini, and took fiendish pleasure in carrying them out—they used the broken roof of the Sepizonium as a latrine—this in the heat of a Roman summer. All the cardinals fell ill: poor Robert of Somercote died in conditions of appalling brutality, and his death was eventually followed by that of two of his companions.

The weeks dragged by and still no definite conclusion was reached: at last in their despair the cardinals elected Godfrey of Sabina, who surprisingly enough appears to have been acceptable both to the Emperor and Matthew Orsini—he took the name of Celestine IV. But Orsini's violence had defeated its own ends, and within seventeen days of his election the new Pope died as a result of his sufferings in the Sepizonium. The other cardinals did not wait for a new martyrdom; four fled from Rome to Anagni and refused to return. Another cardinal died, a Guelf one this time, and all united in begging the Emperor to release his two prisoner cardinals—Jacob of Palestrina and Otto of St. Nicholas, who had been taken at the battle of Giglio—so that another conclave could take place. But the negotiations dragged on for months.

Frederick returned to Apulia, establishing his court at Foggia, and there on the 1st of December the Empress died giving birth to a daughter. Isabella was only twenty-seven: during her six years of married life she had given birth to four children of whom only Henry, born in 1238, and a daughter, Margaret, survived her. The early death of a young woman after repeated pregnancies was not uncommon in the thirteenth century; but Isabella was the third of Frederick's wives to die after a comparatively short married life, and the second to die in childbirth. Inevitably sinister rumours of her husband's having poisoned her, or having caused her death by ill-treatment, were soon current in Guelf circles, and though these were without foundation, it is within the bounds of possibility that the Emperor's Oriental jealousy, which prompted him to keep his wives secluded as if in a harem, may have prevented him from allowing them to be attended by a doctor during their confinements.

Upon her deathbed, Isabella's last thought was to recommend her brother King Henry to the Emperor's good graces. Though no word of this appears in Frederick's stately letter of mourning announcing her death to the King, Henry himself mentioned it in a letter to Frederick two years later—perhaps Margaret Biset or the Empress's English maid had been present when she died and, returning later to England, had described the scene to him. Isabella was buried in the cathedral of Andria, in the same crypt where her predecessor Yolanda lay, and the people of the realm were informed of the death of the Empress, whom they had probably never seen, and the Emperor's mourning for his beloved spouse, in a circular letter couched in moving terms.

The court was again plunged into mourning within the short space of three months; this time it was for the death of the Emperor's eldest son Henry, who was only a few years older than the stepmother who had at one time been proposed as his own bride. For seven years Henry had been a prisoner; first at San Felice, then at Nicastro. According to one story, his father had resolved to pardon him, and had sent orders for his release; but Henry was not aware of this and, fearing a worse fate, he killed himself by riding his horse over the edge of a bridge or a precipice upon the journey to what he thought might be an even grimmer prison. His father's announcement of his death was couched in words of such bitter sorrow that there can be little doubt that the disgrace and death of this his eldest son had indeed been a terrible blow to Frederick. The stern justice to which Henry had been sacrificed did not extend to his family and his son Frederick later served in his grandfather's army and was bequeathed the Kingdom of Austria in the Emperor's will; but he too died young.

Meanwhile the negotiations for the release of the captive cardinals, as the first step towards a new conclave, still dragged on. Cardinal Otto of St. Nicholas had been won over to the Emperor's side, and was released to try his powers of persuasion upon his fellow members of the Sacred College; but Cardinal Jacob of Palestrina, who was a personal enemy of the Emperor, still languished in prison. During the summer of 1242, and again in the spring of 1243, Frederick appeared in the Campagna, ostensibly to hurry the cardinals up into making some decision. The continued papal interregnum dismayed Europe, and St. Louis and the French bishops wrote letters of exhortation to the Sacred College, while in England prayers were said for the election of a new Pope. At last in June 1243 the cardinals, including Cardinal Jacob, specially released for the purpose, met in Anagni and after a short conclave elected Sinibaldo Fieschi, who took the name of Innocent IV.

At first it seemed as if the Emperor's sacrifice of his German interests by remaining in Italy to supervise the complicated negotiations that preceded the conclave and the election of the new Pope had not been in vain. Innocent was of a very different metal from the proud and passionate Gregory; he was about the same age as the Emperor, a shrewd and subtle Church lawyer, whose life had hitherto been spent in political intrigue, in diplomatic missions, and in the dark offices of the papal curia.

The Fieschis were a family of hard-headed, close-fisted Genoese—counts of Lavagna—who were brought up to cultivate ambition and to seek power. To achieve this end most of the sons of the family went into the Church—Innocent's three uncles were all churchmen—and the daughters married into influential families. In spite of their Church connections the Fieschis had a reputation for being Ghibelline in sympathy; they were cultivated, one at least was a patron of the arts— Obizzo, Bishop of Parma, whose name is associated with the building of the famous baptistry—entirely lacking in mysticism, unbigoted, and realists to a man.

For all their alleged Ghibelline sympathies, however, the Fieschis did not join the other aristocratic Genoese families in their conspiracy in favour of the Emperor when his armies were besieging that city in 1241. They were shrewd enough to realise that Lavagna was too important a communications centre to the imperial strategy in Italy for them to be left in undisturbed possession of it if Frederick got Genoa. The Fieschis' sympathies, political or otherwise, were directed only by their personal interests, or that of the family; for it was in their close-knit tribal relationship—and their cunning—that their strength lay. For the advantage of the family they were prepared to go to any lengths, to practise any deception, and with a cold and calculating tenacity to pursue their objective utterly regardless of any moral consideration whatsoever, but in doing so it must be admitted that they displayed very considerable courage.

This then was the formidable clan that the Emperor's two years of diplomatic intrigue had called into power with Innocent at their head; and he was a worthy representative of the stock from which he sprang. To Frederick this worldly and ambitious cardinal had seemed in many ways to be a kindred soul, a man who thought in the same way as himself; with whom he could treat and bargain as he had done with al-Kamil. He greeted Innocent's election with joy, sent an imposing embassy to carry his congratulations to the new Pope, and ordered the *Te Deum* to be sung in the realm.

Then came something of a shock. Innocent refused to receive his ambassadors in person, giving as his reason that it was contrary to papal etiquette for him to see the representatives of an excommunicated prince. The first doubts as to the success of his policy began to creep into the Emperor's mind; afterwards he was to exclaim bitterly, "No Pope can be a Ghibelline"; but he had yet to learn that a Pope of the Ghibelline school of thought, materialistic, worldly, cunning, with a cool duplicity that outmatched his own, was a foe far more terrible than Gregory with all his passionate hatred.

Still, for a while, things seemed to promise well; negotiations for a settlement with the papacy and the Emperor's release from excommunication were set on foot, and appeared to progress satisfactorily. Pietro della Vigna, Thaddeus of Sessa and Archbishop Berard of Palermo were exempted from the Church's ban in order to negotiate; all the old familiar complaints of the seizure of Church lands, release of prisoners, and promises of the Emperor's penitence were quickly disposed of; and then came the crux of the whole matter—the Lombard question. Even in this the Emperor was prepared to be propitiatory and to allow the whole situation to revert to the *status quo* of 1239.

At this stage rebellion broke out in Viterbo, instigated by Cardinal Rainer, a native of the town and a bitter enemy of the Emperor. The imperial garrison took refuge in the fortress, and Frederick moved quickly from Apulia to their relief. Twice he attacked the city and twice he was repulsed. This failure had unfavourable repercussions in Central Italy where several towns

L

went over to the Guelfs; in Germany too it created profound dismay. The Emperor was therefore glad to accept the Pope's offer to reopen negotiations and, treating with his friend Cardinal Otto of St. Nicholas, an agreement was soon reached. The Emperor was to retire to Apulia and the imperial garrison to be allowed to march out with the honours of war. But again Cardinal Rainer wrecked any hope of a peaceful settlement; the imperial troops were attacked and mostly killed as they emerged from the citadel. This dastardly deed roused Frederick to such a fury that he swore that even if he had one foot in paradise itself he would withdraw it if by doing so he could wreak his vengeance upon Viterbo. Nevertheless he recognised that Cardinal Rainer was the real culprit, and peace negotiations were again resumed.

Innocent had made his formal entry into Rome in November 1243; he was greeted with great popular acclamations upon his arrival, but his life was soon rendered exceedingly embarrassing by the importuning of Gregory's creditors, who more or less laid siege to the papal palace. It was a terrible winter, the harvest had been poor, pestilence and famine stalked through Italy and, remembering perhaps the behaviour of the Roman mob on previous occasions of this kind, Innocent barely emerged from his private apartments. Frederick however was far from idle; though the peace negotiations were in progress, he was also treating with the Frangipanis for a share of their fortress built in the ruins of the Colosseum and other strongpoints in Rome.

Nevertheless on Holy Thursday, which fell on the 31st of March, the terms of a provisional settlement between Pope and Emperor were read out in Innocent's presence before a multitude assembled in the piazza before St. John Lateran. The Count of Toulouse, Pietro della Vigna and Thaddeus of Sessa swore to the peace on behalf of the Emperor, and the Pope referred to him as a "devoted son of the Church". The terms were only provisional, the final settlement would have to be ratified; but the Emperor agreed to return to the Church lands, prisoners, hostages, and booty taken in the sea battle of Giglio; and to fast and found hospitals and monasteries as a sign of his repentance; also to address a letter to the kings of Europe stating that he had not opposed the sentence of excommunication from disdain, but because it had not been sent to him with due regard to form. Even a saving formula for the Lombard problem appeared to have been found—the Emperor seemed to be prepared to accept almost anything to obtain peace.

Would this settlement prevail? The Lombards had other ideas. When their representatives arrived in Rome they refused point blank to accept it. The Pope tried to make alterations in their favour, but the imperial representatives stood firm; following the tactics of Gregory, Innocent did not press this point, aware no doubt that in the Lombard question the Emperor had too much right on his side; instead, he demanded that Frederick should return the Church lands and prisoners before the ban of excommunication was officially lifted. It was an impossible stipulation, and Innocent was well aware of it; for once having given them up, Frederick had no guarantee that the Pope would not then discover some other stumbling-block, and his bargaining weapon would have been lost.

However genuine Innocent's desire for peace may have been at first, certainly now he was simply playing for time. Rome was in a restive state; Gregory's creditors became more pressing in their demands, and in mid-April the Frangipanis finally decided to cede part of the Colosseum and another stronghold to the Emperor. The imperial ambassadors were hedging, no doubt while waiting for fresh instructions. Frederick asked for a personal interview with the Pope, which Innocent at first refused, and then suddenly agreed to.

The Emperor's request had given Innocent the chance he wanted, the opportunity he had been seeking to put into operation a plan which had probably been in his mind for some months past. The new Pope had been the witness of Gregory's many vicissitudes; he knew only too well how his predecessor had suffered at the hands of the fickle Roman mob, how on two occasions the Emperor had been within an ace of taking Rome. He was now at the gates of Rome again; and Innocent could scarcely have been unaware of the fact that Frederick had been in negotiation with the Frangipanis, and that he might now succeed in introducing by secret means some Trojan horse of an imperial force into their strongholds. Courage of a kind this scion of the Fieschi possessed, but it was not that of a Gregory who could outface a Roman mob: he sought another way out.

While the arrangements for the interview with Frederick were under way, the Pope held a consistory and created another twelve cardinals: this sudden strengthening of the Sacred College might have served the Emperor as a warning that something was in the wind; in any case he moved to Terni which stands near the appointed meeting-place of Narni. The papal court left Rome during the first week in June, and arrived at Civita Castellana within a few days; there they halted and matters seemed to have come to a standstill. No further progress was made in the final negotiations to arrange the momentous interview between the Pope and the still excommunicated Emperor. On the 27th of June the Pope made some pretext to visit Sutri, which lies a few miles to the west of Civita Castellana, and here he apparently intended to stay. In the small hours, dressed as a soldier, in the company of his nephew William, recently created Cardinal of Sant Eustahio, three other cardinals and six servants, and carrying a large sum of money, the Pope crept out of the silent town, and rode break-neck over the wild hill country that separates Sutri from Civitavecchia.

The secret had been well kept; even his retinue that had accompanied Innocent to Sutri did not discover his escape until some hours after he had gone; the rest of the court were in complete ignorance except four other cardinals who subsequently followed him to Genoa. For this was the reason of Innocent's sudden flight to Civitavecchia: a Genoese fleet was waiting for him in the harbour to carry him to his native Liguria, well out of reach of the encircling imperial forces.

The whole thing had been planned in advance, and was carried out by the Fieschi family and their connections. A Franciscan friar, who was a relation of the Pope's, had been entrusted with a secret letter addressed to his three nephews, Alberto, Ugo and Giacomo, who were then in Genoa; it was an appeal for aid in arranging his escape. Its contents were revealed to the podestà, who was a stout supporter of the Guelf faction, and in a little over a fortnight a fleet of twenty-one fast galleys was ready to put to sea, ostensibly to fight the admiral of the Realm of Sicily whose activities off the African coast were menacing Genoese interests. Two of Innocent's nephews declared that they must go to Parma to be present at a wedding there, where they had family connections. The Fieschi connections with Parma were well known, so there was nothing odd in the two brothers beginning their journey by sea with the fleet, to be dropped, presumably, at their home town of Lavagna to continue their journey overland.

The Genoese fleet set sail on the 21st of June and arrived in Civitavecchia on the 27th, just in time to welcome the Pope. There was no time to lose and, in spite of bad weather, the fleet started on its return journey the following day. The weather grew steadily worse, and Innocent's ship was forced to take shelter in the port of the island of Giglio—of evil memory for any successor of Gregory. The storm did not abate for some time, and it was only on the 7th of July that the papal galley and the accompanying fleet made its triumphant entry into the port of Genoa.

The bells of the city pealed in tumultuous welcome; crowds gathered to cheer, while choirs intoned the psalm "Blessed is he who comes in the name of the Lord"; and, no doubt with a heartfelt prayer of thanks, Innocent stepped from the deck of his galley, which was now festooned with gold brocade, on to the soil of his native land. The Genoese, who have always been renowned for their tight-fistedness, must really have been delirious with joy; for the commune blithely agreed to defray the entire costs of the upkeep of the Pope and his entourage during their stay.

This was longer than the Genoese, in the first flush of their enthusiasm, had probably expected. Innocent fell seriously ill, and withdrew to the quiet of Sestri which was near his ancestral lands of Lavagna. There he learned that his flight had not put an end to his problems, for the kings of Europe displayed a strange unwillingness to accept the unparalleled honour of a sojourn of indeterminate duration by the Sovereign Pontiff upon their national soil. Aragon and England refused outright, and even the saintly King Louis of France, when beseeched upon their knees by the monks of Cluny to give shelter to the illustrious fugitive, said that he must take counsel with his barons—who refused categorically to entertain any such proposal.

The Pope's choice finally fell upon the city of Lyons which, although officially part of the Kingdom of Arles and therefore of the Empire, was in effect an independent entity governed by its commune, and the residence of an archbishop with princely powers. Still suffering from the effects of his illness, Innocent was carried in a litter when he set out on the 5th of October for the journey that was to take him across Piedmont and the Alps. Asti at first closed its doors to him, then came over to the Guelf faction, followed by Alessandria. In spite of these cheering conversions to the papal cause, it was a gloomy journey: thunder was heard without ceasing for fifteen days. The Pope halted for a few days' rest at Susa, where he was joined by the rest of the cardinals who had been left behind at the time of his flight from Sutri, before attempting to cross the Mont Cenis pass which was already covered by the snows of winter. The papal court arrived in Lyons on the 1st of December 1244: it was the first step upon the road to Avignon, and ultimately brought in its train the end of the papal theocracy.

Innocent's flight had taken the wind completely out of Frederick's sails: according to Matthew Paris, "he ground his teeth like a satyr in his rage and exclaimed 'It is written that the unrighteous fly without anyone pursuing them.'" Once again he had advanced to Rome and seemed to be about to come to a final reckoning with a Pope, and once again he found that he had been beating empty air. For Frederick was too shrewd to imagine that Innocent's flight could be interpreted as a victory for himself: for one thing the Pope could now pose before the Christian world almost as a martyr, driven from the Apostolic city by the threats of an overweening Emperor; for another—and this was far more serious—he was now free to call the representatives of the Western world to a General Council, packed with his supporters, which could bring about the Emperor's deposition.

Frederick was now fifty; and the Pope's flight, and all that it implied for the future, probably caused him to take stock of the situation. The years since Cortenuova must have appeared to him as one long struggle for a goal—the defeat of Gregory and the election of a more tractable Pope; this he thought he had attained, only to find that now the prospect of a worse and longer struggle seemed to stretch out endlessly before not only himself, but also his successor. The only solution appeared to be to make peace at any price. Accordingly the Emperor dispatched the Count of Toulouse with a respectful letter to the

Pope in Genoa, in which he marvelled much at Innocent's pre-cipitate departure, but renewed the offers of peace that his representatives had made in Rome.

Frederick had meanwhile gone to Pisa, for he feared that the Pope's presence in the north might encourage the Guelfs there to set the whole country ablaze. He was particularly anxious too about the situation that Innocent's open hostility might now provoke in Parma. This important town, which controls the passes leading from Lombardy across the Apennines to the Tuscan and Ligurian coast, had hitherto been Ghibelline, but the Fieschi lands lay between Lavagna and Parma, and the family had close connections with the city. Three of the daughters had married into powerful Parmesan families—one of them was the wife of Bernardo Rolando de Rossi—and two of the Pope's uncles had held important offices in the church of Parma, where Innocent himself had been educated. The circumstances called for prompt measures, and the Emperor dispatched a strong force to garrison the town: they occupied the towers of the fortified bishop's palace, and arranged for the election as podestà of Teobaldo di Francesco, a Sicilian noble who was a member of the imperial court circle.

These moves strengthened Frederick's position locally, but on the grander scale of world diplomacy he was forced to admit: "When I played chess with Cardinal Fieschi I usually check-mated him or took some important piece; but the Genoese by putting their hands on the chess-board have lost me the game." He was right: Innocent was now preparing the move that would checkmate him—within a short time of his arrival in Lyons the Pope's summons to a General Council had been dispatched to the world at large.

The agenda for the council was set out in the following terms: to return the Church to its honourable state; to save the Holy Land now invaded by the Khwarismians; to throw back the Tartars: relieve Constantinople; and to settle the disagreement between the Papal See and the Prince—Frederick was not even accorded the dignity of his imperial rank. One of the items of this agenda, however, gave the Emperor the chance for yet another peace offensive: Jerusalem and the Holy Land had been lost to Christianity—the first had fallen in August 1244, and two months later practically the whole of the Christian army

had been wiped out at the battle of Gaza. In actual fact the
Holy Land was to remain in the hands of the Turks for nearly
another seven hundred years; but now, at the instigation of the
Patriarch of Antioch, the Emperor offered to lead a Crusade for
its recovery. He said that he would not return to Europe without the Pope's permission for three years; he would give back
to the Holy See the lands of the patrimony which he now occupied; and he would even submit the entire Lombard question to
the Pope's arbitration without reserve.

This was capitulation pure and simple: all that Gregory had
been unable to obtain in the fourteen years of his pontificate,
Innocent now had offered to him after a single year. The
Emperor had returned to Apulia when he made this astounding
offer, which represented the relinquishment of all his dreams, of
all that he had planned and fought for since he had left Palermo
thirty-two long years ago. In this moment of the blackest
depression, Frederick's mind seems to have turned again to the
East with which he was so much in sympathy: he had just
married one of his illegitimate daughters—Manfred's sister—
to the Nicean Emperor, John Vatatzes, who was now threatening the remnants of the Latin Empire at Constantinople.

Vatatzes was older than his father-in-law, and was at the
height of a successful career when Frederick compared his lot
unfavourably with that of the Eastern Emperor in a letter filled
with longing to escape from it all—"Oh happy Asia, oh happy
rulers of the Orient, who fear neither the dagger of the rebel
nor the superstitions invented by priests." As the years wore
on, and the struggle with a foe that he could never bring to
battle in the open dragged wearily by, Frederick may well have
sighed for the fury of combat in the heat of battle against the
Khwarismians, whom he could at least see and smite, instead
of being called upon to parry the interminable underground
machinations of Innocent. To go on Crusade as Frederick now
suggested would have been to admit defeat—but it would have
been an escape.

Fate was not to allow the Emperor this way out, however.
On his way north to the Diet of Verona, to which he had called
the princes of the Empire in the spring of 1245, he devastated the
countryside around the hated city of Viterbo. In the course of
this action his troops created what today we would call border

incidents upon the marches of papal territory. Then, as now, these served as an opportune excuse for the party who was bent upon war at any price—the watchful Cardinal Rainer, who had been left in Italy as the Pope's viceroy. Cardinal Rainer had learnt with dismay that Innocent apparently intended to accept the Emperor's peace offer, and he seized this opportunity to wreck any hope of settlement. The reports that he now forwarded to Lyons so magnified these paltry offences of the imperial troops as to give the appearance of Frederick's playing a double game; and all hope of peace at the eleventh hour was lost.

The Emperor proceeded on his way, oblivious of the consequences of his actions, to hold the last diet in which the Empire was to be represented as a whole; though already there were gaps among the ranks of the German princes. King Conrad came, and the Emperor's new son-in-law—the Emperor Vatatzes—the Archbishop of Salzburg and the Dukes of Moravia, Carinthia, and Austria.

Frederick even had plans afoot for marrying the Duke of Austria's heiress, Gertrude of Babenburg. Much had happened since her father had defied the Emperor from Wiener Neustadt in 1236, when the Emperor had appropriated the Duchy of Austria to himself—only to lose it again when the Duke reconquered his ancestral territories once Frederick's back was turned. Now Emperor and Duke met as friends, as potential relatives, as equals almost; for the Duke was to receive the title of King upon his daughter's marriage to his suzerain. Through all these vicissitudes Frederick had been animated by the same desire—to attach the rich duchy to himself as an additional, and much-needed, family appanage in his northern realms. The only thing that now was lacking was the prospective bride. Apparently Gertrude had been so much frightened by the stories which had been put in circulation by Guelf propagandists, representing Frederick as a bluebeard, that at the last moment she had refused to come. Her absence was indeed an omen of what the papal agents were to achieve in the near future in Germany.

Conrad, who was now seventeen, had not seen his father for some years, but Frederick was not lacking in paternal affection for him. At Christmas in 1239 he had written to Sicily to order two saddles to be made for Conrad in Messina—one for a pal-

frey and another for a war horse. According to these instruc-
sions, they were to be "beautifully worked" for "our dearest
ton". Mindful, no doubt, of the fate which had overtaken
Henry, Frederick wrote constantly to Conrad. Though these
letters were couched in the stylised language of the court,
they showed plainly his affection and anxiety for his son's
welfare: they were a touching mixture of practical common-
sense advice and wise counsels as to the true nature of kingly
dignity and self-discipline.

"People do not distinguish Kings and Caesars above other
men because they are more highly placed, but because they see
further and act better . . . they have nothing to pride themselves
on unless by virture and wisdom they outshine other men",
Frederick wrote in one letter to his son. In others he seems to
be delving back into his own memories of the past and remembering the boy whose actions were "sometimes odd and vulgar
. . . due to the rough company he kept", and who would not
obey his tutor's commands. Thus he wrote to Conrad: "Hence
it is necessary and seemly that thou shouldest love wisdom. And
for her sake it is fitting that thou layest aside the Caesar's
dignity, and under the master's rod . . . be neither King nor
Emperor but pupil . . . we wish to warn thee in hunting and
hawking not to indulge in too familiar converse with huntsmen
and beaters."

Father and son now spent some weeks in each other's company for the last time; a grim future lay before them both.
Though he preserved an outward calm, the Emperor could have
entertained little hope for the outcome of the mission which he
now dispatched to represent his interests at the council which
the Pope had called at Lyons. It was led by Thaddeus of Sessa
and Archbishop Berard of Palermo; for some inexplicable
reason Pietro della Vigna did not take part in what, for all the
foregone conclusion as to its ultimate issue, was in fact the most
important diplomatic mission that was ever to represent the
Emperor. Some had expected Frederick to go to Lyons in
person to reply to the charges that were to be brought against
him, though no formal invitation had been made by the Pope.
But Frederick, who was willing to abandon the causes that he
had been struggling for all his life, and to fight a Crusade in
the hope of making peace, would not lower the imperial dig-

nity so far in the eyes of the world as to appear at the bar as the accused before a bench of hostile priests.

The Council of Lyons opened at the end of June with elaborate ceremonial well calculated to add dignity to the proceedings, though the Emperor had refused, with good justification, to recognise its character as a General Council. In fact it was not truly representative: practically no members of the German, Sicilian or Hungarian Churches were present; and the assembly numbered about one-third of the delegates that had appeared at the last meeting of its kind—the Lateran Council of 1216. Proceedings were opened with the *Veni Creator Spiritus*; then the Pope took his seat upon a high throne. Baldwin, the Latin Emperor of the East, sat on his right hand, the Counts of Toulouse and Provence upon his left; and ranged around him were the Patriarchs of Constantinople, Aquileia, and Antioch, the cardinals, the archbishops and bishops of Spain—England and France were less well represented. A certain amount of embarrassment was caused by the appearance of a Russian archbishop who could speak no Latin, Greek or Hebrew; but when an interpreter was finally found for him, he froze the blood of all listeners with his tales of Mongol atrocities.

The Pope addressed the council saying that he had five sorrows which he likened to the wounds of Christ. He then proceeded to elaborate upon them: they were the Tartar invasion; the schismatic spirit of the Greek Church; the heresies which had crept in, especially in Lombardy; the fall of Jerusalem to the Khwarismians; and the Emperor's enmity to the Church. The first four were speedily disposed of; all who were present—except possibly the Russian archbishop—were well aware that it was the Emperor's sins that were the real reason for the council, and on them Innocent loosed all the powers of his invective. The Saracens of Lucera, the Moslem harems, the Empresses kept in the charge of eunuchs, Frederick's alliances with the Moslems, the marriage of his daughter to the schismatic Emperor, were all produced and painted in the darkest colours. But the Emperor's worst crimes were perjury towards the Church, in not having returned her domains to her, and *lèse-majesté* in not obeying her dictates.

Thaddeus of Sessa then set to work to refute the Pope's allegations point by point, producing documentary proof to back his case. The allegations that the Emperor had broken his promises he countered by pointing out that the Pope had done the same: Frederick could only be convicted of heresy out of his own mouth—this was not possible—and, moreover, he did not allow usury in his domains—the last was a palpable hit at the papal court. The alliances with the Sultans were but common prudence; and if the Emperor used Saracen troops it was because their blood was less precious to him than that of Christians. As for his seduction by Saracen women, they were simply court entertainers whom he would willingly send away. The Emperor wished for nothing more than that the Eastern Church should re-enter the fold and that the Kingdom of Jerusalem should be liberated. The Emperor's advocate then asked for a recess in which to receive fresh instructions. He was backed in this request by the English and French representatives, and in the end the Pope was forced to agree, though by now Innocent appears to have feared that the delay might bring Frederick in person with an army: and he said with perfect truth that he had no taste for martyrdom.

The second session was held in mid-July. The Pope wept as he again addressed the council; but again Thaddeus of Sessa stoutly held his ground. The third session followed shortly afterwards, on the 17th of July. The imperial envoys for whose appearance Thaddeus of Sessa was impatiently waiting had still not arrived; and he must have listened with relief to the delay caused by the complaints of the English delegates against the papal tax-gatherers, and with joy to the Patriarch of Aquileia's attempt to defend the Emperor. This roused the Pope to such a fury that he threatened to demand the return of the patriarch's badge of office—his ring.

Innocent now began his summing up, in spite of Thaddeus of Sessa's continued refusal to recognise the jurisdiction of the council, and of the protests of the envoys of the kings of France and England on the Emperor's behalf. The Pope continued with his peroration, certain that in this packed council he would win the day, rehearsing once again all the Church's old complaints, and winding up with the decree of the Emperor's deposition on the grounds of heresy, sacrilege, perjury and breaking the peace. With awful solemnity the Pope and prelates put out the lighted torches which they carried; and Thaddeus of Sessa, weeping and beating his breast, cried out: "Now the heretics can rejoice, the Khwarismians reign without let and hindrance in the Holy Land, and the Tartars arise in their might and prevail."

When the news of the results of the Council of Lyons reached the Emperor in Turin, according to Matthew Paris his rage knew no bounds. The chronicler says that with fury in his eyes he looked at all around him and exclaimed: "This Pope in his council has deposed me and robbed me of my crown. To what is due this effrontery? To what is due this immeasurable audacity? Where are my treasure chests?" And, ordering them to be brought and opened, he continued, "Show me if my crown is lost"; and when they had found one, he put it on his head, and thus crowned rose to his feet and with a terrifying glance cried out in a loud voice: "I have not yet lost my crowns, and I shall not lose them without shedding blood, neither for the hostility of the Pope nor the decisions of a Council. Could this man of vulgar lineage reach so high as to throw me from my throne? I the first among the princes whom no one surpasses or even equals. With all this my situation is from a certain point of view now bettered: until now I had to a certain extent to obey him, or at least honour him, but from now on I am released from any obligation to love him, to venerate him, or to keep peace with him. . . . For too long I have been the anvil; now I wish to be the hammer."

Gone was the mood of resignation; his offer to capitulate in making the Crusade had been rejected by the Council of Lyons; and the Emperor's fiery spirit awoke again. If it was to be a fight for survival, he would accept the challenge. Two circular letters to the kings, princes and clergy of Europe were the first result of this reawakening of the Emperor's fighting spirit. In them he recognised freely the Pope's power upon the spiritual plane, and his right to consecrate the Emperor, but not to dethrone him. The council had not been sanctioned by the Emperor's own presence or that of the princes of the Empire "who alone have the right to raise someone to the imperial rank, to maintain him there, and depose him from it". His condemnation, he said, had been entirely due to the Pope's personal enmity, and he warned the rulers that if it was now his turn, next time it would be theirs. He urged them to unite with him to defend a cause which was not only their own, but would also be that of their successors, if the Pope once succeeded in establishing the principle that his was the right to depose rulers.

One very telling aspect of Frederick's anti-papal propaganda was his insistence upon the corruption and self-seeking of the Church; for in this the world became increasingly aware that he was speaking nothing less than the truth. Innocent's rapacity, and that of the hordes of relations and hangers-on, who had followed him to Lyons, was fast becoming a byword. Already he had tried to introduce his foreign relations into vacant prebends of the Church at Lyons without the consent of the chapter. The canons resisted him to his face, and told Innocent that they would not intervene if the hostile populace drowned them in the river. The Archbishop of Lyons was so disgusted with the simony and avarice of the papal court that he retired to a monastery. Philip of Savoy, who was not even a priest, was now made Archbishop of Lyons and Bishop of Valence, and given other benefices because his support was useful to the Pope. The exactions of the papal tax-gatherers in England increased out of all bounds, and still the Pope cried poverty, bringing acid comments from English churchmen such as Matthew Paris and even the devout papalist, Grossetete. Vacant dioceses in France and England were filled by the Pope's nephews, to the fury of the local population; riches were heaped upon the Fieschi family. One papal nephew, Percival, became notorious as the richest priest in Christendom. The situation was now an open scandal; scurrilous pamphlets appeared, whose truth was only too well known; and inevitably the reputation of the Holy See as an institution was lowered by the actions of the man who now held the sacred office of Pope. The decay of the papal influence as a universal political institution dated from Innocent's day: with his grasping hands he began the destruction of the spiritual bonds which had knit the mediaeval world together, uniting it to the Holy See.

In such an atmosphere as this Frederick's circular letters inveighing against the greed and worldly corruption of the Church could scarcely fail to find their mark. He wrote to the Christian rulers: "Can you obey the sons of your own subjects? These men with a false appearance of holiness who fatten upon alms, and then wish to use them against the benefactors of the Church. . . . If you offer them your hand they seize your arm up to the elbow. . . . Our intention, as God is our witness, has always been to oblige these ecclesiastics to follow in the footsteps of the early Church, to lead an Apostolic life and to show themselves humble as was Jesus Christ. Once upon a time the anointed of the Lord worked many miracles by their holiness and, not by the temporal sword, they brought Kings to submission. In our days the Church is completely worldly; her ministers, drunken with terrestrial delights, take little care for the Lord. We intend to carry out a work of charity in taking from these men the treasures with which they are satiated, to their eternal damnation. Unite with us, and let us watch together until they, losing their superfluity, from now on serve the Lord and content themselves with little."

The truth and effectiveness of this form of propaganda is borne out by the terms of an agreement signed by the greatest nobles of France, who banded themselves together to resist the encroachments of the clergy. This document read as follows: "Ecclesiastics, although of base origins, absorb lay jurisdiction to such a point that these sons of serfs judge according to their laws the sons of free men. . . ." The French barons had agreed among themselves upon oath not to submit to the ecclesiastical tribunals. This agreement, which was signed by the Duke of Burgundy, the Count of Britanny, the Counts of Angoulême and St. Pol, and many of the barons, is said to have had the tacit approval of even St. Louis himself.

One of the most interesting aspects of the struggle between Frederick and Innocent is that throughout the Emperor had the support of the saintly King Louis IX of France, who steadfastly refused to recognise the validity of the deposition declared at Lyons. This was because St. Louis fully appreciated the dangers of Innocent's policy, not only as a threat to the lay power, but as a danger to the faith itself. He seems to have seen more clearly into the future than any of his contemporaries at the papal court, and to have realised that in pursuing the temporal power, the papacy would lose its real source of might—that of the spirit—as Frederick unceasingly pointed out in his circular letters. And this most Catholic King evidently did not feel that the Emperor was an enemy of the faith in fighting Innocent; though in Gregory's day, and before Innocent's election, he had protested against Frederick's treatment of his ecclesiastical

prisoners after the battle of Giglio and the excesses of his mes-
sianistic propaganda.

Twice in person, and once through an embassy of bishops,
St. Louis interceded with Innocent on Frederick's behalf. On
the 30th of November 1245 he went to see the Pope at Cluny,
accompanied by his mother and wife, many members of his
family, the Kings of Aragon and Castile, the Latin Emperor,
and a great retinue of nobles. He stayed there for seven days,
and had private meetings with the Pope at which only his
mother, Queen Blanche, was present. According to Matthew
Paris, St. Louis departed home indignant at not finding in the
Pope, who was "the servant of the servants of God", true
Christianity. At Easter 1246, again he dispatched his bishops
to try and make peace, but without success.

In the following year even St. Louis's saintly patience could
brook no more the rapacious activities of the papal court, and
he sent his orator to Lyons to make the situation clear, stating
that until now he had kept silence as a devoted Catholic prince
in the hope that things would change. The orator then went on
to outline St. Louis's complaints which, although they were more
calmly stated, repeated in effect all those abuses and encroachments upon the civil power that Frederick inveighed against in
his circular letters. Though for different reasons, the King of
France and the Emperor were at one in thus interpreting the
spirit of an age that had produced St. Francis, and viewed
with grave concern the negation of all spiritual values that was
now represented by Innocent and his court, who should have
been their natural custodians.

St. Louis made one last attempt to achieve peace; it was upon
the eve of his own Crusade, when he was on his way to Aigues
Mortes in 1248. The Emperor had again offered to go to the
Holy Land if the excommunication was lifted and his deposition
rescinded; according to some sources he had even declared
that he would abdicate in favour of his sons Conrad and Henry
if his request was granted. St. Louis, who fully appreciated the
importance of Frederick's assistance in the Crusade, asked the
Pope to look into the state of the Christian world and not to
refuse forgiveness to a prince who asked so humbly for it.
Innocent said, "As long as I live I shall hold firm against this
schismatic, rejected by God Himself, this excommunicate that

the Holy Council has deprived of the imperial dignity"; to which St. Louis replied, "If, as may be foreseen, the consequences of this have a grave effect upon the Crusade, the guilt will be yours." St. Louis failed in his Crusade, where Frederick had succeeded in spite of all the obstacles that Gregory had put in his way, and the world was treated for the second time to the unedifying spectacle of a Pope sacrificing the success of a Crusade to his own political ends.

At the very moment when St. Louis was setting out on his Crusade, the mendicant friars who had been sent as papal agents into Germany were preaching a Crusade against the Emperor—they had received secret orders never to mention the King of France's Crusade in the Holy Land. The old custom of granting indulgence to Crusaders who, if they were subsequently unable to carry out their vows to take part in an expedition to the Holy Land, could acquit their obligation by making a payment in money towards the expenses of the Crusade, was now turned into a sound financial business by Innocent. A vow to Crusade against the Emperor brought with it the same indulgence as for a genuine Crusade, and "Crusaders" of this type were allowed great licence in redeeming their oaths by making a money payment instead. The trade in this type of indulgence became brisk, and many who had no intention whatsoever of taking up arms thus purchased on a cash basis expiation of their sins. No doubt Innocent congratulated himself upon this ingenious expedient for filling the papal coffers and financing his nefarious schemes in Germany; but the seed which he had sown ironically enough bore its fruit three hundred years later when Luther threw down his gage of battle to the Pope; and the aims of the Reformation were very similar to those for which Frederick, albeit for political rather than religious reasons, was now fighting.

This traffic in indulgences is typical of the weapons that Innocent now employed to bring about his enemy's downfall. With greater perspicacity than Frederick, he saw that the true source of the Emperor's power was Germany, and upon Germany he now concentrated most of his forces. His weapons were the reverse of spiritual—bribery and corruption, and the use of insidious agents who played upon the suspicions and jealousies of the princes, were his preferred methods; and with these in the long run he was successful. The ecclesiastical princes, whose power was so great in the Empire, were naturally his first goal —a legate was dispatched to work on them. If they continued to support the Emperor, they were excommunicated, or by devious means forced to resign and their places were filled by Innocent's creatures—thus the Pope gradually achieved a stranglehold upon the German Church. At the same time the begging monks were sent to raise the populace against the Emperor by preaching in the streets and market-places.

Most of the lay princes still stood firm for the Emperor. But Frederick's failure to go to Germany in the early days of the Mongol threat had split the loyalty of the country; and when the papal agents had succeeded in bribing Henry Raspe into standing for election as Emperor in Frederick's stead, he found support among some of the ecclesiastical princes. In 1246 the Archbishops of Cologne, Mainz, and Trier proceeded to elect this new King of the Romans at Veitshöcheim near Wurtzburg; and afterwards the Archbishop of Mainz preached a Crusade against Frederick. The election was not legal as the full number of electors had not participated, and it was not generally recognised, but naturally Innocent gave it his official recognition; though to his great mortification Henry Raspe died in the following year.

Not content with trying to seduce his Christian domains from their allegiance to the Emperor, the Pope now turned his powers of persuasion even upon Frederick's Moslem allies. He wrote to the Sultan of Egypt trying to induce him to break the treaty which existed between his country and the Realm of Sicily: this action provides an interesting comment upon Innocent's pious horror, expressed at the Council of Lyons, of entertaining diplomatic relations with an infidel. The Sultan's reply put the head of Christianity to shame: he wrote, "Ambassadors of the Holy Father of the Christians have come to us and been received with honour. They have spoken of Christ, whom we know how to glorify better than you do, and of your desire to give peace to the peoples—a wish that has always been in our hearts. But you do not ignore that in the time of the Sultan, our father, (May God glorify him) there existed a sincere friendship between us and the Emperor of the Romans. As, if we were to treat with you his agreement is necessary, we will instruct

our envoy at the imperial court to inform him of your pro-
positions."

All the Emperor's Christian friends were not, however, so
unresponsive to the Pope's machinations as this "infidel",
and this Frederick was soon to discover to his sorrow. After
an abortive campaign against the Lombards during the summer
of 1245, the Emperor had retired to Grosseto for the winter:
the wild surrounding country of the Maremma provided excellent hunting, and from it he could keep a close watch upon
Tuscany, whose administration by his vicar-general, Pandulfo
Fasanella, had been giving him some serious preoccupation.
Pandulfo was recalled from office and replaced by the Emperor's
illegitimate son, Frederick of Antioch; but he does not seem to
have been disgraced. In accordance with the customary practice
for an official temporarily out of office, he was in residence at
the imperial court when in March a galley arrived from the
realm with a messenger from Frederick's son-in-law, the Count
of Caserta.

He carried a secret dispatch from Count Richard, informing
the Emperor of a plot that was afoot against his own life and
that of Enzio—they were to be killed at a banquet which was to
take place the following day, and of a rising throughout Italy
which was timed to coincide with it. Frederick could scarcely
believe this terrible news, for the names given as those of the
ringleaders were his dearest friends—men whose families had
been in his service for more than a generation, and others who
owed their advancement in life to his favour—his closest associates who had shared his counsels and his pleasures in the
intimacy of the inner court circle. Pandulfo Fasanella was one;
Jacobo, son of his old friend Henry of Morra, was another;
Andrea Cicala, Roger de Amicis, Teobaldo di Francesco, and
many of their relations were all involved; less surprising was
the participation of the whole family of San Severino, who had
for long been at loggerheads with the Emperor.

Richard of Caserta's information was explicit, however:
Giovanni of Presenzano, who had been in the plot, had turned
informer, and his allegations were rapidly confirmed by the
precipitate flight from the court of Pandulfo Fasanella and
Jacobo Morra. Pandulfo's place of refuge in Rome revealed only
too clearly whose had been the guiding brain behind the daggers

of the would-be assassins: Bernardo Orlando de Rossi had been the agent who had succeeded in seducing many of the conspirators from their allegiance, but he had acted upon the instructions of his brother-in-law, the Pope. It was during his term of office as Podestà of Parma that Teobaldo di Francesco had turned traitor: he it was who led the plot, because he had been promised the Realm of Sicily after the Emperor's death. Such of the conspirators who saved their lives by flight to Rome, and Teobaldo's brother, were in fact given rich rewards for their "loyalty" to the Pope.

The ramifications of the plot were upon a vast scale: they reached from Germany and throughout Italy to Sicily. Henry Raspe was elected and later won a battle against King Conrad near Frankfurt through the defection of a large part of the Swabian forces, whose leader had been bribed by the Pope and offered the Hohenstaufen lands. In Italy, Parma was ready to abandon the Emperor's cause; Cardinal Rainer invaded the imperial territories; there were risings in the realm, where Frederick was believed to be dead; even the Saracens in the island of Sicily rebelled after twenty years of peace.

The Emperor called a hurried court before leaving Grosseto for the realm: Enzio and Ezzelino were left in command in the north, and other emergency measures were taken. At this gathering Marquis Obizzo Malaspina astonished everyone by presenting the Emperor with a broken-down old palfrey of good blood. But Frederick understood the meaning of this curious gift and, looking at it, he said sadly: "This horse was once a noble courser, full of fire and vigour; our Empire, of which it is the living symbol, had like him young and good years; but after being powerful like him, this Empire has fallen low, and its head possesses hardly anything in Italy or Germany, and those who used to tremble before him now despise him as an ally." In his bitterness at his friends' treachery, he saw clearly that other desertions would soon follow, and one of the first was the same Obizzo Malaspina, who was already secretly treating with the Guelfs, and went over to them shortly afterwards, thus depriving the imperial forces of the passes between Parma and the coast near La Spezia.

In the realm, however, Frederick found that the situation was not as grave as might have been expected, thanks to the prompt measures of the Count of Caserta, who had beaten the rebels in a pitched battle, and to the fact that, in spite of the rumours of the Emperor's death which were circulating, they had received little popular support. The rebels had been forced to flee for refuge to the strongholds of Scala and Capaccio. Scala soon fell to Thomas Aquino, another of the Emperor's sons-in-law; but Capaccio was still holding out when the Emperor arrived in the realm. The knowledge that he was alive had given the *coup de grâce* to the insurrection as such; but the defenders of Capaccio, who included among their number many of the ringleaders of the plot, clung grimly on, though the imperial forces had captured the town and they were now confined to the citadel. Probably in their isolation the rebels did not realise that they were alone in their resistance, and hoped for assistance from the Pope: it came in the form of a letter of encouragement which was intercepted by the Emperor.

The ruins of Capaccio are still to be seen from the plains around Paestum; the heat of summer is intense in this region; but with their water supply cut off and subjected as they were to continuous attack, the garrison still held out right into the summer. When the fortress fell at last, Teobaldo di Francesco and the other leaders of the plot were found to be among the hundred and fifty survivors. Why they did not kill themselves rather than fall alive into the hands of the man whom they had so deeply wronged as a sovereign and friend is a mystery. They paid for their treachery with horrible sufferings —they were blinded, their noses and one hand and one foot were cut off before they were brought before the Emperor, who condemned them as parricides: all but five were put to death by being burnt, drowned, hanged, or dragged behind horses. An even more dreadful fate was reserved for Teobaldo di Francesco and his four chief accomplices, whom the Emperor wished to send to the principal courts of Europe with the Pope's letter tied to their foreheads: instead, they were paraded round the principal towns of the realm, for all to see the fate of traitors, and finally burnt. The women of their families were condemned to imprisonment for life; they disappeared into the prisons of the Royal Palace at Palermo and were never seen again.

The first attempt known to history of a Pope having tried to accomplish the murder of an Emperor had failed; and the intended victim had emerged from the ordeal with his position strengthened. Although Frederick feigned unwillingness to name the Pope as the instigator of the crime, he took good care to let the whole world know who was really responsible. In a circular letter to the kings, he openly accused Innocent of having sharpened the dagger which was to strike him, and backed up the allegation by declaring that the Bishop of Bamberg had arrived in Germany from Lyons and foretold that the Emperor would perish miserably at the hands of his own courtiers. Some of the conspirators, too, in their last confession had admitted that they had received their instructions from agents of the Pope; and from documents which are still extant today it is evident that Frederick's accusations were true.

The conspiracy, that had threatened to assume such alarming proportions, had been crushed in a few weeks: Central Italy was now firmly held by the imperial forces, administered for the most part by vicars-general, who were illegitimate sons of the Emperor—Frederick of Antioch in Tuscany; Richard of Theate in Spoleto, Romagna, and the Marches; Enzio had control of southern Lombardy; and Ezzelino of Verona and the east. Even Viterbo had returned to the imperial fold and been forgiven: Isabella's nine-year-old son Henry was sent to reside there as his father's representative. In March 1247 Frederick left the realm; his original intention was apparently to go to Germany to deal with Henry Raspe, but the latter's death diverted him temporarily from this plan.

In the meantime, however, he wished to secure his position on the north-western borders of Italy, now of vital importance because of Innocent's presence in Lyons. The conspiracy had made the Emperor very wary of putting his trust in mere friends, and the conduct of his two young sons-in-law in dealing with the rebels had demonstrated the value of family relationships. So Frederick now proceeded to arrange for the betrothal of his young son, Manfred, to Beatrice, daughter of Amadeo of Savoy, whose lands controlled the Alpine passes in the west. Another illegitimate daughter, Catherine, who was probably Enzio's sister, was married off to the Marquis del Caretto, whose lands marched with those of Genoa. Enzio was remarried to a relation of Ezzelino; his previous marriage to Adelasia of Torres and Gallura had probably by now been dissolved by the Pope.

Thus by a series of family alliances Frederick strengthened
his hold upon Northern Italy in preparation for a daring coup—
for he now intended to take the war right into the enemy's
camp by going to Lyons with his army on his way to Germany.
The way had been well prepared—the friendship of the Count of
Savoy and of the Lord of the Dauphiné opened the passes right
to the gates of Lyons. An imperial diet of the nobles of the
area had been called for Whitsun in Chambery: Frederick was
liked in Burgundy—he had lived more at Hagenau and in the
western confines of his realms than any previous emperor. The
papal court at Lyons, on the other hand, was not popular either
in France or Burgundy; and even in its midst the Emperor had
secret supporters. In spite of his flight, Innocent appeared to
be in danger of again being surrounded by the Emperor and his
allies. True, St. Louis had promised to protect the Pope in the
event of Frederick's using military force against him, but he
had not offered Innocent a refuge in France; and Lyons was,
officially at any rate, a dependence of the Empire.

All Europe waited to see what would be the next move in
the duel between Pope and Emperor; no one knew what action
Frederick really had in mind; probably he intended to force a
meeting with the Pope, but what could be its outcome? Would
the excommunicated Emperor even try to take Innocent prisoner? Frederick had very definitely cleared the decks for
action of some sort; for in April he had created Pietro della
Vigna logothete of the realm of Sicily and protonotary of the
imperial court, thus giving him vast powers, and decentralising
to a certain extent his own responsibilities and freeing his hands.

Part of the imperial armies had actually left Turin for their
journey across the Alps when a messenger from Enzio arrived
post-haste to tell the Emperor that the vitally important city
of Parma had been seized by the Guelfs. Once again Bernardo
Orlando de Rossi had been the instigator: two years previously
there had been suspicion of his being involved in a plot to raise
Parma against the Emperor, incriminating documents had been
found in the Abbey of Fontevivo near the city, but by prompt
action the Emperor had averted the danger, and de Rossi and
his associates fled to Piacenza and Milan.

In May 1247 de Rossi had been in close confabulation with
Gregory of Montelungo in Milan, and the coup whereby Parma

was seized by the Guelfs seems to have been planned at that time. It was daring enough in all conscience—for all his devious ways, this nephew of Innocent's did not lack courage; he was a magnificent-looking man and a great fighter. A small number of the Parmesan exiles—according to some accounts there were only seventy of them—assembled in a field near Parma: they were dressed as pilgrims, with their weapons concealed beneath their clothes. The moment had been well chosen, for all the imperial authorities in the town were celebrating the marriage of the daughter of one of their number. They were called from the banqueting table straight into the battle, and were overwhelmed. The imperial podestà was killed, and de Rossi and his followers first gained control of the gates, and then of the whole city: was there some treachery within Parma itself which enabled them to take command so rapidly? There was treachery everywhere in Italy.

Enzio had been occupied in besieging a castle in Brescian territory when he was hurriedly recalled to deal with the situation. Although he made forced marches, he arrived too late to intervene: the city was already securely in enemy hands. His forces were small, and he encamped near the city while sending a summons for aid to his father. During the short period while he waited for its arrival, what had evidently been a carefully prepared plan of action was put into operation by the Guelfs, and reinforcements poured into Parma from all sides under the direction of Gregory of Montelungo. Fortifications and entrenchments were hurriedly improvised, and by the time the Emperor arrived on the 2nd of July the city was already well defended.

For propaganda purposes, Frederick pretended to make light of the situation, but from his action in instantly summoning aid from all quarters it is evident that he at once realised how very serious the situation really was: the defection of Parma had blocked his one means of communication between north and south on the western side of Italy. As if this was not enough, seizure of Parma caused a general rising of the Guelfs throughout Italy, and in suppressing them he could not bring the full weight of his forces to bear upon the town to make an all-out attack. The Emperor weathered this storm and then gradually set about the reduction of Parma. The first step was to open the road through the passes to La Spezia; Enzio succeeded in pushing his way through, and obtained the submission of one of the Malaspinas, thus reopening this vital road to the south. Slowly the imperial armies succeeded in encircling Parma and cutting it off from the rest of Italy. The besieged had hoped for aid from the gay and frivolous Cardinal Ubaldini, but that luxurious gentleman sat comfortably in his camp at Guastalla.

By winter the encirclement of Parma was complete and, following the same policy as that which he had successfully adopted at Faenza, the Emperor decided to continue the siege. Accordingly he built a winter camp for his troops of wooden hutments, from all accounts a far more elaborate affair than the Faenza camp; it was heavily fortified, and even boasted of houses and streets, a market-place, a palace and a church. As an indication of his confidence in the ultimate outcome of the struggle, Frederick called it Vittoria.

The iron grip of winter now descended upon the besieged Parma, and with it came hunger and pestilence from the unburied corpses of the dead. The poor were reduced to a diet of raw herbs and roots, but still the relentless blockade went on. Gregory of Montelungo was the mainstay of the defence: he raised the flagging spirits of the populace by such ingenious devices as faked letters promising that aid was near at hand; he worked continuously to improve the defences of the city; and, above all, he kept a very close watch on activities inside Vittoria.

As the siege became more and more prolonged, the Emperor's bitterness against his enemies increased. The shock of Teobaldo di Francesco's plot had brought to the fore the Hohenstaufen cruelty, which he had inherited from his father, and he wreaked his vengeance upon the luckless prisoners in his grasp—a number of Parmesan prisoners were executed each morning before the walls of the city: the Bishop of Arezzo was dragged behind a horse and then hanged. Persecution against the Franciscans became widespread in the Realm of Sicily: this was because they were used by the Pope as agents provocateurs; suspicion of disloyalty was often sufficient for people to be subjected to torture which, although practically banned by the Constitutions of Melfi, now became prevalent in this moment of crisis.

In spite of everything, the Emperor was confident of ultimate victory—too confident in fact. Risings in Piedmont had forced him to dispatch some of his troops there, others he was obliged to send to the assistance of his troops fighting elsewhere; but some, the Cremonese, for instance, had been sent to winter quarters in their home town; his son Enzio, an able commander in the field, was away. Early in February Frederick himself seems to have been unwell, but as soon as he was convalescent the Emperor resumed his practice of going out hunting at dawn —there was good sport for his falcons in the marshy country near Parma. On the 18th of February, a Milanese sentry on one of the towers of the city informed Gregory of Monte-lungo of the Emperor's departure, and the Legate ordered a sally to be made on the other side of the city to distract the attention of the Marquis of Lancia, who had been left in com-mand. The ruse was successful: Manfred Lancia set off in hot pursuit, when the entire population of Parma broke out of the city and rushed as one man upon Vittoria, which had been left practically undefended.

Like a wave, the starving people of Parma swept over the defences of the imperial camp: someone set fire to one of the wooden houses, and soon the whole place was ablaze. Thaddeus of Sessa was taken defending the imperial treasure, and both of his hands were cut off. The crowd seized upon the tremendous booty—riches such as they had never dreamed of—gold and jewels, brocades, rich robes and furnishings, the imperial throne and much of the regalia, the imperial seal, a gilded statue that the Emperor was supposed to have worshipped—perhaps some relic of the classical art he loved. The whole collection was seized and borne in triumph back into Parma: a little man called Curtopassi got the crown as his share, and afterwards sold it for two hundred lire. The imperial library was looted, its scientific books, with their charts and maps, giving fresh impetus to the belief that Frederick indulged in magic. Perhaps most sensational of all was the capture of the ladies of the Saracen harem who, weighed down with overmuch baggage, had failed to make good their escape.

Frederick heard the alarm bell of Vittoria ringing far away on the hunting field: instantly he turned his horse's head and galloping back charged into the town. He had arrived too late, and had difficulty in cutting his way out: in the end he escaped

with a few of his huntsmen to Borgo San Donnino (the modern
Fidenza) and, almost without a pause, rushed on to Cremona, a
distance of sixty-two kilometres, to collect reinforcements.
Frederick was fifty-three, and he had spent nearly twenty-four
hours in the saddle without a break; but in four days he had
collected another army and led them back to resume the attack
upon Parma from the smouldering ruins of Vittoria. A council
of war, however, decided against resuming the attack, though
Frederick had the satisfaction of knowing that Bernardo Rolando
de Rossi had been killed in a local skirmish.

The fall of Vittoria was the worse defeat that the Emperor
had experienced in the whole of his long career. It was not
the military results that were so disastrous, as a large number
of troops had not been involved, but the blow to his prestige—
which was little short of disastrous both in Italy and Germany—
and his financial losses: moreover a hostile Parma still endangered his one communication route to the south. The whole
of the Romagna now rose, and Ravenna was lost; but perhaps
most serious of all was the financial crisis which the loss of the
imperial treasure had brought in its train. The hard core, the
real striking force of the Emperor's armies, were the mercenaries, and they had to be paid come what may—his whole
security depended upon it. Taxes and yet more taxes were
imposed upon the realm and the imperial lands in Italy; but
these did not immediately produce the ready money that was
needed, and Frederick was forced to borrow money at exorbitant
rates of interest. Even in these distressing circumstances the
Emperor kept his faith, outwardly at any rate, in his lucky star,
and stressed his own confidence in his ultimate victory. But at
the same time he grew moody and increasingly suspicious of
everyone, even his immediate entourage—the double shock of
the conspiracy and the fall of Vittoria, combined with the strain
of the long-drawn-out struggle with the Pope, were beginning
to tell even on his iron nerve.

In Germany the situation was declining rapidly under the
influence of the Pope's agents. Cardinal Peter Capoccio had
been sent there, armed with enormous sums of money, to
foment discontent and to bring about the election of yet another
candidate for the imperial throne. Conrad's marriage to Elizabeth, daughter of the Duke of Bavaria, had consolidated the

imperial power in the south; but the death without male heirs of the Duke of Austria had produced chaos in his Duchy, a large part of which was now given to Bavaria. Too late Frederick appears to have realised the disasters that his abandonment of Germany at the time of the Mongol peril had brought in its train: he now tried to bind the country to him with fresh bonds —there were negotiations in progress for his marriage to the daughter of Duke Albert of Saxony.

But in the chaos which now reigned in Germany, each man acted for himself. The majority had not actually turned against the Emperor but, under the insidious influence of the preaching of the papal agents—who reiterated that the Emperor only sought the interest of himself and his family, and that he wished to make the Empire hereditary—the princes remained in a state of apathy. Many of them were even content to witness the destruction of the central power, because they believed that it would enable them to seize advantages for themselves. In the northeast, under the influence of the Archbishops of Cologne and Mainz, there was a definite anti-Hohenstaufen party, who now proceeded in the autumn of 1247 to elect Count William of Holland as the new King of the Romans.

The Emperor spent most of the summer of 1248 in Cremona: in the autumn he went to Piedmont to be present at Manfred's wedding with Beatrice of Savoy: in January he returned to Cremona, and Pietro della Vigna was with him. What happened there is a mystery to which neither contemporaries nor the subsequent researches of scholars have ever really provided the key, though theories are numerous. In January Pietro della Vigna was high in the imperial favour, the greatest officer of the court, the Emperor's right hand: in February he was disgraced, a prisoner who had to be rescued from the mob violence of the loyal people of Cremona, and conveyed secretly by night to the fortress of Borgo San Donino.

Some believed that Pietro had betrayed his master to the Pope, though subsequent evidence gives the lie to this; others that he had been guilty of peculation and amassed an enormous fortune for himself by nefarious means—he certainly had plenty of opportunity; another theory is that jealous courtiers succeeded in making the Emperor believe that Pietro had been party to a plot, which certainly did exist, to poison him. The most likely interpretation of the mystery appears to be that della Vigna was indeed the victim of the jealousies of the aristocratic faction at the court: German and Italian nobles whom the Emperor favoured more highly as he grew older—men like the Margrave of Hohenburg, and the Counts of Savoy, Caserta and Walter of Ocra, a nobleman of the Abruzzi who claimed descent from Charlemagne, and was a rising star at court—would certainly have hated and resented a parvenu like Pietro della Vigna. From one of Frederick's letters to the Count of Caserta it seems that the Emperor himself believed that Pietro had been guilty of corruption and peculation. Certainly it would not have been difficult to sow the seeds of doubt and suspicion in Frederick's mind about anyone at this time. To the shock of Teobaldo di Francesco's conspiracy was added another: his own doctor, who he had ransomed from among the prisoners taken at Vittoria, now tried to poison him; and it was in this plot that Pietro della Vigna was supposed to have been involved. The doctor had evidently been suborned by Gregory of Montelungo while he was a prisoner at Parma, and when he was called upon to prescribe a cure for his master for some slight illness, he prepared a poisoned bath and draught of medicine. Frederick had been warned and said grimly, joking, "I beg of you not to give me poison", and, pretending to drink of the draught, spilt most of it, but enough remained to be given to a condemned man, who died instantaneously. The doctor was seized, and Frederick, weeping and wringing his hands, exclaimed, "Woe, woe is me: my very bowels betray me. In whom can I put my trust? Where can I find happiness and safety?"

The Emperor attributed this new attempt against his life to Innocent's agency: he announced it to the kings of the world in a circular letter. He alleged that the Pope's responsibility had been proved by intercepted letters. This may or may not have been true, but it is a fact that Hugh Borgononi, who was a chemist of some renown and an authority on poisons—he wrote a treatise on the sublimation of arsenic—was Innocent's penitentiary from the time of his election in 1243 until 1254, and was afterwards rewarded with various bishoprics.

The doctor was blinded and condemned to perpetual torture until his execution, which took place in the realm. Pietro della

Vigna was also blinded, and the same terrible fate as that which had been awarded to Teobaldo di Francesco was said to be in preparation for him; but he committed suicide by dashing his head against a wall or pillar—some say at San Miniato, some on the outskirts of Pisa. Thus in April 1249, in shame and ignominy, died the man who for so many years had been his master's closest friend and adviser, who, in Dante's words, had once "held the keys to Frederick's heart": no wonder his master, who believed that Pietro had betrayed him, echoed the words of Job: "All my inward friends abhorred me: and they whom I loved are turned against me."

Whether from shock or misery, the Emperor's health seems to have suffered, and he travelled south slowly through Tuscany, refusing to enter Florence because an ancient prophecy had declared that he would die in a place whose name was associated with the word "flower". He appears to have recovered, however; in May he was in Pisa, where he was received with protestations of faithfulness; and from there he embarked upon what was to be his last journey to his beloved realm. His sorrows were not at an end, however, for when he was in Naples news reached him of the death of his son, Richard of Theate, who had been Vicar-General of Romagna, Spoleto and the Marches.

This was a serious blow, but worse was to follow: Enzio was taken prisoner by the Bolognese at Fossalta. It was a mere skirmish, but Enzio was, as ever, in the van of the fighting. He was brave and handsome, and in spite of his youth an able military commander. His capture was a very serious loss to his father, who seems to have loved him and Manfred the best of all his children: moreover there was no commander for the imperial forces in Northern Italy upon whose fidelity Frederick could count as upon his own son. He tried both threats and bribes upon the commune of Bologna, but they replied that they would never free their prisoner, and took an oath to this effect. Enzio was treated with honour, even kindness: although a prisoner, he became a great figure in the city of Bologna, and was finally awarded a state funeral at the expense of the commune: but he lingered on for twenty-three years to witness the extinction of his race, "That brood of vipers", as the Hohenstaufen were now called in the letters which the Papal Legate sent to sow sedition

in the realm. It was no longer Frederick alone who was the
enemy of the Pope, but all his family, and with grim determination Innocent and his successors pursued them to the bitter
end. The year 1249 was the very nadir of Frederick's fortunes:
even his health gave out; he seems to have been afflicted with
some skin disease, brought on no doubt by nervous strain and
worry. But in the autumn he recovered, and set about the
ordering of his realm and the preparation of an expedition to
Lombardy: he even planned to go to Germany—the marriage
with Duke Albert of Saxony's daughter had now definitely been
arranged.

As the months went by, the imperial fortunes appeared to be
reviving everywhere: Piacenza had come over to the Ghibellines
by reason of its rivalry with Parma. It was joined to Cremona
under the governorship of the Marquis Uberto Pallavicini—a
tyrant on the same model as Ezzelino, but an efficient one
nevertheless, who now in some measure replaced Enzio. The
Marquis attacked and defeated Parma. In the Marches, the
Imperial Vicar won a series of victories, and regained Assisi,
Pesaro and Senigalia. In Germany, King Conrad had been
doing well, and induced the hostile archbishops of the Rhine to
seek a truce. Even Innocent was threatened in Lyons by the
renewed fidelity to the Emperor of his subjects in the Kingdom
of Arles: he tried without success to persuade King Henry to
allow him to take refuge in the English possession of Bordeaux.
The Emperor Vatatzes had been sending reinforcements, and
to him Frederick wrote cheerful letters on his future prospects.
Even the disaster of St. Louis's Crusade and capture had brought
grist to Frederick's mill: many people attributed its failure to
the Pope's having prevented his being able to aid the King of
France more effectively than by helping him with supplies.
Louis himself had sent his brothers to insist that the Pope
should make peace with the Emperor.

For some time, however, Frederick's health had again been
causing anxiety, but he refused to give up an active life, and
organised a great hunt in the Coronata. Perhaps he felt that he
would at last follow the advice of his daughter, Violante, the
Countess of Caserta, who had once written to him to ask why
he wore himself out in his constant battles when in his realm
he had all that could make life pleasant; and he had admitted

that her advice had always been sound. He spent the summer in his new castle at Lagopesole, among the fresh greenness of the highlands and beechwoods of the Monte Vulture: some said that he had even fallen in love again.

By the end of November Frederick was really ill, but still he would not rest. He started out from Foggia on a journey to Lucera: he was on a hunting expedition on the way, when he was taken violently ill with an attack of the dysentery from which he had apparently been suffering for some time, but had failed to take seriously. He was carried to the castle of Fiorentino, which was a few miles away, and on the 1st of December he was at death's door. He rallied, but as a precautionary measure the great officers of state were called and he made his will. In the presence of them all—Archbishop Berard of Palermo, Berthold of Hohenburg, Pietro and Folco Ruffo, Giovanni di Procida (his docotor), the Lord Chief Justice, and other justices—he bequeathed the Empire to King Conrad; Henry was to have the Kingdoms of Arles and Jerusalem; his grandson, Frederick, Austria; Manfred received the principality of Taranto and the other lands which had been given to his mother, and he was declared Vicar of Italy. As befitted a Catholic prince, most of the rest of the will was taken up with pious bequests: the Church was to have returned to her all that was her due, having regard to the rights and the honour of the Empire. All old friends and servants of the family were to be provided for out of the Emperor's personal estates, but the royal demesne was not to be touched. Even in this solemn moment, the Emperor still had in mind the practical welfare of his beloved realm; the small detail of a bridge that was being built was provided for out of the income derived from his farm of St. Nicholas at Anfido—perhaps it was the strategically important bridge across the Ofanto at Atella.

After his will was made, the Emperor's health seemed to make progress, but in his heart he was convinced that it was the end. When he had recovered from his first attack and asked the name of the castle where he had been brought, and was told that it was Fiorentino, he was struck by the sinister associations of the name in the prophecy of his death. He had observed that his bed had been placed against a doorway that was blocked up, but which had formerly given access to a tower: when the

masonry was pulled down, he saw that it had concealed an
iron door. The words of the prophecy had been fulfilled: "You
will die near the iron door in a place whose name will be formed
by the word 'flower'", it had run; and, looking at it, he exclaimed: "Oh, my God, if I must give up my soul, Thy will be
done."

On the very eve of his death Frederick's health had improved
so much that he talked of getting up the next day: he had eaten
pears cooked with sugar—according to the *Regimen Sanitatis*
of Salerno, "Bak't Peares a weake stomack doe revive"—they
were regarded as a restorative for internal disorders. But on
the 13th of December he was sinking fast and, true to the
standards that he had imposed upon himself throughout his life,
whatever his inward doubts and questionings, the Emperor was
determined to take leave of it in a manner fitting for a Catholic
prince. He asked for absolution, and, wrapped in the white
habit of a Cistercian monk, he received the Last Sacrament
from his oldest and most faithful friend, Archbishop Berard of
Palermo, who had accompanied him through the joys and tri-
bulations of his life from the day he set out as a boy of eighteen
from Palermo to conquer the Empire.

To Palermo Frederick at last returned: he had asked that his
funeral should take place in the utmost simplicity, but had
wished to be buried beside his father and mother and his first
wife. Nevertheless, his body was accompanied with solemn
majesty to the grave, passing through the Apulia that he had
loved so well: it rested for a night at his hunting castle at Gioia
del Colle, and then proceeded by sea from Taranto to Palermo,
where he was laid to rest in a sarcophagus of porphyry, the
stone dyed with the imperial purple, which he had placed there
twenty years before.

In his tomb his body was robed in a linen garment embroidered at the cuffs with Cufic characters worked in gold,
and over the heart with a cross. This was covered by a red silk
robe, and he was wrapped in a mantle of the same colour,
embroidered with the imperial eagles, and fastened by a brooch
of amethysts and emeralds. His sword, covered with a sheath
of Saracen work, lay by his side: his spurs were attached to
boots embroidered with small deer. On his head he wore a
jewelled crown like that of a Byzantine emperor, and beside him

M

lay the orb filled with earth, but not surmounted by the cross. In death, surrounded by these eclectic emblems of his earthly power, the Emperor had returned to the world from which he sprang—Sicily—the meeting place of East and West, where Arab, German, Italian, and Greek had striven for mastery: and all of them had contributed something to that strange and complex man who was the "Wonder of the World" that could not understand him.

EPILOGUE

WITH Frederick's death the Empire in its ancient and its mediaeval sense came to an end. The title lingered on till the nineteenth century, but no single one of his successors could claim to be regarded as either divine or universal. Within two generations, too, the Hohenstaufen family had vanished from the stage of history.

After his father's death, Conrad continued the hopeless struggle in Germany for a short while; and then came south, abandoning the field to William of Holland. He had some success in Italy, but he died in 1254 at the age of twenty-six. Isabella's son, Henry, had died the previous year when he was fifteen. Manfred, who subsequently became King of the Sicilian realm, was killed in 1266 at the battle of Benevento, which made the victorious Charles of Anjou King in his stead. Manfred's second wife and her children languished for years as prisoners of the Angevin kings—Charles and his successors—immured in the dungeons of the castles which their grandfather had built as his "places of solace". There were tales that one of the sons got away, but the only one definitely known to have escaped this tragic fate was Beatrice who was set free in 1284, and went to Spain to join Constance, her half-sister, the daughter of her father's first marriage, who had married Peter of Aragon. It was due to this alliance with Manfred's eldest daughter that the Aragonese king was welcomed as the liberator of the island of Sicily after the Sicilian Vespers.

In the next generation, Conradin—Conrad's son—who came to claim his family's Italian heritage in 1268, was welcomed with open arms as the true heir. He was defeated at the battle of Tagliacozzo, taken prisoner by treachery, and handed over to Charles of Anjou. His execution at the age of seventeen—a fate unheard of for a King taken prisoner of war—put an end to the Hohenstaufen dynasty in the legitimate male line.

Only Enzio now remained—languishing in his Bolognese prison; he was over fifty, but he tried to escape to fight his

355

family's cause after the execution of Conradin. He was to be carried out of his prison concealed in an empty barrel, but a lock of his fair hair was seen hanging out of the bung-hole, and he was caught; he died two years later.

Frederick of Antioch had died before the battle of Tagliacozzo, but his son Conrad escaped the holocaust of Hohenstaufen adherents which followed, because his mother held two of the Orsini prisoner in her castle at Saracenesco near Tivoli, whom she was able to exchange for her son. Descendants of the house of Antioch were still people of substance in Rome and in the Tivoli area at the end of the fifteenth century, and in the village church of Sambuci there is a tomb inscribed to the "Family of the royal race of Antioch". In the nearby village of Anticoli Corrado, which is said to take its name from the italicised form of the name of Conrad of Antioch, many of the villagers still claim that the surname Corrado denotes their descent from Conrad of Antioch. The women are famous for their beauty, but that is the only heritage which they now possess of the legendary house of Hohenstaufen.

So Frederick's dynasty was extinguished. But the world itself was unwilling to believe that he was really dead. During his lifetime he had been surrounded by such an aura of the supernatural—the divine Emperor, Saviour of the world to his friends—Antichrist to his enemies—that many could not believe the truth of his sudden death; and impostors thrived upon this figment of the popular imagination.

In 1260, a Sicilian beggar, who bore a close resemblance to him, attracted no small following by posing as the Emperor. In Germany in 1284 another impostor arose who, by parading about with "Oriental" attendants and a heavily laden baggage train, tried to prove that he was indeed the Emperor—he had in fact once been a servant in the imperial household. Again in 1295, when if he had lived Frederick would have been over a hundred, there appeared another impostor who claimed that he was the Emperor. For a while both these two men had attracted supporters among the credulous in Germany; sure proof that after the miseries of the great interregnum, and in the continued state of chaos in the country, the days of Frederick's reign were regarded as a golden age to which men looked back with longing.

When even the most credulous could no longer believe
that the great Emperor was alive and wandering in disguise
around the world, the legend grew that he had entered into a
profound slumber, from which he would awake to appear again
as a saviour. In Sicily he was believed to have taken refuge
in the flaming cone of Etna; in Germany he was supposed to
sleep in a cavern in the Kyffhauser, surrounded by his knights,
awaiting the day when by some magic spell he would awake to
succour his Empire in her hour of need.

It was only in the sixteenth century that in this legend
Frederick became confused with his own grandfather—Barbarossa. But still the ancient prophecies which foretold that he
would live for two hundred and sixty-seven years retained something of the truth—for some two and a half centuries after his
death the Reformation awoke in Germany—the Reformation,
one of whose origins was the traffic in indulgences which had
been so extensively used by Innocent IV to bring the Emperor
to his doom.

Frederick of Hohenstaufen had died, apparently defeated by
the powers of his own day, which overcame him; and of all that
he had striven to achieve, only a few castles on the lonely hill-
tops of Apulia, some statues on the gate at Capua, and the
manuscripts of his book on falconry, seemed to live to tell the
tale of his endeavour. For two centuries his ideas slumbered—
then came the new awakening; and in the Renaissance, the
Reformation and the growth of the civil state, they triumphed.
The last of the great Emperors is not dead, his influence lives
with us still, and to the sonorous flow of his titles—Imperator
Fridericus Secundus, Romanorum Caesar Semper Augustus,
Italicus Siculus Hierosolymitanus Arelatensis, Felix Victor ac
Triumphator—might be added the words Immortal Emperor.

Grottaferrata 1953   *Villa Pamphitz 1957*

NOTES

1. Extract from a love poem by Abû al-Hasan Ibn at-Tubi, a Sicilian Arabic poet quoted by M. Amari in his *Storia dei Mussulmani in Sicilia.*"

2. *Transubstantiation.*

The theory of Transubstantiation had been discussed in the Eucharistic controversies of the ninth, tenth, and eleventh centuries, but the actual term is not found earlier than the twelfth century. The fourth Lateran Council in 1215 fully adopted it, but it did not become a dogma, or article of faith, until the Council of Trent at the time of the Reformation. The most recent parallel of a general belief of this kind only being adopted as a dogma after many centuries by the Roman Catholic Church was that of the Assumption of the Virgin Mary, which was officially made an article of faith during the last Holy Year in 1950.

3. *The Style and Titles of Emperor and King of the Romans.*

In mediaeval times the Emperor was entitled to be crowned by the Pope from the moment of his election, but he could not actually use the title of Emperor until the coronation had taken place. Until his coronation he was entitled to the style of King of the Romans. In order to ensure the succession of their sons, the Emperors made great efforts to have them elected Kings of the Romans during their own lifetime, as Frederick Barbarossa had done with Henry VI and as Henry VI and Frederick II did in their turn. For the purposes of convenience, and to avoid confusion, the writer has referred to Frederick as the Emperor-elect until his coronation, as his son was elected King of the Romans prior to this event, and for a while they were both in effect Kings of the Romans.

4. *The Roman Senate.*

When the Senate was revived in 1144 there were fifty-six senators. This continued almost without intermission until 1204, when it became the custom to elect annually only one, or at most two, senators, who were assisted by counsellors. This practice continued with one intermission until 1358, after which the Senator was appointed by the Pope. In the summer prior to Frederick's coronation, Parenzi was Senator, in September or November 1220 (the precise date is uncertain)

Iohannes was elected Senator, and continued in office until November 1221. (A. Salimei, *Senatori e Statuti di Roma nel Medioevo*. Rome, 1935.)

5. *The Aquino Family.*

With one exception—Count Landulf's son, St. Thomas Aquinas. The family bitterly opposed his becoming a churchman and enlisted Frederick's aid to try and prevent it. By one of the ironies of history St. Thomas's religious vocation was ultimately responsible for the Church's acceptance of the Aristotelian philosophy, whose teaching was sponsored by the Emperor at Naples University where St. Thomas studied as a young man, and where he later returned to teach after Frederick's death.

6. *The Emperor's Authorship of the Poems which are Attributed to Re Federico and Federico Imperatore.*

Frederick's authorship of the four poems which are variously attributed to Re Federico and Federico Imperatore ("O lasso non pensai", "Poi che ti piace Amore", "De la mia disianza", and "Dolze meo drudo") in the thirteenth-century manuscript collections of poems, has been called in doubt on the grounds that the title of Re, or King, could not refer to him as he was Emperor, and moreover that phrases that occur in some of these poems, referring to enforced lovers' partings, and those who have the lover in their power, could never have been written by the omnipotent Frederick.

As an alternative it was suggested by various critics that the Re Federico to whom the authorship of the poems was attributed was in fact the Emperor's illegitimate son Frederick of Antioch. In an article entitled "The Authorship of the Poems ascribed to Frederick II, Rex Fredericus and King Enzio", which appeared in *Speculum* in 1927, H. H. Thornton gave both sides of the argument, but pointed out that whereas contemporary evidence exists to prove that the Emperor wrote poetry, there is none whatsoever to indicate that his son Frederick of Antioch did so, nor have any poems survived that are attributed specifically to him, and further that if Frederick II was Emperor, he was also King of Sicily, and that the poems in question were actually written in the Realm of Sicily. Nevertheless Thornton considered that the various attributions to King and Emperor are puzzling.

At the international conference of Frederician studies held at Palermo in 1950 on the seven hundredth anniversary of the Emperor's death, A. Monteverde gave in his address "Federico II Poeta" a detailed analysis of the pros and cons of the case and concluded that the four poems in question, and possibly others, were definitely written by the Emperor himself. He demonstrated that there exists no factual evidence to support the theory that some of the poems in question were written by Frederick of Antioch, and that the theory had been partly based upon a mistaken attribution made in G. Bertoni's *Il Duecento* (which was however corrected in the third edition in 1939), and partly upon the mistaken conception of many critics that the poems were necessarily autobiographical. In Monteverde's opinion the descriptions of enforced lovers' partings, etc., were in fact simply part of the poetic conventions of the period, which the Emperor followed like the rest of his contemporaries.

7. Date of First " Reformation" Letter.

In his *Lo Stato Ghibellino di Federico II* (Bari, 1951), G. Pepe states that even if this letter to the King of England is not of this period, as it was formerly believed to be on the authority of Matthew Paris, nevertheless Frederick's policy towards the Curia undoubtedly displayed great audacity and independence. He also underlines the resemblance between the sentiments which inspire the letter and those of the contemporary anti-clerical Goliardic songs and satires. Nevertheless he implies that the letter could be of a later date; possibly he considers it to be more in tune with the period after the Council of Lyons, when the Emperor's use of this "reformation" type of propaganda is well documented.

8. The Sources of the Architectural Style of Frederick II's Castles.

The distinctive architectural character of the castles of Frederick II has given rise to many theories as to the origins of their style.

C. Enlart in his *Origines Françaises de l'Architecture Gothique en Italie* (Paris, 1894) stressed the influence of the Cistercian monastic builders, and it was indeed an order which held a particular attraction for the Emperor. E. Bertaux in *L'Art dans l'Italie Méridionale de l'Empire Romaine à la Conquête de Charles d'Anjou* (Paris, 1904) considered that the French military architects, especially Philippe Chinard, and French architecture generally had exercised a profound influence upon the castles, but that the Emperor himself was the real "maître d'œuvre" of the Capuan gate and Castel del Monte. C. Shearer in *The Renaissance of Architecture in South Italy* (Cambridge, 1935) inclines to Bertaux's theories, but also stresses the importance of the classical and Oriental element. S. Bottari, in an article entitled "Intorno all Origini dell' Architettura Sveva" (*Palladio* 1951, Rome), quotes the preceding theories, also Agnello's comment that Frederick was the "inspirer of new forms", probably partly absorbed in the Levant, and partly from the Cistercians (G. Agnello, *L'Architettura Sveva in Sicilia*, Rome, 1935), and goes on to draw an interesting parallel between the Frederician castles and those of the Moslems in

Persia, Syria and North Africa, whose debt to Byzantine military architecture is evident.

N. Pevsner in *An Outline of European Architecture* (London, 1953) probably provides the best summing up of the whole question when he says that "the Gothic style came into Germany, Spain, England and Italy as a French fashion. The Cistercian monasteries were the first to employ it. . . . Frederick II's Castel del Monte followed it closely but already in Frederick II's Italian buildings there appear purely antique pediments side by side with the novel rib vaults of France. The appreciative treatment of Roman motifs in Frederick II's Capuan Gate is unparalleled anywhere in the North, and in the South only by Niccolò Pisano's pulpits." In summing up the influences which brought about the thirteenth-century revolution in European military architecture, Pevsner states: "The Crusades caused a complete reform in the planning and building of castles . . . it came from the mighty castles of the Crusaders (e.g. Crack). . . . The Crusaders took it from the Turks, who had in their turn derived it from Roman military architecture." He then goes on to cite English examples of the new style and concludes "for grandeur and daring of conception only the Emperor Frederick II's slightly earlier Castel del Monte in South Italy, again a synthesis of Roman, Eastern and Gothic elements, can be compared".

9. *The Triumphal Gate of Castelnuovo in Naples.*

This gate was built by Alfonso the Magnanimous the Fifth of Aragon and the First of Naples and Sicily, to celebrate his conquest of Naples in 1442, by which he ousted the Angevin claimants from the mainland portion of the Kingdom of the two Sicilies—the Aragonese dynasty had been kings of the island of Sicily since the Sicilian Vespers, and were regarded as the rightful heirs by reason of Peter I of Aragon's marriage to Manfred's heiress, his eldest daughter Constance. Thus Alfonso's triumph could be considered as that of the heirs of the Hohenstaufens over those of the usurping Angevins. The gate itself was built between the two round towers which guard the entrance to Castelnuovo, in the same manner as Frederick's Capuan gate stood between two flanking towers, and E. Bertaux in his *L'Art dans l'Italie Méridionale de l'Empire Romaine à la Conquête de Charles d'Anjou* (Paris, 1904) regards the Capuan gate as the source of inspiration for that of Castelnuovo; a comparison is also drawn by C. A. Willemsen in his *Kaiser Friedrichs Triumphtor zu Capua* (Wiesbaden, 1953).

10. *Furnishing of Castel del Monte.*

A. Use of Classical Statues.

Of Frederick's use of classical statues for the decoration of his castles there are several instances: the Greek bronze rams at Syracuse (G. Agnello, *L'Architettura Sveva in Sicilia*, Rome, 1935). In 1241 the Emperor had classical bronze statues of a man and a cow removed from the monastery of Grottaferrata (Chronicle of Riccardo San Germano). In the imperial registers for 1240 there is a letter from Foggia ordering classical statues to be brought overland from Naples to Lucera. (*Constitutiones regum regni utriusque siciliae mandate Federici II Imperatoris per Petrum de Vinea*, ed. G. Carcani, Naples, 1786.)

B. *The Emperor's Love of Books, taking them on his Travels.*

In the letter which he sent with his present of translations from the works of Aristotle to Bologna University, Frederick wrote: "Since our youth, before we assumed the responsibilities of government we have sought always after learning and breathed her balsamic perfumes. Now the cares of state require most of our attention, but the little time we have left . . . we spend in pleasurable reading . . . meditating upon the manuscripts of all kinds, classified in order, which enrich our cupboards." (G. Paolucci, *Le Finanze e la Corte di Federico II di Svevia*, Palermo, 1904.)

According to the Malaspina Chronicle Frederick took the works of Aristotle and Avicenna with him to Castel Lagopesole in coffers on the backs of pack-mules, and he evidently had books with him in camp during the siege of Parma, for in 1264 or 1265, Gulielmus Bottatus of Milan wrote a letter to Charles of Anjou offering to sell him a magnificently illustrated book on falcons and dogs, bound in gold and silver, which he stated had been taken as loot by the people of Parma in the Emperor's camp at Vittoria. (Letter in the Bouches du Rhône Archive quoted by Casey A. Wood and F. Marjory Fife in *The Art of Falconry*, London, 1956.)

C. *General Furnishing of the Period.*

Italian thirteenth-century frescoes and miniatures give some idea of the very simple furnishing of the period, particularly frescoes of the Last Supper, the Annunciation, and Visitation, such as those to be seen in the remote Abruzzi churches of the thirteenth century at Fossacesia, Bominaco, and Fossa. The miniatures of the Exultet Rolls, which were common in Southern Italy at that period, show several examples of the thrones of popes, emperors and bishops, and fald stools, nearly always covered with cushions. Benches which surround the walls, like those which still exist at Syracuse, Gioia del Colle, and Castel del Monte, appear in these frescoes, usually with cloth hangings that cover the wall halfway up behind them. In the thirteenth-century French poem "Guillaume de Palerme" there occurs a graphic description of the royal palace at Palerno, that describes the rooms decorated with mosaics that still exist, and it is believed that the poem must have been inspired by travellers' descriptions. It says that the rooms of the palace were curtained round with "dras de soie a or ouvrés" and that the trestle stools and seats were also worked with gold. (N. Zingarelli, *Guillaume de Palerne*, Palermo, 1907.) The furniture of rich and luxurious houses was modelled on church furniture (A. Schiaparelli, *La Casa Fiorentina*, Florence, 1908) of which some examples have survived; notable among them is the thirteenth-century carved wooden abbot's chair in the Abbey of Montevergine at Avellino near Naples, that closely resembles those which are portrayed in contemporary frescoes and miniatures. The use of lecterns for supporting the immensely valuable illuminated manuscripts of the time is familiar from many contemporary miniatures of the evangelists.

D. Cushions.

Cushions, as is evident from the frescoes and miniatures, were in general use, but the making of embroidered cushions was a speciality of the Moslems of Lucera. In an order of Charles II of Anjou, made in 1301 after the fall of Lucera, stating that the various types of craftsmen are to be assembled and sent under guard to Naples, he specifically mentions the cushion embroiderers. (E. Bertaux, *Les Arts de l'Orient Mussulman dans l'Italie Méridionale*, Papers of the French School of Rome, 1895.)

E. Lamps and Candlesticks.

Candlesticks of rock crystal and enamelled bronze of the thirteenth century exist in the treasury of San Nicola in Bari. No fewer than three lamps made in the form of an elephant with a tower on its back, made in Germany in the thirteenth century, are shown in the *Encyclopédie de la Lumière* (G. Henriot, Paris, 1933). According to E. Bertaux (op. cit.), the imperial elephant went to Colmar.

F. Carpets.

Carpets were much in use in Italy during the Middle Ages; there was a great vogue for Oriental ones at the time of the Crusades, and in inventories they are usually differentiated as being Turkish or Tartar (A. Schiaparelli, op. cit.). There was considerable trade between Italy and the Black Sea, and by 1250 the Genoese had their own trading stations in the Crimea (G. Bratianu, *Recherches sur la Commerce Génois dans la Mer Noire au XIII siècle*, Paris, 1929). There are also references to carpet-makers in the Sicilian realm in the imperial registers of 1239–40. (Carcani, op. cit.)

G. Plate and Linen.

Long flowing tablecloths are usually conspicuous in contemporary frescoes of the Last Supper. Matthew Paris and Roger of Wendover give a description of the fine workmanship of the magnificent plate, including the silver saucepans, that formed part of Princess Isabella's dowry, and Salimbene in describing in his chronicle the loot taken in the imperial camp at Vittoria, outside Parma, says that there were vessels of gold and silver, much treasure of gold and jewels, and clothes of purple and silk, which were afterwards sold to merchants who came from all over Lombardy.

H. Bed-coverings.

The imperial registers for 1239–40 contain a letter ordering a mattress covered with cendal, and a bed-covering of the same silk, for the nephew of the King of Tunis, whom Frederick held as a prisoner of state. No doubt his own bed was also covered with silk or something even more magnificent. There are several orders in the registers for rich stuffs of silk worked with gold, and mentions of the specialised artisans who made them. (Carcani, op. cit.)

11. *Percival Doria's Poem.*

> Kome lo giorno quand è dal mattino.
> Chiara e sereno—e bell' è da vedire,
> Perche gli ausgelli fanno lor latino
> Cantare fino—e pare dolze udire.
> E poi ver mezo il giorno cangia e muta,
> E torna impiogia la dolze veduta,
> Che mostrava;
> Lo pellegrino, ea sicuro andava,
> Per l'alegranza delo giorno bello
> Diventa fetto—pieno di pesanza,
> Cosi m'a fatto Amore, a sua pesanza. (First verse.)

O. G. Rosetti's translation.

> Even as the day when it is dawning
> Seems mild and kind, being fair to look upon,
> While the birds carol underneath their awning
> Of leaves, as if they never would have done;
> Which on a sudden changes, just at noon
> And the broad light is broken into rain
> That stops and comes again;
> Even as the traveller who held his way
> Hopeful and glad because of the bright weather
> Forgetteth then his gladness altogether;
> Even so am I, through love, alas the day! (First verse.)

(D. G. Rosetti, *Poets from Ciullo D'Alcamo to Dante Alighieri*, London, 1861.)

12. *Translation of Enzio's Poem.*

Go my little song, and salute my lord,
Tell him of my misfortune,
Those who have me in their power hold me so closely
That I cannot live.
Salute for me Tuscany, who is Queen of all,
Where Courtesy reigns,
Go to the plains of Puglia—the great Capitanata,
There where my heart is night and day. (The last verse.)

13. *Translation of Enzio's Second Poem. D. G. Rosetti's translation of " Sonnet on the Fitness of the Seasons".*

There is a time to mount; to humble thee
A time; a time to talk, and to hold thy peace;
A time to take thy measures patiently;
A time to watch what Time's next step may be;
A time to make light of menaces,
And to think them over a time there is;
There is a time when not to seem to see. (First verse.)

(D. G. Rosetti, op. cit.)

14. *Longevity of Pike.*

C. H. Haskins quotes the incident in his *Studies in Mediaeval Science* (Cambridge, U.S.A., 1927), but points out that the Emperor was not in Germany in the year 1230. The Romans believed that pike could live for a very long time, as much as a hundred years, and some modern sources say as much as 250 years (*Everyman's Encyclopaedia*), but it is evidently a subject upon which it is difficult to produce concrete evidence.

15. *Comparisons between the Size of the Armies of Barbarossa and Frederick II.*

It is difficult to arrive at a reliable estimate of the size of mediaeval armies, because, as Ferdinand Lot states in his *L'Art Militaire et les Armes au Moyen Age en Europe et le Proche Orient* (Paris, 1946), the chroniclers' accounts cannot be relied upon as they usually tend to exaggerate. However, he points out that the army which Barbarossa took to Italy in 1158 was so large that it was divided into four parts to cross the Alps, using as many different passes, while there is no mention of any of Frederick II's armies having to be divided into more than two forces to undertake the crossing of the Alps—in 1236 knights coming from the Low Countries and the Rhineland were ordered to assemble in Basle to cross by the Swiss passes, while the German ones assembled as usual in Augsburg preparatory to crossing by the Brenner, though these assembly points may have been dictated by reasons of geographical convenience, and not by the size of the forces concerned.

The *Gesta Friderici* claimed that Barbarossa had as many as 15,000 *knights* in 1158, apart from foot-soldiers. Lot considers that this was certainly an exaggeration, but he also considers that Pietro della Vigna's claim that Frederick II disposed of 10,000 *men* at the battle of Cortenuova was also an exaggeration. Even allowing for exaggeration on both occasions, and possibly proportionately greater exaggeration of Barbarossa's forces in 1158, there is so great a disparity between the claim of 15,000 *knights* in the first instance and 10,000 *men* in the second as to make it evident that even when Frederick called up all the German and Italian forces that he could muster for his Lombardy campaign, the size of his forces could not be compared with those of his grandfather, though, admittedly, at the battle of Cortenuova he had sent part of his forces to Cremona as a feint.

Basing his estimate on the numbers of knights which the most important princes had to produce in time of war as part of their feudal services, Lot considers that Barbarossa really disposed of a force of some 6,000 knights, though that some of these may not have succeeded in crossing the Alps. According to the annals of Verona (a Ghibelline city at the time and therefore more likely to exaggerate the size of the Emperor's army) Frederick had only 2,000 knights at the battle of Cortenuova.

This disparity between the size of the forces of the two emperors is probably partly to be explained by the changing currents of the thoughts and feelings of the times. In Germany the Empire had far greater power as a symbol in the days of Barbarossa. The intervening period of civil war between Philip of Hohenstaufen and Otto IV, and Frederick's own policy of relinquishing the imperial rights in favour of the princes, had loosened the ties which bound these last to the Emperor. In part it was also no doubt due to the difference in the personalities and tastes of the two men themselves—Barbarossa was, above all, the Emperor of Germany, completely identified with his own country, in spite of his dreams of greater dominion. Frederick II was in point of fact a Norman Sicilian, in spite of his name, and although he exercised an extraordinary fascination over his German subjects, after reigning over them for twenty-five years, as he had done at the time of Cortenuova, he had only spent nine of these among them. In view of these factors it is not surprising that Frederick was unable to draw the same number of his German subjects into his Italian adventures as his grandfather had done.

BIBLIOGRAPHY

Among the numerous works consulted the following are suggested as of special interest for further study both of Frederick and of his period.

BIOGRAPHIES

M. BRION: *Frederic de Hohenstaufen* (Paris, 1948).

E. KANTOROWICZ: *Kaiser Friedrich der Zweite* (Berlin, 1927).

T. L. KINGTON: *Frederick II, Emperor of the Romans* (London, 1862).

E. MOMIGLIANO: *Federico II di Svevia* (Milan, 1948).

H. DE ZIEGLER: *Vie de L'Empéreur Frédéric II de Hohenstaufen* (Paris, 1935).

GENERAL HISTORY OF PERIOD

Cambridge Mediaeval History (Vols. 5 and 6, Cambridge, 1936).

A. J. CARLYLE: *Mediaeval Political Theory in the West* (London, 1955).

Histoire Générale du Moyen Age, ed. G. Glotz (Vol. 5, Paris, 1937).

A. HUILLARD BREHOLLES: *Historia Diplomatica Friderici II* (Paris, 1859).

G. B. PARKS: "The English Traveller to Italy" (*The Middle Ages to 1525*) (Rome, 1954).

C. W. PREVITÉ-ORTON: *Outlines of Mediaeval History* (Cambridge, 1929).

H. RASHDALL: *The Universities of Europe in the Middle Ages* (Oxford, 1936).

THE CHURCH, RELATIONS BETWEEN CHURCH AND EMPIRE, FREDERICK'S PHILOSOPHY OF IMPERIAL POWER

J. BRYCE: *The Holy Roman Empire* (London, 1941).

C. DE CHERRIER: *Storia della Lotta dei Papi e degli Imperatori* (Palermo, 1862).

A. DE STEFANO: *Federico e le Correnti Spirituale del suo Tempo* (Rome, 1922).

—*L'Idea Imperiale di Federico II* (Florence, 1927).

M. ESPOSITO: "Una Manifestazione di Incredulita Religiosa nel Medioevo" (*Archivo Storico Italiano*) (Rome, 1931).

F. FAVA: *Le Idee Religiosi di Federico II di Svevia* (Messina, 1899).

E. GEBHARDT: *L'Italie Mystique* (Paris, 1899).

E. GILSON: *La Philosophie au Moyen Age* (Paris, 1947).

P. Hughes: *A History of the Church* (London, 1948).
C. H. C. Pirie-Gordon: *Innocent III* (London, 1907).
W. Ullman: *Mediaeval Papalism* (London, 1949).
—*The Growth of the Papal Government in the Middle Ages* (London, 1955).

NORMAN BACKGROUND

F. Chalandon: *Histoire de la Domination Normande en Italie et en Sicile* (Paris, 1907).
A. de Stefano: *La Cultura in Sicilia nel Periodo Normanno* (Messina, 1932).
C. H. Haskins: *The Normans in European History* (Boston, U.S.A., 1915).
—*The Renaissance of the Twelfth Century* (London, 1927).
E. Jamieson: "The Sicilian Norman Kingdom in the Mind of Anglo-Norman Contemporaries" (*Proceedings of the British Academy*) (London, 1936).

ARAB BACKGROUND, RELATIONS WITH MOSLEM RULERS, CRUSADE

M. Amari: *Storia dei Mussulmani in Sicilia* (Florence, 1872).
T. Arnold and A. Guillaume: *The Legacy of Islam* (Oxford, 1931).
S. Runciman: *A History of the Crusades* (Cambridge, 1954).

THE EMPEROR'S FAMILY AND PRINCIPAL PERSONALITIES AT COURT

W. Cohn: *Hermann von Salza* (Breslau, 1930).
A. Huillard Breholles: *Vie et Correspondence de Pierre de la Vigne* (Paris, 1864).
D. Young: *Richard of Cornwall* (Oxford, 1947).

ARCHITECTURE AND SCULPTURE

G. Agnello: *L'Architettura Sveva in Sicilia* (Tivoli, 1935).
E. Bertaux: *L'Art dans l'Italie Méridionale de l'Empire Romaine à la Conquête de Charles d'Anjou* (Paris, 1904).
L. Bruhns: *Hohenstaufenschlosser* (Leipzig, 1937).
G. Chierici: "Castel del Monte" (*Monumenti Italiani della Reale Accademia*) (Rome, 1934).
C. Diehl: *L'Art Byzantin dans l'Italie Méridionale* (Paris, 1904).
—*Palerme et Syracuse* (Paris, 1907).
G. di Stefano: *L'Architettura Gotico Sveva* (Palermo, 1935).
C. Enlart: *Origines Françaises de l'Architecture Gothique en Italie* (Paris, 1894).
R. Fedden: *Crusader Castles* (London, 1951).
G. Fortunato: *Il Castello di Lagopesole* (Trani, 1902).

N

A. Haseloff: *Die Bauten Hohenstaufen in Unter Italia* (Leipzig, 1920).

J. Ross: *Land of Manfred* (London, 1889).

C. Shearer: *The Renaissance of Architecture in Southern Italy. A Study of Frederick II of Hohenstaufen and the Capua Triumphator Archway Towers* (Cambridge, 1935).

C. A. Willemsen: *Kaiser Friedrichs Triumphtor zu Capua* (Wiesbaden, 1953).

POETRY AND LITERATURE

G. Bertoni: *I Trovatori d'Italia* (Modena, 1915).

—*Poeti e Poesie del Medio Evo e della Rinascenza* (Modena, 1922).

—*Il Duecento* (Milan, 1930).

G. A. Cesareo: *La Poesia Siciliana sotto gli Svevi* (Catania, 1894).

—*Le Origini della Poesia Lirica e la Poesia Siciliana sotto gli Svevi* (Palermo, 1924).

A. de Stefano: *La Cultura alla Corte di Federico II Imperatore* (Palermo, 1938).

D. G. Rosetti: *Poets from Ciullo d'Alcamo to Dante Alighieri* (London, 1861).

C. Salinari: *La Poesia Lirica del Duecento* (Turin, 1951).

SCIENCE

C. H. Haskins: *Studies in Mediaeval Science* (Cambridge, U.S.A., 1927).

—*Mediaeval Culture* (Oxford, 1929).

G. Sarton: *Introduction to the History of Science* (Baltimore, 1951).

L. Thorndyke: *History of Magic* (New York, 1923).

A. Wood and F. M. Fyfe: *The Art of Falconry, being the De Arte Venandi cum Avibus of Frederick II of Hohenstaufen* (for Editor's Notes and Commentaries), (London, 1956).

COSTUME AND FURNITURE

A. G. I. Christie: *English Mediaeval Embroidery* (Oxford, 1938).

INDEX

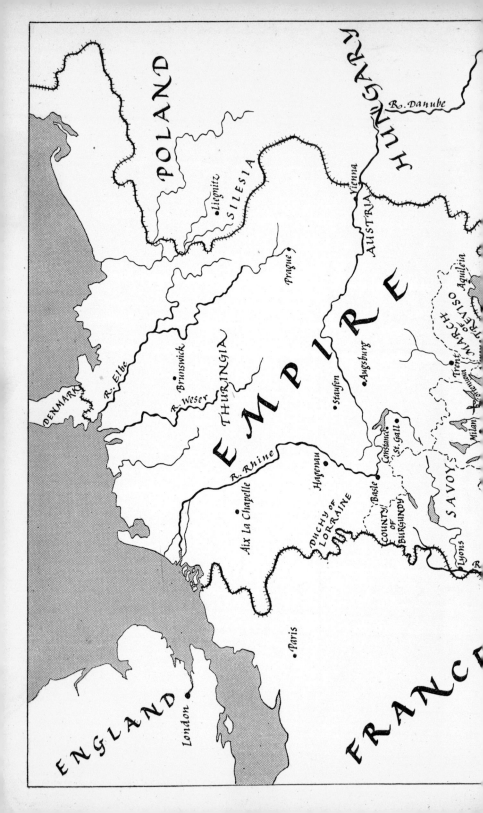